EL ALTO, REBEL CITY

A book in the series

Latin America Otherwise: Languages, Empires, Nations

SERIES EDITORS:

Walter D. Mignolo, Duke University

Irene Silverblatt, Duke University

Sonia Saldívar-Hull, University of Texas, San Antonio

ABOUT THE SERIES

Latin America Otherwise: Languages, Empires, Nations is a critical series. It aims to explore the emergence and consequences of concepts used to define "Latin America" while at the same time exploring the broad interplay of political, economic, and cultural practices that have shaped Latin American worlds. Latin America, at the crossroads of competing imperial designs and local responses, has been construed as a geocultural and geopolitical entity since the nineteenth century. This series provides a starting point to redefine Latin America as a configuration of political, linguistic, cultural, and economic intersections that demands a continuous reappraisal of the role of the Americas in history, and of the ongoing process of globalization and the relocation of people and cultures that have characterized Latin America's experience. Latin America Otherwise: Languages, Empires, Nations is a forum that confronts established geocultural constructions, rethinks area studies and disciplinary boundaries, assesses convictions of the academy and of public policy, and correspondingly demands that the practices through which we produce knowledge and understanding about and from Latin America be subject to rigorous and critical scrutiny.

EL ALTO, REBEL CITY

SIAN LAZAR

SELF AND CITIZENSHIP IN ANDEAN BOLIVIA

DUKE UNIVERSITY PRESS ✳ DURHAM AND LONDON 2008

© 2008 DUKE UNIVERSITY PRESS

ALL RIGHTS RESERVED

PRINTED IN THE UNITED STATES OF AMERICA

ON ACID-FREE PAPER ∞

DESIGNED BY KATY CLOVE

TYPESET IN QUADRAAT BY KEYSTONE TYPESETTING, INC.

LIBRARY OF CONGRESS CATALOGING-IN-PUBLICATION

DATA APPEAR ON THE LAST PRINTED PAGE OF THIS BOOK.

for Steve Lazar, 1947–2007

CONTENTS

All photos are by the author unless indicated otherwise.

ACKNOWLEDGMENTS

My greatest debt is to the *vecinos* of Rosas Pampa and to the members of the Executive Committee of the Federation of Street Traders of the city of El Alto, who were so kind to me and so willing to share their lives with me. I am particularly grateful to Doña Rosalia, Vero, Doña Juana, Bertha, Doña Encarna, Doña Vicky, and Silvia for their friendship, forbearance, and stories. They appear in these pages under pseudonyms. I would also like to thank Don Ruben, Don Linu, Don Agustín, and Cleto; and Darío, Jhonny, Luigi, Eva, Osvi, Nena, and Flora for cheering me up on so many occasions and accompanying me down my street past the rather ferocious dog that lived opposite. All of the leaders of the Federation of Street Traders were very generous with their time and inspirational in their struggle. I cannot mention them all by name, but I am especially indebted to Don Braulio Rocha Tapia, Doña Antonia Narvaez, Don Jorge Mamani, and Don Roberto Mancilla. There are many other general secretaries of different associations who took time to explain their association's concerns to me and who welcomed me to meetings, parades, and demonstrations, and I am very grateful to them all. Edgar Ramos has been enormously helpful, and my sociology students at the Universidad Pública de El Alto were similarly generous with their opinions and inspirational in their political commitment.

Ineke Dibbits and the women of Grupo Solidaridad introduced me to Rosas Pampa in the first place. Others in Bolivia who have helped and taught me over the years include Silvia Rivera, Don Juan de Dios Yapita, Don Vitaliano Huanca, Ricardo Calla, Alison Spedding, Cristina Bubba, Felix Patzi, Bruno Rojas, Esteban Ticona, and Luis Tapia, and various NGO workers and politicians who consented to be interviewed for different research projects. I would also like to acknowledge the support of my friends in La Paz: the Zalles family, the Antezana family, David, Marco, Selma, and Andrea.

This book has benefited from comments on my work at various stages of elaboration, and I would like to thank Victoria Goddard, Sophie Day, Cris Shore, Brian Morris, and Stephen Nugent at Goldsmiths College, London. Thank you also to my fellow postgraduate students there for friendship and discussions, especially John McNeish, Caitlin Scott, and Helen Cornish. I am very grateful to Penny Harvey, Pilar Domingo, Tristan Platt, Maxine Molyneux, Natalia Sobrevilla, Flavia Fiorucci, David Lehmann, Sarah Radcliffe, Andrew Canessa, Alpa Shah, Fiona Wilson, Lucy Taylor, Mao Mollona, John Gledhill, and David Nugent for suggestions, comments, and encouragement. I very much appreciate the constructive comments of the anonymous reviewers from Duke University Press, and the work of Valerie Millholland and Molly Balikov there. Most important, I would like to thank my supervisor, Olivia Harris, for her guidance during and after my PH.D., for her incredibly insightful commentary on multiple versions of this work, her generosity with ideas, her faith in me, and her patience, especially at the most stressful moments.

The errors or omissions that undoubtedly remain are of course my responsibility alone.

Funding for field research and writing between 1997 and 2001 was provided by Economic and Social Research Council studentships at the master's and doctoral level. An RAI/Sutasoma award in 2002 provided additional support. My fieldwork in 2003 and 2004 was funded by the Centre of Latin American Studies of the University of Cambridge (CLAS) and research grants from the University of Cambridge. The Centre of Latin American Studies also supported the production of transcriptions of some interviews, for which difficult job I am grateful to Karen Paz. I thank Dr. Geoffrey Kantaris and Dr. Charles Jones of CLAS for their past and on-going support institutionally and intellectually.

Part of chapter 2 has been published as "Personalist Politics, Clientelism and Citizenship: Local Elections in El Alto, Bolivia," *Bulletin of Latin American Research* 23, no. 2 (2004): 228–243; portions of chapters 2 and 3 have been published as "Citizens Despite the State: Everyday Corruption and Local Politics in El Alto, Bolivia," in *Corruption: Anthropological Perspectives*, edited by D. Haller and C. Shore (London: Pluto Press, 2005), 212–228; an earlier version of chapter 7 has appeared as "In-betweenness at the Margins: Collective Organisation, Ethnicity and Political Agency among Bolivian Street Traders," in *Livelihoods at the Margins: Surviving the City*, edited by James Staples (London: Left Coast Press, 2007); and parts of chapters 1 and 8 in "El Alto, Ciudad Rebelde: Organisational Bases for Revolt," *Bulletin of Latin American Research* 25, no. 2 (2006): 183–199.

Finally, I would like to express my gratitude to my mother, Sue Lazar, for her love and encouragement; to my siblings, Sam, Sophie, Seth, and Sebastian, for love and arguments; to my son, Zach, for being simply joyful; and to Milo for being so sweet. Thank you also to my partner, Dave, for emotional and technical support far beyond the call of duty. He commented on innumerable draft chapters, editing them, extracting the points I was making from the shapelessness of the early versions, and giving me some of his own arguments; he provided IT support for some of the data analysis, participated in many of the events described in this book, and even conducted informal research when he lived with me in Bolivia. Beyond all that, he looks after me every day. Lastly though, I want to thank my father, Dr. Steve Lazar, who died when this book was in the later stages of production, but at least got a chance to see the proofs. He was truly a great man and a wonderful father, who was always immensely proud of me. That pride, together with his unshakeable belief in me, has inspired me throughout my life. Paps, you won't get your signed copy now, but this book is dedicated to you.

We could defend ourselves if we all unified and paralyzed the country. There's no other option. One hundred percent is now privatized. This Mallku [Felipe Quispe, an Indianist leader] has spoken well, saying "We have to make them listen to us, and paralyze [the country] until the government listens to us." His aim is war. . . . I want the poor people to progress; people with three or four houses just want more houses. We'll only win by cutting their nails. During the strikes, rich people will have all their money in vain, they'll die of hunger the same as us, and the president will have to listen to us. It's like that.—Doña Josefa, interview, August 2000

[In October 2003] all the organizations mobilized themselves, and with one voice said "We don't want the gas to be sold [and exported] either through Chile or through Peru." . . . The fight began in El Alto from the 12 of October. . . . We ourselves were with the FEJUVE [Federation of Juntas Vecinales] comrades and with the different neighborhood councils, the vecinos [residents of each neighborhood], confronting the army.—FEJUVE leader, interview, January 2004

We mobilized, we held vigils, we didn't sleep at all, day and night; we had to stay up all night, keeping fires going in the marginal neighborhoods of El Alto. . . . We worked, as mothers, as Bolivians, children, grandchildren, we all worked, we all went together to each demonstration.—Doña Gertrudis, interview, January 2004

We asked for a change for our dear Bolivia, but we left this change half done, because it actually meant changing everything, so that the people govern, as it should be; and the q'aras [white people]—as they say, no offense intended—should go to their proper place. They say we're racists, but it's not that in reality, instead it's rage. I know that not all [white people] are guilty, no, the guilty ones are the ones in government. . . .

For me, October 2003 was a triumph for the Bolivian people, the people of El Alto . . . and I admire them for their bravery, to rise up against Sanchez de Lozada, armed simply with stones and sticks when he has a whole regiment, well-armed, shooting left and right, without control, without seeing that there were children, old people there, who were simply asking him to go, because they could put up with it no longer. And the chap became very stubborn, defiant, he said "I'm in charge, period," like that. They say to kill an Indian makes a fatherland, don't they? But that's not it. I think that to kill a president makes a fatherland—a bad president, of course.—FEJUVE leader, interview, January 2004

Over the past few years El Alto has been building an identity as an indigenous city. Indeed, in the last census, 74 percent of its residents self-identified as Aymara, one of the main indigenous groups in Bolivia.[1] Part of El Alto's identity is bound up with a political radicalism that has exploded in the past few years: in February 2003, riots against tax increases in La Paz and El Alto forced the Bolivian government to renegotiate the terms of its budget surplus with the International Monetary Fund. In October 2003, protests centered on El Alto and coalescing around opposition to the export of natural gas—the Gas War—forced the president to resign. In January 2005, the government promised to rescind its contract with the privatized water company in the city in response to a general strike called by the citywide residents association. The conflict continued over both issues (the water and the gas) locally and nationally, to the point where in March 2005, President Carlos Mesa threatened to resign, saying that Bolivia had become ungovernable as a result of the power of oppositional social movements. Protests against the president's plans for natural gas exploitation continued thereafter, and by June of that year forced his resignation for real. Evo Morales, the leader of the coca growers' movement, became president in the elections of December 2005, and on 1 May 2006 nationalized the natural gas production facilities.

The actions of ordinary Bolivians have sparked considerable excitement among international networks of alternative globalization activists, who look to these events, among others, as sources of inspiration in what they see as the fight against neoliberal globalization. Bolivia has often been something of a model for different political groupings internationally: from its enthusiastic implementation of structural adjustment under Jeffrey Sachs's tutelage (Arbona n.d.; Kruse 2004), through the constitutional changes and decentralization measures of the mid-1990s, to the perceived struggles against neoliberalism of recent years. In April 2000, the citizens of Cochabamba were the main protagonists in the eyes of the international media during the so-called Water War, led by a group called the Coordinator for Water and Life, but since then El Alto has moved to center stage. And yet as a city it remains largely unknown to or misunderstood by those who do not live there, even in Bolivia. In the inevitable simplifications that accompany the international flow of information, the contemporary political developments in El Alto and Bolivia have been understood through narratives of desperation and poverty, or the image of a noble and naturalized indigenous concern for Bolivian sovereignty over natural resources. In contrast, in this book I provide a more profound and long-term analysis of the state–citizen relationships that made the events of October 2003 and 2005 possible. By this, I do not mean to present a teleological narrative that sees either as the culmination of the processes I describe. Instead, I consider more everyday practices and experiences of citizenship that structure alteños' relationships with the state in both ordinary and extraordinary times at the beginning of the twenty-first century.

The nature of citizenship in this indigenous city indicates that we cannot understand citizenship in non-Western contexts as purely a legal status consisting of the individual ownership of a set of rights and responsibilities vis-à-vis the state. Specifically, I examine the tension between collective and individual senses of self and political agency, and I consider how individualized, liberal understandings of political action interact with collectivist traditions, which draw on indigenous communal practices, Trotskyite trade unionism, anarchosyndicalism, and other threads, a logic of combining that is a long-standing, if often misunderstood, feature of Bolivia. It is not simply a question of the imposition of Western notions of individual rights and citizenship onto a kind of indigenous collectivist self; rather, the citizens of El Alto creatively combine these different political resources according to the circumstances and their political aims. I therefore address particularly important issues about how citizenship can be constructed and experienced in ways completely different from those envisaged by more Eurocentric perspectives.

An ethnographic approach to citizenship in the particular context of El Alto begins to explore exactly how political subjectivities are produced in the interaction between state and nonstate actors and histories. It is highly productive because it provides insights into local-level understandings and embodied experiences of citizenship. Some of the best anthropological discussions of citizenship have focused on the articulations between transnational (or cosmopolitan) and national citizenship (Ong 1999b, 2005; Hannerz 1990; Miller and Slater 2000). In contrast, I focus more on the articulations between *local* and national citizenship. In El Alto, the relationship between citizens and the state is mediated by a well-established structure of collective organization that is parallel to the state and that interacts with it at multiple levels simultaneously. I explore what it is that enables these organizations to get people out onto the streets in order to enforce their political views, and I find that much of it has to do with the ability of such groups to construct collective and relational senses of self among their members, against the pull of individual interests and factional conflicts. Rather than being based purely on a straightforward exchange of participation in the group in return for benefits or rights, these identities are built through ritualized and embodied practices, gossip and suspicion, and the development of notions of reciprocity, authority, hierarchy, and obligation. The groups that mediate these state–citizen relationships have to work hard to create and to maintain this sense of collectivity and of obligation to the group.

CITIZENSHIP

Part of my aim is to counter the emphasis on rights and responsibilities in accounts of state–citizen relations in recent social theory, which usually draws inspiration from T. H. Marshall's now normative definition: "Citizenship is a status bestowed on those who are full members of a community. All who possess the status are equal with respect to the rights and duties with which the status is endowed" (1983 [1950]: 253). Marshall equated community with the nation and viewed membership of that community as primarily a sort of individual ownership of a basket of rights and corresponding duties. From Locke onward, liberal citizenship has been seen as a status of the (predominantly male) individual. The rights associated with this status in theory allow individuals to pursue their conceptions of the good life, as long as they do not hinder others' similar pursuits (Oldfield 1990). This is the essence of liberal tolerance, and the state protects this status quo. In return, citizens have minimal responsibilities, which revolve primarily around keeping the state running, such as paying taxes or participating in military service when the state is threatened.

Anthropologists are not alone in arguing that the constitution of any given community requires a considerable amount of work, and that meaningful membership is more than the possession of a particular set of rights and responsibilities. Political theorists have also viewed citizenship as a set of practices, especially related to participating in politics (Yuval-Davis 1997; Oldfield 1990; Lister 1997; B. Turner 1993). The theory of citizenship practice is influenced by a tradition of civic republicanism which goes back to the Greek democracies described by Aristotle (1992) and Thucydides, who recorded Pericles's (1999) famous funeral oration. The duty of political participation was emphasized by Cicero and, much later, by Machiavelli (Heater 1999; Oldfield 1990). Civic republicanism influenced the revolutions in America and (in part) France, both of which were inspirational for early republicans in Latin America. Through the nineteenth century, it was sustained by Hegel and then Tocqueville, and the most distinguished twentieth-century proponent of civic republicanism was Hannah Arendt (1998 [1958]).

For these philosophers, the participation of citizens in politics was an essential part of creating the sense of community necessary for political life, which Aristotle called "concord." That participation was mediated not through voting, but through speech and deliberation, in the *agora* (lobby) and the *ekklesia* (assembly), in the case of the Greek democracies (Castoriadis 1992). Aristotle considered the state to be an aggregation of its citizens, and the citizens to be those eligible to participate in office, or government. Castoriadis points out that this implies that universal citizenship cannot therefore exist in a state based upon liberal representative democracy, but only in one where all those who are being governed are able to participate directly in government (cf. Fotopoulos 1997). Such participatory philosophies have their contemporary echoes in the calls of social movements in Latin America for more participatory and direct democracy (Dagnino 1998; Nugent forthcoming) and in initiatives such as participatory budgeting, for example in Brazil and Argentina.

Citizenship can therefore be analyzed as a bundle of practices that constitute encounters between the state and citizens,[2] rather than simply a legal status accorded to those who are "full members of a community." Key to this are the processes and practices that make someone a full member of a given community, rather than the end result itself. Historically, citizenship has always been understood in part as a project to work on the self in order to create good citizens, and this ethical dimension of citizenship is central also to contemporary understandings (Dagger 2005). In Athens, creating a sense of duty toward the polis was considered an absolutely crucial element of citizenship and implied the creation of particular kinds of persons with the sense that the individual was part of the collectivity and defined by it (Castoriadis 1992), alongside the development of a masculine notion of civic virtue, or selfless devotion to civic duty.[3] Rousseau also advocated a program of citizenship education, and education is still inherent in citizenship, whether implemented through political participation, schooling, or citizenship classes for immigrants.

Through these different practices, societies organize and challenge political participation and exclusion (historically, of workers, women, illiterates, and children). The challenge comes from two principal directions: first, the more liberal version of seeking inclusion for those excluded, so that all people become "full members" (a universal category of citizenship); second, from those who argue that treating everyone the same ends up favoring dominant groups, who therefore propose some form of group rights (Little 2002; Kymlicka 1995). This is particularly important in highly stratified societies like Bolivia, where a small, Creole (white) elite controlled the government from Independence until December 2005. For Saskia Sassen (2003), these tensions mean that citizenship is an "incomplete" category which develops through a dialectic whereby the practices of those excluded from full citizenship come to define or influence the terms of their subsequent inclusion. We might also point to a third challenge to dominant notions of citizenship in the case of Bolivia, arising from more radical Aymara groups who wish to take over the state, an increasingly popular political project. In Latin America, such challenges arise as part of the long-standing assertion by social movements, particularly those of indigenous peoples, of their right not only to "inclusion" but also to redefine the very terms of political participation and government (Dagnino 1998). These contrast with the conservatism of the civic republicanism, or "political" communitarianism that stresses the citizen's duty to participate in politics at the expense of an active role in creating the terms in which politics is discussed.[4] Latin American indigenous activism has challenged dominant constructions of citizenship through the use of both a collective sense of citizenship, such as in demands for group rights during the 1980s and 1990s, and more individualized liberal versions of political agency, such as voting for indigenous candidates in national and local elections.

The latest wave of regional indigenous movements began with the organization of the Shuar Federation in Ecuador in 1964, gained steam with the transitions to democracy of the late 1970s and 1980s, and peaked with the organization of the opposition to the 1992 Quincentenary celebrations (Wearne 1996; Van Cott 1994; Brysk 2000). The Bolivian indigenous movement in the highlands, the Kataristas, was one of the earlier ones to organize, with the declaration of the Tiwanaku Manifesto in 1973; the Amazonian indigenous groups organized themselves into the Confederación de Pueblos Indígenas de Bolivia (CIDOB; Confederation of Indigenous People of Bolivia) in 1982.[5] Subsequently, the Bolivian movement has been one of the most prominent on the regional stage, whose key moments were the 1990 March for Territory and Dignity from the Amazonian lowlands to La Paz and the success of the Aymara vice presidential candidate, Victor Hugo Cardenas, in the 1993 elections. Indigenous activists in Bolivia and Latin America have generally phrased their demands of the state in terms of group rights, and states have responded in kind, specifically with constitutional reforms that recognized the pluriethnic and multicultural nature of the different nations and provided (principally) for some degree of indigenous self-determination in terms of territory, recognition of customary law, and bilingual education (Sieder 2002a; Van Cott 1994, 2005; Yashar 2005; Assies, van der Haar, and Hoekema 2000). Together, these reforms represent at least potentially a radical restructuring of the state and citizenship away from the liberal republicanism of the recent past. Scholars of such developments have moved from a fairly optimistic position in the 1990s (Albo 1991; Wearne 1996; Van Cott 1994) to greater discussion of the difficulties with the actual implementation of such reforms (Sieder 2002b; Assies et al. 2000). Others have begun to interrogate the very notion of a reasonably coherent indigenous movement, beyond making the basic point that the "movement" is really many "movements." For example, Gow and Rappaport (2002) describe very effectively the ways that the conflicts on the inside of indigenous movements shape those movements but do not prevent activists from joining together at particular moments to present a united front to others, at national and international levels.

Robert Albro (2003) has made a similar argument for Bolivia, documenting how an alliance of urban popular sectors, peasants, and unionists in Cochabamba in April 2000 came to be understood as part of the indigenous movement. Much of this has to do with international solidarity activism and with how protagonists choose to present themselves on international stages; although Oscar Olivera, the figurehead for the Cochabamba Coordinator of Water and Life, does not claim to be indigenous himself, he projects an indigenous identity for the Coordinator internationally that is at odds with its political projects in more local spheres. Evo Morales is similarly adept at presenting himself in the most effective way to different audiences (Canessa 2006). In fact, both have quite clear trade unionist political trajectories, which in the past would have been associated with traditional, class-based leftist political parties. They also tend to present themselves at home more as anti-neoliberal and anti–United States than as either indigenous (Evo) or quasi-indigenous (Olivera), largely because this is a more successful political strategy. Albro's discussion of plurality is a useful way to approach the indigenous movement in contemporary Bolivia without simplifying it into a politics based solely upon ethnicity, but without denying its indigeneity either, and this book is in part a contribution to that intellectual strategy. I investigate the political practices of people who see themselves as indigenous but are not part of explicitly Indianist political organizations. My central point is that when Bolivian Aymaras and Quechuas do choose to join actions that later become part of indigenous mobilization to national and international eyes, they often do so on the basis of collective action, principally blockades and mass demonstrations, and in favor of collective demands, such as autonomy, self-determination, "collective economic development" (Sieder 2002a), and cultural rights.

CITIZENSHIP, COLLECTIVISM, AND INDIVIDUALISM IN THE ANDES

In June 2002 and December 2005 the indigenous and popular classes in Bolivia also pressed their case through voting, the archetypal liberal citizenship practice of engagement with the state. In the election of 2002, Evo Morales came in second, with just over 20 percent of the vote;[6] Felipe Quispe, the Mallku, came in fifth, with 6 percent. This was unprecedented; it meant that about a quarter of the deputies in the Congress came from indigenous and popular parties. In 2005, Evo Morales won a staggering 54 percent of the vote and became president; his party gained 72 out of 130 deputies in Congress and 12 out of 27 senators. The Mallku's vote fell to just over 2 percent.[7] Evo's electoral success is indicative of the rising power of indigenous people within Bolivian society and also of the ways the social movements have mobilized individualized liberal forms of political agency alongside the collectivist forms described earlier. A number of political scientists have even seen ethnicity-based political parties as the maturing of the indigenous movement in some Latin American countries, including Bolivia (Yashar 2005; Van Cott 2005).

As I discuss in chapter 3, in El Alto there are important collectivist elements operating behind the supposedly universal and individualized exercise of citizenship through voting. Yet it would be false to propose a model of the Western imposition of liberal individualism on indigenous societies that are somehow naturally (or even predominantly) collectivist. In the case of the Andes, the rhetorical split between traditional collectivism and modern individualism has been particularly delicate politically. From the *indigenistas* of the 1920s, scholars have tended to seek out the persistence of unchanging precolonial cultural values among indigenous peoples in the rural parts of the region. Within anthropology, the influence of John Murra and Tom Zuidema has encouraged the study of continuity between pre- and postconquest cultural, cosmological, social, political, and economic systems in the Andes (Harris 2000c: 9). In 1991 Orin Starn launched a blistering attack on this tendency, which he labeled "Andeanism," the local version of Orientalism. He argued that anthropologists of the Andes had focused on symbolic and cosmological continuities and therefore depicted Andean communities as bounded and static and somehow out of modern time. As a result, they missed the more modern elements of Andean society that provoked the rise of Sendero Luminoso in Peru in the 1980s, such as migratory movement, widespread and grinding poverty, and the desire for political change. It is generally agreed that Starn overstated his case somewhat (Mayer 1991; Harris 2000c), and he has subsequently recognized this (Starn 1999). But his criticism of an essentialized construction of Andean communities as relics of the pre-Columbian past remains valid and has been taken very seriously by other scholars (Harvey 1994b; Abercrombie 1998; Salman and Zoomers 2003).

The problem with this, however, is that promoting an interpretation of contemporary indigenous peoples as survivors of the pre-Columbian past (with the implication that little has changed culturally and socially) has been particularly important for different indigenous movements, as the "discovery" of precolonial values enables activists to claim authenticity and thus gives them considerable rhetorical power. Furthermore, as Olivia Harris (2000c) has pointed out, the voices of indigenous intellectuals have been increasingly central to the academic debates, at least in Bolivia, and one political and analytical strategy of theirs has been to promote the otherness of their nations and to assert their premodern or precapitalist natures. This is one part of a strategy that is explicitly anticolonial, which argues that the othering has been part of the processes of internal colonialism that have also created the economic conditions highlighted by Starn and others. Even during the *indigenismo* of the early twentieth century, and the heyday of the concept of *lo andino* in the 1970s and early 1980s that was so criticized by Starn, the positive valuing of Andean culture by anthropologists was a response to prevalent stereotypes of Andean peasants as poor, backward, undeveloped, uncreative, and without culture (Mayer 1991).

With respect to the question of citizenship, this paradox problematizes any discussion of community in Bolivia because much of the power of claiming that particular ways of organizing society have pre-Columbian authenticity lies in the fact that the *ayllu* in particular is associated in the popular imagination with a very strong sense of community solidarity.[8] Anthropologists have participated in this association, stressing the structural coherence of the ayllu, as displayed symbolically and enacted ritually, and focusing also on the organization of communal work practices, networks of mutual aid and reciprocity, and a sense of obligation to the community, especially expressed through holding office (e.g., Isbell 1978; Harris 2000c; Urton 1981, 1992; Carter and Mamani P. 1989 [1982]; Rasnake 1988). Bolivian scholars have also stressed the importance of solidarity within the ayllus, where the communal structure overcomes individual desires and the attendant factionalism (Albó 1977), or where there is a clear distinction between autochthonous community structures in the countryside and the peasant unions, seen as Western, factionalist, and individualistic and imposed by the post-1952 Bolivian state (Rivera Cusicanqui 1990; Choque and Mamani Condori 2003). They have also asserted the democratic nature of the ayllu (Rivera Cusicanqui and Equipo THOA 1992; Rivera Cusicanqui 1990; Ticona Alejo 2003; Fernández Osco 2000) and emphasized the economic and social importance of collective landholding and the difference between ayllu-based forms of landholding (both individual and collective) and the more Western notion of land as property (Untoja 2000; Patzi Paco 2003).

A close reading of the works produced by such intellectuals shows how careful they are to avoid essentializing the Aymara-Quechua peoples as either premodern and unchanging or inherently collective. But the processes by which such discourses pass into popular imagination filters out the shades of gray, for good reason. When I was teaching an undergraduate course in urban sociology at the Public University of El Alto, I proposed to the students that ayllus might not always have been as egalitarian as we think, and that there may have been internal disputes and hierarchy. A few students agreed with me, but the most politically active ones argued forcefully that I was wrong and that I could not possibly know the truth because my knowledge is of "official" history, that is, written history, rather than that which is known by virtue of indigenous descent. They would no doubt have been horrified to read Arij Ouweneel's assertion that the ayllu was "established as part of a lordship . . . [but then] became more egalitarian during the Spanish period because of Spanish pressure to rotate its principal office and to secure it within fixed boundaries" (2003: 92). This Dutch historian's analysis is notable because of the common association between ayllu democracy and rotative leadership systems, something I discuss in detail in chapter 8. In the conversation with my students, I realized that it was easy for me to question ayllu solidarity from my position as outsider. My instinct was to try to separate political opinions or rhetoric from academic analysis of reality, which is an operation of power in itself. Claims about collective or individualistic understandings of political agency and experiences of citizenship are therefore sometimes of more than just academic interest in contemporary Bolivia.

Recently, Bolivian intellectuals and activists have drawn upon the association of indigenous communities with collective values and extended it to proclaim a more democratic popular sphere in general, in contrast to the corruption of elite party politics and state institutions (e.g., see Lechín W. 2003; Garcia Linera et al. 2000; Gutierrez et al. 2002). For them, the democratic nature of the popular sphere lies in its creative mixing of indigenous traditions of community organization with trade union traditions and new forms of collective organization around the defense of local sovereignty over natural resources and control over the means of social reproduction (Garcia Linera 2001). Some argue that this is a local manifestation of the "multitude" (Hardt and Negri 2000, 2005), which is becoming increasingly successful in its ability to articulate a positive vision of democracy that is an alternative to the neoliberal version of normative politics (Gutierrez, Garcia Linera, and Tapia Mealla 2000; Garcia Linera 2001). It is too early to tell whether their optimism is misplaced, but it is certainly the case that the social movements in Bolivia at the start of this century are coming up with creative alternatives to normative institutional democracy at the levels of rhetoric, theory, and practice. Moreover, their power to constrain the government is growing, as presidents are no longer able to implement IMF proposals with the freedom they enjoyed in past decades, although there is the ever-present danger that this situation will produce a military coup. The social movements have even produced a president who will need to balance their demands and expectations against the exigencies of Bolivia's participation in the global economic system.[9] The collective political subjects that are at the heart of this growing strength are the subject of this book.

Subjectivity and the Self in Political Theory and Anthropology   In El Alto, adults organize themselves as workers and petty capitalists in trade unions or as residents (vecinos) in neighborhood councils and in the parents' associations of the schools their children attend. These groups have their own citywide organizations, and there is a further layer of national civic organizations. At all levels, the organizations represent their affiliates in negotiations with each other and with different parts of the state, negotiations which can be both consensual and highly conflictive. The organizations thus mediate between their members and the state at the different levels, and citizenship is multitiered (Yuval-Davis 1997). Importantly, the organizations often also substitute for the state, doing the work of regulation of their members in its place, and vigorously defending this position. The first part of the book focuses on the importance of residence (vecindad) as a collective category of citizenship, emphasizing in particular the local civic bodies at the neighborhood level. The second part explores how citizens, specifically street traders, construct themselves as collective political subjects through their membership in trade unions and examines the complex interrelationships among such civic organizations and their interactions with the state.

Investigating the generation of community and a collective sense of political agency in El Alto requires consideration of the notions of person and self operating there. Liberal citizenship depends upon a particular conception of the self, since the focus on universality and the presumption of equality is a "shared civic identity" (Kymlicka 1995: 173) premised upon an "abstraction of self" (Yuval-Davis 1997: 70). John Rawls is the most distinguished recent proponent of this abstraction. The procedural model of politics he described in A Theory of Justice (1972) assumes a type of abstracted subjectivity that has been criticized by both feminists and philosophical communitarians (Okin 1991; Kittay 1997; MacIntyre 1981; Sandel 1992; Walzer 1992).[10] The individual behind the Rawlsian "veil of ignorance" is the epitome of rationality, but without sex or emotions; in addition, that individual is not allowed to consider community or familial ties which might make him or her think differently about how best to structure society (Frazer and Lacey 1995; Sandel 1992). Such an asocial individual, or "unencumbered self" (Sandel 1992), is impossible to envisage for most communitarians, anthropologists, and psychologists. In fact, one does not have to dig too far to realize that, since there is nothing to differentiate the individuals in the original position, there is, effectively, only one individual: the Kantian rational man (Barron 1993; Pateman 1988).

Liberal citizenship theory presupposes a particular form of subjectivity for those subject to liberal political structures, which have been enacted in Bolivia as neoliberalism. The rational, autonomous (implicitly male) individual as the basis for liberal political thought implies that the rights of this citizen become the inevitable language of political expression (Barron 1993). Communitarian thought tends to replace rights with responsibilities, but the individual retains priority, although this time embedded in community (or "encumbered" by community; Sandel 1992; MacIntyre 1981; Etzioni 1993). Both assume a possessive and individual model of the person (Strathern 1988; Macpherson 1962).

Both liberalism and communitarianism are static versions of the relationship between person and self as defined by Marcel Mauss. Mauss differentiates between *personne*, as cultural category, and *moi*, usually translated as "self" and meaning an individual's "conscious personality" (Mauss 1979 [1938]: 61; Morris 1994). Mauss's version of the modern notion of the person constitutes itself as a psychological being, so in effect he collapses personne and moi together (Mauss 1979 [1938]; Carrithers 1985). Later anthropologists pointed to the frequent tension between personne and moi, arguing that individual consciousness and identity operates within a dialectical relationship to cultural prescriptions of the person, both influencing and being influenced by culture and cultural, social, and political institutions (Cohen 1994; Rosaldo 1984). During the 1970s and 1980s, anthropological work on the self was oriented around the dichotomy of individual versus collective senses of self, tending to leave little scope for concepts of the autonomous individual outside of Western culture (Morris 1994).[11]

Therefore, my focus on the "collective self" in this book is somewhat against the grain of much recent anthropology of the self, which in the 1990s enjoined anthropologists to take into account the importance of individual responses to highly collectivized and socially determined notions of the self, personhood, and behavior (Rapport 1997; Cohen 1994;

Morris 1994). In contrast, I am seeking to resurrect the collective to some extent. Nonetheless, I attempt to do this without slipping into an overly deterministic interpretation of the relationship between the self and society or the group. This kind of determinism has been a feature of much sociology (and anthropology) since Durkheim first delineated the proper areas of investigation for the discipline. Within anthropology of the self it has its reflection in the concept of the "sociocentric self," most clearly outlined by Shweder and Bourne (1984). They argue that Western cultures produce selves that are predominantly individualistic ("egocentric"), while non-Western cultures produce more collectively oriented selves ("sociocentric"), following a distinction first made by Marcel Mauss (1979 [1938]) and then developed by Louis Dumont (1986; see also Macfarlane 1978). Nigel Rapport points out the connection between the sociocentric self and communitarian political thought:

> In this view it is their deep and diverse collective attachments which give people their particular identities, it is their roles and group membership which willy-nilly are constitutive of their persons. . . .
>
> Communitarian politics treats the group as a given, as sui generis, and individual members as derivatives therefore; it will never accommodate the specificity (rightful, inexorable) of the individual. (Rapport 1997: 189, 193; cf. Young 1990)

Both the communitarian version of self and the sociocentric self suffer from the problem of denying individual agency, or the ability of self as psychological being to break out of the constraints of person as cultural category. This is the reason for communitarian conservatism, because the implication is that people are completely bound by their insertion in their community, which is static and uncontested. The egocentric self maps onto the liberal model of citizenship and political agency assumed by most contemporary government and development agencies; in this conception self equals person and is prior to the collectivity. This is why liberalism cannot take into account the fact that people are embedded in communities, and therefore ends up creating everyone as white, rational, property-holding man. Neither are adequate on their own as an explanation of how most people experience their selfhood, and thus their citizenship.

Some contemporary psychologists do identify a sociocentric or collective self and argue that the collective self and the individual self coexist within individuals and societies, even if the balance between the two types is culturally and historically contingent (Triandis and Trafimow 2001). What is important is a sense of dynamism when we think about the self, and the recognition that "society may use all sorts of devices in the attempt to make the self in the social image" (Cohen 1994: 54), which may or may not be successful at any one time and with any one individual. Such devices and processes operate at both moral and experiential (embodied) levels (Csordas 1994). Ethnographers of the Andes have tended to stress the importance of communal work, ritual, and systems of office-holding to social cohesion, often making a structuralist analysis of the symbolic universe expressed in such practices (Heath 1987; Urton 1981, 1992; Carter and Mamani P. 1989 [1982]; Saignes 1993; Stobart 2002b; Fernandez Juarez 1995; Abercrombie 1998). However, although scholars do recognize that people participate in the symbolic universe to different degrees, that participation is often left uninterrogated, or analyzed implicitly in terms of interest-based calculations of the benefits of belonging to the group and the sanctions for nonconformity. The notion of the person as interest-bearing individual has much in common with notions of the person assumed in Western ideas of citizenship: a "commoditized" vision of the person (Strathern 1988) as a bounded individual who "owns" a set of rights, responsibilities, and interests.

Cholo Citizenship   The dominant citizenship projects of the nineteenth and twentieth centuries represent the ways that these notions of the person have been put into practice politically in Bolivia, and the existence of the city of El Alto demonstrates their failure. During the period of Liberal Party hegemony between the 1880s and 1920s, the version of citizenship presented to the Indians by the political elites was essentially one of exclusion from the imagined nation of Bolivia, even though the Indians themselves consistently resisted that exclusion. That period saw the most concerted attacks on communal landholding through, on the one hand, the expansion of the large haciendas, especially in the northern altiplano (highlands), and other attempts to transform the Indians into individual property-holding yeoman farmers, for example through the 1874 Ley de Exvinculación (Law of Disentailment; Platt 1984; Larson 2005). The census of 1900 notoriously predicted "the slow and gradual disappearance of the indigenous race," arguing that "if there has been a single source of retardation in our civilization, it is the indigenous race, essentially resistant to all innovation and progress" (cited in Choque and Mamani Condori 2003: 148). By the mid-twentieth century, the project of assimilation through *mestizaje*, in the Mexican mold, had become dominant, as evidenced in the legislation that followed the 1952 revolution, principally the agrarian reform and the introduction of universal suffrage and primary education. The revolution's "citizenship option" for the Indians was that of assimilation—as workers and peasants who would eventually develop into modern *mestizos* through education and individual property-holding citizens who participate in politics by means of voting. Both exclusion and assimilation are consistent with the liberal focus on homogeneity among the citizenry, which is how the idea of universal citizenship was translated into practice across Latin America. However, by the mid-1990s, Bolivia was at the forefront of Latin American moves to design a new relationship between individuals, communities, and the state that took into account a more differentiated citizenship. Constitutional and legislative reforms, for example those establishing intercultural education and popular participation in local development, heralded a citizenship project that improved upon the liberal Hobson's choice of assimilation or exclusion. Nonetheless, differentiated citizenship has proved very hard to achieve in practice, not least because the political will to make the reforms work has been lacking. In practice, the citizenship projects of exclusion, assimilation, and multiculturalism coexist in contemporary politics.

And *alteños* are a reminder of the failure of all of these projects. Neither fully assimilated nor fully excluded, they are a constant presence for the political elites of La Paz, looking down threateningly and reminding them of the fragility of their privilege on a daily basis. They are neither fully Indian nor fully white, Creole, or even mestizo; they are *cholos*. Cholo is an ethnocultural category which has been used since colonial times to describe an Indian who has moved to the city and who is therefore somewhere between Indian and mestizo. In the colonial period, cholos were also known as Creole Indians (*indios criollos*), or "successful Indians" (*indios con éxito*), that is, the Indians who moved to the cities and worked in urban trades such as mining and commerce (Abercrombie 1991). As Thomas Abercrombie points out, these urban Indians were, for the Spanish and mestizos, a "particularly pernicious form of debased Indianhood" (114). As Brooke Larson has detailed, several key Bolivian writers of the early twentieth century continued the theme of the cholo as the principal threat to the pure racial categories of Indian and non-Indian.[12] Politically, the cholo came to signify the vice-ridden, degenerate, and semiliterate mob, in contrast to the "prepolitical" and uncorrupted Indian (Larson 2005: 244); intellectuals of the time deployed anticholo discourses to attack popular politics, urban labor mobilization, and incipient indigenous social movements (245).

Cholo is still a highly politicized racial and social category. Like many words for ethnicity, the term alters its meaning according to the speaker and context, but it is often pejorative, possibly deriving etymologically from a word meaning "mongrel" or from a term used of the lower classes in Early Modern Madrid (Peredo Beltrán 1992). Qualities of uncleanliness and excessive sexuality are often attributed to the chola (Weismantel 2001). These kinds of negative associations have much to do with the threat that cholos represent, as Linda Seligman (1993) has argued, because of their "in-betweenness" in ethnic and political terms. This is linked to the association of cholo ethnicity with particular economic activities. Economically, cholos are indelibly associated with the urban service sector and the informal economy: transport, commerce, and, in earlier times, mining. The chola is stereotypically a market woman, the intermediary between the rural (Indian) producers and urban (mestiza, white) consumers. The cholo often transports the products to the markets. These stereotypical activities of cholos are a good description of what the residents of Rosas Pampa, discussed in the first part of this book, do for a living, and the street traders who are the subject of the second part of this book are the classic cholas. They are "in between" in terms of cultural categories, but also economic positioning, as the intermediaries between rural producers and urban consumers, a position which has given them a considerable amount of economic and political power. For the urban mestizos and whites are dependent upon the cholos, and the cholo intermediaries are able to withhold the produce they usually sell (Seligmann 1993). Their familiarity with the peasants means that they are often on their side, a situation which has done much to shape El Alto's role in recent political upheavals. Increasing migration to the cities has meant that cholos are increasing in numbers and in their awareness of themselves as a separate and potentially powerful political constituency.[13]

Economic positioning, exchange relationships, gender, and ethnicity are all intertwined with political agency in El Alto, and this book is also an ethnography of cholo life beyond the strictly political. Certainly, the city market and exchange relationships have been very fruitful prisms for Andean anthropologists to view issues of gender and ethnicity more widely, precisely because of the ways that chola market women disrupt a bifurcated racial categorization of Indian and non-Indian. They have shown how fluid and relational ethnicity is in the Andes, as women shift their ethnic identification according to what they do, how they dress, and how they relate to consumers and other producers in the markets in which they sell (Paulson 2003b; Seligmann 2001; Sikkink 2001; de la Cadena 1996). People in El Alto rarely explicitly self-identify as cholos without prompting. However, they do often describe single, young, pretty women as *cholitas*, the diminutive of chola, and the phrase *gran chola Paceña* (great chola from La Paz) is used admiringly about women who have been very successful in commerce. The most common signifier of being a chola or cholita is dress, principally layered gathered skirts, called a *pollera*; for that reason, the term *mujer de pollera* (woman of the pollera) is more polite and more frequently used than chola.[14] For special occasions, women wear a shawl of vicuña wool, which is very expensive, and their best bowler hats, which are an Italian make called Borsalino; they also wear large gold brooches and earrings. These clothes are much more expensive than those of *mujeres de vestido*, the women in Western clothes.[15]

Ethnicity is therefore clearly something that people can control to a certain extent, by making what Mary Weismantel (2001) calls "indexical statements" through their clothes and what they buy and eat, even if they do not explicitly self-identify as chola. One friend of mine dressed as a cholita for a photograph she took in order to register for a computing course. The photograph would eventually go on the certificate confirming that she had passed the course. She told me that she did so because more and more offices were looking to hire mujeres de pollera. Market women also self-consciously assume what Lynn Sikkink (2001) calls an "ethnicity for consumption" by the purchasers of their products. But ethnicity is also attributed to them by others, including consumers of higher or lower status in the ethnic hierarchy. Ethnicity is inseparable from gender, as those women who remain in the countryside to work the fields become more Indian than the men who move between the two spheres, while those who travel to sell their produce in the cities come to be the archetypal chola, with all its associated ambiguities and threatening overtones (de la Cadena 1996; Weismantel 2001). Having said that, many women do both, changing their clothes as they move from one place to the other, becoming chola or Indian depending on circumstance (Paulson 2003b).

Like the cholos and cholas themselves, cholo life in El Alto is a fluid and processual mixing of rural and urban, a theme which runs throughout this book. These two ideas are very important in Andean anthropology and political life, as the idealized and collective Andean discussed earlier in this introduction is most definitely a rural person; the Aymara and Quechua of the Katarista indigenous movement are similarly romanticized as rural figures, despite the fact that the leadership of this movement has mostly consisted of urban Aymara intellectuals. It is only recently that indigenous leaders have really been able to capitalize on the ways that urban Aymara—cholos—in El Alto straddle the rural and the urban or maintain links with the peasants. How rural culture, including collective values, have translated to the cities is a matter of some debate: either the city is seen as a debased space where people lose their collective morals and succumb to (implicitly Western) individualist consumerism, or they bring their rural traditions to the city and automatically create rural, collective life there. The extent of collective organization in El Alto is surely unusual for a city of its size, and in this book I do focus on that aspect of daily life. However, throughout I emphasize the work that is involved in the maintenance of collective political agency and the interplay of individual and collective values and senses of self within the day-to-day operations of such organizations.

METHODS AND STRUCTURE OF THE BOOK

I conducted the fieldwork for this book over several visits to La Paz and El Alto between 1997 and 2004. The two principal periods of fieldwork in El Alto were over twelve months in 1999–2000 and two visits in 2003–2004, from April to September 2003, then December through January 2004. These visits spanned a crucial period in Bolivia's recent political history, from the Cochabamba Water War and the peasant blockades in April 2000 to the forced resignation of Gonzalo Sanchez de Lozada in October 2003. My interest throughout was the experience of citizenship at the local level, because my previous research in Bolivia and other countries in Latin America had brought out how the regional social movements were using citizenship as a central theme for organizing their demands from the mid-1990s onward (Molyneux and Lazar 2003; Dagnino 1998, 2003). Nonetheless, this book has of necessity been shaped by the political events of 2000–2003, and I have become much more focused on explaining the background of this political history than I was initially.

It became clear to me from early on that civic organization was key to citizenship in El Alto, but I also knew that my original focus on one zone had provided an incomplete picture. So in 2003 I returned with the aim of grasping a sense of the city as a whole. I decided to research the work of occupational-based collectivities. Those months were fairly tense: in the aftermath of the burning of the Town Hall in February 2003, relations between the mayor and the more radical civic organizations, including the Federation of Street Traders, had become estranged. Political meetings in El Alto discussed the events of Black February with a view to learning from them for future mobilizations, and the Universidad Pública de El Alto (UPEA) was riven with factionalism over the issue of autonomy for the university. So I was present at what in hindsight I know to be the buildup to the events of September and October 2003, as the local civic organizations recovered from state repression after February 2003, when some leaders had been imprisoned. By August, they were gearing themselves up to mobilize over the question of local house registration procedures, the *formularios maya y paya*.[16] I knew that El Alto was an angry and rebellious city, as a civic leader strikingly expressed it to me in an interview back in 2000. I also knew that support for the peasants who blockaded the roads in April and September 2000 had been widespread, and opposition to neoliberal political parties at the national level was similarly strong. I did feel that El Alto as a city was more radical politically in 2003 than it had been in 1999–2000, but I attributed that to the fact that I was spending more of my time with people who had chosen to take an active part in the city's politics.

Nonetheless, October 2003 surprised me precisely because I had been immersed in the sectoral politics of the civic organizations in the city and could not see how the question of the natural gas exports would have brought all the different entities together against the government. I therefore returned for a month in December 2003 and January 2004 to find out what had happened from the people I knew in the Federation of Street Traders and in Rosas Pampa. My experience of some of the most politicized spheres of El Alto in mid-2003 and my surprise at hearing what happened a few weeks after I left have shaped my analysis of the events of October. I am inclined to see it as a highly contingent coming together of different sectoral interests that exploded into something much more once the government ordered the army to kill the demonstrators. I would argue that the question of the export of Bolivia's natural gas has provided some coherence to these events in retrospect and from the perspective of public intellectuals in Bolivia and internationally. The fate of the natural gas was part of the set of demands by all of the different organizations, but so were other questions, such as the tax code and the Law of Citizen Security, which criminalized road blockades. However, the natural gas situation came to symbolize a long-standing dissatisfaction with neoliberal economic policies and the political elites both nationally and internationally. Such dissatisfaction was evident back in 2000, and so, although the fact that the demonstrations happened as they did and when they did was a surprise to me, the fact that *something* happened was less surprising. I choose to see October 2003 as a turning point, when the city of El Alto irrupted into the national political sphere, and April 2000 as the beginning of the latest cycle of political upheaval that has shaped what some of my interviewees called El Alto's "awakening." The protests are a good hook for my analysis in this book but a relatively small part of its subject matter, as they are a small (albeit important) part of alteños' experience of citizenship.

Chapter 1 discusses the city of El Alto in more detail and introduces the two main focuses of this book: the neighborhood of Rosas Pampa and the Federation of Street Traders of the City of El Alto. The book is then divided into two parts. Part 1 examines citizenship practices and senses of identity and collectivity that derive from belonging to a particular place, principally the neighborhood of Rosas Pampa. I pay particular attention to the ways people of Rosas Pampa imagine and constitute themselves as a collective political subject, the "zone" (i.e., neighborhood, but the Spanish term most frequently used was *zona*).

Chapter 2 introduces the status of vecino of Rosas Pampa, arguing that this is the equivalent local term for citizen. I use the issue of development as a means to explore how the vecinos constitute themselves as a community, examining how they have literally constructed the zone and the role of state and private authorities in this process. I also discuss the theme of corruption to illustrate how the vecinos exercise accountability and imagine themselves as a collective via their expectations of their authorities. Chapter 3 continues the theme of corporate political imagining in an analysis of the local elections held in December 1999. Although suffrage is usually seen as an individualized relationship between citizen and state, I show that both individual and collective interests operate before and during the election campaigns through clientelistic politics. I argue that clientelism cannot be dismissed as simply dysfunctional and antidemocratic, and seek out the agency of the clients as they choose between patrons and make decisions about whom they will support. However, simultaneously, their talk about the corruption of politics emphasizes the distance that they feel between ordinary voters and politicians.

In chapter 4, I discuss the ritual of the annual anniversary fiesta of the zone and use a focus on dance and movement to argue that people experience collective belonging and a relationship with place in very physical ways. While Andean ethnography has often focused on fiesta rituals and fiesta sponsorship as means of building social cohesion within communities, the analysis has predominantly been symbolic, with the exception of some more recent work that addresses more performative aspects (Goldstein 2004). I complement this focus with a phenomenological analysis that places the physical experience of the fiesta at its center. Chapter 5 picks up on the emphasis on the body and the religious aspects of the fiesta and develops it to explore the senses of self that are the foundations of vecindad (the status of being a vecino). The "colonial Catholicism" of the fiesta devotion reveals a relational self that involves being part of a network of social relations that include place and the spirits. In this chapter, I oppose this version of self to the "anticommunity" promoted by Evangelical Protestantism in order to consider a different way of being part of a collectivity, mediated through an individualized sense of self built on the experience of a one-to-one relationship with God.

The second part of the book complements the place-based emphasis on a single neighborhood to examine the constitution of political agency among a specific occupational group which is spread throughout the city: street traders. Since this part examines labor organizations, I discuss the reorganization of the local economy as a result of neoliberalism in a much more explicit way than the first part. Chapter 6 examines the ways the street traders unions create a sense of collectivity among their members in an environment—the informal economy—often characterized as one primarily of competition between individuals. As with previous chapters, I highlight the embodied and physical nature of these processes, without assuming their automatic success. The example of the values and conflicts surrounding the exercise of leadership provides a particular case study of the fragility of the development of collective senses of self, where people attempt to assert values of collectivity in the face of the (perceived) pursuit of individual interests to the detriment of the group. Such dynamics are crucial to how the street traders unions construct themselves as collective political subjects with the capacity to confront and negotiate with the state, the subject of the following two chapters.

Chapter 7 discusses the relationships among commerce, ethnicity, and political agency in El Alto. I focus on the case study of the fish-sellers and examine the nature of their relationship of mediation between their members and the state and substitution for the state, a position that can cause considerable tensions and difficulties for the leaders of associations. The fish-sellers are an example of the in-betweenness (Seligmann 1989) of cholo market traders in El Alto, as they are positioned between the rural and the urban and in chains of production and distribution of goods. The example of the fish-sellers also allows me to explore how the in-betweenness of citizens of El Alto translates into political power through the connections between that city and its rural hinterland. The Aymara peasants of the La Paz countryside were extremely important protagonists of the national upheavals of 2000 and 2003; their alliance with alteños in 2003 probably explains the greater success of those mobilizations and will certainly continue to be an important factor in the development of politics in Bolivia in the future. It is, however, an alliance that cannot be taken for granted, as the potential for conflict and fractiousness is as great as if not greater than that for unification and political power.

Chapter 8 completes the move in part 2 from the self back to citizenship, perceived as the relationship with the state, and brings the book's discussion back to political philosophy through the argument that collective organizations in El Alto both model and enact a type of democracy that looks very different from that assumed by liberal political science. Democracy is "vernacularised" in different sociocultural and historical contexts (Nugent forthcoming; Michelutti n.d.). A political science informed by modernization theories flattens those differences into a simple line from less to more democratic, such that democracy can be brought to countries simply by importing liberal institutions. In this final chapter I therefore explore in detail how street traders associations model democracy, addressing practices such as the dynamics of general assemblies and values associated with the importance of speech, discussion, consensus, and leaders serving the bases, or grass roots. I would argue that these are fundamental to the exercise of citizenship in El Alto today. Bolivia has a long tradition of collective organizations that have throughout their history been both co-opted by and antagonistic to the state at different times and to greater or lesser extents, depending often on the balance of power between leadership and grass roots. So the kind of democracy under investigation in this chapter has more than localized relevance.

My conclusion starts with the point that citizenship cannot simply be understood as a legal status consisting of a sort of ownership of rights and responsibilities, as Western scholars and politicians tend to represent it. Such a conceptualization relies upon an understanding of the self as a rights- or interests-bearing individual, a "commoditized" version of the self (Strathern 1988) that is incompatible with actual practice, in El Alto at least. Looking at the practices of citizenship operating in one particular context, and the conceptions of the self and person underlying such practices, we are able to achieve a more nuanced understanding of how people actually experience their own citizenship and political agency and the implications of such alternative experiences as a factor that will continue to impede global neoliberal governmentality projects in the future.

The city is the dominant arena for much citizenship action today, and Bolivia is no exception. The argument of this book is that national citizenship must articulate with local forms of belonging or citizenship, and the setting for my discussion of those local forms is the city of El Alto. For a while its political importance as a city was underestimated by most of those who commented on Bolivian political life in the national media. However, the events of September and October 2003 have proven to be something of a turning point; since then it has become impossible to ignore El Alto. At that time, mobilizations that began as sectoral and local became national in scope, as protests over local house registration procedures in El Alto merged with those of the altiplano peasants with similarly localized demands. They were the first and most effective political alliance of Aymara peasants and El Alto residents at a time when the principal civic institutions in the city were unified and, with the exception of one, run by leaders whose politics were squarely oppositional to the national government. Those institutions were crucial to the organization of the protests and to their success.

El Alto was so central to the protests for three reasons. First, the general strike there effectively besieged the city of La Paz, a tactic of protest that has a long and poignant historical heritage, going back to the rebellion of Tupac Katari in 1781. Food and other household supplies could not get down to La Paz. Second, the repressive military response to the demonstrations in El Alto that were blocking the movement of supplies came to symbolize the inhumanity of Gonzalo Sanchez de Lozada's regime more generally and enraged alteños (i.e., residents of El Alto) and other Bolivians. In this it is crucial to remember that "Goni" is the single figure most associated with neoliberalism and its attendant structural violence in Bolivia, which has been most acutely felt in El Alto (Gill 2000). More specifically, twenty-six protestors were killed and over a hundred were injured when they tried to stop gasoline tankers from leaving the neighborhood of Senkata, and more deaths followed in other parts of the city (Ramos 1998). During the week of 12–17 October, protests demanding Goni's resignation spread to middle-class areas of La Paz and to other cities in Bolivia. Though accusations that Goni was a murderer were abundant, the opposition focused as much if not more on the question of the export of natural gas. Third, the physical politics of the waves of large numbers of demonstrators marching down from El Alto every day to join those in La Paz reinforced the sense that it was the Bolivian people in general rather than a small and localized minority who were demanding Sanchez de Lozada's resignation. The city's subsequent restiveness has always referred back to October 2003, each mobilization holding the implicit threat of a repeat. That threat was fulfilled when Carlos Mesa resigned in June 2005, prompted by street protests across the country in which El Alto took a leading role.

El Alto's political importance came into sharp focus in October 2003 but is not confined to those specific events. It is of much wider and longer term significance politically, a significance that derives from what makes it distinctive as a city. This chapter is an attempt to outline some of those distinctive elements, highlighting movement, commerce, the strength of local allegiances, the city's relationship with its rural hinterland, and, most important for this book, the high levels of civic organization there. As such, it also serves as an introduction to El Alto as city and ethnographic field site.

CITIZENSHIP, COMMUNITY, AND THE CITY

El Alto is important to our understanding of citizenship only in part because of its entry into the national political sphere; the more local citizenship of the city itself is of equal theoretical importance. Indeed, the nature of the city more generally is central to how we understand citizenship (Holston 1999a; Isin 2000; Goldstein 2004). Engin Isin (forthcoming) has argued that the state must articulate itself through the city. Throughout history, according to Isin, states, empires, leagues, and republics have all been performances enacted in practices that can happen only in the city, instead of entities as such. We might not wish to go quite this far for the case of Bolivia and other countries with considerable rural populations, but we could certainly highlight the importance of the city as a locus of political action in the twenty-first century, as the protests in El Alto and other cities such as Cochabamba have underlined with such force. This recognition pushes us into a consideration of how urban, local citizenship operates and interacts with national citizenship in particular contexts. In modern Western political thought, which Isin characterizes as "scalar," spaces and territories are conceived of as nested scales: cities are subordinated to provinces, which are subordinated to the state in a hierarchical and exclusive relationship. National citizenship thus in theory overtakes and seeks to replace urban citizenship, certainly in the juridico-legal sense of the terms. However, modern (nation-) states in Europe and Spanish America emerged from states that were a conglomeration of separate self-governing towns. The Spanish community of natives (naturales), as it developed during the sixteenth through the eighteenth centuries, was conceived of as a community of "local citizens," for whom the legal status of citizen (vecino) was granted on the basis of their demonstration of loyalty to the local community through their behavior (Herzog 2003). So national legal citizenship was constituted on the basis of local urban citizenship. This vision of citizenship translated to the New World (Herzog 2003; Thurner 1997), and it retains considerable importance today, once we look beyond citizenship as juridico-legal status and seek to analyze it in a more political and social sense.

Indeed, citizenship has always been about working on the self to create certain kinds of citizens who will behave in particular ways toward the local (rather than national) community, from Aristotle (1992) and Pericles (1999; Castoriadis 1992) through Rousseau, to contemporary talk about "good citizens" (Dagger 2005) and the idea that children can learn citizenship in schools through participation in locally based voluntary projects, as in contemporary citizenship education programs in the United Kingdom. In the Modern period, states attempted to remove all layers of allegiances between the individual and the state, but failed to do so, leaving what is often called "civil society" as intermediary. It is that intermediary sphere that is the subject of this book, especially as expressed through local organizational forms based upon residence and occupation. It is important to remember that the state does not subsume such localized intermediaries, and different allegiances can come into conflict and overlap with each other, overflowing the boundaries between them (Isin forthcoming).

The local public sphere incorporates much more than the institutions of government, having been widened in part by social movements' contestations over public space (Isin 2000; Holston 1999b). Urban public spheres include the streets where people demonstrate as well as the many forms of association where people negotiate the building and defining of society, even where citizens act violently toward one another (Holston 1999b; Goldstein 2004). If citizenship is a practice as well as a status, as I argued in the introduction, the question is, Where does that practice occur? The logical realm for political action for most citizens has always been their local area, and people are often suspicious of those who choose to extend their political action beyond that and become professional politicians rather than citizens (Lister 1997). Furthermore, as Nikolas Rose (2000: 108) has argued, urban governmentality inheres in various arenas, and there has been a "displacement of an earlier notion of social space by the micro-moral territory of the community, and the emergence of new games of citizenship that operate in terms of the relations between community and subjectivity, between collective responsibilities and an ethic of personal obligation. It is in terms of this new ethical space of the community . . . that all our new forms of urban governmentality operate." More concretely, it is in the public spheres of the city that these games of citizenship are negotiated, and governance enacted and resisted.

As the quote from Rose indicates, the nature of community takes center stage in social and political theory of citizenship. However, as anthropologists have often pointed out, community cannot be taken for granted (e.g., see Amit 2002; Cohen 1985). Much anthropology of the Andes, which has focused predominantly on rural areas, indicates the constructed nature of community there. Anthropologists have seen the expression of collective values in ritual and symbolic structures (Isbell 1978), patterns for organizing work (Urton 1992; Skar 1982), the categorization of people as full persons (jaqi) or not (Canessa 1998), office-holding pathways (thaki), and rotative leadership systems (Abercrombie 1998; Carter and Mamani P. 1989 [1982]; Ticona Alejo 2003). Yet internal contestation over collective values is mostly analyzed in terms of differential participation in such systems (e.g., Buechler 1980), or as a structural principle (Albó 1977), rather than through the practices of those taking part (although see Klemola 1997). The misrecognition of internal differentiation is particularly acute in the popular stereotypes that distinguish starkly between (rural) indigenous communality and (urban) Western individualism.

Such discourses have parallels with Anglo-Saxon communitarianism in the way they assume away conflicts internal to communities, tending toward a homogenizing vision of community itself (Gutmann 1992; Rapport 1997; Mouffe 1992). Iris Young (1990: 300) argues that communitarians do not provide us with a solid basis for a politics that can deal with diversity: "Community is an understandable dream . . . but politically problematic . . . because those motivated by it will tend to suppress differences among themselves or implicitly to exclude from their political groups persons with whom they do not identify." This is the problem with attempts at differentiated citizenship based on group rights. But the liberal answer to such problems, namely, universal individual citizenship, is also inadequate. Young uses the modern city as a model for overcoming some of the tensions between communitarianism and liberal universalism. Proposing an idealized version of "the unoppressive city," defined as "openness to unassimilated others," as a model for a "politics of difference," she argues against the ideal version of community that implies and relies upon face-to-face communication and values sharing (319). In what is admittedly a discussion of ideal types, she overstates the opposition between the mixing of the city and the face-to-face communities of tradition. However, her vision of the city as a place where people meet and interact with others who are not like themselves is widely shared (Holston 1999a; Isin 2000; Phillips 1993). El Alto is a particularly good example of a city based on the mixing of people, and therefore a productive arena for research into questions of urban or local citizenship.

INTRODUCING EL ALTO

The city of El Alto fans out from the area known as the Ceja (the eyebrow) to the north, the west, and the south, flowing around the airport. Maps of the city often describe it as a *mancha urbana*, or "urban stain," and it does appear to have spread as if it were spilled liquid. The streets and buildings stretch out over the high plateau between the East and West Andes. Only the mountains themselves can, it seems, stop the city's progress. Visitors to El Alto may wonder whether they catch their breath because of the thin air at that altitude (4,100 meters above sea level), or because of the great expanse of space, the flatness of the land, the immensity of the sky,

1. Huayna Potosí, from the outskirts of Rosas Pampa

the clarity of the atmosphere, the quality of the light, and the frequent glimpses of the beauty of the mountain peaks of Huayna Potosí, Chacaltaya, Mururata, and Illimani.

To the east of the Ceja is the ridge of the bowl-like crater in which La Paz is built, and if you peer over the precipitous cliffs, you can see houses spilling down the steep banks, which are called the *laderas*. On occasion, this is more than a metaphor, as landslides are common. At times La Paz seems to be collapsing in on itself, sliding down the banks, or retreating behind locked gates and private security in the wealthy southern neighborhoods. Alteños tell stories of a future flood that will fill the bowl with water. La Paz is claustrophobic, El Alto expansive: the cold mountain air moves there.

El Alto is a new city, formally recognized as such only in 1988. Prior to that, it was part of the city of La Paz, the result of La Paz's spilling over the edges of the bowl-like crater. The first urban settlements there were in the early years of the twentieth century; El Alto has grown to its present population of around seven hundred thousand as a result of migration from the Aymara- and Quechua-speaking countryside and mining centers. El Alto is therefore intrinsically linked to La Paz, having begun as the outgrowth of its indigenous periphery. However, the administrative separation of El Alto from La Paz in 1985 has begun to mean something in the past few years, and El Alto is emerging with a distinctive identity as an indigenous city. It has its own business districts, albeit based upon street markets; its own administrative centers where the alcaldía (town hall) and the offices of the important civic organizations are located; its own transport system; a newspaper since 2002; and a public university since 2000. In the past most alteños worked or studied in La Paz and returned to the city to sleep, giving rise to its nickname *ciudad dormitorio*; they even had to travel down to La Paz to pay their monthly utility bills. Today, the term ciudad dormitorio is accurate only for some neighborhoods (principally Ciudad Satelite and Villa Adela). Many alteños do not need to "go down to the city" (*bajar a la ciudad*) during their daily lives—although the use of the term la ciudad to refer to La Paz does betray the hierarchical relationship of the two cities in ordinary people's minds. Now, many go only for special reasons, such as for family gatherings, to participate in political demonstrations outside the seat of the national government, to make special wholesale purchases, or to collect salaries. Nevertheless, the connections between the two cities remain important, politically and socially. Many alteños have family in the peripheral areas of La Paz, who migrated earlier and built houses there before land became too expensive. Many still work in the city or study at the Universidad Mayor de San Andres (UMSA) there, and the two main roads between the two cities are full of traffic, especially in the mornings and evenings. However, El Alto is more than the impoverished satellite or suburb of La Paz, and its role in the recent political upheavals underlines its distinctiveness.

El Alto is also very different from other Latin American and Andean cities. As Daniel Goldstein (2004) argues, when we visualize such cities on a map, we see the city center as highly detailed, with plazas and landmarks, and as we move outward to the periphery, "bare spots on the map" appear, seemingly empty spaces devoid of complexity, plazas, or named landmarks. These are the marginal districts of the squatter settlements, unrecognized by the state or deemed illegal, clandestine, and disordered, and as such usually un- or underserved in terms of public utilities and basic services such as health and education. Increasingly, these peripheral areas are accompanied by wealthy suburbs, gated communities of residents escaping a crowded and dangerous city center and leaving it for the tourists and some brave businesses, but not for the poor, who are moved out (Caldeira 2000). In contrast, El Alto has a spoke-like spatial structure.

Its centers are the commercial districts of the Ceja, which is also the point at which you leave El Alto to travel to La Paz, and to its north the 16 de Julio, which hosts an enormous market on Thursdays and Sundays. Two main roads branch out from the Ceja, one going south to Oruro and thence to Potosí and Chile, one north to Lake Titicaca and then Peru. The airport and customs depot lie between the two roads. The mestizo residents of El Alto are concentrated in the middle-class districts of Ciudad Satelite in the south and the up-and-coming Villa Adela district to the west of the airport. They mostly work either in La Paz or in the El Alto municipal administration. The central districts around the Ceja and 16 de Julio are indigenous or cholo, mostly commercial, and by now they have the basic infrastructure of water, sewage systems, and electricity; the roads are paved and the houses are well established, often two stories or more, and made out of brick rather than adobe. The very outlying districts, especially those in the northern part of the city, are the poorer and newer ones, with less infrastructure and more first-generation migrants. Between the two lie middling zones, where public utilities may exist but coverage is patchy and not everyone has signed up to receive services; houses are mostly adobe with some made of brick; and some, but not all, roads are paved. So the city certainly has hierarchies of class and race within its borders, but the racial stratification and segregation so evident in La Paz, Quito, Lima, Cochabamba, and other Latin American cities is less stark here.

That is in part because almost the whole city is marginal. El Alto is certainly poor: the census of 2001 reported that 48 percent of its residents lived in moderate poverty, 17 percent in extreme poverty, and 0.5 percent in "marginal" conditions; 25 percent live "on the verge" of poverty.[1] Its residents have particularly suffered the consequences of the neoliberal economic policies of the past two decades. Many are former miners, "relocalized" (i.e., fired from the state-owned mining companies) in the mid-1980s. The state has gradually withdrawn from most forms of social provisioning, including health services, education, pensions, and public services, as well as programs to subsidize food and gasoline. Building a house is difficult in El Alto because the land market is subject to the (often criminal) activities of those selling plots of land, the loteadores, and actual construction relies on self-exploitation and the mobilization of kin networks. Local municipal administration has become more effective in recent years but remains corrupt and underresourced, and nongovernmental organizations (NGOs) have stepped into the breach, providing patchy health and education services, among others (Gill 2000). Many parts of the city do not have effective sewage systems, and residents are finding it increasingly difficult to pay the rising bills charged by the private companies who control public utilities such as electricity and water. Crime is increasingly serious: pickpocketing is common and burglaries of the most prosaic things, such as gas canisters (for cookers), are more frequent now than even five years ago. In an unfortunate but by now familiar pattern, the policing of crime has been largely privatized: while the wealthy in the southern suburbs of La Paz protect themselves from the threat of crime by locking themselves away and hiring private security, some residents of El Alto have resorted to lynching (cf. Goldstein 2005).

Yet, although these are all indications of social fragmentation, and El Alto can be analyzed very effectively in this way, the city is also more than the sum of its social problems. Lesley Gill (2000) warns us against the romanticization of poverty, and of the poor's ability to survive under neo-liberalism through either self-help or entrepreneurialism, not least because it elides the role of the state in the immiseration and oppression of the poor. Writing about El Alto's social problems and about what it lacks in terms of basic services is a way to make a claim on state resources for the city. However, much that is written about the city along these lines is done so with a pervasive sense of crisis and emergency, as in this extract from an important survey of the city conducted in the 1980s and 1990s: "The city of El Alto is in more than one sense the clear expression, not only of the global crisis that still affects this country, but also it exemplifies the conjunction of problematics that characterize Bolivian society. . . . El Alto is a city traversed by problems from all sides" (Antezana 1993: 9–13). The theme of poverty combines with that of violence, emphasized in crime and domestic violence statistics and newspaper stories, as well as scholarly analyses of the structural violence of discrimination and internal colonialism or the violent ruptures of migration itself (Cottle and Ruiz 1993). The problem is that such characterizations are also uncomfortably close to the racist stereotype of the city and its residents as violent, ignorant, desperate, and backward: la indiada from the countryside but in the city, the Indian masses who are a potential time bomb far too close to La Paz, and who threaten the whites both physically and by undermining the perceived modernity of the city (cf. Goldstein 2004).

Several authors, including Gill, also recognize the importance of collective organization in El Alto (Sandoval and Sostres 1989; Sostres 1995; Anze O. 1995), and Goldstein (2004) points out how even lynch mobs are an expression of collective identity and a collective demand to be recognized by the state. Neoliberalism has reconfigured social relations in the city, but not totally at the expense of collectivity, even if the more traditional forms of class solidarity typified by the unionized miners no longer exist. El Alto is not entirely an anonymous city, then, since small communities have been created within it, based upon place of residence or birth, occupation, or kinship networks. In this, it is not unlike places in other Andean cities where rural–urban migrants have settled (Altamirano 1984a; Long 1984; Paaregard 1997).

POSTCARDS FROM EL ALTO

The dialectic between the way that the neoliberal economic climate has influenced collective organization and cooperation on the one side and social fragmentation and individuation on the other mirrors the tension between face-to-face communities and anonymous city and makes El Alto a productive subject of research into the politics of the "unoppressive city." The latter is a tension that also appears when conducting anthropological research in cities, especially given the emphasis on participant observation in ethnographic research. The difficulties posed by the sheer size of most cities are both methodological and representational: How can we know and describe an entity that is a collection of seven hundred thousand people? Any response will of necessity be partial, but one answer is to look for a village-size population within the city, a face-to-face community. Another is to approach the city as a series of networks and flows, perhaps a "space of flows" rather than a "space of places" (Castells 1989: 348). The two strategies are not mutually exclusive, and this book combines both, because alteños experience their citizenship in and through both of these types of locations and movements. This requires privileging particular networks, communities, and flows over others.

This section explores two networks or flows and one face-to-face community that make up El Alto. It comprises "snapshots" or "postcards" (Van Dam and Salman 2003) from three of El Alto's locations or shapes. The first snapshot is of the Ceja, which is the hub of El Alto and the busiest place in the city on a day-to-day basis. It is also the most important spatial location for the construction of occupation-based identities, which are the subject of the second part of this book. I then describe the more face-to-face community of the zone of Rosas Pampa, the subject of the first part of this book. The third postcard introduces a different set of relation-

2. Weekly market in Santiago II, the zone adjacent to Rosas Pampa

ships, which combines networks, movement, and face-to-face communities. These are the networks that migrants from the same part of the altiplano countryside build when they move to the city. There has been a fair amount of literature devoted to this third location,[2] so, although these networks are a presence in this book, they are not its focus. Nonetheless, they are crucial background for understanding the nature of El Alto and its relationship with its rural hinterland, which is, in turn, central to alteños' encounters with the state.

The Ceja   The Ceja concentrates El Alto's main economic activities, principally commerce and public transport. It is thus a key location for the construction of occupation-based identities and one of the sites where El Alto's distinctive identity as an Aymara city crystallizes. It is rare to see someone simply wandering through the Ceja. Everyone is there with a purpose: to travel through or to buy or sell. In the multiple networks of social relations that make up El Alto, the Ceja is a crucial node, connecting people through commerce as well as through transport. In the Ceja, commerce is not so much the expression of an economy embedded in social relations as it *is* those social relations themselves. The Ceja is a fierce engine of trade, traversed by hierarchies and competition as well as by solidarity and collective organization. It is dynamic, pulsing with the changing seasons and hours of the day. The noises, smells, and colors there overwhelm the senses.

Several networks that make up El Alto touch down spatially at the Ceja. The Federation of Street Traders ("the Federation") has its office there, along with the COR (Central Obrera Regional, or Regional Workers Center) and the FEJUVE (Federation of Juntas Vecinales). It is also one of the two main locations for alteño street traders (the other being the 16 de Julio market on Thursdays and Sundays). I describe the Ceja here both to contextualize the activities of the Federation of Street Traders and also to use the Ceja as a metonym for the El Alto of flows and networks. Representing it as a metonymic field site in this way assists in analytically grasping the city as a whole, while retaining the use of ethnographic description that remains of necessity place-centered (cf. de Certeau 1984).

The Ceja itself is a group of streets crammed full with market stalls, *ambulantes* (mobile street vendors), minibuses, *micros* (buses), customers, and people traveling from one side of the city to the other, from El Alto to La Paz, or from both cities out to other parts of the country. It is the place that links different parts of El Alto together and is the predominant link between El Alto and La Paz, and La Paz and everywhere else. Almost all public transport routes go through the Ceja. Travelers who want to go anywhere in El Alto take a minibus or micro into it, then catch another one which exits along one of three roads. The minibuses and micros then turn off from these spoke roads at different heights according to the residential zones they serve. A pamphlet distributed to advertise the municipality's plans for traffic redirection measures in the Ceja in 2003 stated that 50,988 vehicles pass through the Ceja an hour: 55 percent are minibuses, 11 percent micros, 28 percent cars (taxis and private vehicles), and 2 percent interprovincial coaches.

The Ceja is multiple flows of people. In the early mornings, people are traveling to work, school, or university, either in El Alto or in La Paz; on Thursdays and Sundays they travel from their homes to the market in the 16 de Julio zone, either as vendors or as buyers, and return during the early afternoon; around midday on weekdays many who work in El Alto travel home to eat their lunch or travel to the Ceja to have their lunch there; once they have done so, they travel out again and return at 7 or 8 P.M. after an afternoon at work; later the travelers are mostly students returning from evening classes at the UMSA in La Paz.

Women struggle through the crowds carrying goods that they have bought or are intending to sell in brightly colored *awayus*—square textile carrying-cloths that they knot around their shoulders, with the contents on their backs. Some carry their baby or toddler in an awayu and move through the streets at the pace of another child who is holding their hand. Awayus are woven in stripes of red, white, pink, purple, blue, or green on a background of one of those colors. Fashions in awayu colors change slowly, as they are very hardwearing. The combination of colors of the awayus, the produce on sale, and the clothes of the people flowing through makes the Ceja a striking visual experience.

Along the streets are shops and shopping centers, selling clothes, computers, music instruments, amplification equipment, typewriters, stereos, TVs, meat, wholesale dry goods—almost anything other than fruit and vegetables. Increasingly they also house Internet cafés, video game arcades, and mobile phone shops and repair centers. Dotted throughout are restaurants selling one or two kinds of lunch, and "broasters" with chickens turning on a spit just outside the door. Every so often you catch a glimpse of a covered alleyway with women sitting behind mountains of oranges or other seasonal fruit. Fruit and vegetables are also sold from the market stalls that line the curbs and the middle of the bigger roads, where you can also find clothes, shoes, electrical goods, and ingredients for ritual offerings. In the Ceja, it is possible to buy almost anything you need.

There are different kinds of market stalls, from metal constructions that the stallholders lock up at night to open wooden stalls sheltered by ch'iwiñas. The ch'iwiña is an umbrella-like construction of blue or red plastic stretched over wooden poles. Banana sellers sometimes use yellow plastic because it makes the bananas look better. The ch'iwiñas are set at about eye level for a gringo/a, making walking down the middle of two lanes of stalls a hazardous experience. Weaving through the stalls, the traffic, and the shops are ambulantes selling fruit, juice, milk drinks, safety pins, and other goods, often from carts or wheelbarrows. Other ambulantes put down a small tarpaulin on the pavement outside a shop, sit down, and spread out their goods to attract customers: herbs, toothpaste, batteries, rat poison, lip balm, woolen hats, small piles of vegetables, and frozen sweet tubers from the countryside—the altiplano's ice cream. Stallholders and ambulantes are predominantly women, as are their customers.

On busy corners, teenage boys and girls dressed in neon waistcoats and carrying a mobile phone attached by a chain to their wrist sell phone calls to those who use their own phone only to receive calls. This was new to me when I returned to Bolivia in April 2003, two and a half years after the previous time I visited. Another novelty was the (male) private security guards patrolling the streets in pairs, dressed in black, with dark sunglasses and what looked like bulletproof vests. The backs of the vests announce the often very macho name of the firm: Men in Black (from the film) or RIP (presumably Rest in Peace), for example.

Commerce in the Ceja changes over the day: the vegetable sellers do their most brisk business in the mornings, as women buy produce to cook for the main meal of the day at lunchtime. From midmorning to midday, the streets are dotted with women cooking meals on gas stoves, serving them to customers squatting nearby. Some of the market stalls are restaurants, with wooden benches for their customers under the blue plastic. They stay open throughout the day. The smell of cooking lingers and by the end of the day combines with the smell of rubbish. During the day, the rubbish builds up in mounds, which the dogs come to pick over in the afternoon. Overnight, the private company subcontracted by the municipality clears it away if the workers are not on strike for lack of pay. Vendors are responsible for cleaning around their stalls.

Furniture, clothes, and toy stalls usually open around midday or early afternoon; in the evening the hair trinket stalls and ambulantes selling slices of cake come out to catch the students returning from school or university or the workers coming home at the end of the day. On Thursday and Sunday mornings the Ceja is calm because many vendors have taken their wares to the 16 de Julio market. In reality, the Ceja is never anything but busy during the daytime, but relatively speaking it seems subdued. In the evenings, especially Fridays and Saturdays, the bars, discos, and brothels open; the majority of vendors pack up their goods and take them home, and traffic lessens. As people walk through on their way home, one or two drunken men stagger through the streets or try to take a minibus home by disguising their drunkenness, although drivers and customers are rarely fooled. Others just pass out on the pavement and remain there until the following day. At this time the smell of alcohol fills the air outside bars. It is also particularly strong just after Carnival (Mardi Gras), when stallholders have ch'alla'd their stalls for the year.[3]

The products on sale change according to season: there are school uniforms when the school year starts and around Independence Day, when students have to parade. On special days, vendors organize more stalls, so that they can sell, say, fireworks at San Juan (21 June); cards, flowers, and gifts in the days before Mother's Day; streamers, balloons, water pistols, and alcohol at Carnival time; gifts, panettones, and wrapping paper at Christmas; grapes and red and yellow underwear over New Year's.[4] Around Christmas, several of the roads are closed to traffic, and the streets fill to bursting with stalls, customers, and pickpockets.

Commerce in the Ceja is organized spatially as well as temporally. Around the outer edges on one of the main spoke roads, the Avenida 6 de Marzo, are mechanics workshops and high-value industrial-scale goods, such as parts for trucks and cars and hardware in general. On the other side, transporters park their trucks, filled with one kind of vegetable they have brought in from other parts of Bolivia or with wholesale dry goods brought from the borders. Market stallholders and small shopkeepers buy their goods there and transport them to their shop by taxi. In the center of the Ceja, traders sell high-volume, low-value goods. On the streets where women mostly sell vegetables, the vendors put out small mounds of, say, tomatoes or carrots, and buyers know that this amount costs 1 Boliviano.

I used to catch my minibus home from a crossroads in the middle of the Ceja, where the Avenida Tiwanaku crosses Calle 1. Down the Avenida Tiwanaku in one direction on the right-hand side there are a few stalls selling powdered milk, coffee, and breakfast cereals, then some small-scale vegetable and meat stalls. Opposite them, down the middle of the road, rows of metal kiosks sell pharmaceutical products and then pans, washing-up bowls, buckets, and plates. On the other side of the road, still down its middle, you can buy toys, children's shoes, and clothes; opposite them, vendors sell small pieces of hardware: screws, nails, and so on. On the corner is a dairy kiosk that sells milk, yogurt, and butter. Turning around, down the Avenida Tiwanaku still but in the other direction, the stalls sell, in the first line on the left, gifts for graduation events or birthdays; in the middle are stalls for watch and shoe repair, followed by stalls selling goods for ritual offerings, then fish; on the right are vegetable stalls. Along Calle 1 in both directions you can see shops and stalls on the side of the street, with people edging along in single file between them and the nose-to-tail minibuses elbowing their way through two abreast.

When you want to buy furniture, you go to the street where the shopkeepers exclusively sell furniture; they display their wares on the road outside. If you want to consult a yatiri (a ritual specialist), you go to the roads that are on the edge of the cliffs leading down to La Paz. They have a good view of the mountain ranges from here, which is important for their work (Fernandez Juarez 1995). If you want to buy meat, you should go to one of the streets or covered markets where the butchers are. One of the few products for which I did not find a street is coca: coca sellers are dotted about the Ceja. Under their scarlet ch'iwiña, the women position themselves behind two large bags of coca, one holding the deep green leaves of higher quality, the other holding cheaper ones. The women also sell cigarettes, pure alcohol, and lejía, a substance that is chewed with the coca leaves in order to release their flavor.[5]

If you develop a good relationship with a coca seller, she will give you some extra leaves after she has weighed out the amount you asked for. This extra is called the yapa, and experienced buyers always ask for a yapa when they buy vegetables or fruit by weight. They also bargain, asking the vendor, "Rebajáme, pues"—"Discount it for me, go on." As a gringa, I was only sometimes successful when I made this request. My comadre, however, is particularly good at bargaining down prices.[6] She is well aware that the yapa often only compensates for the "inaccuracy" of the weights and measures, so she takes along her own, more trustworthy hand-held spring scales when she buys food by weight.

Prices of goods are fixed by negotiation and depend upon the relationship between vendor and buyer; if they are caseras, which means that the buyer is a regular customer, the buyer is usually confident that she is getting a good price or a generous yapa. Otherwise, prices are remarkably consistent for the same goods in the same street, even though vendors I knew swore to me that they didn't fix prices between themselves. Prices change according to the season: at the beginning of the new school year, for example, sober-colored trousers and skirts, sportswear, and exercise books rise in price. In winter, coca and cigarettes go up in price. Nonetheless, vendor friends frequently complained to me that people now want to "buy cheap" and are forcing prices down as the competition gets more acute.

Aside from the confusion of colors, the noise of the Ceja is the dominant sensual experience. The mobile phone boys and girls cry out "Llamadas celulares!" (Mobile phone calls!); vendors with carts that have megaphone systems advertise the price of their goods, especially ballpoint pens and exercise books; ambulantes selling chocolate milk shout out the product and its price; and shopkeepers play loud music, although stallholders rarely shout out their wares. The minibuses in the traffic jams usually have their radios tuned to Radio Chacaltaya, which plays tropical music and has an instantly recognizable jingle. Other drivers prefer the sermons and hymns of Evangelical radio stations or their tapes of Morenada and other folkloric dance music. The younger ones play *tecno* (i.e., pop music). The minibuses rev their engines and beep their horns, and the *voceadores* in the back shout out the names of the neighborhoods they will pass through. The drivers go as slowly as they can until they fill up their vehicles, which usually hold fourteen passengers. They battle with the police trying to keep the traffic flowing, who blow their whistles to tell them to move on. Above the general hubbub of the traffic, thousands of buyers are talking to each other or negotiating with stallholders.

The voceadores are usually young men or boys who are related to the minibus driver. As well as shouting out the minibus route, they also collect the fares. When the minibus is full, the voceador stands at the side of the bus, hunched over to fit in around the passengers. Passengers can hail a minibus at any point and alight at any point, although drivers prefer to set passengers down and pick them up at street corners. Women with babies or large bundles of produce squeeze their way in to the front seats of the main compartment. Mujeres de pollera very rarely take one of the two seats next to the driver; they leave these for men, young mujeres de vestido, and gringos. Sometimes it is possible to catch the correct minibus simply by hearing your destination in the route shouted out by the voceador. More usually passengers know which part of the Ceja the route passes through and make their way to the appropriate street. Passengers must also make a calculation of how close to the beginning of the route they should get into a minibus, because there is a trade-off between sitting in traffic for a long time and getting a seat. There is no standing room.

Minibus fares are set by the municipality in discussions with the drivers trade unions. However, these are also dynamic and drop at off-peak times, for example when drivers want to get down to La Paz in the afternoon so that they can pick up a full load of passengers for the journey back. This gives rise to one of the Ceja's most distinctive sounds, as the voceadores shout out the fare and compete with each other for passengers at the beginning of the road that leads down to La Paz. Micros sometimes also have voceadores, either for the whole journey or at the beginning of routes, boys who hire themselves out to shout out the route for different drivers. Micros are cheaper than minibuses but go much slower. Like the minibuses, they don't have set stops; in La Paz, the authorities have tried to institute such a scheme several times with little success, and they have never tried such a scheme in El Alto.

The Ceja, then, is a place of movement—of ebbs and flows of people, vehicles, and produce. Goods come in with one person and leave with another; people come in from one side of the city and leave to go to the other side or to another city. People rarely meander; they usually come into and go out of the Ceja with a purpose. It is the connecting point for the whole city. Some people live there, above their business or in back streets, but it is primarily a commercial and transport center.

Rosas Pampa   The Ceja's hustle and bustle contrasts strikingly with the calm of the second main location of this book, the neighborhood—or zone, from the Spanish word *zona*, used most frequently by locals—of Rosas Pampa, which is in the south of El Alto. It has approximately a thousand households and fifty-three hundred inhabitants, or vecinos, and it is bordered on its western side by the highway to Oruro and on the other by precipitous cliffs that lead down to the valley of Achocalla. A railway line, along which a few freight trains pass each day, runs parallel to the Oruro highway. The central avenue (Avenida 4) cuts the zone in half between these two points, and lateral residential streets branch off it like a square version of the veins of a leaf.

Walking down Avenida 4, I feel protected, safe, in contrast to the danger of the outer limits of Rosas Pampa, especially the railway line. Assaults were relatively common along the railway, and in 2000 a young local girl was murdered and left there. Avenida 4 runs down from the earth street at the top (north) of the zone to the football pitch, the focal point of the whole neighborhood. Just at the bottom of the football pitch is the market, the public toilets, built in the early 1990s, and the Community Center, the ground floor of which was completed in mid-2000. At its northern end is the health center, with a basketball court out front, and on the other side is the local state school, the Unidad Educativa Bolivia. Small shops line the street at that point, selling sweets, household supplies, and stationery. There are also two *locales*, rooms that can be hired for parties. One or two dogs roam the edges of the street, sniffing at the shop wares or fighting each other. Women and children attend their stores, playing, gossiping, or just sitting and watching Avenida 4. I lived on one of the lateral streets, and within a short time they all knew me, at least by sight, and said hello as I passed by.

On Avenida 4, the muted conversations of women and children walking to one of the stores, the odd dog fight, and occasional minibus or micro cocoon me in a comfortable silence. The football pitch opens up to the blue sky, and the zone also feels expansive. Four times a day the street fills with children and noise as they are going to and leaving school. Their

3. General purpose shop in Rosas Pampa

uniform is navy blue and white, and the little ones wear white lab coats to protect (and perhaps disguise) their clothes. Older girls walk arm in arm with their friends, boys hang out in small groups; they buy sweets, jelly, and lollipops and make their way home for lunch or tea. After about half an hour, the zone settles down again. At night, the silence is even more absolute, as the normally low level of traffic noise quiets further. The sky becomes black, and the stars are usually clearly visible. On some nights, the full moon lights up my room like a streetlight. There are streetlights in the zone, but the dark sky swallows up electric light, and the moon and stars take over.

When I walk down the street I live on, I leave the safety of Avenida 4 and run the gauntlet of the dogs menacingly protecting their owners' homes. Seasoned vecinos, including children, pelt any aggressive ones with stones as they hurry past. In 1999–2000, there was a particularly unpleasant dog, Rocky, almost opposite to my house, which attacked me on one occasion; like a few of the children, I was scared of him. In the middle of my first stay there, his owners moved closer to Avenida 4, opposite Cepillo, a dog that always barked when people passed by but never actually attacked. The two dogs set each other off. It is important to know the character of the dogs on any particular street; some will attack seemingly without motive. My landlady told me to mutter under my breath "San Roque, San Roque" to appeal to the patron saint of dogs so that they wouldn't attack. I would also cross my fingers as I walked by. By 2003, both Rocky and Cepillo were gone; people said that Rocky disappeared overnight, perhaps poisoned by a neighbor fed up with him scaring their children. People can lose their *ajayus* (souls) if they get a fright, and they then become ill, and children are more vulnerable than adults. For this reason, several people felt that Rocky needed to be dealt with.

The houses in Rosas Pampa are predominantly made of adobe bricks with corrugated iron roofs. They consist of three or four separate one-room buildings clustered on one level around a courtyard. As people have time and resources, they add more rooms to their compounds, which are surrounded by high adobe walls. Each time I return to Rosas Pampa, more red-brick two- or three-story houses have appeared. During dry weather, everything is covered with dust. The sun reflects off the light-colored streets, and everything seems faded in comparison with the intensely blue sky above.

Rosas Pampa and the nearby town of Achocalla used to be part of a hacienda, which was divided among the former serfs during the agrarian reform in 1953. The foundation of Rosas Pampa as urban zone is usually considered to be 1975, when the Junta Vecinal de Villa Rosas Pampa (Neighborhood Council of Villa Rosas Pampa) was established, an event marked by the first fiesta in the zone. Despite its age, the infrastructure of Rosas Pampa is not at a level comparable to other well-established zones in El Alto. This is probably due to struggles during the 1970s between the vecinos and the railway company, which wanted the land for its employees (Musch, Valdez, and Gondrie 1994). In 1984, public taps for drinking water were installed, and in 1994, with support from the Dutch NGO Projecto de Fortalecimiento de la Atención Primaria en Salud Distrito III—El Alto (APS; Project for the Strengthening of Primary Health Care Services in District 3—El Alto), domestic sewage and drinking water systems were put in. Most people have water in their home, usually a tap in their yard. In 1988 a small medical center was built, replaced in 1993 by a new building, funded and run by APS, who also organized the materials for the new Community Center (Musch et al. 1994). In the late 1980s, the junta vecinal managed to get public lighting and electricity for the zone. By 1999, though, the streets were still not paved. This was the principal difference from other comparable zones in El Alto, and the resulting dust was the main complaint of vecinos in a survey I conducted in 2000 with the youth group of the local Catholic church at the time. By 2003, the main trunk roads through the zone had been paved or tarred and the residential streets in the northern half of Rosas Pampa had been cobbled. Where this had not been done, or had been done badly, the few weeks of rain or snow each year meant that the streets became so muddy that they were almost impassable.

The zone has its own market and also around eighty small shops, where women purchase bread, sugar, oil, soft drinks, and other sundries and stop to chat with the shop owner or with other customers. It is these trips once or twice a day that constitute the daily maintenance of social networks in the zone. As soon as any procession comes through, such as an election campaign meeting or a rehearsal for a dance for the fiesta, people come out of their houses to watch. Children share information and gossip at school. In the afternoons, if they are not in school and have completed their homework and chores, small groups play on the streets that do not have dangerous dogs or in the churchyard.

Adults meet for organized meetings of the junta vecinal or junta escolar (parents association of their neighborhood school), or when they must register their children at the beginning of the school year, or when they attend school events such as the physical education and music fairs. Men in particular also meet while watching or playing in the weekend football matches. Two or three establishments open up to sell beer to the men, who sit outside on benches or metal chairs around a small table, getting gradually drunker throughout the day. Otherwise there are no bars that open regularly. Some adults meet frequently for Evangelical services (cultos); others belong to microcredit groups. Every so often there is a party held in one of the halls in the zone, which involve family members from within and outside of Rosas Pampa. Everyone living in that half of the zone knows about these because they can hear the music, and the air outside the hall doors smells of alcohol. Sometimes when I lie in bed at night I can hear music from parties in houses a few streets away.

The vecinos of Rosas Pampa are mostly first- or second-generation migrants from rural areas. My informal impressions were confirmed by the survey I conducted. This showed that 46 percent of all the respondents to the survey and 61 percent of those over sixteen were born in the countryside. Those over sixteen had lived in Rosas Pampa for an average of just under ten years and three months. Seventy-one percent could speak both Spanish and Aymara, and only 20 percent were monolingual Spanish-speakers. For the children (under sixteen), the picture was reversed, but still 18 percent said they were bilingual in Spanish and Aymara. This is likely to be an underestimation, since many children I knew could understand Aymara but not speak it, something common across El Alto (Guaygua, Riveros, and Quisbert 2000).

Rosas Pampa can be said to be a middling zone of El Alto. It is poor, but its residents are generally fairly well-established migrants, many of whom came to the city or moved up from La Paz in the 1970s, a time of expansion for El Alto in general and Rosas Pampa in particular. People's migration stories vary: some came individually as children because of maltreatment by their parents; some came as a couple because their land in the countryside was not producing enough or because the man found a job in the city. Some moved straight into commerce; others worked for several years as domestic servants in La Paz before marrying and moving up to El Alto.

The Third Flow: Migration　　A third location through which one can study El Alto is that of the networks of connections between rural villages and the city. Flows of migration shaped El Alto's growth during the twentieth century and have created its highly distinctive identity as an indigenous city. People from the same *pueblos* (birth villages)[7] have maintained their kinship networks in the city, frequently settling near each other so that zones tend to have very strong links with specific rural areas. Once living in the city, people move backward and forward between there and their pueblos to help with agricultural tasks, to visit family, or for the annual fiesta. Some people have houses or land in both spaces; others work between the two, transporting produce from the countryside to the city.

At the beginning of the century, the land that is now El Alto belonged to about five or six large haciendas (Sandoval and Sostres 1989). Initially, urban settlements began at the Ceja, at the time a crossroads and the only route out of La Paz. Some people settled to conduct commercial activities in the service of the railway company, which constructed the first line through the altiplano in 1904. Other important constructions were the airport and flying school, built in 1923, and the offices of Lloyd Aereo Boliviano, the national airline, which opened in 1925 (Sandoval and Sostres 1989). Some of the early inhabitants of El Alto were veterans of the Chaco War (1932–1935) who were offered plots of land near the Ceja for 50 cents.[8] In the 1940s, a number of the hacienda owners there saw the commercial opportunities of urbanizing their lands and selling off plots.

Julio Tellez Reyes was the first to follow this route, and the first zone of El Alto, Urbanización Villa Dolores, was founded on 14 September 1942 and named after his wife. The process of urbanizing hacienda lands was accelerated as a result of the agrarian reform of 1953. The Revolution of 1952 which gave rise to the agrarian reform was also the first time that many of the eleven thousand inhabitants of El Alto participated in mass mobilizations as organized communities (Sandoval and Sostres 1989).

The agrarian reform sparked the first big wave of migration to La Paz and El Alto from rural areas (Albó, Greaves, and Sandoval 1981). Former serfs were free to move, and in many cases the individual parcels of land given to them were not sufficient to support them and their families. In addition, around the time of the reform, there was severe drought and famine on the altiplano; I was told stories of people eating grass because they were so hungry. People came to the city and settled on the laderas of La Paz and in El Alto. The next wave of migration was linked to the construction boom of Hugo Banzer's dictatorial regime in the 1970s, fueled by foreign debt and U.S. aid (Dunkerley 1984). Between 1960 and 1976 the population grew from about 30,000 to 95,434 (Obermaier, Perez Garriga, and Donoso Paz 1999). As El Alto grew, increasing numbers of people, especially young second-generation migrant couples, moved up from La Paz, seeking space and affordable plots of their own.

The 1980s saw the third and most recent wave of migration to El Alto from all parts of Bolivia, triggered by the neoliberal restructuring of Paz Estensorro's New Economic Policy and the notorious Decree 21060 of 1985. As a result of these measures to make labor flexible, many, in particular miners, lost their jobs, and large numbers of those, known as the "relocalized" (relocalizados), migrated to El Alto.[9] Between 1976 and 1992, the population of El Alto grew at the remarkable rate of 9.23 percent annually, to 405,492 in 1992. The census of 2001 recorded a population of 647,350, and the rate of growth between 1992 and 2001 was 5.1 percent annually.[10] In the midst of this third wave of migration, Bolivia became democratic in the transition of 1982–1985. In 1985 local government legislation brought in elected mayors for the first time; previously mayors had been appointed by the president (Calderon and Szmukler 2000). Having been a district of the city of La Paz since 1970, in 1985 El Alto was granted a separate municipal administration of its own as capital of the fourth section of the Pedro Murillo province. In 1988, it formally became a city in its own right, changing its name from El Alto de la Paz to Ciudad de El Alto.

Bolivian scholars have investigated the links between rural–urban migrants and their places of origin to great effect, beginning in the early 1980s, when El Alto was still part of La Paz; an example is the seminal four-volume work, *Chukiyawu: La Cara Aymara de La Paz*, by Xavier Albó, Tomas Greaves, and Godofredo Sandoval (1981, 1982, 1983, 1987). El Alto is not unique as a migrant city: in the late twentieth century, Lima underwent what some scholars have called "Andeanization" as a result of large-scale migration from the mountains (Altamirano 1984a; Paaregard 1997). Some *residentes* (i.e., members of rural communities who live in the city) are more formally organized than others. Their links with each other and with their common pueblo are maintained in institutional arrangements such as residentes associations in the city or at events such as football competitions and fiestas in the city and the pueblo (Paaregard 2003; Albó et al. 1987). Some associations send money back to the rural community, particularly for the building of schools. They can also be political groups, putting pressure on the central government for resources for their pueblos (cf. Altamirano 1984b).

Links are also maintained and forged more informally, such as when women return to their pueblos to look after family members (Criales Burgos 1994). Many people maintain land in their pueblos and go there to sow and harvest potatoes, quinoa, and other crops; if they don't have land of their own, they may travel to their pueblos at these times to assist family members (Llanos Layme 1998; Canessa 1998). First- and second-generation migrants in Rosas Pampa maintain very strong links with their pueblos. Around a quarter of those I surveyed in 2000 visited their pueblo between two and four times a year, and about a fifth more than once a month, or "very frequently." Only about a fifth said that they never visited. Others visit once a year for the anniversary fiesta. Some women go once or twice a month if their pueblos are nearby, while others go less often but stay for a fortnight or even a month or two, particularly at harvest time. They bring potatoes and other supplies back with them to the city, sometimes to sell but mostly as stocks for family consumption. In the city, more established residentes often assist new migrants by providing accommodation or employment (Gill 1994; Rivera Cusicanqui 2002; Long 1984; Altamirano 1984b).

I knew a network of migrants from the pueblo of Quilloma, in Aroma province, between La Paz and Oruro. They talked of arranging a residentes association, but as of 2003 had not done so. Instead, they met frequently to rehearse a dance for the annual fiesta in Quilloma or for kinsfolk organizing a dance for the fiesta in another zone of El Alto; at festival times in El Alto, such as Carnival or Todos Santos; or for family events in the city, such as weddings, baptisms, and funerals. It was not always possible for them to organize a dance for the Quilloma fiesta, as the cost meant that only a few would take on the commitment of *pasante* (dance group organizer). Even if they did not dance at the fiesta, though, many visited Quilloma at that time to participate in the football competition, if nothing else.

The network of quillomeños in El Alto combines the face-to-face quality of the extended family group and the pueblo itself with a more diffuse network of extended kin that touches down at particular points of the city. The quillomeños I knew lived in the southern parts of El Alto, in zones along the highway to Oruro; a few lived in Villa Exaltación, some in Rosas Pampa, and in the past few years several have bought land in the zone of Senkata, further out along the highway. The move south has happened as new generations become adults and have families of their own. They buy land in the cheaper and newer districts and construct their houses there. One family had a house in Senkata but remained as tenants in Rosas Pampa, near their parents' house, because Senkata does not yet have a good school for their children. In 1999, another family—a mother (Doña Josefa) and her daughter, son, and grandson—rented a house on my street in Rosas Pampa, next to Doña Josefa's sister's house. In 2000, they moved to Villa Exaltación to rent a house next to Doña Josefa's other sister; by 2003, both Doña Josefa and her daughter had bought land in Senkata (on credit) and moved out there to build their houses. So inward flows of migration combine with flows outward toward the edges of the city, a fluidity that operates on a different time scale from that of the Ceja.

The relationship between El Alto and its rural hinterland is crucial to understanding it as a city, despite its common characterization as merely a satellite city of La Paz, the ciudad dormitorio of the stereotype. In Rosas Pampa, only 12 percent of adults worked in the city of La Paz, while the majority worked in the zone itself or elsewhere in El Alto. For other alteños, El Alto is less a satellite of La Paz than an extension of its rural and semiurban hinterland, perhaps even one of the ecological niches in which peasant communities have members. Although the principle is similar, it would be stretching the analysis a little too far to call El Alto one part of people's ayllu. The majority of alteños come originally from the department of La Paz, where the ayllus were severely weakened by the nineteenth-century expansion of haciendas and where peasant unions have been historically strong. There are attempts to reconstitute local ayllus, headed by the Consejo Nacional de Ayllus y Markas del Qullasuyu (CONAMAQ; National Council of Ayllus and Markas of Qullasuyu) (Choque and Mamani Condori 2003), but as yet these initiatives have not included El Alto in their remit.

However, September and October 2003 marks an important moment when the indigenous movement finally began to capitalize on the links between alteños and their birth villages in the countryside. The Confederación Sindical Única de Trabajadores Campesinos de Bolivia (CSUTCB; Sole Trade Union Confederation of Peasant Workers of Bolivia) began their hunger strike at the beginning of September in the buildings of Radio San Gabriel on Avenida Bolivia in El Alto. Local residents held bonfire-lit vigils outside the buildings in order to protect the peasants from rumored army interventions. Accordingly the peasants' protest was brought firmly into the middle of the city, that is, the "middle" as seen from the perspective of the countryside: the geographical center of El Alto rather than the Ceja. This decision meant that the peasant blockade had much more impact than the blockades of 2000 and 2001, even though more peasants had participated then and even though there was also widespread sympathy in El Alto for the peasants at that time.[11] I suspect that it was not a random decision: in political meetings during mid-2003 which evaluated the tax riots of the previous February, analysts and politicians (including the Mallku himself) debated the importance for the Indianist movement of gaining a foothold in the cities, particularly El Alto. Subsequent mobilizations in El Alto, especially in 2005, were based more on localized urban concerns such as the nature of the contract with the privatized water company, or national concerns such as the nationalization of natural gas resources. Bringing the indigenous or Indianist movement into the city of El Alto would not be an easy task, but it is no longer one that can be overlooked.

MAKING THE CITY, CONSOLIDATING ITS IDENTITY

The ways that El Alto provides a link between rural and urban Andean Bolivia are one of the principal reasons for its political importance in recent years, but not the only one. The other key factor is the level of civic organization in the city. Given the multiplicity of dimensions and perspectives of El Alto and its relative youth, it is pertinent to ask what it is that makes El Alto a city rather than a slum, a suburb, a marketplace, or a transport hub. My answer is that different actors, in both the state system and in nonstate places, are in the process of making a distinctive and separate identity for El Alto. That identity is of course not singular, but is becoming increasingly bound up with political radicalism and indigeneity. In recent years intellectuals and community leaders have become better able to articulate El Alto's identity as an Aymara city and to convert that identity into political action. On the official side, El Alto was declared a separate administrative area on 6 March 1985; the city's anniversary is celebrated every year on that date with parades by schoolchildren and adults. The municipal authorities of El Alto have also developed specifically alteño symbols, such as its flag and anthem.

Civic mobilization has also been vital to the development of a specifically alteño identity, something particularly evident in the story of the establishment of the Public University of El Alto in 2000. The UPEA is an infrastructural development that is very important to the project of building alteño identity. It was achieved through a dialogue between civic organizations and the state system that was driven by the political mobilization of different groups in civil society. In early 2000, the national government began discussions with the mayor of El Alto about the establishment of a public university there; in parallel, groups of students and staff began registering applications for a public university in El Alto, reaching a total of (some claimed) ten thousand students. On 1 May, a large group took over the buildings of the UMSA technical annex in Villa Esperanza, in protest at delays in the process of establishing the university. The fact that the government was keen to avoid another series of riots like the recent Water War in Cochabamba meant that they agreed in principle to the idea of the UPEA.[12] Nonetheless, the protestors kept up pressure from the day the decree was signed. Throughout the following months, students and staff held multiple protests, in El Alto and La Paz. They also continued the process begun early that year of organizing the university structure and giving courses, while the government began to discuss the establishment of the UPEA with civic leaders.

In September 2000, the UPEA was finally created, to be regulated by the Consejo de Desarrollo Institucional (Council for Institutional Development), a group of representatives of the UPEA staff and students along with the most important civic institutions in El Alto.[13] The need for mobilization did not stop there, however, as the law establishing the UPEA also stipulated a transitional period of five years before the university would be granted full autonomy, a status which means the university has the ability to control its own budget, hire staff, and elect its own rectors rather than have a rector chosen by the government. After years of protest, factionalism, and intrigue, Carlos Mesa finally granted autonomous status to the UPEA in late 2003. The commitment of the students to the UPEA in its first years was quite remarkable: they had little time and few funds available for study but were prepared to undertake courses in an establishment of dubious institutionality and support the version of the UPEA that they believed in through their presence in class and at demonstrations.

Students argued that the Bolivian government wanted tight control over the UPEA, at least in its first few years, because they were scared of the kinds of political effects that might result from the education of Indians. If this is true, then the government's worst fears have been realized: since 2000, UPEA students have usually been at the forefront of revolutionary activity in the city. They were blamed for the burnings of the Town Hall in May 2000 and February 2003 and were enthusiastic participants in the October 2003 protests. One student told me that he went out by cover of night to the less radical zones to set up barricades so that the vecinos there would join the general strike. The UPEA buildings in Villa Esperanza were put at the service of the Central Obrera Boliviana (COB; Bolivian Workers Center) for meetings and to house miners who had marched to the city; some people used its furniture to make weapons with which to confront the army.[14] Although the students do not lead citywide mobilizations in El Alto, they are one of the most important sources of its radicalism. It is no coincidence that El Alto's move to center stage in Bolivian politics has coincided with the institutionalization of the university there.

Civic Organization in El Alto It should be evident that El Alto is a highly organized city, something that has been crucial in shaping its entry into national and international political life and one of the most important aspects of its residents' citizenship. The mobilizations in favor of the UPEA and during October 2003 and early 2005 built upon a long tradition of civic organization, as alteños drew on "repertoires of collective action" (Tilly 1978, 1993) familiar to them from previous struggles with the state. Those who have migrated from rural areas usually have experience of some form of community organization there, as members of ayllus or peasant unions or as ex-hacienda workers. Those who migrated from the mines have an illustrious tradition of trade unionism (Lora 1977). A number of studies of El Alto have recognized the vibrancy of community organization there (Sandoval and Sostres 1989; Sostres 1995; Anze O. 1995). From the beginning of settlement in El Alto, vecinos organized themselves into juntas vecinales to demand the provision of basic services from the state. The juntas vecinales combine with trade union structures and the juntas escolares to create a structure of civic organization that is parallel to the state and very powerful in El Alto.

Most adult alteños also belong to trade unions in the informal sector. In the case of the predominantly male jobs (as drivers or artisans), the collective organizations are called unions (*sindicatos*), and in the case of the predominantly female street traders, they are called associations (*asociaciónes*). An association consists of all the women (and men) who sell in the same area in markets which are held weekly, twice weekly, or daily, depending on the neighborhood. Associations mediate between individuals and the state and represent the traders in negotiations with the other civic bodies in the zone where they work, principally the junta vecinal and other associations of traders. The associations are affiliated with the citywide Federation, which mediates any conflicts between two associations and assists associations when they must deal with the state authorities. The Federation is led by the Executive Committee, the head of which is the executive secretary. The juntas vecinales and juntas escolares both have citywide federations like the street traders do. The other main organization at city level is the COR, a coordinator of workers trade unions, including factory workers, teachers, journalists, artisans, and the federation of market traders.[15] There is a further layer of civic organizations at the national level. At all levels, the organizations represent their affiliates in negotiations with each other and with different parts of the state, as illustrated in figure 4.

Negotiations with the state are not necessarily characterized by co-optation and acquiescence and can often be highly confrontational. Between 1999 and 2003, multiple demonstrations were organized by different collective bodies to protest reductions in state expenditures on health, education, and pensions, income tax increases to fund the servicing of external debt, the export of natural gas, and more. In such mobilizations, alteños expressed their increasing levels of anger at the effects of the neoliberal policies of successive governments (Arbona n.d.). After demonstrators had ransacked and burned the El Alto town hall in May 2000, one union leader told me that El Alto is an "angry city," and that its people are "vigorous, and always prepared to fight, sometimes without measur-

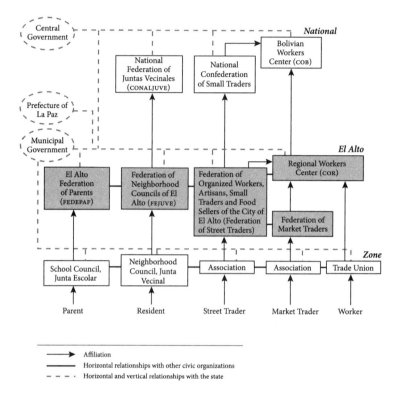

			Affiliation
			Horizontal relationships with other civic organizations
			Horizontal and vertical relationships with the state

4. Civic organizations and the state in El Alto

ing the consequences. The alteño is capable of offering up even his life [for the struggle]." The deaths of over fifty alteños in October 2003 testify to the accuracy of his comment.

October 2003 is a significant turning point in the development of the distinctive identity of the city of El Alto. Leaders of the FEJUVE and the Federation of Street Traders consistently used phrases that indicated El Alto and its population's "awakening." They said, for example:

> As of last year [2003] I think that the alteño community has become conscious of many things. They've oppressed us for more than five hundred years. . . . Now I think that thanks to many institutions and educated people, especially those who have studied, et cetera, we've realized what is going on in the country. (Don Miguel Sanchez, FEJUVE)

Everyone was the bravest: the artisans, the traders, [people from] the markets, from the schools, parents—that is to say, we all totally united. Those who had never before come together, came together. So there's no doubt that now, that is to say, since now we're united, I think that's given more force to the citizens of El Alto. Not only alteños, but we can say this at a national level, because bit by bit they have woken up. (Doña Maxima, FEJUVE)

The experience of October 2003 can fit into a dominant characterization of the city of El Alto from the perspective of La Paz, which is to see it as a time bomb because of its social problems and abandonment by successive national and municipal governments. However, as well as being the outcome of anger and desperation on the part of the alteños, the events of October 2003 and January through July 2005 also built upon longstanding traditions of collective organization and protest. Furthermore, they incorporated creative proposals for the democratic renovation of the Bolivian state that came out of alteños' experience of their citizenship on a local and a national scale. As one civic leader said, "El Alto, especially El Alto, has now become conscious of all these things, and it's going to be very difficult from now onwards for governments to decide by themselves. Instead it's going to have to be in a consensual way." Don Braulio Rocha, the executive secretary of the Federation of Street Traders in 2003, said, "I think we've made a very important forward step at the global level, because today the city of El Alto is recognized, and the foreign governments have recognized it because it has been at the vanguard [of political struggle]. Today the city of El Alto is the sentinel of [democracy in] Bolivia."[16] Another friend said that El Alto "se ha hecho respetar" ("made itself respected"), as alteños moved from the margins of Bolivian politics to its center. In the process El Alto is constituting itself as a city in its own right, Latin America's first indigenous city. In the chapters that follow, I explore some of the dimensions of citizenship on which these developments are founded.

Alteños experience their citizenship of Bolivia as mediated through their membership in a number of collective entities, and two of the main forms of collective identity are place-based and occupation-based. The chapters in part i focus on the former and discuss how the residents of one zone, Rosas Pampa, construct their collective political agency as vecinos of that zone. I move from obviously political processes of local development, community leadership, and municipal elections, to more symbolic and phenomenological constructions of collective subjectivity. Throughout, I argue that individualism and internal differentiation and contestation of the ideal of community are central to the construction of the real community.

If citizenship is a mediated relationship between the individual and the state, then the community authorities are one of the hinges in that relationship. The two main authorities, the junta vecinal and the junta escolar, have increasingly become the means by which the state relates to its citizens, channeling available resources to the zone through them and using them as the motor of local development. In the absence of any overall development plan, community authorities become supplicants to the state for resources for their neighborhood. The state's way of administrating development thus creates Rosas Pampa as a meaningful political unit represented by the two juntas. Across El Alto, this process can therefore be a means of interpellating the juntas into state projects and government but can also be turned against the state, as when the juntas organize demonstrations in opposition to the government. However, the community authorities also have to respond to the vecinos, and the vecino–junta relationship is a crucial means of creating the zone as collective political entity. That relationship is not easy, and often the community leaders' perceived individualism becomes the foil for the collective ideal, and thus internal contestation over their ability to represent the community creates a notion of what that community is.

Even where citizenship is supposedly direct and individual, as in the case of voting, it is also mediated through membership in the zone. In El Alto the "time of elections" (Auyero 2000), when the state comes closest to its citizens, consists not only of election day itself and the campaign immediately before, but also of the moments in the years running up to the election when potential candidates seek to gain support through clientelistic mechanisms. At all of these times, citizens engage with the state in a corporate as well as an individual way. They seek to ally themselves with particular patron–client groupings (the political parties), but also to gain advantage for themselves or for their zones by playing off the different patrons against each other. Both these processes of mediation between citizen and state can be seen as the alteño version of what Aihwa Ong (1999a: 54) calls citizenship capacity, which she describes as "the ways citizens in different democratic countries seek to realize particular interests, including resources and citizen dignity, and the kind of political accountability they expect from their government."

The construction of a collective political subject, the zone, is critical to the forms of mediation discussed here. But administrative and political processes of construction are only part of that. Collective political agency requires collective political subjectivity, and the production of individual selves that are fundamentally part of a collectivity based upon relationships with other vecinos and with the zone. Chapters 4 and 5 examine that process of constructing collective selves through symbolic and ritual activity. Chapter 4, on the dance, introduces the concept of "nested affiliations," another way of conceptualizing the state–citizen relation. Citizenship of the "imagined community" of Rosas Pampa is dependent upon insertion into smaller face-to-face communities based upon kin or occupational networks, in the same way that citizenship of the imagined community of Bolivia requires the mediation of face-to-face communities based upon residence, kinship, or occupation. The fiesta provides a good example of communitas (V. Turner 1969) through intense and effervescent bodily experience of togetherness (Durkheim 1965 [1915]), but also exemplifies how that is conditioned by hierarchy and distinction within the collectivity of participants. So the collective entity that is the zone and is perceived as such administratively and politically is not homogeneous or undifferentiated.

This last point is underlined most strongly by the final chapter in this part, which discusses competing projects of selfhood. On the one hand, the sense of self promoted by the "colonial Catholicism" (Harris 2006) expressed in the fiesta and in rituals to the Pachamama (Mother Earth) and the *achachilas* (ancestral spirits) is a relational one that creates a very strong sense of connection with a place made sacred. It is a particularistic form of community rooted in the local achachilas and the local instantiation of the Pachamama in the home and in the zone. Individual selves are permeable and inserted in a complex network of social relations that includes the local deities. On the other hand, Evangelical Christianity promotes an antagonistic form of community detached from localized place and based upon a set of bounded and autonomous individuals whose concept of the self is ontologically prior to the collectivity rather than created in dialectical relation to it. Both are projects of the self that require more or less work, although the Evangelical one is particularly demanding. Their models of sociality and the self influence how the vecinos of Rosas Pampa relate to their community and to those in power and as such are a central part of their experience of citizenship.

The fieldwork on which these chapters are based was principally conducted over twelve months from 1999 to 2000, and over six months during 2003–2004, when I lived in Rosas Pampa. While there, I divided my research into different spaces. For some time I taught in the local school as a substitute English teacher, and throughout my time in the zone I attended school ceremonies. Toward the end of my first period of fieldwork I was allowed to conduct some group interviews with seventeen- and eighteen-year-olds, most of whom I knew through the local church group or through having been their English teacher. I also attended meetings of the junta vecinal committee and the general assemblies of both the junta vecinal and the junta escolar. I conducted taped interviews with a number of the members of these two committees, and my landlady, Doña Gregoria, was the treasurer of the junta escolar. The local catechist, Don Roberto, was another important local figure and became a good friend of mine. He helped me to design a quantitative survey of households in the zone, which members of the church youth group carried out. These young people (ages fourteen to twenty) surveyed areas near their homes, picking every fifth house, and asking questions about how many people lived in a particular household, where they were born, what kinds of civic activity they participated in, what kinds of public services they used in the zone, what they wanted for their zone, and what their basic family income was. The total sample was 179 households, approximately 18 percent of the total number of households in Rosas Pampa. I coded the survey sheets and analyzed the results and presented them to Don Roberto and the local priests before I left, as a thank you for their support and as a small contribution to their activities. The survey data are not the cleanest, but the young people gained much more access than I would have been able to do by myself and appeared to have enjoyed learning about their zone through conducting that survey.

I also went along to meetings of two microcredit groups, participating in day-to-day discussions with the women present and also conducting semistructured taped interviews with a number of them. Toward the end of my stay I attended services and other activities run by a small Evangelical group whose church was on my street. My partner came out to Rosas Pampa for the final six months of my fieldwork in 2000. Not only did he provide moral support and intellectual discussion, but he also conducted informal research of his own, which I could then follow up in my own work. In addition, he participated in a number of the events that inform this part of the book, most importantly the fiesta dancing. I danced in two fiestas in 2000, one in the pueblo of Quilloma and one in Rosas Pampa, my partner joining me in the latter. This meant participating in rehearsals as well as the fiestas themselves. I visited Quilloma a number of times with friends, returning for the fiesta of 2003, although I did not dance that time. Needless to say, much of my research involved eating and drinking with friends, spending time on the streets of Rosas Pampa, talking with shopkeepers while I bought provisions, traveling through El Alto on my way to La Paz or to the markets, and going to the markets with Doña Gregoria and accompanying her to her pueblo.

I begin my exploration of local citizenship practices and the tensions between individual and corporate forms of citizenship with an examination of politics in Rosas Pampa. Citizenship in Rosas Pampa, or the relationship between individual and state there, is mediated by the local community authorities. Through a discussion of questions of local development, in this chapter I examine the two parts of that mediated relationship: the relationship between the (national and local) state and community authorities on the one hand, and that between community authorities and individual citizens on the other. The community authorities are therefore a kind of hinge between individual and state. The vecinos of Rosas Pampa have built the zone both figuratively and literally, constructing a sense of community in part by organizing themselves to develop their zone. This has happened as a result of the vecinos' own initiatives and the ability of the local authorities to gain services for Rosas Pampa from the state and private providers. The zone thus constitutes itself in part through its relation to the state: in a negative way as attested by the self-constructed nature of development in Rosas Pampa in the absence of the state, and in a positive way as the alcaldía of El Alto (the municipality) distributes resources through community authorities. This is crucial to my argument about the collective nature of citizenship in Rosas Pampa, because the state creates the community of Rosas Pampa as an administrative entity, first by requiring the vecinos to develop the zone without the state's help (often despite the state), and later, by administering local development through the articulation between the municipal government of the city, NGOs, and the authorities of the zone of Rosas Pampa. The vecinos themselves have also created the zone as a collective political subject through their actions of self-construction and through the ways they organize themselves.

The community leaders are subject to formal and informal mechanisms of control, which show how the vecinos also imagine themselves as a collective entity through their expectations of the authorities and exercise of accountability. The theme of corruption illustrates this point, as through rumor and gossip vecinos hold their leaders to account preemptively, establishing a sense of the public good and an obligation on the part of the leaders to serve that good, expressed especially in the successful achievement of public works for the zone. The collective of vecinos attempts, not always successfully, to keep control in the face of the individual leaders' personal interests. These day-to-day practices around the provision and protection of the means of social reproduction (Garcia Linera 2001) at the zonal level are one of the foundations of the collective political agency that is actualized at extraordinary moments, such as October 2003 and the first part of 2005. Those mobilizations were led by the citywide Federation of Juntas Vecinales (FEJUVE), the umbrella organization of the local-level residents committees. An analysis of the committees' dynamics at a localized and everyday level helps us to understand what it is that makes them the expression of or channel for alteños' citizenship, and therefore why the FEJUVE takes on a structural position between alteños and the state that enables it to represent and mobilize the residents of El Alto against the state.

VECINDAD

Latin America as a region has had a strong tradition of community organization, through trade unions, Christian Base Communities, indigenous authorities, and women's groups, for example. Whereas in the Andes this tradition is more often associated with the rural areas, this chapter investigates urban communalism through the optic of the concept of vecino. There is considerable debate in the anthropological and sociological literature on rural–urban migration about whether migrants become more individualistic once they move to the city, a debate which echoes early sociological concerns about the anonymity of urban life and the dangers posed by increasing urbanization to the life of face-to-face communities. Much of the literature stresses a more individualistic and less collective orientation on the part of those who move to the city (Altamirano 1984b;

Gill 1997b; Canessa 1998; Rivera Cusicanqui et al. 1996; Llanos Layme 1998; Roberts 1995; de Soto 1989). However, scholars also recognize migrants' need to organize collectively, and some argue that rural–urban migrants actively seek out new forms of collective allegiance once in the city (e.g., Sandoval and Sostres 1989; Albó et al. 1983; Gill 1993; Calderon and Szmukler 2000; Perlman 1976). These come to form distinctly urban practices, but ones that are based in part upon the articulation between values of duty, prestige, and material gain that are discussed in ethnography of the countryside (e.g., Klemola 1997; Abercrombie 1998; Carter and Mamani P. 1989 [1982]; Buechler and Buechler 1996; Buechler 1980).

Those adults who have made the decision to move to, and stay in, Rosas Pampa are known as vecinos. In this context the term means neighbor, thus implying a person-to-person relationship, but it is also a category that roots someone to a particular space, meaning a resident or inhabitant. People frequently described themselves to me as vecinos of their zone. The term zone is administrative: El Alto is divided into six urban districts and one rural, which are then divided into zones of varying sizes. At the head of the local government of El Alto is the alcalde (mayor) and Council, and the alcalde nominates sub-alcaldes to preside over each district. Each zone has a junta vecinal (Residents Council), voted for by the vecinos and called by them the authorities or leaders of the zone (autoridades/dirigentes de la zona). The zone indicates the territoriality of people's sense of allegiance to place and to other people with similar allegiances.

In many ways, the term vecino also indicates this sense of place and territoriality. In common use today, the term also has a substantial historical heritage, as it has been used to indicate the legal status of being a member of a town in Spain since medieval times: citizenship in the Classical, or ancien régime, sense.[1] Vecindad was enjoyed by homeowners who were usually born in a particular town. Vecinos had various rights, such as access to common land, and they attended open council meetings, at which they called themselves collectively the community or the Republic (la Republica; Nader 1990). The use of the latter term demonstrates that similar ways of imagining collectivity translated to the New World, where government was structured into two republics, that of the Spanish and that of the Indians. The notion of vecino itself translated directly, largely because the Conquistadors had a fundamentally urban outlook (Nader 1990; Herzog 2003). The tension between the particularity of vecindad and the universality of the liberal ciudadanía (citizenship) was as central in the past as it is today. The citizenship projects of the nineteenth century in Latin America were built on the understanding of what it meant to be a vecino and were also defined against it (Carmagnani and Hernandez Chavez 1999). Francois-Xavier Guerra (1999: 42) points out that "contrary to the modern citizen, who is an individual component of an abstract collectivity—the nation or the people—the *vecino* is always a man who is concrete, territorialized and rooted." Guerra considers the two categories to be fundamentally opposed. However, early republican legislation defined citizenship through vecindad, for example making only vecinos into citizens, as in the case of Mexican electoral legislation of the early nineteenth century (Carmagnani and Hernandez Chavez 1999), and in Rio de la Plata, where eligibility for voting was determined on the basis of vecindad (Herzog 2003). As Tamar Herzog has shown, this drew on Spanish practices, whereby the national community was in many ways seen as a community of local citizens or vecinos. The right to colonize was given only to Spanish natives (naturales), and the most common way of proving nativeness was precisely through acting as a vecino of a particular local community, which proved a sense of loyalty and obligation to that community. These linkages show the coexistence of a plurality of definitions of citizenship at the time, and in particular the corporate nature of Latin American society: the nineteenth-century Mexican commentator Mariano Otero called Mexico "a society of societies" (Carmagnani and Hernandez Chavez 1999: 374).

In Rosas Pampa today, vecino is a less exclusive category than it was historically, referring to both homeowners and those who have rented their homes for a long time. Nonetheless, it is a contemporary form of older versions of urban citizenship as historically constituted in articulation with national citizenship. I first realized its importance as a category when I asked women in a microcredit group how they knew each other. For many, kinship relations were most important, but some were simply vecinas who were known to them, *conocidas*. Some anthropologists have used vecino as an ethnic or class-based category of mestizos or local notables, often explicitly or implicitly presented in contrast to the more "authentic" Indian *comuneros*, even in conflict with them (Abercrombie 1991; Crandon 1985; Weismantel 2001; Isbell 1978; Skar 1982). The common factor is that vecinos dwell in a town; in my experience a more inclusive use of the term as well as an emphasis on territoriality rather than ethnicity is more faithful to the local uses of language in Rosas Pampa and El Alto today. Not only does the term vecino persist, but the corporate, rooted, and physical form of citizenship that it implies is central to local understandings of citizenship in Rosas Pampa.

Community Organization: The Juntas People's attachment to their zone is one crucial aspect of their relationship with the local and national state, and hence their construction of their citizenship. This citizenship, understood as lived experience rather than legal status, is lived in part through responsibilities to the zone as a communal entity. Those responsibilities are especially acute for leaders as they mediate the relationship between individual vecino and the state, and they are the focus for much of the contestation over collective values that is a central part of the construction of those same values and the sense of community they engender. Hence the focus of this chapter on the community authorities, that is, the junta vecinal and the junta escolar, which are two of the most important hinges in the relationship between individual citizen and the state in El Alto.

Adult residents of Rosas Pampa are represented by one of the two zonal juntas vecinales (also called junta de vecinos), and if they have children at the local school, as most of them do, by the junta escolar. Rosas Pampa has about a thousand households in total, two hundred of which are in the area known as the *barranco*, the edge of the zone. I lived in the part of Rosas Pampa covered by the main junta vecinal, which is led by an elected committee of fourteen who meet roughly every two or four weeks, and weekly around the time of the fiesta. The composition of these meetings fluctuated while I was there, but the president would always be present, and usually around six committee members would attend, with more in the runup to the fiesta. Every two to three months they would hold a general assembly of all the residents of the zone, which about 150 people would attend.

Given that there are eight hundred houses covered by that junta vecinal, not all of which are occupied, attendance at assemblies is reasonably high. In the survey I conducted over the whole of the zone, a remarkable 77 percent of respondent households said that they regularly attended some form of civic activity, and most of them went to the general assemblies. Of course, this is likely to be an overestimation, but it shows at least that attendance was seen as something they should do. Usually the heads of households attend, and certainly the *jefes de calle* (literally, chiefs of the street), who are then supposed to inform the residents on their street about the meeting. Some streets have more formal organizations and meet regularly to discuss issues such as security and the decisions of the general assembly. Junta vecinal leaders do not have to work particularly hard if they do not want to, as the president tends to do most of the work, with one or two others. Their primary responsibility throughout the year is to obtain *obras* (public works) for the zone. Public works could be a sewage system, electricity, street lighting, a square, or a park. They are also in charge of organizing the anniversary fiesta every 14 September.

The junta escolar consists of three leaders (president, vice president, and treasurer) who work alongside the headmaster of the school and two or three times a year call a meeting of all the parents of children at the school. They are responsible for implementing decisions taken by the Federation of Juntas Escolares in El Alto regarding mobilizing parents for marches and demonstrations, and, with the headmaster, they coordinate the parents' involvement in obtaining various obras for the schools, from political parties, the municipality, the Federation of Juntas Escolares, and NGOs.

Not everyone who lives in Rosas Pampa goes to the general assemblies of the junta vecinal or the junta escolar, although between the two they probably manage to convene most residents at some point. If an adult cannot go, he or she will often send an older son or daughter as a representative. Although attendance at meetings has dropped in recent years, important information does filter through; for example, when there was a possibility that the municipal government would pave the streets, it was announced in a general assembly that individual households had to make sure they had organized the building of the curb outside their houses, otherwise the street would not be paved. In the following few weeks, I noticed one resident of my street out finally building the curb outside his house (most people on the street had done this years before). Our jefe de calle had probably asked him to get the work done.

The junta escolar has a rather more authoritarian way of organizing its members: the parents have special identity cards, which note how many of their quotas for building work and other expenses they have paid, and fines, often for not coming to demonstrations. If they are not up to date, their children cannot get their school records, which means that they cannot register at any school at the beginning of the academic year. So, although not every parent comes to the meetings, the vast majority contribute financially to the junta escolar's work. Usually, people feel that if they have to contribute financially, they want to go to the meeting to supervise what is happening with their money. The junta escolar meetings, which are less frequent than those called by the junta vecinal, are often better attended. The gender balance of those attending junta escolar meetings is almost the inverse of the balance at junta vecinal assemblies: roughly two thirds female and one third male. The junta escolar meetings are held on Saturday afternoons, which is a time when more women than men are in the zone, as many men work on Saturdays; junta vecinal general assemblies are held on Sunday mornings, when the men are back from work. There is also an obvious connection between perceptions of women's responsibilities for their children's schooling, associated with their reproductive responsibilities, and of men's status as head of household when discussing community affairs—a division of labor in working for the community.

The issue of gender balance raises an obvious question: Whom do the juntas represent? On the surface, the answer would seem to be that it is the men who decide for the community, and certainly in both sets of meetings it is predominantly the men who do the talking.[2] During the general assemblies I attended, the women sat on one side of the circle, taking up around a quarter to a third of the space. The men all remained standing, occasionally stepping forward to speak. The problem is that it is difficult to isolate which interests might differ along gender lines, because people did not represent conflicts in that way. While I was there, there was consensus between men and women on the priorities for the zone and the juntas, despite the fact that the men appeared to make the decisions; for example, much decision making occurred in the very male arena of the weekend football matches, when the junta vecinal leaders would drink beer and watch the matches together, along with other prominent male members of the community. However, during the week, more general discussions occurred at home or in the female spaces of shops, the market, or in the microcredit group meetings. The children also discussed matters of import to the zone, at school and while playing, and reported back to their parents. At the general assemblies, the women present did make their opinions known through the comments they made among themselves: they positioned themselves right next to the leaders, whom they knew would hear anything they said.

The involvement of women in the creation of formalized and public community consensus depends to a certain extent on how gender relations are negotiated in the household, and it is often the case that women are in charge there (Harris 2000a [1978]). Many men who are at work for most of the week get much of their information on community public opinion from their wives' involvement in local social networks during the week as well as from the discussions around the football pitch on a Sunday. However, it is important not to take this too far but to remain skeptical about the policy initiatives and NGO rhetoric that privilege the juntas as the only legitimate grass-roots organizations, which do not just *represent* the community, but in many senses *are* the community. Some feminist NGOs in El Alto argue that the juntas vecinales in particular exclude women, and the NGOs have a number of development programs that are based on capacity building for female leaders so that they can gain important positions in the juntas vecinales (Molyneux and Lazar 2003; Ruiz 1993). In Rosas Pampa, the only female junta vecinal committee member in 1999–2000 was in charge of women's issues (*vinculación femenina*) and very rarely came to meetings. By contrast, one of the three leaders of the junta escolar, the treasurer, was female.

LOCAL DEVELOPMENT AND THE "SELF-CONSTRUCTION" OF ROSAS PAMPA

Local development, understood as the provision of the means of social reproduction (Garcia Linera 2001; Gutierrez et al. 2000), is a key arena for citizenship practices in the zone, as community membership mediates the relationship between individual citizen and the state. Both the state and parastate organizations such as NGOs have been crucial in the construction of community in Rosas Pampa, in concrete ways and in terms of creating a sense of community. The day-to-day administration of El Alto relies upon the junta vecinal and junta escolar positioning themselves as brokers at neighborhood level, and they have become nodal points for the coordination of the service providers to the zone of Rosas Pampa because of their ability to stand in for the community and the grass roots. The 1990s reforms, principally the Law of Popular Participation and the Education Reform Law, have meant that the local junta vecinal and junta escolar stand at an interface between the state and civil society.[3] They are part of the process through which government channels development money to Rosas Pampa. International NGOs also channel money through them and are often better patrons than the local or national government for Rosas Pampa.[4] Rosas Pampa has come into being through the complex interactions between vecinos, the state, and NGOs. The vecinos expect the juntas to deliver local development. This section outlines some of the ways that has happened and some of the contemporary difficulties the juntas face in delivering on those expectations in the context of neoliberal development orthodoxy.

Local Development in the Absence of the State   Rosas Pampa was originally part of a hacienda whose land was distributed among its former peons in the agrarian reform of 1953.[5] Thirty peasants gained two hectares each, for which they had to pay compensation to the former owner of the hacienda. They then organized themselves as an agrarian union to supervise division of the land, and in the mid-1960s began the process of legal recognition as an urban area. They eventually achieved this formal status in April 1983, although the date from which people count the founding of the zone of Rosas Pampa is September 1975, when they changed the agrarian union to a junta vecinal. During the 1970s, the vecinos of Rosas Pampa conducted a long struggle against the railway company, which at various points attempted to take control of their land, often by dubious measures. Although the vecinos could not meet during the day, because this was in the time of the dictatorship and they were prohibited from doing so by the police, they met at night in order to plan street blockades, demonstrations, and strikes. They were ultimately successful in repelling the railway company, despite reports of generous compensation for vecinos who agreed to move away from Rosas Pampa and for the leaders who persuaded them to do so (Musch et al. 1994).

In 1999–2000 only a couple of residents actually mentioned this struggle to me, while another pointed me to the book by Mirjam Musch et al. (1994) as an authoritative source for the zone's history. However, many had a sense of a "before," when Rosas Pampa and, indeed, El Alto, was "empty really, pure prairie." Nowadays, the zone is full of buildings and "has everything," according to Don Julián, the junta's secretary: electricity, water, a sewage system.[6] People recognize the role of the junta vecinal in mobilizing the community to gain development for the zone, sometimes contrasting today's incumbents with their more active predecessors, as in the following quote from a middle-aged woman: "The juntas, well it seems as though they don't care about the zone. Before they were good, the zone's juntas, but now, they just become leaders, and . . . it's not like it was before."

Many, whether committee member or ordinary vecino, attributed the waning enthusiasm for their authorities to the fact that most of the battles had been won. Since the vecinos no longer need to band together to get infrastructure for the zone, people are less interested in participating in general assemblies, much less in paying monthly quotas to support the activities of the leaders. However, most of the vecinos have experience in working together to gain benefits for the zone, whether through paying quotas for the building of classrooms in the school or taking responsibility for building their own curb before the municipality will pave the streets. Many also contributed labor to build the Health Center and the football pitches and to install the electricity and sewage systems, and nearly every homeowner has built his or her own house. They have therefore built Rosas Pampa in very concrete ways, contributing to what one worker from a cultural association called El Alto's "self-constructed" nature. Their willingness to do this is reflected in a particular strand of current development orthodoxy, neoliberal in focus, which seeks to minimize the state as far as possible, privatizing public service functions so that they are taken over by NGOs, and putting communities themselves in charge of their own development—a form of self-help as participation. This has particular implications for citizenship, as it translates into the neoliberal ideology of the active citizen who does not rely upon the state. While neoliberal policies are based upon the creation of individual citizens responsible for their own welfare (Rose 1999; Lazar 2004), this active citizenship outside of the state does rely upon collective groupings. Their experience of self-construction has brought the vecinos of Rosas Pampa together as a community and created a sense of Rosas Pampa as an entity with certain needs for obras, such as paved streets and a square. The vecinos accept an active role in meeting those needs and making Rosas Pampa better.

In the past, they also turned to international NGOs for help in the development of their zone. Most of the obras procured for the zone and the school by the juntas were funded by the Dutch NGO APS, which was active in the zone during the 1980s and 1990s. The municipal government had provided streetlights and some help with the installation of the sewage system, but APS helped with Rosas Pampa's electricity, water, streetlights, a health center, and the sewage system, as well as a significant expansion of the school's classroom facilities and a toilet for the pupils. They provided the materials for the buildings, and the residents the manual labor. In 2000 they funded the construction of a community center using surplus from the quotas that vecinos had paid for the installation of the sewage system.

Development agencies' privileging of NGOs notwithstanding, APS's service provision was not particularly good. At several general assemblies and in informal conversations, the residents complained vigorously about poor treatment at the health center, for example. Several people that I knew would not go to the health center if they were ill, but would go to the center in the neighboring zone of Santiago II because they were treated better there. In the general assemblies, there were complaints about the behavior of the nurses, but primarily the problem was that the center was not open all the time, as promised. In particular, it was not open at 7 A.M. or on weekends, which are the only times some people can attend. One resident pointed out that when his daughter had an accident on a Sunday afternoon, he could not go to the center at 4 P.M. because it was closed: "[To say they are open] twenty-four hours is just making fun of the vecinos. We aren't toys, nor are we animals." The junta vecinal wrote a letter to APS about the fact that their twenty-four-hour center was anything but, and they received a letter back informing them that there was nothing that could be done.

In fact, although they did not explain this in the letter, APS was undergoing serious restructuring, as the Dutch government no longer wanted to fund the health center projects it had initiated over much of South El Alto. So they were negotiating with the new mayor to have the municipality take charge of the centers. Eventually, the running of the centers was taken over by Radio Fides, a Catholic charity. The whole process took months, so it is in some ways unsurprising that the junta vecinal failed to get anywhere. However, the NGO in effect simply ignored the junta vecinal and would not make its doctors fulfill their responsibilities to the zone. What this example shows is that the junta had no means by which to force private service providers to fulfill their obligations. Building things was easy: they were given the materials and then organized the work. However, when it came to service provision, all they could do was write polite letters requesting good service, which were often simply ignored. They were in a similar position with private companies, such as Clisa, the rubbish-collecting company, and Electropaz, who were responsible for the street lighting.[7]

There are also signs that the willingness to participate in the zone's development is diminishing, or at least has its limits. Parental involvement in construction of classrooms was primarily through the payment of quotas for workmen's wages rather than the provision of voluntary labor, as one might have expected from NGO accounts of these kinds of projects.[8] At one general assembly, a young jefe de calle proposed that the vecinos get together to pave their streets; he was voted down because other people pointed out that it was the municipality's responsibility, since that was what they paid their taxes for. This highlights an incongruity in the neoliberal vision of the active citizen based upon an ethos of public service and often justifying state evasion of responsibility (Rose 1999, 2000): eventually the active citizens begin to ask what the state should do as its part of the bargain. The way development is administered in El Alto places the vecinos in the position of supplicants, consumers of development services in a highly unequal power relationship where they need to appeal to a mixture of state and private bodies for assistance, rather than being citizens with some sort of legitimate expectation of the state and with the ability to hold the state to account if it does not deliver. Private providers are not bound by those kinds of citizen expectations, and there is no real accountability toward those that they choose to help (Edwards and Hulme 1995; Molyneux and Lazar 2003). Neoliberal constructions of citizens as consumers (see Yuval-Davis 1997) disregard these kinds of power differentials.

Local Government, Local Development, and Popular Participation   The issue of development illustrates what happens when the state delegates or evades its responsibilities in a place like Rosas Pampa. Where it is present, the local manifestation of the state is often little better than private bodies such as NGOs. Local government inefficiency is the main reason that El Alto is so self-constructed. Both juntas in Rosas Pampa had to negotiate with the alcaldía in order to develop the zone, a process that was understood as successfully bidding for obras, but this was no easy task. Until 2000, no one entity was in charge of urban development at the municipal level. Largely because of the weakness of municipal government, the central government had bypassed the alcaldía by creating the position of presidential delegate for El Alto, who was responsible for channeling central government money and some money from international NGOs. By 1999, he was publishing draft proposals for El Alto's urban development (Obermaier et al. 1999) and supervising the participatory planning processes that were in theory the responsibility of the alcaldía. Not that he was particularly effective himself, or that such plans were ever implemented. In 1999–2000, after the changeover in municipal administration, the new mayor, Jose Luis Paredes, sought to regain some sort of control for the alcaldía, as the example of the reorganization of APS's health centers shows. He also engineered the sacking of the presidential delegate. By 2003, some improvement was evident, as various infrastructure projects had been implemented across the city, albeit predominantly in the zones that supported Paredes's political party. He was considered by many to be a reasonably good mayor and was reelected in December 2004.

The Law of Popular Participation of 1994 was a remarkably ambitious attempt at creating an effective system for local development in Bolivia, as well as being an attempt to take into account the corporate nature of Bolivian society (Gray Molina 2003; Secretaría Nacional de Participacion Popular 1997). The legislation provides resources which should enable the municipality to pay for obras and a framework through which alteños can demand obras. It does require a minimum of institutionality from the municipalities, especially in areas of high population. In El Alto, as else-where (McNeish 2001; Postero 2006), its proper implementation has been severely retarded, suffering from the inefficiency, corruption, and politici-zation of local government. The alcaldía of El Alto was notoriously chaotic during the Condepa (Conciencia de Patria party) administrations of 1989–1999: people were constantly moved around different offices or just hired and fired as corruption scandals led to the resignation of one mayor after another. As different parties gained control over different departments in the municipality, their supporters would come into those jobs.[9] This made it very hard to follow the process of obtaining an obra for the zone from beginning to end.

The junta vecinal's main priority in recent years has been getting the streets paved. When I asked women from Rosas Pampa in 2000 what their wishes for the zone were, nearly all began with paving the streets; in the survey I conducted, 37 percent of respondents mentioned paving the streets as a priority wish. This was clearly something that they could not appeal to NGOs for, and the procedure for dealing with the alcaldía was incredibly complicated. The whole process is called a tramite, and went as follows. First, the junta vecinal had to formulate a solicitud, a letter request-ing a particular obra. If this got the support of the Supervisory Committee (Comité de Vigilancia) it would get included in the Annual Operative Plan (Plan Operativo Annual) for that year. This turned it into a carpeta (i.e., a file) to be acted on (in theory), making its way through the alcaldía's processes for design, budget allocation, tender, and eventual work. How-ever, this last stage was extremely fragile. Functionaries supporting a carpeta might get moved to a different job, or they would ask for some-thing in the file to be rewritten, often several times and requiring the services of lawyers; budgets would be allocated, then taken away; and election imperatives could come into play (one functionary offered to speed up a carpeta in late 1999 if the junta could get various people out to demonstrate for his party in Rosas Pampa). All sorts of things could go wrong. If my personal experience of getting a student visa is anything to go by, these are probably classic examples of bureaucrats slowing down processes in the hopes of being given money to speed them back up again. This is the reason the actual system is so difficult to pin down: because there isn't a system in any coherent and immediately obvious sense (de Soto 1989, 2000). Around the time of the municipal elections and the subsequent change of administration, the changing of offices, departments, responsibilities, and personnel as a result of the election combined with extrasystemic organizational measures (i.e., bribery) to make the whole system very opaque. A further complication within Rosas Pampa was the changeover of presidents, discussed below. There was a period of a good few months when the zone lacked a president, and when the new one really began work he was preoccupied with the fiesta.

The juntas had to play a very careful party-political game, and their tramites were vulnerable right up to the point when the work was actually completed. Rosas Pampa's switch from Condepa to MIR (Leftist Revolutionary Movement) in the local elections probably paid off. Although they did not receive as important an obra as the more loyal MIRista zone of Santiago II, by mid-2000 work had begun on the first stage of paving the central avenue. There was no obvious strategic benefit to paving this particular stretch of road, as it was used only by traffic coming into Rosas Pampa and not that traveling through El Alto. But clearly those in the alcaldía had understood the junta vecinal's need for work that would be visible to most people in the zone. The paving of this part of the street also provided a focal point for the fiesta, and the junta was very concerned that it be completed in time. When the work was under way, comments about the junta vecinal were extremely positive, and the fact that the street was paved that year benefited the reputation of the incumbent president. People felt that he had been working hard, in contrast to previous presidents. In fact, most of the running had been done by the previous president, and the process of putting the work out to tender was launched in late 1999, prior to the local elections and the changeover of presidents of the junta. Around this time, the Condepa administration was probably trying desperately to show its ability to deliver results, as it felt the election slipping from its grasp. Nevertheless, the new MIRista government officials could

5. Work paving the central avenue in Rosas Pampa, Avenida 4, in 2000

very well have buried that particular tramite had they wanted to, and so the credit for the work fell to the MIR and the new junta president. In subsequent years, the paving was extended the full length of Avenida 4, Avenida Cívica was covered with asphalt, and work began on cobbling the lateral residential streets of the zone.

The struggle for development for Rosas Pampa illustrates a complex process whereby outside entities, that is, the municipal government and international NGOs, have a part in constructing the community as a bureaucratic entity, represented by the juntas and dealt with as a consumer of or petitioner for development. Making collective citizenship meaningful is very hard in this environment. The leaders of the community find it difficult to deliver the citizenship expectations (Ong 1999a) of the vecinos, namely obras. They are unable to demand what the vecinos see as their due because there is no consistency in the relationship between citizen and state, or in what the agents of the state recognize as their responsibility and what they prefer to delegate. The state is constantly aiming to dodge its responsibilities for the well-being of its citizens (Gill 2000), but private entities such as commercial companies and NGOs are equally inconsistent, as well as much less accountable and even more fleeting than the state.

While the previous section focused on the Rosas Pampa–state part of the mediated relationship between individual citizen and the state, this section focuses on the individual–Rosas Pampa relationship. I examine the issue of leadership and how vecinos assert their own expectations of their authorities. My argument is that community leaders do not always serve the interests of the collectivity, but their failure to do so does enable the construction of a notion of what those interests might be. Occasionally, the collectivity defines itself against, or despite, the actions of its leaders through accusations of corruption, which in a circular way reinforce a notion of a common good that can be violated through corrupt practices. Here, rumor and gossip are means of constructing public opinion and conducting local politics and are therefore very important citizenship practices. As well as being a serious problem in local administration, corruption is also one of the ways through which zonal politics is articulated, highlighting the parallels between zone, municipal, and national levels of government. The following chapter explores corruption talk as a discourse through which people represent their relationship to the state, but many similar issues arose when people talked about public office at the zonal level. When people talked about community leaders being corrupt, they meant that they were seeking to use the zone's money to serve their own interests rather than those of Rosas Pampa. Other ways of describing the same thing was calling people *personalistas* or *interesados* (self-serving, self-interested). Corruption was the most important trope through which rumor and gossip were used to make and resist claims for power or leadership positions, as well as being a way to evaluate community leaders and articulate values about the use of power. Accusations of corruption are an important element in how the vecinos exercise accountability and ensure that their leaders are working for the benefit of the zone. They are therefore a crucial citizenship practice. Exercising leadership in this context is a very delicate proposition.

Rumor, Gossip, and Direct Accusations of Corruption   In Rosas Pampa, corruption was used via rumor to articulate political allegiances or struggles and to maneuver for positions of power, as well as to resist such maneuvers. Accusations of corruption serve both to highlight the moral integrity of the accuser, as well as to throw some mud (not always undeserved) at the accused. An example of this occurred in the junta escolar. In 1999, the leadership had been in position for about six years. They were elected because they had been particularly vocal during meetings in questioning where the fines and quotas charged to the parents actually went (the rumors at the time were that parents' quotas were spent on birthday celebrations for the teachers). They were generally reckoned to be very successful leaders, having negotiated with APS to build six classrooms and toilets for the children during their term of office. However, beginning in March 2000, rumors started to build that they had begun to steal building materials and money.

People were asking when the leaders would "give in their accounts" (rendir cuentas bien). I was told by some that the rumors happened when they did because a particular group of people was "running around" in order to take over the leadership of the junta escolar. This was not unusual: the catechist Don Roberto said that people always complained when the time for voting for new leaders was approaching, but they never actually proposed alternatives, so the same ones remained in position. Doña Gregoria, one of the incumbent leaders of the junta escolar who was being accused of corruption, and those on her side accused the rumormongers of wanting to become leaders simply in order to "extract money" (sacar dinero). She said that it was people from the barranco, the edge of the zone, who wanted to become leaders. However, they had mostly built their houses illegally, according to her, and did not hold proper title to their land, which meant that they could simply run off with any money they collected. Don Roberto confirmed that it was people from the barranco who were disgruntled, telling me that they had approached him to be involved as a future leader. He felt, "It's all self-interest now, they just see money." In mid-2003, a small group finally succeeded in dislodging the junta escolar leaders, mostly because people in the zone felt that it was time for a change. The incumbent leaders themselves agreed and therefore did not defend their position as vigorously as they might otherwise have. There were accusations of accounts not being rendered fully and therefore some suspicion of quota money going astray, but they were relatively mild.

Even when there were no upcoming elections there were constant rumors about community leaders being corrupt. For example, it was commonly known (or thought, at any rate) that most of the leaders of the junta vecinal, like previous committee members, had houses or land in other zones, particularly Senkata. Senkata is a district a bit further out of El Alto along the road to Oruro. Land there is available and cheap, and the belief was that successive junta vecinal committee members had used their positions to accumulate enough money (or building materials) to buy a plot there and build a bigger house than their property in Rosas Pampa. Even in taped interviews women made comments about the junta vecinal's tendency to "sacar dinero":

> I would say that the junta should—well there are times when they say "give us a bit of time" [to show how they have spent the money], really, but frankly they can't say that any more; people say that they help themselves [to money] anyway. People have helped them [with money, quotas], but they've just redirected it to their houses. Yes, they even buy houses for themselves, and with the money make everything nice, that's what people say. . . . People say that they really just take advantage [se aprovechan]. . . . The authorities change, but they all do the same. A new one comes in, and away he goes with the money.

> Every single president has to take advantage [tiene que 'provechar], really.

Both interviewees used the verb aprovechar, which is common in altiplano Bolivia. It means "to take advantage of, or exploit, an opportunity or situation." Although it is not always a negative thing to do, it is ambiguous. The second woman thought that, although you can see the obras of the junta escolar, "there's always some for their pockets. . . . They never use up all the money they collect, they're always fining people."

The junta vecinal probably had more opportunities for corruption than the junta escolar. There were many stories alleging diversion of the money raised from quotas collected for the installation of almost all of the public services. For example, Don Rolando, the president during 1999, had apparently charged quotas of 10 Bolivianos (US$1.70) per house for work paving the three main streets of the zone, but he said that someone had broken into his house and stolen it, a scandal I discuss below. Doña Gregoria thought that Don Rolando was particularly personalista. She said that when the junta escolar had obtained funds for the school toilets he had demanded to be the builder in charge of their construction since he was also the president of the zone at the time. Later on they discovered that stones and cement had gone missing. For that reason, she prevented him from working on the classrooms they built in 1999, even though he had again asked to be involved.

These stories show a struggle between the perception that personal material gains are the most important motivation for leaders (a "politics of the belly"; Bayart 1993) and a strong conception of communality.

Leaders are supposed to work for the benefit of the community rather than for personal interest, and people had a strong sense of what public service was; for example, Doña Gregoria felt that people (other than, of course, herself) were no longer doing things for the zone. She connected this individualism to Bolivia's underdevelopment, claiming that if people were honest and worked for the benefit of their zones, then Bolivia would progress more, a good articulation of the neoliberal philosophy of active citizenship and development as self-help. There was a general consensus that junta vecinal and junta escolar leaders had stood for election because they wanted to work for Rosas Pampa. In one general assembly, the president of the junta escolar said of the junta vecinal, "A leader has become a leader in order to work for the good of the zone." The "good of the zone" was a frequent theme in conversations, meetings, and interviews. Leadership positions in Rosas Pampa were elected, usually through acclamation (rather than secret ballot) during the general assemblies of the vecinos and the school parents. Leaders stand for elections, but generally say that they were asked to do so for one reason or another. They give the impression that they are (often reluctant) servants of the community. Many were called upon to be leaders because they had been vocal critics of previous administrations, as in the case of the junta escolar leaders of 1993–2003. Others were called upon because of their long residence in the zone; Don Ronaldo, the newly instituted secretary of Sports and Young People in the junta vecinal of 2000, said, "They gave me the position of sports secretary because I, well, I've lived in this zone it must be since about '76. I'm really one of the first vecinos and since I get on pretty well with the young people, for that reason they gave me this position, of secretary of Sports and Young People." When asked if he could have refused the job, he said not really: "Also, people know you. They know that you're on the side of the young people. I don't think that you can [refuse] because when someone speaks, I think that if you're going to talk you have to respond by working too." He felt that he could not refuse partly because, like the leaders of the junta escolar, he had been criticizing the previous leaders, implying that he could do better.

Don Ronaldo's comments hint at another reason for qualifying as leader, which is simply that if you are able to do the job, at some point it becomes your turn. This is very similar to what happens in the countryside, where leadership positions rotate among households (Klemola 1997; Carter and Mamani P. 1989 [1982]; Abercrombie 1998). There is some flexibility, though. In April 2003, the junta vecinal committee's term of office had come to a close, and it was time to choose new leaders. In a general assembly called in part for that purpose, a delegate from the FEJUVE suggested that the vecinos had two options: they could organize an election or they could ratify the present incumbent, Don Teodoro, and his committee. After general discussion, the vecinos decided to hold a vote then and there on that question, and Don Teodoro was ratified. The vecinos then began the process of filling the positions on the committee that had become vacant because leaders had abandoned them. This they did first by promoting those members of the committee present, on the recommendation of Don Teodoro; for example, a general secretary who had worked well and come to meetings was promoted to vice president. Once that process was over, there were a few positions left to fill, including that of secretary of sports, and so the junta vecinal committee and the regular audience members suggested names and asked those people if they would be prepared to fill the position. Several people refused, saying that they did not have the time; one man explained that he was a tenant rather than a homeowner, so did not qualify, and one woman said she could not because she could not write. Not all candidates were able to come up with convincing excuses, however, and eventually enough people agreed and the new committee was ratified and congratulated by those still present. By lunchtime most of the audience had drifted off. Clearly it is possible to avoid election by simply not being present at the meeting where this happens. Another way to avoid the responsibilities of being a leader, which I also saw frequently in the street traders associations, is to abandon the position, that is, simply to stop working and turning up at meetings. This can be a prelude either to a resignation for some personal issue, or simply to the replacement of the committee member at the next available opportunity. The junta vecinal committee of Rosas Pampa has sixteen nominal members, but this large number is probably an insurance policy on the basis that not all will be able to work conscientiously; indeed, usually only around six or seven do so.

Given these ways of avoiding leadership responsibilities, in general the system works quite well and people do not usually get involved in zonal business if they are not in some way willing to become leaders when they are needed or it is their turn. The ways by which leadership committees of each zone are constituted are important in enabling them to function effectively as mediators between vecinos and the state. They take on that hinge position because they are both outside the community and of it, and the expectation placed upon them to serve the zone helps to create an understanding of what the zone as collective political entity actually is. They become leaders through the exercise of community democracy, which in Rosas Pampa is based upon systems of rotative leadership often pointed to as indicative of Andean forms of local democracy (Ticona Alejo 2003). However, in a dynamic also common among the street traders associations (see chapter 6), good leaders also stay in position for a long time, as the vecinos ratify them for each new administrative period. Thus, committed leaders who serve the zone well are kept in place until they are no longer effective. This is in part because the vecinos recognize that being an effective mediator between them and the state is difficult, not least because of the weakness or absence of the state.

Andean ethnographies tend to view community leadership in the countryside as an obligation that is usually very expensive: prestige and duty prevail over material interest (Klemola 1997; Carter and Mamani P. 1989 [1982]; Abercrombie 1998). The committee members of Rosas Pampa themselves were often vocal about the fact that they were spending their own money on all the work they did. Don Julián pointed out:

> It's hard work being a leader, because really the Junta de Vecinos doesn't have money, or resources for fares or even for food, when we go to the alcaldía. We don't even get our monthly quotas, because since the zone now has everything [i.e., public utilities infrastructure], people are not interested in going to meetings, and no longer give their monthly 1 Boliviano. Since we're eight hundred [households], really there should be 800 [Bolivianos] monthly for the leaders to use. But there isn't, we just about raise 20 or 30 Bolivianos, so we leaders use our own money.

In practice, people are understanding up to a point, accepting that nobody works for nothing. Leadership of a community is hard work, an obligation but also a job, and one does not work entirely for free, particularly in the context of a serious economic recession. People are prepared to recognize that leaders of the junta escolar and junta vecinal should be recompensed in part, at least for their fares and lunches, when they have to go to the alcaldía to ask for things on behalf of the zone. Rather pointedly, one woman said to me, "They don't get paid anything either. Who's going to work for free? They get hungry." For her, voluntary work did not make sense. So, for example, Doña Gregoria received a salary for the construction work on the new classrooms she did as a representative of the junta escolar. When I began work as a substitute teacher, many people said that I should ask to be paid for what I did; when I attempted (unsuccessfully) to volunteer at the school, there was considerable suspicion about the fact that I did not want payment. Antero Klemola (1997) provides a contrasting picture for the rural community of Kila Kila, where accusations that leaders were being paid for their work were tantamount to corruption allegations, in that payment indicated that a leader was working for personal interest rather than the communal good.

Payment for community activity is an ambiguous issue in Rosas Pampa, as well as in the countryside. These ambiguities mean that the leaders tread a fine line between being fairly recompensed for their work and spending the zone's money on themselves. Doña Gregoria told me of friction between herself and another leader of the junta escolar. There were rumors that he had taken a typewriter that had been donated to the school and that he had been selling parents' attendance cards for more than they were worth. She, of course, considered herself to be completely honest, and felt that his actions might reflect on her; she thought that they should be very careful to be above suspicion. On other occasions, though, she told me of things that could have become grist for the rumormongers' mill. Buying things for the school, which requires a lot of walking, is very tiring, and the leaders of the junta escolar work hard ("mucho sacrificio"; a lot of sacrifice), so on one occasion the headmaster offered her a blanket or some money as payment—at least to cover her expenses.

Don Pablo, a former president subject to corruption rumors over the destination of quotas he raised for the sewage system, maintained to me that he had been working very hard for the benefit of the zone in ways that were not necessarily visible to ordinary residents. He had supervised all the tramites to get the legal status that enabled the zone to access money from the Law of Popular Participation (the zone's *personería jurídica*). He felt that the criticisms easily made a leader become discouraged, that people notice the president only when he is failing a little bit, not when he is actually working: "Sometimes, being a leader, we want things for the good of the zone, but it doesn't turn out like that. Sometimes the opposite happens. . . . But the vecinos . . . think that we are trying to steal, get a little bit for ourselves. . . . Life's like that, isn't it? They've criticized me too, they went to the press, to the radios, they criticized me, you know." As of September 2000, nearly two years after his term had finished, he had not provided the accounts for his presidency and did not seem likely to.

The corruption stories have as much to do with highlighting the moral integrity of the teller as anything else. Everyone is involved; I was even told the story of how some priests had offered previous leaders of the junta escolar US$3,000 each to turn the school over to the Catholic Church.[10] And no one is involved; the person who told me this was doing so to prove his moral integrity in turning down the offer. If they were bad people they would have taken the money, and, he went on, they probably should have since the school would now "shine," and anyway people don't appreciate the sacrifices made by the junta escolar for the benefit of the school. For leaders, operating in such a context is difficult since trust is not straightforwardly conferred upon them but is conditional.

Corruption, Accountability, and Obras The trust between community and leader sometimes appears whimsical. If leaders do succumb to the temptations of corruption and upset the balance between working for the zone and gaining personal recompense, there is in practice a fair degree of acceptance, as Don Rolando's case shows. By March 2000, the vecinos of Rosas Pampa had had enough of the president. At a general assembly, he and his vice president were forced to resign and were replaced by other members of the leadership committee. I had been unable to go because I was ill, but I asked Doña Betty about it later while buying provisions from her shop. She called over Don Arturo to explain it to us. It was a case of embezzlement: Don Rolando had "misspent" (*malgastado*) US$2,000 from the money set aside for the Community Center. Doña Betty had heard that the figure was $25,000 and that he had bought a piece of land in the alteño zone of Atipiris with the proceeds and taken building materials from the Community Center in order to build a house there. According to Don Arturo, Don Rolando had actually spent the money on a mistress in Santa Rosa. He was apparently still living in Rosas Pampa but had gone to ground. Doña Betty said that she thought he should show his face, to say whether he had stolen the money or not. She thought he was a coward and not a real man. Both she and Don Arturo agreed that it was all right for him to spend his own money on a lover, but one shouldn't "play with the zone's money." Earlier in the year, he had been so stressed at creditors and builders asking him for the money he no longer had that he had actually poisoned himself and been taken to hospital. As Doña Betty put it later in an interview, "He squandered the money, then he poisoned himself, it came out in the paper, everything, it was all over the press. It's a real disgrace."

Don Roberto later told me that the Community Center money had come from various nongovernmental institutions, and the money that had been "misspent" was from that allocated for the provision of furniture. He said that the same sort of thing had happened in many administrations. None of the juntas vecinales have given an account of what they spent; each administration has to start from scratch, as no one keeps any documents. He had been arguing strongly for some sort of community archive, which would hold documents from previous juntas and allow for knowledge to be passed down. He thought that Don Rolando had a weak character, even though he knew a lot, whereas the other leaders were stronger in character but lacked knowledge. My neighbor Doña Emiliana thought that leaders "shouldn't do these things"; perhaps a woman would poison herself, but a man shouldn't. Regarding community authorities in general, she said, "We can't say anything, they won't listen to us. It's the same in [my pueblo], they defraud just the same, it's their job." I asked why they do it. She said, "I ask myself the same thing. Perhaps because there's no money around." Don Ronaldo, the sports secretary, was also fairly sympathetic:

> It makes you really angry, doesn't it? I mean, I think he was in a really critical moment, no, in a moment—I think that you only do that sort of thing when you are desperate. When there's no way out, and to do, to get to that extreme, I think he must have been really desperate to do that, really, to sell his reputation. Because a lot of people more or less thought he was very able, they believed in him, but since he's done this, no, they think he must have been really desperate, he must have had debts, to get to the point where he sold his prestige, really just threw away his good name, his person [su persona].

People disapproved of Don Rolando's actions, but they were mostly unsurprised and resigned to its being the way things are. I suspect that was because by the time the story got out the processes of accountability had failed, and everyone knew that the money had been spent and was unrecoverable. Doña Gregoria said that as treasurer of the junta escolar she was very keen to keep good records and be careful with the money, because "people talk." In this sense, accountability is about prevention, with the sanction of people talking. The stories act as examples and serve to keep other leaders in check. As the sports secretary put it, as a leader, one does not want to lose one's prestige, one's good name. It is tempting to suggest that this sanction is no longer effective in an urban context, where people can simply move to another zone as Don Rolando did, to his house in Senkata. However, he had certainly suffered, losing his status, even his masculinity, in the eyes of residents of Rosas Pampa. He could not show his face in the zone. One wonders what his wife felt about all this.

People will always talk about their leaders, though, even if they are honest (cf. Parry 2000). As a leader the only way to avoid excessive criticism and overt accusations of corruption is through obtaining obras for the zone or the school; obras constitute the acknowledged legitimate expectations of the citizens, whether citizens of Rosas Pampa or of El Alto. From the vecinos' point of view, the achievement of obras was both necessary for the zone and evidence that the junta was making an effort and achieving results (trabajando bien, "working well," or caminando bien, literally, "walking well"). The leaders were well aware of this. At a meeting toward the end of October 1999, they were discussing an appropriate time to hold the next general assembly. They decided that it was a good idea to have a meeting soon, since they had the newspaper advertisement for the tendering of the contract to pave Avenue 4 and had nearly finalized the contract for building the Community Center. They decided that they should wait until the latter had been finalized so that they could present the two as concrete achievements and thus forestall criticism from the vecinos.

The junta escolar was under similar pressure to produce obras but had had more success than the 1999 junta vecinal. When asked their opinion about the junta escolar, many of the women I interviewed made comments about how the school had progressed, how ugly and small it was before, when children had to have classes outside in the playground.

They've worked, the school's pretty now.

Yes, with them things have gone well. They mobilize themselves, they mobilize for milk, for the children. They mobilize in order to improve the school.

Yes, they [as opposed to the junta vecinal] have worked hard.

You can see the obras.

The women I interviewed were well aware that my landlady was one of the junta escolar leaders, so they were probably not as critical as they could have been. However, the general consensus did seem to be that they had done a good job, or that they were bien nomás (okay). I heard criticisms from closer friends that they had been in their posts for too long and should give someone else an opportunity. There were also those rumors about corruption. Overall, though, the assessment of the junta escolar was more favorable than that of the junta vecinal because they had quite clearly improved the school. You could see where they were spending the money they charged in quotas and fines. With the junta vecinal, results were not so obvious. So the women made comments such as the following:

Up until now, you can't see anything.

[The leaders] have forgotten about the zone. They've totally forgotten. Now, recently, there seems to me to be a little bit of interest in the zone. . . . But they've never had any interest in the zone. [I asked, "What good things have the junta done?"] No, they haven't done anything, there aren't any obras.

They haven't moved themselves. . . . For example, this avenue [Avenida 4], they had to do that last year. It seems as though the authorities are there more for money than anything else. They don't move themselves, they don't mobilize for the zone. Because if the authorities, if the president of the zone, had actually mobilized themselves, I think the zone would have progressed much better. But they don't care, that's why it's like it is.

People weren't universally critical: one woman pointed out that "it's difficult to be a leader" and that people don't understand, they "talk behind their backs" and don't realize how much work the leaders put in and how much it costs. Others said that they were okay, that they had provided the zone with a sewage system, water, electricity—some leaders are good, some bad. One pointed out that they were making an effort, in conjunction with the market women's leaders, to get the market improved and make it more hygienic.

One result of the fact that obras are so important in Rosas Pampa was a series of highly ritualized inauguration ceremonies for the obras that had been completed during the year I lived there. The junta vecinal ceremoniously poured alcoholic libations for the newly built Community Center, with the relevant NGO people present. The same NGO people came to the ceremonial opening of the four new classrooms at the school. Both ceremonies consisted of long speeches from various important adults, and poetry readings and dances from schoolchildren, then an official ch'alla[11] and a toast of "champagne" (cider) and biscuits, followed by food and, if those present were lucky, beer. The grandest ceremony was when the mayor came to open the newly paved Avenue 4 on the morning of the first

6. The community center, built by the junta vecinal, in 2000
7. The community center in 2003, with additional floor and extension

day of the fiesta in September 2000 and supervised the civic parade of the schoolchildren that traditionally opens the festivities. Such rituals of accountability marked the triumphs of the authorities in a far more powerful and important way than rendering well-kept financial accounts could ever do. The vecinos of Rosas Pampa have various ways of asserting their expectations of their leaders and controlling their actions, particularly through accusations of corruption. Corruption is both the means by which citizens stake their claim to these obras and the context which makes such concrete evidence of activity essential.

COLLECTIVE CITIZENSHIP

This chapter has described some of the practices by which the vecinos of Rosas Pampa constitute themselves as collective citizens, a collectiveness that was recently recognized by the Bolivian state in its provisions for local government. The vecinos' sense of collectivity involves a strong conception of active responsibility toward the community, which varies according to the person but is most acute for the leaders. Nearly everybody has participated in some way in the development of the zone, and most people are well aware of zonal politics through informal networks as well as formal structures. The vecinos of Rosas Pampa have constructed their zone over the past thirty or so years on their own initiative and by appealing to the state and to NGOs for the provision of services and infrastructure.

One consequence of that history is the emphasis on results, on obras instead of accurate accounts, as a means of measuring the success or failure of local politics. Politics coalesces around concrete local issues, and if the juntas do not provide obras, then they have failed in the eyes of the vecinos. The corruption talk is a way of explaining the failure to secure obras: either the juntas or the local government is deemed corrupt. In turn, the demand for obras is a means of reducing the damage done by corruption, because, at the very least, some money has been invested in the community. Corruption talk is also an example of the practices by which women redress the gender imbalance of the public face of community politics. Where much of local politics is conducted through rumor and gossip, female networks are crucial to the forming of public opinion. Finally, it also expresses and imposes the vecinos' expectations of their leaders, holding future leaders to account preemptively with the threat that they will be discussed in the same demeaning way as Don Rolando was if they succumb to the temptation to divert the zone's money for their personal interests. Future leaders know that in order to be successful they should hold to their commitment to be active in favor of the zone. Thus, corruption talk creates an understanding of the public and the zone as well as drawing on that understanding.

Creating that sense of collectivity also becomes actualized as collective political agency at less mundane moments. The daily experiences of managing the relationship with the state in order to administer the means of social reproduction collectively provide the foundation for mobilizations against the state when it becomes predatory. The FEJUVE enforced participation of the different zones in the general strike of early October 2003 through the committees of the local juntas vecinales. Some of the more radical ones used attendance lists and fines to enforce vecino participation on barricades and at marches. In other instances, the impetus to participate came from the vecinos themselves. This was the case for Rosas Pampa, where vecinos told me that the president of the junta vecinal had gone to ground for most of the week of 12 to 17 October. They said that he showed his face only when the zone was conducting a wake for one of the victims of the army; he shouted at them, saying that he had told them not to go to the demonstrations and therefore they should not blame him for the death. Their explanation for his lack of leadership was that he was a MIRista, thus connecting what they perceived as his self-preservation instincts to his self-interest as an individual co-opted by a political party. This is a good example of how criticism of the leader as individualistic and acting against the interests of the zone can create a notion of the zone as a collectivity with much more authentic political instincts. The vecinos who went on the marches from El Alto down to La Paz found out about them principally by listening to the radio or from the people who came through the zone ringing bells and informing them about the demonstrations. They went in part because of their personal anger at Gonzalo Sanchez de Lozada and in part as representatives of their zone. This was important not least because rumors had it that zones which did not participate in the demonstrations would be considered pro-government and therefore risked being looted. The member of the junta vecinal leadership committee with responsibility for carrying its standard in marches and civic parades went to all of the protests, and thus proved the participation of the zone of Rosas Pampa in the mass mobilization.

The constitution of the zone as a collective political subject is dependent upon internal and external dynamics. Internally, discussions about corruption and community leadership enable vecinos to imagine themselves as a single political entity. That collectivity, however, is riven with suspicions and tensions, as the vecinos attempt to counteract the apparent self-interest of the leaders. In addition, the zone must interact with external forces, such as the state and, in the state's absence, the NGOs. The community authorities mediate the problematic relationship between individual citizen and the state, but they are not always uncontested representatives of the community. In fact, that contestation is much of what actually makes the community.

THREE *CITIZENS DESPITE THE STATE*

At election time, the relationship between individual citizen and the state becomes in theory much more direct and individualized than the day-to-day administration described in the previous chapter. However, an investigation of the 1999 local elections in El Alto shows a mix of individual and collective interests and strategies at work. The official political system in El Alto is the theme of this chapter, which examines electoral democracy from the point of view of the voters and citizens themselves. Voting is the archetypal citizenship practice and expression of political agency in liberal democracies, both the duty and the right of citizens. Universal suffrage (associated with the Revolution of 1952 in Bolivia) is central to twentieth-century liberal rhetoric about a universal and equal category of citizenship. That universalism is undermined in practice through the operation of clientelism and personalist politics. Paradoxically, this situation both exacerbates the distance between electorate and elected and brings them closer together, at least during the time of the election campaign. Both these effects create different collective political subjects: as well as the patron-client grouping, a collective sense of "the people" against, or despite, the politicians.

The smooth operation of a representative democracy implies the depersonalization of both the elector and the elected, as we become abstracted individuals making rational choices. Yet the people of Rosas Pampa destabilize both the abstraction and the individuation, principally through the logic of the patron–client relationship. Clientelism does not, however, mean complete passivity on the part of the clients, who use it to assert an engagement with the state in the person of the politician and a greater representativity of politics as they develop personalized relationships with him or her. Although individuals seek to establish themselves as clients of the political parties for personal reasons, this coexists with a desire to gain collective benefit from the patrons and constitute the zone itself as a client. Clientelism here appears as a means by which the clients seek to overcome the depersonalization of electoral politics to create a more direct and less delegative local democracy.

Meanwhile, a pervasive disillusionment with politics expresses itself in narratives of politicians' corruption, which articulate the powerlessness people feel with regard to political (and economic) elites. Through narratives of politicians' corruption, the people of Rosas Pampa assert their expectations of the state and attempt to hold politicians to account, thus representing the nature of the state and the reality of their citizenship back to themselves. This has the effect of distancing them from the state and the political elites and is an expression of the lack of representativity in the political system,[1] but it also constitutes Rosas Pampa and the "people of Bolivia" as collective entities—as citizens betrayed by venal politicians. Despite this, the operation of the actual election is taken very seriously in Rosas Pampa, and the vecinos act *as a zone* and assert a collective pride in their right to vote and to do so meticulously. The election is also therefore a part of the process of constituting the sense of community in Rosas Pampa.

THE POLITICAL SCENE IN EL ALTO

In the December 1999 local elections in El Alto, the stakes were high. The alcaldía had been run by the same political party for the previous decade: Conciencia de Patria, or Condepa. The Condepa administrations were notoriously corrupt and inefficient, and the party had fragmented since the death of its founder in 1997 and its subsequent electoral success and entry into national government as a coalition partner. In 1999, the situation looked ripe for an upset in their final stronghold, El Alto. Sure enough, the Movimiento Izquierdista Revolucionario (MIR; Leftist Revolutionary Movement) put an end to Condepa's reign. Their candidate, Jose Luis Paredes, also called Pepelucho, gained around 45 percent of the overall vote, and the MIR won an unprecedented seven out of the eleven council seats on offer. Rosas Pampa too had been Condepista for the previous ten years and similarly switched to the MIR in 1999, the result mirroring the overall vote for El Alto.

Condepa was founded by Carlos Palenque, who rose to prominence in the 1960s as a charango player,[2] a *folklorista*. His move to more obviously political spheres began in 1980, when he started a radio show called *La Tribuna Libre del Pueblo* (The Free Tribunal of the People). The show is still broadcast; its format is that ordinary people come to the microphone to appeal for help, publicize events, denounce a crime, and so on. In 1985 he bought a TV station, enabling him to broadcast the *Tribuna* on TV as well as on the radio. In 1988 the TV and radio stations were closed down temporarily by the government, and he and fellow workers at the channel, including his pregnant wife, famously went on a hunger strike to protest. It was soon after this that he founded Condepa and they ran in the municipal elections of 1989, coming first in the department of La Paz, much to the surprise of the Bolivian political classes (Saravia and Sandoval 1991; Archondo 1991). In 1997 Palenque died of a heart attack just before the presidential elections, leaving a political and communications empire to be squabbled over by his daughter, Veronica Palenque, his fellow TV presenter and rumored mistress, Remedios Loza, and his recently estranged widow.[3] Condepa was part of the national governing coalition from 1997 until late 1998, when the party split and left the coalition. Remedios's faction moved into opposition, while Veronica's "rebels," although not part of the coalition, continued to vote for the government. Palenque's death, however, proved impossible to overcome. The 1999 municipal elections were the moment when Condepa lost its last remaining stronghold, El Alto, even though the much-loved Remedios was a candidate for mayor. Her candidacy was a last-ditch attempt to rescue the party from division, escalating corruption scandals, and the gaping symbolic hole left by Palenque's death. In the 1997 presidential elections Remedios herself had filled this hole, as an indigenous woman and Palenque's most faithful ally, but by 1999 this was no longer enough. She was tainted by rumors about her style of leadership, as well as the phenomenal corruption of Condepista administrations in the previous decade in El Alto and La Paz. By the 2002 presidential elections Condepa's support, even in the department of La Paz, had dwindled to almost nothing.

The MIR's campaign, culminating in December 1999, is one of the more recent examples of a trend of local-level populism in Bolivia that began in the mid-1980s with Condepa (Blanco Cazas and Sandoval 1993; Mayorga 1991; Archondo 1991). As with other Latin American populist movements, Condepa and MIR appealed at both pragmatic and affective levels. In the mid-twentieth century, Latin American populism's pragmatic appeal for voters tended to rest upon its association with redistributive economic policies, the archetypal populist movement being Peronism in Argentina.[4] For most populist movements, economic redistribution was organized along clientelist lines, and the neopopulists of recent years continue to rely heavily on distribution of patronage (Blanco Cazas and Sandoval 1993; Auyero 2000). The clients use this distribution of patronage for their own ends. They seek to do this in part through the development of a personal, direct relationship with the patron; that is, they place great importance on the more affective side of politics.[5] They actively shape and take advantage of opportunities that arise during election time for bringing the political process closer to home, thus gaining benefit and substantiating their citizenship in practice, albeit temporarily. This contradicts much of the literature on clientelism, which misrepresents the clients as passive, unsophisticated, and uninformed—purely subjects of control.[6] In fact, as many are acutely aware, there is much at stake for the clients: the zone might miscalculate and therefore be forgotten by the alcaldía for the next five years, or it might enjoy the benefits of being known as a zone that voted for the winning party. In addition, whole families' livelihoods depend upon making correct calculations about party allegiance, since their future employment may be linked to party membership.

"GETTING PEOPLE": THE PRAGMATICS OF CLIENTELISM

This section is a detailed discussion of one aspect of the citizenship practice of voting: the calculations that voters make during election campaigns. By addressing the operation of clientelism from the perspective of the clients, I explore the ways clients exercise their political agency according to both individual and collective interests. The general marginalization of the poor from political power is less solid at the local government level, and in particular at election time. The system of campaigning tends toward face-to-face interaction with the candidates in the years prior to election and during the campaign. Javier Auyero (2000) has noted something similar for Buenos Aires, where people talk of the "time of elections" as a palpably different period in the relations between politicians and poor districts. As in El Alto, in the runup to the elections, residents of poor urban neighborhoods suddenly find that they count, that their support is being sought, and that politicians are visiting their zone frequently in order to court them. This gives at least the impression that politics is for a short while more representative of the poor, that politicians are more accountable, and consequently, that citizenship is more meaningful. Robert Gay (1998) points out that the vote of a poor person has the same value as that of a rich person, and it is cheaper to buy the votes of the poor than those of the rich.

For political parties during election campaigns, it is extremely important to "have people" (*tener gente*), since the party with the most people is the one that voters expect to win and are therefore most likely to vote for, in a snowball effect. Before I examine the slow and incremental process of gaining people, in the sense of gaining goodwill, in the years prior to the election, I address the election campaign itself. I look at the more instrumental side of how political parties gain their people through clientelism and how this is viewed by those whose allegiance is sought, as well as at the role of spectacle during the campaign in demonstrating the people you have and gaining more.

Clientelism During the Campaign   I went to a meeting of the MIR women's group with a seventeen-year-old friend, Victoria, during the final week before the elections. I was the seventy-fourth woman to register as a *militante*, or party activist, even though I can't vote in Bolivia. About forty-five to fifty women attended the meeting at the beginning, and around thirty stayed the whole time. The others left after registering their attendance and collecting plastic mugs that were given out to the women who had attended a campaign event on the previous Sunday. Many then went home and returned to collect wool that they had been promised as payment for their participation in demonstrations and for having registered as militantes. This was a derisory amount, worth 2 Bolivianos (about 30 U.S. cents at the time), and was only enough wool for a baby's hat. It was also available only in orange and blue, the MIR colors. Many of those who were given the rather violent orange wool looked as though they felt distinctly cheated, but they signed for it anyway. During the meeting I asked why the women came, and one said "in order to vote." I asked if it was necessary to come to a meeting in order to vote, and she said that it was, and "they also give you cups and wool." Certainly it seemed that the primary motivation among the women was the wool, but many also evidently enjoyed the chance to get together with friends, discuss children, and gossip. In general, political parties promise rice, sugar, wool, and sometimes toys for children in return for the work of campaigning. In this they draw on voters' cultural expectations of gift giving in return for work, which have a long history rooted in the exchange relationships between hacienda owner and peon and mirroring that between poor women and NGOs, whereby women are paid in foodstuffs for work on public projects (Albro 2000). The political parties often deliver very small amounts, but some women, if they have time, sign up for as many parties as they can in order to gain maximum benefit. Victoria herself signed up for two parties and received more wool from the second. But it is hard work: she had to go to various demonstrations, which took up whole days, during which time she was on her feet with her baby on her back. For that she was given a few Bolivianos' worth of wool.

This does not seem adequate payment, and there were many who grumbled quietly, during and after the meeting. However, the short-term strategies of taking advantage of small amounts of payment for campaign work need to be balanced against more long-term considerations. Even if the immediate benefits don't measure up to the amount of work put in, having what is called *aval político*, a record of involvement in party activity, can be beneficial in the long term and can lead to employment after the election. The range of jobs that depend upon party allegiance is wide, in all parts of the civil service, public health structures, and education, and from construction workers to hospital auxiliaries and school porters. One auxiliary nurse I knew had been fired after eleven years when General Banzer won the national elections in 1997; she had been replaced by a woman who owned a café and had only had one year's training. Her situation was not atypical. Among the ramifications of such practices are widespread inefficiency in public services and the lack of trust on the part of the service users.[7]

When new politicians take up their posts, they fire hundreds of workers in order to make space for their supporters and generally do not pay the wages for the last three months (or so) of work, let alone redundancy benefits, and the state does not pick up the slack. A salaried municipal civil service job may not bring in much money per month, and wages are often not paid for three or more months, but it is still a job. If you lose that job, you need to quickly find new ways to earn money. In Victoria's case, her mother, Doña Josefa, had worked in the municipality for a number of years as a result of her status as a Condepa militante with a good record of aval político. She knew that Condepa would lose this election, and she would therefore lose her job, so she encouraged Victoria to sign up for other parties as a way of spreading her family's forces. Her strategy was for Victoria to get a job from the MIR after the election, thus replacing her mother as the family member earning money from political involvement and enabling her to financially support the entire family (her mother, brother, and baby son, as well as her partner, who was still at school).

The issue of party-related public service jobs impacts in a very real way the strategies for economic survival available to many poorer residents of El Alto. It is a gross understatement to say that the insecurity that comes from the political nature of jobs makes life very difficult. However, there is a sense in which the jobs are not simply the gift of the winning political party, or an effect of corruption; rather, they are part of the citizens' expectations of the state, part of what Aihwa Ong (1999a: 54) calls their "citizenship capacity." So, some months after the election, when the new mayor, Jose Luis Paredes, had not given as many jobs to MIR militantes as was expected, some people felt cheated.[8] (And, of course, those who feel cheated or betrayed may not vote for the same party again.) They felt that if you put in the work for the party, you should be rewarded—paid—as long as you are able to do the job. As a result of this type of clientelism, at the lower levels of the civil service there are high levels of participation in government, so that it is almost as though Doña Josefa and Victoria were standing for election themselves. This is an intriguing paradox, given what I have previously said about the distance between the political process and the popular sectors, although the civil service levels to which Victoria might have future access do not hold any actual power.

My second example, on a more collective level, is about the local school. During the runup to the elections, the school held several political events to which parties donated materials. One such event, about three weeks before the elections, was an opening ceremony for two new classrooms funded by an NGO. After the ceremony, and with great fanfare, the Movimiento Nacionalista Revolucionario (MNR; National Revolutionary Movement) representative arrived, accompanied by a few local militantes, to present much-trumpeted desks. However, instead of desks accommodating two or three children, as most had expected, they brought twenty single chairs with a resting place for books on the arms. Despite the obvious disappointment, the parents and children present politely heard the MNR representative's speech and eagerly collected the hats, exercise books, and almanacs he handed out.[9] The headmaster spoke, saying rather half-heartedly that we should support the MNR because they were demonstrating their commitment to the zone with deeds.

Later, the Acción Democrática Nacional (ADN; National Democratic

Action, the party of then-President Banzer) asked the leaders of the junta escolar to organize a convoy of parents to go to a demonstration in another zone, promising more than twenty bags of cement for the school in return. So around twenty mothers went to cheer and collect flags, hats, soft drinks, and whatever else they could find. But, as it turned out, "weeping with the effort, they just about gave us five bags of cement," as Doña Gregoria said. This was a serious embarrassment for her, since she had gone to a lot of trouble to get the twenty women out for the ADN on the promise of cement for the school. Five bags of cement cost about US$5 and are not enough to be used for anything; twenty would at least have been useful for some improvement to the school. The mothers who had gone campaigning were not happy.

These two parties' election strategies had backfired, at least in Rosas Pampa. Doña Gregoria pointed out to me that the ADN's actions showed how they would behave if in government, as they did not fulfill their promises. Likewise, the MNR had promised desks but brought twenty "little chairs" (sillitas), no use to a school with class sizes ranging from thirty-five to fifty-five. On an earlier occasion, the MIR had brought ten bags of cement; they had also brought a typewriter and provided a PA system for school events and basketball hoops for the school (painted in MIR colors). When telling me all the things they had donated, she said, "They're corrupt, but at least they keep their promises." Meanwhile, the junta escolar and the school authorities had between them at least got three political parties to provide some cement, a few chairs, a typewriter, and other things for the benefit of the school. Politicians are notorious for forgetting poor zones once in power; the campaign period is perhaps the only time the school is noticed and can play parties off against each other for its own benefit, again giving the lie to the characterization of clients as passive.

The junta vecinal tried to implement a similar strategy with the political parties during the election campaign, although with less success, probably because of the overt affiliation of the main leaders with Condepa, which did not have as much money as the MIR, partly because campaign money from the National Electoral Court had been withheld because of corruption accusations. At one meeting, the president told how he had been talking with the architect in charge of planning at the municipality, who was also a candidate for an offshoot of Condepa. This candidate expected to come to Rosas Pampa but wanted people to be there, cheering him on. In return, he was prepared to speed up the approval process for the second phase of the paving of the main avenue. The president said that there would be no problem getting residents of the zone to cheer him on, and anyway, "of course, the vote is secret," meaning that residents could vote for whomever they chose at the actual election. Unfortunately, the candidate did not come to the zone, and ten months later, the second phase of paving had yet to be approved.

Face-to-Face Politics: The Campaign Rally   Quite early on, it was clear to most of my informants that the MIR would win the election in El Alto, "because they have a lot of people" (*porque tienen mucha gente*). This generally referred to the people who had signed up as *militantes* or who had done some work for the party. But simply having people is not enough for a party to win, they must *show* that they have people, and get their people, or at least people who *look* like they are their people, out on the streets. This dynamic has also been recognized in classical anthropology of patronage politics; the Swat Pathan lords, for example, paraded their clients as if for war in order to underline their strength (Barth 1977). Along with TV, public displays are the main way politicians stake their claims to electoral success, and street demonstrations are the best way for voters to assess the chances of particular political parties. They are a crucial element of the affective politics of creating allegiance (Auyero 2001); they appeal to voters' sense of fun, curiosity, and business and are a means of demonstrating parties' wealth and generosity.

One Friday, Doña Gregoria's children came to tea brimming over with excitement because they had heard that Jose Luis Paredes was going to visit the school the following day. They wondered what he would bring: hats, flags, cups? The music teacher was a fanatic MIR militante and had arranged everything: Pepelucho would turn up at 10:30 A.M. I arrived at 10:20 to the strains of thumping pop music. The kids from the graduating class were kicking a football around, the builders working on the school were cementing the outside of the classrooms, and the music teacher occasionally appeared, looking important. A loudspeaker announced that we would shortly be receiving a visit from a very important person. The banner outside the school entrance was prepared, along with awayus and teddy bears. An hour later, Bolivian music was put on the loudspeaker, the kids formed a corridor, and the music teacher called together everyone, including parents, "because it's for the good of the school." However,

8. Banner welcoming Jose Luis Paredes to the school during the election campaign of 1999

despite all the excitement, the gathering broke up with no Pepelucho. The music teacher and his fellow MIR militante scuttled around some more, making phone calls on a mobile to Paredes's people, with little success.

At midday, the candidate from another political party, the Movimiento Bolivia Libre (MBL; Free Bolivia Movement), drove in. Or, more precisely, his militantes came in on a bus, and he followed in a car. They drove to the MBL office, a large house on one side of the football field, where a small crowd had collected. Various people spoke, in Spanish and in Aymara, advocating participatory democracy and stressing the fact that the candidate was from El Alto. They sang songs accompanied by pan-pipes (which are associated with Aymara music), distributed flags, and drank soft drinks. After the candidate spoke, he drove off. His militantes hung around for a bit, chatting, until 1:30.

At 12:40 things seemed to be collapsing in the school. Half an hour later, most people had become bored and gone home to eat, as it was clear that Pepelucho was not going to come. The disappointment that he had not turned up, along with the effort put in to welcoming him properly, somehow created an atmosphere whereby he became special. I went for lunch, and Doña Gregoria asked me what things the MBL—the party that had actually turned up—had brought. Unfortunately, this time the answer was nothing, not even a leaflet with any kind of manifesto promises. The MIR office in the zone also had no copies of the Plan Progreso, Paredes's much-touted manifesto. One got the sense that politicians can, as one seventeen-year-old said to me, "invent policies." They can sweep into a zone, promise what they like depending on their audience, and leave.

A week later, Remedios Loza, Condepa's candidate, also passed through the zone, on a gleaming green tractor, presumably one of the alcaldía's, which somewhat ironically were subjects of several rumors of theft by municipal agents. This was in fact the only big event that Condepa put on in Rosas Pampa during the whole electoral campaign and was supervised by junta vecinal leaders of the time. They were out early in the morning with a table for people to register as Condepa militantes. The pages in that book stayed remarkably clear. Only about an hour late, Remedios came through, with a large garland around her neck, smiling and waving like a queen. Lots of people came out to look at the spectacle and collect the posters and calendars her people were giving out. Occasionally some would go up to her to put confetti on her head and talk to her. She spotted me, with my camera, and waved directly at me. I was too shy to go up to her, even though a couple of years previously I had interviewed her for my master's thesis. Later, a number of people told me that I should have gone to talk with her, telling me that she's very approachable. Remedios's sweeping visit to Rosas Pampa reflects the reverence accorded to the most popular politicians, symbolically shown through garlands and confetti. Reverence and respect, though, does not mean that the politicians were unapproachable. All the same, like the other politicians, Remedios did not even stop to tell us her proposals, to the chagrin of Doña Gregoria. Perhaps Remedios felt that this is not really the point. People do not vote for particular politicians according to their proposals, since they mostly feel that all political promises are empty.

In the three weeks prior to the actual elections, the political parties shifted up a gear and came through the zone of Rosas Pampa every weekend. Even Pepelucho eventually visited. The final citywide rallies for each political party were attended by hundreds of activists and onlookers eager to see what was happening and catch any present that might come their way. The MIR seemed able to convene the most people. They closed their election campaign on one of the two principal roads in El Alto. There was a carnival atmosphere, with people selling popcorn, kebabs, sweets, drinks, everything, and a stage show of pop stars and wrestlers. The main leaders of the MIR showed up, demonstrating the party's commitment to winning El Alto and the fact that they thought it a key constituency for Jaime Paz Zamora's possibilities for the presidency in 2002. They stressed the need for hope, for progress, for a future for El Alto. Jose Luis Paredes declared that his *obra estrella*, or star obra for El Alto would be the achievement of "credibility" before the citizens of El Alto, international organizations, and the media, and that he would turn El Alto from the poverty capital of Bolivia into an industrial and export capital.

The experience of effervescence (Durkheim 1965 [1915]) during such spectacles reinforces feelings of similarity with others and being part of the crowd. It also evokes a feeling of an almost personal connection with the leader, in a way that television does not. Pragmatically, as a voter you can assess how many others are likely to vote with you and the likelihood of your party winning; you can also go to various campaigns and get free entertainment for the day and possibly a baseball cap, flag, or soft drink. Thus politics in El Alto have an extremely important sensual side to them. Through shouting slogans, singing songs, and listening to passionate speeches, politics becomes oral and aural; it is about gratifying taste when you are given a soft drink during a campaign rally or biscuits in a militantes' meeting; about seeing hundreds of people wearing orange and blue baseball caps and waving orange and blue flags (or red, white, and black, or pink, or brown),[10] and feeling part of that, part of the crowds and the dancing. These expressive and affective dimensions present a dilemma for a public code of sober, rational, representative democracy, since the one thing that big campaign rallies do *not* allow voters to do is assess the merits of different political parties on the basis of their proposals for government, reflecting a weakness of the public sphere, according to Claudio Lomnitz. He argues that "at any given local level, the relationship between public discussion and ritual is negative: ritual substitutes for discussion and vice-versa" (1995: 21).

I would argue that the rallies are one aspect of politics as the development of a personalized relationship between elector and elected. That may be achieved through actually meeting the candidates, on campaign or in their office, at a distance (mediated by the stage) or close up. Television and local radio also play an extremely important part, even if they are not quite as direct. It is not the case that an ideological position or a program of government is unimportant to voters in El Alto, but few of the parties will commit to one. Most voters expect them to promise everything and then not fulfill those promises. In this context, it makes sense to look to other ways of assessing suitability, asking whether this candidate might be more likely than the others to fulfill at least some of his or her promises. Granting support visibly through campaign rallies or through placing confetti or garlands on the candidate are also cultural forms for attempting to oblige politicians to return the favor and fulfill their promises, as their reciprocal duty to the electorate.

Before the Campaign: Preparing the Ground   Formation of the corporate identity of the patron–clients grouping is far from automatic and requires patient work on the part of the patron, which draws on cultural codes known by all. For years, Jose Luis Paredes had been carefully maneuvering himself into the position of leading contender for mayor of El Alto. He was backed up by the MIR's party machine, and to a certain extent its money, although he invested much of his personal resources both during the campaign and in gaining favor in the years running up to the election.[11] In the event, the voters were not voting for the MIR, they were voting for him.[12] Despite attacking Condepa's use of symbols, he himself very capably used a number of key symbolic threads in his campaign. In particular, he staked a claim to two very important symbols: the mantles of two key populist leaders of the 1990s. Paredes made this explicit, saying that he based his political identity on two examples: "that of Don Carlos Palenque, his sensibility and the way he had of treating people, and that of Don Max Fernández, with his donations of modest public works."[13] Although I felt that Carlos Palenque was patronizing in his TV show, many people I knew thought that he had a particularly good rapport with ordinary people (see also Lazar 2002b). Max Fernández was a similar figure, although his power base did not derive from the media. Like Palenque, he had risen from humble roots to become a successful businessman, owner of the national brewery. He used that position to gain political power through donations of beer and obras, founding a political party, the Unión Cívica Solidaridad (UCS; Civic Solidarity Union), in the late 1980s.[14] After his death in a plane crash in 1996, the leadership of the party passed uneventfully to his son, Jhonny.

The deaths of both Palenque and Fernández provoked large-scale and extreme manifestations of grief. The site of the plane crash that killed Max Fernández became an instant shrine. People came from all over the country to offer flowers and alcohol and pray for help. Newspapers reported scenes of multitudes of crying people at Palenque's funeral, and there were shouts that he should not be buried because he might be resurrected.

Later, a stone known for displaying the faces of saints and virgins began to show the face of Palenque (Lazar 2002b). He was a very important figure for most of my informants; I heard more than once the rumor that Palenque had been murdered because he was defending the poor. People commonly believed that Palenque would have helped the poor had he become president. I am somewhat cynical about this; on the evidence of his very plush house in the wealthy zone of Calacoto it is possible that he was using the poor for his own personal advantage, like any other politician. However, one informant felt that the expensive house was fine because Palenque had done well for himself and he was still the ally of the poor among the wealthy (cf. Bayart 1993).

Although upper class, white, and a fully paid-up member of the political classes, Paredes did not denigrate Palenque, as many others in a similar position had done; in fact, he showed reverence and respect for him. But his invocation of Carlos Palenque's example was largely symbolic. He appropriated both Condepa campaign songs and their slogan; in Paredes's hands, the Condepista "uka Jach'a Uru jutaskiway" became "ha llegado el Gran Día" (the Great Day has arrived), a direct translation from the Aymara to Spanish.[15] He combined this skillful manipulation of symbol with a great deal of hard work, following Max Fernández's example of "civic behavior" (civismo), defined as a vocation of service to the community expressed through obras (Mayorga 1991). He claimed that since 1992 he had invested between US$2,000 and US$3,000 a month in building materials given to different communities of El Alto, through the social department of his television station, Channel 24.[16] The basketball hoops in the Rosas Pampa school had been provided by the MIR and painted in MIR colors. Channel 24 also came to the zone to film a football match, which had proved very popular with the residents, according to Don Roberto. And there were jokes going around that there was hardly any school in El Alto without a television set from Jose Luis Paredes as godfather.

It is difficult (and largely academic anyway) to disentangle which of the various gifts to different zones came from Pepelucho as an individual, which came from MIR money, and which from Channel 24. The point is that little by little, Pepelucho had been building personal ties with the residents of El Alto through cultural forms such as becoming padrino de promoción (godfather of the graduating class in a school) or just providing some cement or bricks for school buildings or donating equipment. The padrino de promoción is responsible for funding at least part of the various high school graduation ceremonies, such as the toma de nombre ceremony. when the graduating class takes the name of their godfather prior to the end of the year, and the graduation ceremony itself. The padrino does not provide food or drink for the parents that come, but may fund the hiring of the hall, a meal for the teachers, pennants, and flowers or badges given to each of the graduates. The padrino is mainly responsible for funding an activity, usually a vacation, for the class. Being a padrino de promoción is not cheap. However, it does mean that you are known as a generous person in the zone, not to mention godfather to fifty young people, who, beginning in 1994, can vote at age eighteen. Furthermore, the padrino de promoción becomes compadre to the parents of his godchildren. Donating equipment such as a television can also put you in the position of being compadre. Of course, an added advantage for Paredes of giving televisions to schools is that there is a better chance of people seeing his television channel; perhaps more important, it underlines his position as owner of that channel and an important player in El Alto. It may even be that Paredes was consciously aping Palenque's position as owner of a TV channel.

The *compadrazgo* relationship is a very powerful one in Andean societies, and the links between the godparent and the parents of the godchild are often stronger than those between godparent and godchild. Compadrazgo serves mainly to cement friendships and alliances and can be between people of the same class or where the godparent is of higher status or class than the parent (Mintz and Wolf 1977; Bolton and Mayer 1977; Long 1984). Clearly, the compadrazgo that results from being a godparent through sponsoring the baptism of a child is a much stronger link than that from being padrino de promoción. However, the latter reflects the former and thereby shares some of its power. Being a *padrino de televisión* (i.e., a godfather who has donated a television) also benefits from the association with stronger forms of compadrazgo, even though everyone is aware of why politicians are donating televisions or other equipment. Palenque had put a great deal of stress on compadrazgo, calling Condepa militantes and all of those who came to his television show compadre or comadre. He was el Compadre Palenque, and Condepa militantes were supposed to call each other compadre (Lazar 2002b; Saravia and Sandoval 1991).

Furthermore, in consciously imitating Max Fernández's strategy of "modest obras," Paredes was able to call on peoples' allegiance through compadrazgo, and also to demonstrate his willingness to invest in the community. The latter meant that out of a sense of reciprocity, people were prepared to vote for him because he had at least given them something. People also felt that the fact he had put his own money into obras implied that he would be prepared to put the municipality's money into even bigger obras. Fernández had used the same logic, as a statement from the National Directive of the UCS in 1989 makes explicit: "If we give the people bread today, when we are the government, we will give them work. If we give them medication today, when we are the government, we will give them health. . . . If we give them bricks today, when we are the government, we will give them houses. If we give them pencils today, when we are the government, we will give them education" (Mayorga 1991).

Personalism: Working to Become Electable The development of a personal relationship with politicians is an important citizenship practice for alteños as they seek to assess the suitability of their prospective leaders and patrons and to engage them in a reciprocal relationship where they feel obliged to serve the people in return for their electoral support. As Paredes's activities show, the politicians recognize that elections are primarily a character assessment exercise, and that personal contact with the voters is central. A surprisingly large number of ordinary people, both particularly politicized and relatively apathetic, had met with the candidates. For example, Don Roberto had made a specific effort to meet up with Paredes prior to the election campaign. Condepa had built up its power base through personal contact with party militantes and ordinary people on a daily basis on the TV program *Tribuna Libre del Pueblo*. However, with most parties, such personal contact is usually possible only at campaign time and before, when the candidates are trying to charm potential voters. After they achieve power, they can hide behind multiple layers of bureaucracy, and accountability is almost nil.

In their assessment of candidates' characters, voters will reward perceived qualities of approachability, sincerity, honesty, generosity, and wealth, all the qualities of a good patron. Rubén, my neighbor's nephew, explained to me that he had offered himself as organizer of the Morenada dance group that we took to Quilloma in April 2000 (discussed in chapter 4) largely because he was thinking that some time in the future he might like to be a candidate for that particular municipality: "My aim is to get myself known by the people there, because they look at your character, they have respect for what you do. You have to help people, and then they vote for the person that helped them. If you give them support, invest a little bit for them, they'll vote for you." He had not decided which party he would represent; he had relatives in the ADN who might help, he said, but local people "who used to be in Condepa" (meaning that he did not know what party they would join after the elections) had also said they would support him, and his teacher at the UMSA was an important member of Movimiento al Socialismo (MAS; Movement toward Socialism), whose Trotskyite ideas were very attractive to Rubén.[17]

The Movimiento Bolivia Livre (MBL; Free Bolivia Movement) candidate for El Alto had been in a similar position, in that he had to weigh up offers from different parties. Jose Luis "Tren" Martínez is the son of a prominent and successful alteño businessman. In an interview, he told me that their firm has for many years invested in what Martínez called "the urban growth of El Alto."[18] He has been involved in collaborations with international donor agencies to provide rural electrification, and has a large leisure center in the north of El Alto, with a sauna, swimming pool, and squash courts. Through such activities, he has achieved a high profile in the city and was first invited to be a candidate for another political party, the Movimiento Sin Miedo (MSM; Fearless Movement). However, he felt that he could not work with the MSM in El Alto, so he picked the MBL, who seemed less selfish and controlling and closer to his own ideas.

Martínez is perfect material to be a good local patron, since he is known (conocido) in his area and through his father's business has been involved in various good works for alteños. He is well aware of the need to play the various games of local politics. As such, in 2000, he agreed to be padrino de promoción for eight classes of high school graduates, including the one in Rosas Pampa. He maintained that it was "a little bit about growing in the popularity aspect," but also that he wants to encourage "vocation for service" in his seven hundred godchildren, "actually training people who have a feeling towards their society, and also take up the challenge to achieve something for their El Alto." He linked it very closely to enabling alteños to "demand their rights," which was an important part of his political stance during his candidacy. He planned seminars and workshops for his godchildren, to orientar, or guide them. This also fits in with his electoral strategy: his promotional material (called Plan Identidad) stressed his youth, one slogan being "A young city with a young mayor."[19]

When he was present at the toma de nombre ceremony held for the Rosas Pampa graduation class, to which he arrived four hours late, he took great care to press the flesh with all the parents, drinking at least one glass of beer with each family. Many people, including my Condepista friend, Doña Josefa, were very keen to get their picture taken with him, and one could see the personal relationship beginning. I left before the seminars for the students were scheduled to take place and am not even sure if they happened, but it seemed a very sensible tactic to draw in the young people through "capacity building" and "orientation." I have no doubt that the sole fact of being padrino de promoción will not be enough to get the parents voting for him, but it is a start. As Paredes proved, maneuvering oneself into a position of electability takes a long time and is not solely, or even possibly mostly, to do with having the right ideas.

OBRAS AND CORRUPTION

As with community-level politics, corruption and obras are central themes of local elections and the relationship between citizen and state in the context of municipal government. Together, they are tropes through which citizens attempt to assert their expectations of their leaders and hold them to account so that the threat of accusation of the former leads politicians (one hopes) to build the latter. Since most people felt all politicians to be equally corrupt, the issue of corruption did not enable alteño electors to choose between the political parties. However, discourses of corruption do reveal some of the values underlying political life, as well as perhaps discursively constituting political life and subjecthood. As Akhil Gupta (1995: 376) argues, "The discourse of corruption [is] a key arena through which the state, citizens, and other organisations and aggregations come to be imagined."

The nickname Pepelucho stressed Paredes's approachable, personable side. But he was also called "El Doctor," a respectful nickname that highlighted a paternal side and also a high level of education and therefore status. This, coupled with the stress that the MIR placed on the fact that they were the only party with a real plan for government, emphasized their fit with a very important technocratic and nonaffective side to Bolivian politics, which is, Gamarra (2003) argues, evidence of the authoritarian legacy of the dictatorship era. For the 1999 elections, the MIR in El Alto produced a document entitled the Plan Progreso, which was extremely detailed and replete with targets and pledges that were impossible to meet in their entirety. What was important about the Plan Progreso was that the MIR was able to present itself as the modernizing party that would fund obras for El Alto. This was accomplished mostly through proclaiming the existence of the government plan, even if it was hard to get hold of a copy in outlying zones such as Rosas Pampa.

As in the community politics described in the previous chapter, the emphasis on obras must be placed in the context of a pervasive view of politicians as corrupt. This was a very important theme in the local electoral campaigns of 1999.[20] The Plan Progreso helped the MIR to put clear blue water between itself and Condepa, stressing that it would be more efficient and less corrupt than the previous administration. El Alto, which had been run for ten years by Condepa, was in a terrible state by 1999, as everyone knew. Doña Gregoria told me about the scandal of missing tractors (hence the irony of Remedios turning up on a gleaming green tractor during her campaign). Don Roberto told me that, in order to get anything done in the municipal administration, you had to pay small bribes all the time. However, as Doña Josefa pointed out, the system of sharing out departments according to each party's electoral strength meant that corruption associated with what were MIRista departments reflected badly and unfairly on the Condepista mayor. She reckoned that the Development Department was the worst, and it was run by MIR people. This of course did not stop Jose Luis Paredes appearing on TV one evening with his "whip against corruption" (*chicote contra la corrupción*) in his hand.

Corruption Talk, Accountability, and Representativity   I often heard from friends of all classes that although Bolivia has everything in terms of natural riches, the politicians steal everything, so Bolivia has not been able to "advance." I was told that Bolivian politicians even steal international aid; one friend (not a development worker) estimated that only a quarter ever reached its destination. The piles of secondhand clothes sold wholesale at the markets in the Ceja have usually been diverted from humanitarian aid packages sent from the United States to Bolivia, and there were rumors that, at the time of an earthquake in Aiquile in 1997, almost none of the aid sent from international donors reached the earthquake victims, but Goni (the president at the time) ended up with a shiny new presidential airplane. At a more local level, the Popular Participation legislation is also the subject of numerous corruption rumors. In all these stories, from the colorful to the more sober, corruption explains underdevelopment in a departure from *dependista* explanations such as the anti-neocolonial discourses of nationalist and leftist (and also some rightist) politics. Here, the subalterns blame the elites: Bolivia is not underdeveloped because its citizens are backward (which one does occasionally hear from Bolivians of all classes), or because of an inauspicious environment, or because of its place in the global economy. Rather, a country that could be wealthy is betrayed by elite leaders, who are personalistas and interesados. Thus self-esteem and pride in the country, land, environment, and the masses of the people can be maintained. The people telling these stories are collectively imagining themselves as citizens despite the state, rather than citizens that are constituted through a positive relationship with the state.

At the same time, something is being said about the distance between politicians and other elites and the masses in terms of democracy and social class. The stories told around corruption and the rumors and suspicions that abound regarding anyone in power can tell us something about people's relation to the state, their country, and their community—that is, their citizenship. I overheard the following comment in a taxi: "We queue up in order to pay taxes, they queue up in order to steal." In such talk about politics, the lack of felt representativity becomes apparent, and the democratic nature of the Bolivian delegative democracy is opened up to criticism. Corruption is a reason or trope for feelings of disenfranchisement and marginalization. One of my neighbors purposely spoiled her ballot paper in the 1999 election because "they're all corrupt and liars." Another friend felt that corruption was linked to democracy itself. He told me that in Cuba they used to shoot corruptos, so there was no corruption: "This democracy law, it makes people manipulative."

However, as the previous chapter showed, disentangling what we mean by corruption is by no means easy—there are many stories told every day. Corruption is both everywhere and nowhere because it is never made explicit. And, of course, what to one person is corruption is another person's way of being paid for the work he or she does. Telling a story about corruption generally serves more to highlight the moral integrity of the teller than anything else: corruption is always somewhere else, perpetrated by someone else. Comments from the two aspiring politicians introduced earlier, my neighbor's nephew Rubén and Jose Luis "Tren" Martínez, reflect some of the ambiguities of corruption talk.

Rubén was weighing the possibility of standing for election in his pueblo, and Martínez was the MBL candidate for mayor of El Alto in 1999. Both spoke of corruption in politics as a result of the investment required to be elected. When asked for his assessment of Paredes's new government, Martínez said, "I at least think that they have made a big investment in order to enter local government, and the symptom you can see straight-away is a return on that investment." He was talking about Paredes in the same way that Paredes spoke in the interview quoted earlier, where he pointed out how much of his personal resources he had invested in becoming mayor.

Rubén thought that in Bolivia there is "too much corruption," as politicians go into positions of power purely to "extract benefits." He wanted "to work more for people, get something out of it, but not much." Notable here is his view that there can be "too much" corruption, implying that there are degrees of corruption, some of which are appropriate. Rubén was a close friend of mine, and it is reasonable to assume that he was more frank with me than Martínez had been regarding his own ambitions. He was probably being realistic about politics: being a candidate for any position is an investment, and one usually expects returns on investments. He estimated that he had spent US$700 to US$800 on taking the Morenada to Quilloma, and, if he decided to continue in politics, he knew he would have to find the money for something more concrete, and more expensive. For him, it was therefore only reasonable to expect some return. It is the *level* of return that is contestable, along with the amount of work you do to benefit your people or your village. This is reflected in the common assessment of one of the most successful mayors in Bolivia, Manfred Reyes Villa, nicknamed El Bombón, and mayor of Cochabamba for three successive terms during the 1990s: one often heard people say, "He steals, but at least he does something."

Corruption and Obras Although people talk so often and so negatively about politicians being corruptos, I suspect that *paceños* (residents of La Paz) and alteños who almost longingly talked of Bombón would rather have a corrupt mayor that did obras than a completely honest one who did nothing visible. The focus on obras is unsurprising given the needs that actually exist in residential zones of El Alto, and anyway, at high levels of power complete honesty is often thought impossible (cf. Parry 2000). Electors assess the value of a politician despite and beyond his or her presumed corruption. Doña Gregoria's comment about the MIR reflects this: "They're corrupt, but at least they keep their promises." The default position for politicians is that they will steal public money.[21] Given this, when looking closer at the newspaper reports, the picture becomes much muddier: Are politicians who say they've made "mistakes" corrupt or inefficient or stupid? (Probably all three.) There are differences between mal-

versación de fondos or *fondos malgastados* (embezzlement, misspent funds), getting a return on one's investment, and stealing, depending upon the position of the person narrating that particular corruption story.

Corruption is culturally specific. It is difficult to pin down, mixed up with rumor, exaggeration, euphemism, and storytelling. As such it is a good means for understanding Bolivian political life, both for outsiders and for Bolivians. Corruption talk enables people to make evaluations of those in power, according to how *personalista* or *interesado* they are. The diversion of public money for private gain is a widely accepted definition of corruption (Haller and Shore 2005), and although understandings of public and private cannot be assumed to be the same cross-culturally, my informants made a clear distinction between Bolivia's money and personal resources: corrupt politicians clearly steal the former. What is at issue is the *extent* to which public money is diverted for personal gain, or, more important, redistributed to the people through obras or jobs, these being linked because it is the *militantes* who get the jobs to build the obras. Of course, the evaluations that people make of politicians do slip and vary according to context and person, but their mobilization illuminates the kinds of expectations people have. This is an indication of what Bayart (1993) calls a "politics of the belly." He argues that in Cameroon politics is about the accumulation of wealth and its subsequent redistribution to satisfy and increase a politician's clientele. Politicians are not viewed as public servants, following a Western bureaucratic paradigm of work for the common good. They are entitled to, and expected to, accumulate wealth personally and use it to benefit their social networks, including, above all, their family. How acceptable this is in Bolivia varies according to the context, but what is similar is that Bolivian patrons are expected to redistribute their wealth, and the wealth of the state, through the provision of jobs to their clients. In the Bolivian case, corruption, and political life in general, cannot be understood apart from the expectations and needs people have for obras as tangible evidence of political activity.

Hence the frequent repetition of increasingly unrealistic promises of obras for El Alto during election campaigns. One time, when the election campaign was nearly over and several political parties had come to Rosas Pampa to promise obras and then leave again, I was joking with young friends about the La Paz MIR candidate's promise to build a system of cable cars between the two cities if he were elected. One young man proposed a "star obra" of a system of tubes so that people could slide from the heights of El Alto down to La Paz![22] Obras are (often literally) concrete evidence that politicians have been working in the people's interests, however much money they might have siphoned off for their own benefit. Ironically, although it is largely true that mayors and councilors make a lot of money through bribery and stealing while in office, the largest part of a municipality's budget goes to wages (Blanco Cazas and Sandoval 1993). While Condepa was in power in El Alto, half of the budget went to wages, a third to debt servicing, and less than a fifth to new obras.[23] It is here that parties are caught between two imperatives: the need to give jobs to their militantes and the need to fund obras, again linked together, but this time in a negative way. Condepa held the allegiance of many people because they "helped poor people" through clientelistic party mechanisms, even if they did not pay back the zones with many actual obras. However, that tolerance was extended only up to a point. Remedios Loza was unable to replicate Carlos Palenque's aura of incorruptibility, partly due to the factionalism within the party and partly because, after ten years and given the presence of a promising alternative, enough alteños were fed up with having an inactive municipal administration to vote Condepa out.

ELECTION DAY

On Election Day in December 1999, despite the fact that most people said to me at one point or another that politicians were liars and corrupt, the actual process was taken very seriously. Voting is compulsory, and travel is forbidden for forty-eight hours around Election Day, as is the selling of alcohol. There is an almost festive atmosphere in the zone, with children playing out on the streets, which are empty of cars and buses. People voted in the school, in ten separate classrooms, which is where the votes were also counted at the end of the day. The "table delegates" held up every single ballot paper (there were around two hundred papers at each table) in front of party delegates so that they could confirm the accuracy of their count and argue if a vote was unclear. Each of the party delegates noted down how many votes had been cast for each of the parties in their room. At the same time, prominent men of the community went around each classroom noting down the votes for the different parties. I took the opportunity to do the same.

Given the oft-repeated expressions of disillusionment with politics, one would perhaps expect high levels of voter apathy. However, turnout in Rosas Pampa was reasonably high: 63 percent of those registered, and, of the votes cast, only 7 percent were void or blank. Although voting is compulsory, the voting register includes people who registered for previous elections and subsequently moved away or died (Gray Molina 2001). I counted 1,719 votes cast in Rosas Pampa, which represents a good turnout for a zone of one thousand households. It seems that on Election Day itself the local residents were determined to make sure that no corruption would occur in their school and that the forms of democracy for which they themselves were responsible would at least be properly observed and accountable to them. Their performance, in Judith Butler's (1990) sense, of a proper election can be seen as a kind of resistance, a refusal to simply abandon themselves to political corruption. In this way, they used formal citizenship practices to maintain collective dignity and stake a claim to accountability.

During the campaign, and on Election Day itself, one of the complaints that I heard most often was that successive mayors had forgotten about the zone of Rosas Pampa. The attempts to develop a personal relationship with politicians are a response to this tendency for faceless bureaucrats to marginalize poor areas. This is not peculiar to Bolivia, of course. As Robert Gay (1998: 16) points out, in Brazil, the "least privileged elements of . . . society" unsurprisingly "embrace clientelism as a hedge against what is often perceived not as democratisation but as bureaucratic indifference and exclusion." However, clientelism is not purely a hedge against social exclusion. This chapter has shown some of the ways in which residents of El Alto endeavored (and often succeeded) in turning the "time of elections" (Auyero 2000) to their advantage. This quite clearly demonstrates the working of a set of political strategies attuned to the realities of local administration. Robert Albro (2000:41) calls it "sound Andean logic," whereby politicians exchange gifts for political capital in reciprocal arrangements.[24] As Robert Gay (1998: 14) says, "The problem is that we have become so accustomed to thinking of clientelism as a mechanism of institutional control—often referred to as corporatism—or the product of 'false consciousness'—often referred to as populism—that we have failed to consider the possibility that clientelism might be embraced as a popular political strategy." The popular strategies of clientelism during these election campaigns can be understood as attempts to substantiate citizenship; the popular sectors here are using clientelism to temporarily redress the normal balance of unrepresentative politics. Most obviously, politicians have to deliver *before* they get the vote, and, since voting is secret, even that is not a given (Gay 1998). In the process, politicians gained benefits for the zone and also asserted the right of Rosas Pampa to receive obras once the winning party took over the alcaldía.

In this way, we can see that clientelism is a modern practice, functional to the contemporary Bolivian political system. As with many aspects of Bolivian life, it combines new situations with the more classical features of clientelism: individualistic, dyadic connections between client and patron; the existence of a set of brokers in a chain of patronage that leads up to a single powerful figure; a sense of reciprocity between patron and client in the exchange of gifts for work and votes; and the development of a personalistic connection between the two (Albro 2000; Lande 1977; Wolf 1977). El Alto also embraces a "corporate clientelism," identified by Lande in Italy, where whole communities become clients of specific patrons in return for development projects. While Lande saw this as part of a development from the traditional politics of dyadic patron–client ties to modern, interest-based politics (implicitly along class-based divisions), in El Alto it is clear that no teleological progression has occurred; rather, all these forms of politics coexist there. What is peculiar to the current democratic conjuncture is the existence of several possible patrons in the urban sphere, in the shape of competing political parties. Local elections have occurred in Bolivia only since 1985, and national elections have included a constituency system only since 1997. In 1999 El Alto shifted from one patron, Condepa, to another, Jose Luis Paredes; it was therefore a moment of opening up for the clients.

Political parties in Bolivia are not quite institutional forms of interest mediation, in the way that they should be according to much political science (e.g., Mainwaring and Scully 1995; Mainwaring and Soberg Shugart 1999; Diamond, Linz, and Lipset 1989; O'Donnell 1986; Van Cott 2005). They are more like ways of channeling patron–client relationships (Dunkerley 1998; Mainwaring and Scully 1995). Whether this is truly democratic or not is beside the point; the point is that this is how people understand electoral politics, and that they do gain some benefit through this understanding. It is evident that the poor of El Alto often accommodate rather than resist existing power structures, choosing vertical patronage linkages over horizontal linkages based upon their class interests. This is usually the case when it comes to electoral politics, especially at the local level, but is not necessarily true of the politics of civic organizations, as the second part of this book makes clear. What follows is the recognition that politics is mixed and that electoral success for any candidate in El Alto rests in large part on his or her ability to deliver benefits to clients, both corporate and individual. Political parties must do considerable work to convince alteños that they will do this once in power, and that requires mobilizing considerable numbers of people and preparing the ground a long time before the actual election happens. This is what the MAS did in the runup to the December 2005 national elections, but the fact that they had been unable to fully consolidate their people by December 2004 meant that despite widespread sympathy for their ideology and leader, most of El Alto voted for the person who in their eyes had delivered on his promises in the local sphere: Jose Luis Paredes.

The vecinos of Rosas Pampa practice their citizenship as much if not more through their preelection participation in clientelist politics as through the infrequent, though meticulous act of voting. Through the development of a personal relationship with the candidates, clients and voters attempted to make them directly representative. In fact, in some ways clientelism makes politics even more representative than the normative, delegative, electoral democracies envisioned by liberal citizenship theory. The fact that civil service jobs at so many levels depend upon political affiliation does create incentives to corruption and maladministration. However, it also means that when people engage in campaign activities on behalf of political parties, they are in a sense standing for election themselves—not for mayor or councilor, but for office assistant, nurse, or school porter. This issue of representativity and democracy is not a purely abstract theoretical question. One day, as the election was nearing, Don Roberto muttered that "exactly the most corrupt people" were leading the MIR campaign in the zone in the hopes of jobs afterward. He recognized implicitly that he was voting not only for Paredes and the MIR councilors, but for the people who would take up roles in all of the tiers of public administration in El Alto.

The engagement between citizens and the state encouraged by clientelism contrasts with the sense of estrangement expressed by the corruption stories that I heard during my fieldwork. They are ways of narrating democracy, as the focus on politicians' propensity to steal public resources emphasizes the distance between the people and the elites. Corruption explains underdevelopment by labeling politicians as unpatriotic thieves who have stolen all Bolivia's natural resources. At the subaltern level, corruption narratives become a way to understand and express the powerlessness Bolivian citizens feel when it comes to holding their rulers to account. They are also about class: at the heart of most corruption talk is a dispute over the correct distribution of economic resources—to the people, or the personalista politicians and elites. This dispute became more heated in the last two decades of the twentieth century because of the hegemony of neoliberal economic politics, although private ownership of resources viewed as national has been an important issue for Bolivia for the whole of the century because of the tin mines (Dunkerley 1984; Nash 1993 [1979]). Dubious distribution of privatization contracts is a source of corruption allegations worldwide (Sneath 2002); again, this is a dispute over the correct destination of "public" resources in terms of their associated profits. Allied to the talk of politicians stealing Bolivia's resources is a widespread disapproval of the selling off of Bolivia's resources in the form of privatization. Narrating corruption serves as a means for people to represent and explain not just their political marginality but also their position in the distribution of economic power. Yet the nuances and ambiguities of people's feelings about corruption reveal a further layer. If it is generally understood that political office is an economic investment, and that politicians want a return on that investment, the voters are happy for this to happen as long as the politician in question also builds obras.

The common factor in these processes of engagement and estrangement is the extent to which the vecinos of Rosas Pampa imagine themselves collectively, either as a body of clients of one politician or through constituting the zone itself as a client, or through portraying themselves as the Bolivian people betrayed by venal politicians, what I have called citizens despite the state. The corporate approach to politics culminated on Election Day itself, as many individuals based their calculations upon what would be best for Rosas Pampa and collectively performed a "proper" election. The zone asserted its control over democracy at that moment, and its pride in the fact that at least there the election was beyond question. Citizens clearly value local democracy, and their feelings about it are markedly less cynical than their opinions of politicians. The performance of a scrupulously observed election was a way for the vecinos to confirm the importance of the zone and stake their claim to collective membership of a democratic Bolivian state. In other words, there is a dialectic between individual and community at the heart of the political process as individuals exercise their citizenship through different corporate groupings in order to gain the best outcomes they can.

The foundational act of Rosas Pampa as urban zone in 1975 was the organization of the junta vecinal, and one of their first acts was to establish the patronal fiesta of the zone (Musch et al. 1994). Today the organization of the fiesta is the main responsibility of the junta and one of the most important ways in which the vecinos of Rosas Pampa constitute themselves as collective political subjects. Annual cycle ceremonies, particularly the annual anniversary fiesta (held on the patron saint's day), are central to how people experience their membership in local and national communities in Bolivia. Dance is one of the main focuses of the fiesta,[1] and this makes dance a central citizenship practice for El Alto and highlights the embodied nature of citizenship if viewed from the perspective of the citizens rather than political structures and institutions. Since Durkheim, it has become standard practice in anthropological theory to highlight the role of ritual in the building of senses of community and belonging, and the political implications of this have occasionally been acknowledged in political anthropology.[2] However, although Rousseau recognized the importance of ritual in any discussion of citizenship with his work on "civil religion," most discussions of citizenship theory fail to address ritual, or religion, seriously.

Through movement, the vecinos of Rosas Pampa perform, define, and reproduce their sense of community, or collective belonging. This sense of belonging consists of three main sets of relationships: first, relations with the zone; second, a sense of commonality and togetherness with other vecinos; and third, a sense of the distinctions and hierarchies between members of the collectivity. The community, then, comprises all the relations between people and also between people and locality in Rosas Pampa which are experienced as sacred. Those relations are experienced and talked about mostly as obligations on the part of the individual member—responsibilities rather than rights, but responsibilities in a context of expected reciprocity from all participants in those relationships, including the zone itself. Juliana Ströbele-Gregor (1996: 79), in her article "Culture and Political Practice of the Aymara and Quechua in Bolivia," sums it up thus: "The available ethnographic data clearly demonstrate how the idea of community is celebrated and continually reconstituted in ritual festivities. The point is not only to reinforce group cohesion but also to strengthen the ties to the supernatural force." In this chapter, I add a physical focus to the available ethnographic data in my emphasis on the importance of bodily movement in the processes of community building, which I explore using phenomenological approaches (Csordas 1999).[3]

THE FIESTA

Not every resident of El Alto will dance in a particular fiesta, but most who are not Evangelical Protestants will at some point in their lives dance, either in the annual fiesta of the urban zone in which they live or work or in their (or their spouse's) pueblo. Some dance every year, if possible, in one, or even both, of these fiestas. Fiestas in pueblos in the countryside are often very important for urban migrants who originally came from there. Migrants often go back to their pueblos only once a year, on the date of the fiesta, and this may involve taking a group of dancers, called a comparsa, to perform a dance. In April 2000, I went to a pueblo called Quilloma with a comparsa of Morenada dancers. Rosas Pampa holds its fiesta on or around 14 September each year, the day of the Señor de la Exaltación, Christ's exaltation on the Cross. The religious element interacts in a complex way with the intensely local nature of the celebrations to heighten their importance for the majority of vecinos. Supervising the zone's anniversary fiesta is probably the most important responsibility of the junta vecinal, more important even than gaining obras for the zone. I participated twice in the Rosas Pampa fiesta, once as spectator and once as dancer of the Kullawada.

The Rosas Pampa fiestas of 1999 and 2000 followed similar timetables. On Friday morning, the schoolchildren paraded around the zone, finishing in the football field in 1999 and in front of the school at the end of the newly paved part of the street in 2000. Then, in the afternoon, the comparsas danced through the zone in full costume. This is called the *Entrada*. Led by the members of the junta vecinal, the comparsas begin at the beer factory, which is on the outskirts of the zone, and move through the zone, ending in the football field, to display their steps in front of the members of the junta vecinal, who are stationed on a lorry to judge the dancing along with any visiting guests. This part is called the *palco*, and the parade stops here, but the dancers continue in their groups to a gathering at the church to pay their respects to the figure of the Señor de Exaltación and for refreshments. There is not a formal Mass at this time.

Throughout the ritual of the fiesta, the secular, formal, and civic merge with the religious. For example, the guests are secular and civic: in 2000, the junta invited a representative of the FEJUVE to judge the dancing. Another illustration of the merging of more formal citizenship practices with the fiesta is the importance of the civic parades by schoolchildren on Friday morning. They follow the same route as the later Entrada and are also judged, in 2000 by the mayor of El Alto as well as the junta vecinal. The judges led the procession, followed by a group of female members of the junta escolar, then the schoolchildren of the zone from both the local state school and the private Lutheran school. The Entrada is in many ways an adult analogue of the children's civic parade, although the distinction between the adult and the child form of citizenship practice is symbolic but not total: adults participated in the schoolchildren's parades and the children also participated in the Entrada as a comparsa organized by the school. The timing of the two on the principal day of the fiesta is no coincidence. They are equally important, but the more formal and civic part of the festivities must happen while people are still sober and needs to be finished before the fun can start.

After the Entrada finished, each comparsa went to drink at their organizers' houses or at a room hired for the occasion. The following morning, there was an early Mass at the church, followed by what is called the *Diana*, when the dancers danced the same route in street clothes. After this, there was the prize-giving at the palco, followed by more drinking and celebrations in the football field. Spatially, the football field, not the church, was the center of action during the fiesta, as it is under normal circumstances in Rosas Pampa. At this point in the fiesta of 2000, many people left to sleep off the effects of the alcohol, returning that evening for more drinking at the organizers' houses. On Sunday morning there was more drinking and preparation for dancing during the bullfight held in the football field in the afternoon, when the comparsas traditionally enter the ring with the bulls and dance round the outskirts.[4]

The Entrada is extremely popular; whole families sit at the side of the road and watch the dancers, munching on popcorn and encouraging them as they progress. Men, women, and children go up and down the streets selling popcorn, sweets, biscuits, and other food. There is also usually a funfair for the children. The Entrada is free and available to everyone. The costumes are beautiful and the dances, when properly rehearsed, impressive. Nearly the whole zone as well as people from other zones come out to watch the dancing. The zone is on display to others. Although zones do not compete with each other, there is a great deal of pride attached to putting on a good show. In the two fiestas I attended in Rosas Pampa, there were four comparsas dancing, each comprising thirty to fifty people. The neighboring zone of Santiago II managed eleven comparsas, and bigger zones such as the commercial area of 16 de Julio can have over thirty. The biggest fiestas in Bolivia, with up to seventy comparsas participating, are Carnival in Oruro, the Entrada del Señor de Gran Poder in La Paz, and the Entrada Universitaria in La Paz.[5] The comparsas compete good-naturedly for prizes: in 2000, our Kullawada won the prize for *danzas livianas* (light dances, i.e., not Morenada, which is the most prestigious). We did not win the overall prize of best dance, because that had to go to a Morenada group, but some dancers thought that we were acclaimed so loudly at the palco that we should have won.

In all these fiestas, the physical form is the same. The comparsas dance one of several different types of dance, which have different steps but the same general format. They parade in turn along a specific route and are accompanied by a brass band who usually walk at the back, unless the group is large enough to require two bands. At the front of the group there are mascots, who might be children, young women, or a couple dressed in particularly ornate or symbolic versions of the costume worn by the other dancers. They are followed by the dancers in lines, either in single-sex groups or in couples, depending on the dance. The people at the head of the lines are called guides, and they dictate which steps the dancers behind them will dance. There is a basic step which enables the dancers to move forward and about four to six special steps, which are based on the basic formula but might involve turning, swapping positions, or jumping in the more energetic dances. The elaborateness of such steps depends on a number of factors, such as the age of the dancers, their energy, and the amount of time they have spent rehearsing. The steps can be very simple. The dancers dance the basic step until the guides indicate with their hands the number of the special step they want the dancers to dance and whistle to prompt the group to move into that step. Much effort goes into creating the costumes and practicing so that everybody in the comparsa does the correct steps at the correct times. The effect is quite spectacular. The bands are highly skilled and very entertaining, with coordinated clothes and their own dance steps. (Video footage illustrating the fiesta dances can be found at http://www.sianlazar.net.)

INDIVIDUAL, COMMUNITY, AND SPACE: TOGETHERNESS

The fiesta is central to the collective experience and expression of community in Rosas Pampa. The importance of the fiesta for the vecinos is highlighted by the role of the community leaders in its organization. The junta vecinal is not only a central agent in the performance of the fiesta but also the primary agency responsible for organizing it. And organizing the fiesta is their one yearly responsibility. Even if they have been less than successful in their other role, that of obtaining basic services and development for the zone from the municipal government, this is the one time when they can discharge their obligations as leaders. For some of the more minor members of the junta, the runup to the fiesta was the only time they attended meetings with any regularity. The junta had to coordinate with the organizers of the comparsas, invite dignitaries to judge the dance competition, decide on the final route and timetable, sell lots for people to set up food and drink stalls, and more. It has not always been the case that juntas vecinales have played a leading role in the organization of the fiesta. Hans Buechler (1980) noted that during the 1960s and 1970s, the juntas tended to have limited involvement in fiestas in La Paz; he argued that this reflected their general lack of political importance. Where the juntas' political functions were well developed, particularly in marginal neighborhoods, they took a more prominent role in organizing neighborhood fiestas (172–174).

Helping with the fiesta was also seen as a responsibility for those vecinos who could contribute. The wealthier ones, such as the transport unions, the local Taquiña beer factory, local businessmen, and I, were approached by the junta vecinal to provide trophies for the dance groups, beer, or prizes (called *enjalmes*, usually blankets) for the participants in the bullfight. Such people are well known, relatively wealthy, and have often given in previous years. As one member of the junta vecinal told me, they give because "they're vecinos, conocidos, they have to give." They give because it is their zone. The nature of collaboration for the fiesta is illustrated by the story of one vecino in the runup to the fiesta of 2000. The fiestas were generally organized on the basis of who had collaborated in previous years. However, in 2000, the junta did attempt to prevent this man from bringing in his group of young men to taunt the bulls and, more important, from running a bar in the football field for the duration of the fiesta. His story shows the intertwining of the fiesta, ordinary zonal politics, and the obligations of a vecino, as well as the ways in which the junta vecinal regulated the community.

Calixto's Story: Organizing the Community   Just prior to the general assembly in August, some of the junta vecinal leaders had raised concerns about Calixto's bar during the fiestas, arguing that Calixto had become *bien vicioso* (really immoral, antisocial) lately. The fiesta bars are notorious for staying open all night so that people get very drunk, and in some zones this has led to fights and even deaths. At the very least, people are unable to sleep. Furthermore, the group of young men that Calixto had brought in to run with and taunt the bulls the previous year were rowdy and drunken, throwing stones at people, for example. The junta vecinal asked the vecinos present at the assembly whether they thought that Calixto should be allowed to run his bar again, and they said no. Calixto had not been present at this general assembly, but he turned up at the junta vecinal committee meeting on 1 September to argue his case.

When he spoke, he was extremely polite and formal and thanked them profusely for allowing him to come. He also pointed out that he had begun to put in a curb outside his house, as he had been asked to by the junta vecinal and his jefe de calle. This was important at the time because the alcaldía's scheme for paving some streets in El Alto relied upon the vecinos providing curbs outside their house. Most of the vecinos of Rosas Pampa had done this a few years previously, when they had received grants of materials from the alcaldía, but there were a few "lazy" people who were now being pressured by their jefe de calle. If they did not do it, the whole street would not be paved. Calixto was very keen to show that he was making good his previous errors and being a responsible citizen. He was well aware that his errors were partly responsible for his missing out on an important business opportunity.

On that point, he argued that he was a responsible bar owner and that the really noisy drunken bars were the province of women coming in from other zones, who bring their customers with them. He even said that these women had claimed to have paid various juntas vecinales more (i.e., bribed them) for the privilege of staying open later than they should. He considered that, as an old vecino, one who had lived in the zone for a long time, he should not be penalized. His friends on the junta vecinal committee backed him up; they felt it was important that those running bars should be vecinos of Rosas Pampa, not people coming from Santa Rosa, who are "pure thieves." But others felt that the junta is responsible if the bars attract "people of poor quality." They argued that they had a responsibility to implement decisions taken by the general assembly and that Calixto should have been present then to argue his case. Those who had attended the general assembly, the *bases* (grass roots), were the "maximum authority" (*maxima autoridad*). In the end, they agreed that Calixto would be able to have his bar, until midnight only, but that he could not bring in his young friends for the bullfight. Calixto gratefully said that this was acceptable to him, that he did not want "bad blood" simply for one or two days of business during fiesta: "I'm ready to collaborate with my zone because it's my zone: I don't want to be an enemy of my own zone." He then brought in soft drinks and beer for all of us at the meeting to thank the junta, show his willingness to be trustworthy, and seal the agreement.

On the one hand, Calixto had a strong commercial imperative: a bar in a prime site during the zonal fiesta is extremely good business. On the other, the rowdiness, drunkenness, and criminality associated with such bars worried the vecinos, and many would have preferred to have none at all. The compromise position was to try to limit the running of bars to people from the zone, who were more easy to regulate. Even women from Santa Rosa or Santiago II, which are neighboring zones, were outsiders and suspect because they were not conocidas. Calixto had at least been around for a long time. Since I did not know him, I cannot comment with authority on the sincerity of his expressions of desire to collaborate with his zone. But his situation illustrates the complex mixture of self-interest and commitment to the zone that encourages people to collaborate with the junta vecinal in the organization of the fiesta. Calixto's comments that he did not wish to become an enemy of his zone and that he wanted to collaborate "because it's my zone" answer my question about why those who donate trophies, beer, and prizes agree to do so: "They have to give." They are *obliged* to give what they can because it is their zone and because they are wealthy enough. Collaboration enables the demonstration and recognition of prestige and wealth, and also means a friendlier relationship with people around you. It is akin to the expectations that wealthy and successful politicians will give something back to those who have supported them. Collaboration in the fiesta is something more than a responsibility, a compulsory sacrifice, or a gift to the zone, particularly to El Señor de Exaltación, the patron saint. However, that obligation is matched by the fact that if all members of the zone have given well, in return El Señor usually looks after the zone, and therefore the individual vecinos.

Movement and Experience   The commitment to the zone evident in the obligations associated with organizing the fiesta is even more keenly felt and constructed through movement on the day itself. As Jane Cowan (1990: 132) argues, "Participating in the dance can provoke that sense of recognition—which though not inevitable is still by no means rare—that one is morally part of, just as one is now corporeally merged with, a larger collectivity, a recognition that, as a profoundly visceral knowledge, carries the force of absolute conviction." Her theory is similar to older anthropological approaches to dance influenced by Durkheim. For example, in *The Andaman Islanders* (1922), Radcliffe-Brown argued that dancing produced a subconscious feeling in individuals that one's personal value depended upon collective harmony. My focus here, which draws on dance scholarship,[6] is on the experience of a performance itself, from the point of view of both audience and performer. Analyzing music and dance performances in Bolivia has enabled Michelle Bigenho (2001: 23) to develop the useful concept of "experiential authenticity," the fleeting feeling of sharing the experience of a performance with others, and thus becoming "root[ed] to places through bodily movement and the achievement of a performative 'oneness' . . . with sonorous events and other people."

My personal experiences of experiential authenticity while dancing in and watching the fiestas illustrate the importance of dance in the construction of a sense of community and citizenship. These experiences began with rehearsals, which usually start up to four months before the fiesta. The rehearsals I attended were generally a time to gather with friends and relatives, chat, and practice dance steps. Those who were particularly confident or experienced decided on the steps and taught the rest of us, who followed them, dancing in someone's courtyard for the Morenada or, in the case of the Kullawada, on the street outside the market. The *pasantes* circulated, distributing *trago*, which is burnt alcohol mixed with squash and is drunk in small shot-size glassfuls that are knocked back in one. During the evening, as the tragos began to take effect, the dancing became easier and less embarrassing, and chewing coca helped to ward off fatigue. Although the basic steps are very simple and I am generally a competent dancer, the rhythms were unfamiliar to me and initially difficult to grasp. Only a few months later, I found that my physical memory of the steps had almost entirely disappeared. My Bolivian friends had been listening to the music and dancing these particular rhythms all their lives, and as a result they slipped into the "groove" of the music (Bigenho 2001) much quicker than I did. Some people came to only a few rehearsals, some came to all, and levels of ability varied greatly among the dancers.

As people rested, they would chat with friends and family. This was particularly the case for women at the rehearsals for the Quilloma fiesta. They were mostly relatives, and many did not live in Rosas Pampa, so they enjoyed the opportunity to socialize collectively. Not all the women present at the rehearsals ended up dancing, and even if they did they decided not to have any particularly difficult special steps. They were all experienced Morenada dancers so did not need much practice. The rehearsals were also the only opportunity to discuss practical arrangements: halfway through, and once everyone had arrived, the dancers would gather around the pasante to discuss quotas, costumes, and traveling arrangements and collectively to make any decisions necessary.

Dancing in the Entradas and Dianas themselves was an incredible experience. Dancing at high altitude for five or six hours at a time was exhilarating, but also hot, tiring, and hard on my feet. The costumes for the Entradas were extremely difficult to dance in: I had to negotiate very high heels for the Morenada and a baby (a doll) on my back and a beaded hat, which was very heavy and did not fit me, for the Kullawada. But my exhaustion, embarrassment, and irritation with my costume were alleviated by the frequent stops for drinking beer and tragos, and it was, as my partner said, "a very proud experience" for both of us. By the time we reached the palco we were enjoying ourselves hugely. On the home stretch, hundreds of people cheered us on, and at the palco the reception for the whole group was very enthusiastic. (See video at http://www.sianlazar.net.)

The dancing affirms a sense of common belonging to the zone of Rosas Pampa, common status as members of a community. For me, the feeling of experiential authenticity and some sort of (visceral knowledge of) common belonging came through the physical experience of participating in a shared "affective culture," defined by Joann Kealinnohomoku (1979: 47) as "those cultural manifestations that implicitly and explicitly reflect the values of a given group of people through consciously devised means that arouse emotional responses and that strongly reinforce group identity." The performers and spectators were in collusion in this, in contrast to the musicians, who came from outside the zone and were hired for the purpose of the fiesta. They were the experts, and they put on their own shows, moving in unison, twirling cymbals, and jumping. The distance between expert dancer and audience, such as in ballet, was not relevant. The boundaries between performers and spectators were blurred because the performers were the same people as the spectators; we all knew each other. Vecinos lined the streets, and people, especially those who knew us, shouted encouragement or brought us beer when we took breaks. I was pulled out by a student of mine and given a better shawl; my landlady tried to sort out my hat for me; and on a couple of occasions women I knew helped me by retying the awayu holding my "baby," which kept falling out. As the dance scholar Sondra Horton Fraleigh (1987) points out, the body and self, and in particular the self in relation to others, are lived through dance precisely because of the relation between performer and audience in dance. The fiesta is being-in-the-world experienced as being-with-others through dance (Tamisari 2000).

Furthermore, the overall impression of the dancing is one of groups of people moving forward in uniformity. Everyone follows the people in front, and those at the head of the lines, the guides, are the ones who dictate when the group moves into rehearsed special steps. The movement is highly choreographed, and there is no improvisation other than the guides' decisions to begin the steps. Contrast this to dance styles such as salsa, where choreographed steps are used but in an improvised order, or a ballet performance, where small units of movement are combined in a fixed choreographed sequence (Cohen Bull 1997). In the former, the agency of the individual dancers is paramount, while in the latter, the choreographer has individual and primary agency. Bolivian brass band dances like the Morenada are entirely different: a more diffuse agency rests in the collectivity, led by the guides.

The aesthetics of the dances require conformity: stepping out of line or getting out of sequence breaks the flow and the overall impression of the performance. And those aesthetic values work on the spectators and the dancers. When rehearsing the Kullawada, my partner and I were keenly

9. The Morenada in Quilloma, 2003

conscious of our difference, particularly since everybody seemed to be looking at us to see how we would do. What made us stick out was in part the different way we moved, in part the fact that we were taller than the other dancers. I felt this sense of not belonging more acutely while rehearsing and dancing than under normal circumstances by that time, which was toward the end of that period of my fieldwork. However, when I ignored that sensation and relaxed into the movement, my sense of togetherness and coherence became very strong too. When all the dancers are moving in unison, the effect is quite breathtaking for the spectators and the participants.

Part of the mascot's job is to maintain this uniformity; when we danced the Kullawada we were told that every so often we should circle the groups dancing behind us and discipline the dancers if they made mistakes. Our authority was buttressed by our different costumes but also our ability to go against the general forward direction of the movement by turning around to circle the group. Fortunately for us, we did not need to learn and keep to the special steps, although we rehearsed with all the other dancers; we were outside of the aesthetics of uniformity (and control) in this sense. This positioning gave us special responsibilities too: as we were approaching the end of the procession route, spectators kept shouting to us "More joy!" (Más alegría!), encouraging me to smile and the both of us to move more expansively. Before and during rehearsals, we were told that our joy was essential if we were to win the dance competition. This effervescence was not restricted to the dancers. During the fiesta, day-to-day living is put on hold for three days, and people can (and mostly do) enjoy themselves by dancing, watching dancing, and getting drunk; they are "reinvigorated by living, for a few moments, in a life that is less strained, and freer and easier" (Durkheim 1965 [1915]: 427). Ritual moments are a "bracketing off" of normal time (Kertzer 1988), moments to experience *communitas* (V. Turner 1969). Dancing serves many functions: from safety valve and catharsis, to a means of conflict, self-assertion, or self-generation for society; from an organ of social control and education to (controlled) release from social norms (Hanna 1979; Peterson Royce 1977; Spencer 1985).

The function I wish to highlight is connected to the aesthetics of unity in forward motion, which map out people's collective relationship to their zone. The Entrada creates a shared sense of identity through movement, and this sense of identity is intimately connected with place as the dancers proceed through the zone. Moving through space thus constitutes the relationship of person to locality; in this sense, the dancing of the Entrada reflects the highly spatial nature of the local terminology of citizenship, namely, zone, vecino, and pueblo. Bigenho (2001) notes the importance of movement through space for rural areas and contrasts this form of (physical) mapping, which marks out territory but focuses on central points, with the (paper) mapping of territory for bureaucratic purposes, focused on boundaries and limits. In the Rosas Pampa fiesta, the route (the mapping) spirals in, from the outer reaches of the zone to the most important central public spaces, principally the football pitch.

INDIVIDUAL, COMMUNITY, AND SPACE: DISTINCTIONS

The overwhelming emphasis in anthropological literature on dance and ritual is one of drawing people together (Lange 1975; Spencer 1985; Radcliffe Brown 1922). The only way of avoiding being drawn together through dance is by nonparticipation. For example, Hans Buechler's (1980) work does much to examine the ways in which fiesta rituals generate information about social life but implies that looking at fiestas as generative of social integration means that it is impossible to look at their expressive elements, a zero-sum choice. For him, the generation of information requires choice, and social control its absence; or at least the only choice is whether or not to participate. However, a more nuanced and porous vision of social integration than both of these may be more useful. People experience as much or as little of the festivities as they want and take from them many different meanings, some of which can reinforce a sense of common belonging and social integration. Yet this is not the exclusive set of meanings expressed by the dancing. Aesthetics of conformity and uniformity notwithstanding, there are important distinctions among members of the community of Rosas Pampa, which are revealed and experienced during the fiesta. In contrast to the homogeneous community of communitarian political theory, ethnography of the fiesta demonstrates that even at the most intense time of collective effervescence individual vecinos experience their collective identity through distinctiveness and hierarchy (cf. Sallnow 1987). Hierarchy within the community is underlined throughout the festivities by, for example, the prominent position of the junta vecinal in leading the Entrada and then judging the dances and by the forms in which the different dance groups are organized (Anze O. 1995). Gender and age distinctions are also expressed within the dances.

The sonorous experience of the fiesta marked out membership of the general collectivity in a complex way. Since I was dancing at the front of our group, it was very hard to hear the band at the rear and very easy to get confused with the band of the comparsa in front. The pasantes in front of me kept to their own rhythm but were far enough out in front for that not to matter. I found myself torn between what I could hear from behind and what I could see in front of me. The sonorous distinction between dance groups is blurred for at least some of the dancers as an effect of the bands bringing up the rear of each comparsa. For spectators, though, the impression is one of flows of sound going by one after another, each with a separate identity that is given physical shape by the dancers. Scholars have noted the importance of musical cacophony in rural highland fiestas in Bolivia (Bigenho 2001; Stobart 2002a), and much the same can be said for the urban fiesta, at least from the spectators' point of view. In Rosas Pampa, after the comparsas had displayed their steps at the palco on Saturday morning, the dancers went to the football field and continued dancing to their bands, buying beer for each other and for the band. As in rural fiestas, the bands always played the same music, which became something of a theme (cf. Bigenho 2001). The impression on an observer is of a territory being marked out by sound into distinct smaller spaces; as with pools of light, observers move from one pool of sound to another. But the inhabitants of each pool of sound are unaware of the others, not least because by this time they are drinking heavily. This is one metaphor for social relations in Rosas Pampa: distinct groups, although with blurred boundaries between them. These groups mediate the relationship between individuals and their zone—nested affiliations that are also evident in the organization of the fiesta and the dance groups.

The junta vecinal shares the organization of the fiesta with the *preste* and the pasantes. Traditionally, being preste would mean being responsible for funding and organizing nearly the entire fiesta (Buechler 1980), although in 2000 the preste organized a comparsa and paid for the main church service during the fiesta. Pasantes are the organizers of individual comparsas. They are usually a couple but are represented in organizational meetings by the man. The junta vecinal's role was essentially supervisory, and the fiestas were organized on the basis of who had participated the previous year. Continuity was very important, and from the outside the fiestas seemed almost to organize themselves. The Rosas Pampa Junta Vecinal knew who the pasantes should be, since they were chosen by the previous pasantes during the fiesta and danced on the final day at the front of the group with red, yellow, and green ribbons on their breasts.[7] Some weeks beforehand, the president of the junta vecinal went informally to the pasantes to confirm that they would be entering the fiesta and asked the president of the junta escolar if the school would join in. The assumption was that every group that had danced in 1999 would dance in 2000, and the responsibility for getting them out on the streets fell to the pasantes.

The pasantes were responsible for convening people and providing the drink and PA systems necessary for all the rehearsals, which were held on Sunday nights. They also contracted the band. Traditionally, the pasantes pay for the band, but in both comparsas in which I participated each couple dancing paid a quota. We also paid for the hire of our costumes, but the pasante organized it all. At the time of the fiesta, the pasantes provide food and sometimes lodging (in the case of returning to the countryside) for the dancers. As Buechler argues, Bolivian urban and rural fiestas are ritual spaces for exchange relationships. Participation in fiestas is dependent upon insertion into particular kinship and social networks, and the bases of such social relationships are, in the ritual context, "various types of exchanges of alcohol, food, coca and cash" (1980: 13). Prestes and pasantes often call on the fact that they have previously provided services (beer, for example) to relatives or friends in similar circumstances and expect those people to return the service in the form of urban *ayni* (reciprocal service). Dancing is also part of the exchange, in the sense that it should be reciprocated: if you have been a pasante, in future years you should dance for those who danced for you (Buechler 1980).

There are two main types of networks that are mobilized for the purpose of organizing dancing groups: kinship and friendship networks and occupational networks.[8] The main comparsa, run by the overall preste, consisted of many of the vecinos of Rosas Pampa, organized through friendship and kinship networks. The other comparsas were formed from occupational groups; the mechanics formed another Morenada comparsa. The third comparsa, who danced the Kullawada, consisted of women who sold in the local market, along with their husbands; and the final comparsa was the school, whose pupils danced the Tinkus.

But participation in the dancing does not automatically result from participation in the relevant set of social relationships. In 2000 there were rumors about problems with the mechanics' comparsa, since the pasante had been somewhat arrogant when asking people to take part. He had announced that the quota for band and costume was 300 Bolivianos and if they wanted to dance they could give him the money. There were mumbles that they could dance elsewhere if he was not prepared to ask them politely, actually to almost beg them to take part. Hans Buechler (1980: 179) provides a detailed description of how prestes had to visit people, sometimes twice, bringing beer, cigarettes, and coca, in order to invite them to participate. In my experience, pasantes sent out invitations and informed people where rehearsals would be held.[9] Nonetheless, there is a reciprocal obligation to dance for people who danced for you and a responsibility to help out family members by dancing for them. A number of people who danced with the market women's comparsa came from different zones in El Alto but were related to the pasantes. The market women's union even resorted, it was rumored, to fining people who would not participate.

Being preste or pasante is very expensive, and because of that brings status. Rubén, the pasante of the Morenada we took to Quilloma, estimated that he had spent about US$800 in total. He is a student and a taxi driver, and he told me later that he had done it because he was hoping to stand for mayor of Quilloma at some point in the future. He wished to get himself known there and show that he was generous, relatively well-heeled, and prepared to give something to his pueblo. In rural areas, being prestes for community fiestas is part of a defined series of leadership positions that couples hold as they move up in society (Abercrombie 1991; Sallnow 1987; Buechler 1980). Rosario Anze (1995) found a similar situation for urban zones in the southern part of El Alto near Rosas Pampa. As the comments over the mechanics' comparsa show, being pasante or preste requires an understanding of etiquette and cultural norms and the ability to stay on good terms with kinsfolk and occupational associates; it is a delicate and responsible position. As Rubén told me, "It's difficult to get people together." He relied very much upon the support of his parents,[10] particularly since, unusually for a pasante, he was unmarried at the time.

The connections between political authority and having been preste or pasante are a further example of the overlapping of formal politics and ritual obligations, an overlapping similarly testified to by the importance of the junta vecinal in fiesta organization. The structure and organization of the dancing in the fiesta reveal something about how individuals relate to their community, in that their membership is mediated by membership in a corporate entity, such as mechanics, the school, the market, or a particular kin group. Citizenship here is a multitiered construct (Yuval-Davis 1997) of membership in various collectivities that nest and overlap.

Reading the Signs of the Dancing: The Morenada   The experience of the distinctions within the collectivity also rests upon shared cultural competence in reading the signs of the dances. As with any other symbolic activity, the symbolic dimensions of the dances not only reflect differences but also constitute them. Structuralist dance anthropologists saw dance as language (Spencer 1985; Hanna 1979; Williams 1996; Peterson Royce 1977), and Adrienne Kaeppler (1995) has argued that dance performers and audiences need shared levels of linguistic competence (in the Chomskyan sense) in the language of movement in order to be able to "decode" movements. However, any attempt to do this will necessarily be partial, since the meanings of dances can exceed the limits of verbal language (Thomas 1993). In a sense, this is how it should be: the meanings should be just beyond the grasp of words; as Isadora Duncan said, "If I could tell you what it meant, there would be no point in dancing it" (quoted in Peterson Royce 1977: 155). Thus, recognizing the partiality of my account, I read the signification of the dances through costume and movement, although any significations are dependent upon context. I look here at two main forms of distinction and illustrate them with the example of the Morenada.

According to Antonio Paredes-Candia (1984), the "dance of the *Morenos*" is first mentioned in an article published in the La Paz Geographical Society magazine in 1898. The oldest Morenada group that still dances in the Oruro Carnival dates from 1913. Elssa Paredes de Salazar (1976) argued that the Morenada arose in the first years of Independence. She maintained that the Morenada tells of the experiences of Afro-Bolivians in wine presses in the region of the Yungas. Brought over from Africa during colonial times to work in the mines of Potosí, the slaves were unable to acclimatize to the hard work and cold weather of the mining region, so were moved to the warmer regions of the Yungas. The movements of the dance mimic the movements of grape pressing. Other commentators think that the dance refers to the journey that slaves took to the mines of Potosí from Central America (Rocha n.d.), while the website of one of the Morenada fraternities of the Oruro Carnival describes it as about both the mines and the wine presses.[11] Still other authors maintain that it originated in the altiplano village of Taraco, near lake Titicaca (Asociacion de Conjuntos Folkloricos del Gran Poder 1999). Everyone agrees, though, that the Morenada is about the African slaves and the name *moreno* refers to people of dark skin. It is traditionally the backbone of the fiesta in La Paz of the Señor del Gran Poder, the zonal fiesta of the commercial zone of Chijini in La Paz. (See video at http://www.sianlazar.net.)

In Rosas Pampa, the Morenada was generally agreed to be the most prestigious dance of all. Its prestige derives, according to informants, from the expense involved, either for the dancers or for the organizers. Bands who play the Morenada charge more for their time than the others, and the men's costumes are the most elaborate and cost the most to hire (see also Buechler 1980). Perhaps more important nowadays, the women dancing the Morenada need to buy new outfits, consisting of pollera, shoes, and shawl, and a different set for the Diana the following day. The polleras worn by members of a comparsa should ideally be of matching material. The whole ensemble could cost around US$250. When dancing, the women wear their best and most expensive gold earrings and brooches. In their new polleras and shawls and dripping with gold, the Morenada dancers underline their commercial success (as cholas),[12] probably a reason for the popularity of the Morenada during the Entrada of Gran Poder.

10. Men dancing the Morenada, fiesta of Gran Poder, 2003

Originally, in fact, the Morenada was danced only by men, even in the early 1970s (Asociacion de Conjuntos Folkloricos del Gran Poder 1999; Buechler 1980), and their costumes are certainly the most spectacular (see figure 10). A consistent feature of the Morenada dance has been the *matracas*, or rattles, that the dancers, particularly the men, carry. The matracas used to be fish or armadillos, but now often indicate the dancers' profession or affiliation; for example, taxi drivers will have taxis, and groups of vecinos might have matracas shaped like beer bottles. In the Entrada of Gran Poder in 2000, the men of the comparsa from the market of Eloy Salmón carried matracas shaped like stereo players because the Eloy Salmón market is where black market electrical goods are to be found in La Paz.

The migrants from Quilloma would not consider dancing anything other than the Morenada when going back to the Quilloma fiesta: it enabled them to say to their pueblo that, although things in the city might be tough, they could at least afford to dance the Morenada. Their willingness to spend is a mixture of snobbishness and respect—they would not be cheap when it came to their pueblo—but it also says that they have made a success of the migration to the city. Such motives, however, are expressed as obligation or necessity. When we returned from Quilloma on the bus, the men sang raucously:

> You have to dance Morenada
> Once a year
> Even though it's hard for us to pay
> What will we take with us
> When we die?
> Cholita paceña.

> Hay que bailar Moreno,
> al año una vez,
> aunque nos cueste pagar
> Que cosa vamos a llevar,
> Cuando nos vamos a morir?
> Cholita paceña.

The Morenada also expresses something about adulthood, dignity, and appropriate gendered behavior. It is meant to be danced by older married people, such as the group who went back to Quilloma to dance. When younger people dance the Morenada in the Oruro Carnival or the Entrada Universitaria, the boys' movements are much more athletic than the older men's, involving more elaborate jumping and twisting, while the girls dance in flirty mini-polleras instead of the full pollera worn by the older women, a fact commented upon with disapproval by one of my (younger) friends. The issue of dignity addressed here is not only about women of different ages wearing different clothes, but also about the ethnicity of the dancers. With her snorts of disapproval at the short skirts, my friend expressed a view that mestiza women are more flirtatious and less dignified than stately chola women, who move in a more measured fashion and wear more demure clothes. This example shows that understandings of age, ethnicity, and gender influence and reveal readings of signs in the "cultural artifacts" of fiesta dance events (Cowan 1990; Kaeppler 1978).

The Morenada comparsa has both corporate groups of dancers doing the same steps and several mascots at the very front, or at the front of a subgroup. When we went to Quilloma, I danced at the front as china. I was able to hire my costume, which meant that I did not have to go to the expense of buying a pollera and all the rest. My costume consisted of high-heeled thigh-high boots, a mini-pollera, and a matching top, all in black and gold. The ensemble was topped off with a gold bowler hat with a feather in it. The part of china is usually played by young single women (although traditionally it was played by cross-dressing men), who dance coquettishly at the front of the comparsa. Being not fully adult yet, they are not part of the well-heeled collectivity who process in dignity behind them.

The contrast between mature woman Morenada dancer and china figure is not only one of costume; movement is also very important.[13] The Morenada is a very dignified and stately dance. When married women dance the Morenada, they tend to stick to the basic dance step with only a few elaborated special steps. The basic step moves forward, with steps to each side, but the women's movement is focused upon swishing their luxuriant skirts, so they emphasize the swing to each side with their hips moving in an almost horizontal plane while they face forward most of the time. The Quilloma women had two special steps, one of which was based on the basic step and involved turning to the front, left, back, and right, to come back to facing forward and proceeding along their route with the basic step. Women also carry matracas, which are smaller than the men's and which they operate in time to the steps and the music. Their posture is very contained: limb movement is kept to a minimum, as if the dancers are in a cocoon, and they do not move their heads a great deal, although there is no stiffness. There is no sense of abandonment in limb or head movement, even when the women become very drunk, but there is a sense of flow, elegance, control, and reserve. The cliché that they look like fleets of galleons processing along the sea is actually rather accurate. I was told that the Morenada was easy for women to do because it does not require much physical exertion.

The china dance is simpler. I had to do only one step, although I have seen more expert chinas dancing several special steps. Their movement is choppier than the older women's swishing from side to side; with the smaller skirt comes a smaller range of movement for the arms and legs, and the hips are supposed to swing from side to side in the vertical plane rather than swinging around in the horizontal plane, as with the older women. All this gives the impression of prim and haughty coquettishness.

My partner had not arrived in Bolivia when I began rehearsing for the Quilloma Morenada, although he was present at the actual fiesta. This made it possible for me to dance as a single girl. By the time rehearsals began for the Rosas Pampa fiesta a few months later, I had managed to

11. Women dancing the Morenada in Quilloma, 2003

12. The Kullawada of 2000 in Rosas Pampa, with Awila and Waphuri in front. Photo by David Campfens.

persuade him to join me in dancing. As participants in the Kullawada comparsa in Rosas Pampa, we also danced as mascots, but as a couple. He was the Waphuri, and I was the Awila, a grandmother. The Waphuri is supposed to direct the movement of the dance (Asociacion de Conjuntos Folkloricos del Gran Poder 1999; Rocha n.d.; Paredes de Salazar 1976). He wears a (very heavy) mask with a big nose and hat, plus a hired shirt, belt, and trousers. He brandishes a large spindle, which is extremely heavy; I wore a smaller hat and a blouse, and carried a doll. My pollera this time was that of an adult woman: by dancing with my partner, I had matured from a flirty china to an adult woman with a baby.[14]

The important point is that it is very unusual to dance alone; in theory, even chinas should dance with others out in the front of the group. The wives of the male mascots dance with the other married women. Dancing these days is meant to be done as part of a heterosexual couple, particularly for the mature dances such as the Morenada and the Kullawada. In other dances, such as Caporales, Tobas, and Tinkus, which are mostly danced by younger people (because they are very athletic), gender roles are not as tightly circumscribed; for instance, I have seen women dancing male Caporales dances, even in small Entradas such as that in Santiago II.[15] The pasantes also should be married, and if not, as was the case for Rubén, they need to be accompanied by a female relative for the dancing and also to organize the food, drink, and accommodation for the comparsas. In Rubén's case, it was his mother who filled this role. This requirement of some form of male-female couple to hold leadership positions is similar to Aymara requirements for political office-holding, as numerous ethnographies have shown (e.g., Harris 2000a [1978]). Sponsorship of dances occurs at particular stages of individuals' life cycles, and in this sense, public fiestas are also individual rites of passage (Buechler 1980). Full selfhood for adults is dependent upon being part of a stable heterosexual couple, and this has implications for various citizenship and political practices, including, in this case, dance.

DANCE AND BOLIVIAN IDENTITY: NESTED AFFILIATIONS AND CITIZENSHIP

Local Entradas can tell us much about national as well as local citizenship, principally because they reveal the way that nested affiliations shape vecinos' citizenship. Dancing also shows how the cultural projects associated with multiculturalist politics at the national level actually retain strong assimilationist tendencies, and suggest that this is the case for the more political projects of citizenship. By holding an Entrada, vecinos of Rosas Pampa express a national sensibility as well as the very localist one described above. Dance is central to Bolivianness for Bolivians of all social classes. One vecino of Rosas Pampa told me, "We Bolivians are thuqiñas [dancers]," using the Aymara word. Dance and alcohol are also commonly used to explain Bolivia's underdevelopment; I was often told that Bolivians have too many fiestas and drink too much, and this is why the country has not progressed. Furthermore, the dances included in the Entrada enact national belonging as well as local belonging. As well as being influenced by rural fiestas, in many ways the Rosas Pampa and Quilloma Entradas mimic, or refer to, the famous city-based national Entradas, particularly those of the Oruro Carnival and the Gran Poder festivities in La Paz (Anze O. 1995). An examination of that citation through dance reveals the ambivalence of Rosas Pampa vecinos' positions in the national chain of belonging.

National Entradas have grown at a remarkable rate in recent years. The first Entrada of Gran Poder was held in 1966, and the Entrada Universitaria is even newer, having been instituted in 1988. The Oruro Carnival has a longer history and has taken many forms throughout precolonial and colonial times. The oldest folkloric dance associations that participate in that Entrada each year date from the beginning of the twentieth century, but most were formed in the 1970s and 1980s.[16] The Entradas are all televised and attract large audiences of Bolivians of all classes. Beer companies prominently sponsor the big dance festivities and use images of dancers to illustrate Bolivian identity in their advertisements. For example, the beer company Paceña, which is from La Paz, brought out a TV ad in 2000 which showed a group dancing the Tinkus on the salt lake in Uyuni, which is between the city of Potosí and the Chilean border. Such a combination of localized images (La Paz beer plus northern Potosí dance plus national tourist site) to create a national sensibility creates an almost exact commercial reflection of the "pluri-multi" approach to Bolivian identity of 1990s policymaking (Patzi Paco 1999), no longer Creolized and integrationist, but one of unity in diversity. By dancing dances that come from specific regions of Bolivia, vecinos of Rosas Pampa were emphasizing their belonging not only to Rosas Pampa but also to Bolivia.

Although my informants viewed the Morenada primarily as a prestigious dance that was expensive to participate in, and no one told me that it was about African slaves, they would certainly have understood the Morenada to be about Morenos, or Africans. The regional differences of the dances would have been evident to them through the names and through what they learned about these dances in schools, even if they did not consider themselves authoritative enough to pass on this knowledge to me or if they thought such references were too obvious to merit mention. Other dances danced in Rosas Pampa are similarly region-specific: Tobas refers to indigenous groups of the eastern lowlands of Bolivia, and the Tinkus is a dance that supposedly derives from the famous tinku fights in northern Potosí. Dancing each dance enacts a Bolivianness that is composed of multiple regional and ethnic identities, and dancing cross-culturally, as the urban Aymara do when they mimic indigenous peoples from the eastern lowlands or tinku fighters from northern Potosí, simultaneously reinforces and breaks down those identifications.

However, the citation of national Entradas also means that the Entrada of Rosas Pampa participates in their more assimilationist aspects, principally in the folkloricization of dance culture. In this logic, dances can be celebrated, but must be bracketed off from normal Bolivian time, rather like ritual time is bracketed off. Contemporary Bolivian media tends to present the famous Entradas as tourist attractions, something exotic and colorful—folkloric remnants of an indigenous past. The Bolivian government encourages such an interpretation, for example in its campaign to get the Oruro Carnival declared a "Masterpiece of the Oral and Intangible Heritage of Humanity" by UNESCO. As Thomas Abercrombie (1991: 119–120) argues with regard to Oruro, the Entrada is a way city people can exorcise and domesticate the Indian within them.

History, especially precolonial history and the history of resistance during the colonial period, is mobilized by intellectuals to make claims for the cultural importance of dances like the Morenada. But an unfortunate side effect of this mobilization of history is that the dances are taken out of the present time—they become exotic, traditional, a "*folkloric* demonstration of protest against the colonial epoch" (from a description of the Morenada on the official website of the Asociacion de Conjuntos del Folklore-Oruro, http://www.acfo.org; my emphasis). Clearly, these processes can work the other way, highlighting the ways the colonial epoch is reflected or perpetuated in modern times. But there is a danger of weakening the power of such claims through folkloricization. And the vecinos of Rosas Pampa partake of that folkloricization, for example through learning (and teaching) dances in school as folkloric and somehow out of time or in the past rather than contemporary. This runs the risk of creating a form of ethnic consciousness that Blanca Muratorio (1980: 51) aptly terms an "alienated folkloric consciousness." This kind of consciousness exposes the assimilationist side to multiculturalism, and is of course not new. In a book on Bolivian dances published in 1976, Elssa Paredes de Salazar argued that the fiesta should become "a remembrance of a traditional and romantic past which is, each time, receding further and further into the distance"; she describes the Oruro Carnival as "really a folkloric fiesta where typical costumes are exhibited" (32).

Yet, as this chapter has shown, the fiesta is much more than an exhibition of dance and costume; it is a central part of the annual cycle of modern Bolivian communities. When vecinos of Rosas Pampa dance the Morenada or Kullawada in their Entradas they are asserting their collective belonging to the nation of Bolivia as vecinos of Rosas Pampa. They cite *both* the folkloric national Entradas *and* rural fiestas that they either remember from their childhood or continue to participate in when they visit their pueblos. Dancing is an ambivalent activity in this sense, and the Rosas Pampa fiesta partakes of this ambivalence. Having said that, dance is experienced during the local fiesta in context, and the bracketing off of ritual time takes place within an identifiable community. Furthermore, the fiesta is also great fun, the dangers of folkloricization notwithstanding.

To be a citizen in El Alto is to be part of a zone, and in some ways the fiesta is a metaphor for the zone, a means for individuals to define and physically experience the collectivity. Local politics are intimately connected to the fiesta. The route of the Entrada maps the territory of the zone, spiraling in from its boundaries to its center (the football pitch) and asserting the vecinos' relationship to place. The collectivity symbolically takes in the whole zone during the procession but breaks up into small groups once the dancers have displayed their steps to the judges. Citizenship of the imagined community of the zone is dependent upon insertion into smaller face-to-face communities and networks, marked out by sound, movement, and costume. The importance of networks that underpin vecindad in Rosas Pampa is also reflected in the organization of the fiesta into comparsas that consist of kin or occupational networks. On a more individual level, the dances reveal much about the nature of personhood, specifically adulthood, with their stress on dignified movement, the heterosexual couple, and conspicuous consumption.

If dance is a citizenship practice, then the citizenship here is not an abstract status or category of belonging, but concrete, physical, and embodied, involving a sense of collectivity which includes a common relationship to place but which cannot be taken for granted. That collectivity is neither homogeneous nor uncontested; indeed, the community is constituted precisely through hierarchy and distinction and is split into smaller collectivities. Any one vecino can be a member of different networks that make up the larger political entities, and such communities are overlapping, varied, and contingent. That this nested nature of belonging in Rosas Pampa is a characteristic of national citizenship is evident in the way that the Rosas Pampa Entrada cites the big national Entradas and in the dances themselves. The fiesta is both a moment of intense local belonging and an expression of Bolivian identity. As the vecinos of Rosas Pampa dance cross-culturally, mimicking Bolivians from other parts of the country and enacting a smaller version of events that have come to symbolize Bolivianness, they dance their Bolivian nationality. That nationality is dependent upon their insertion into a set of smaller communities: the Andean region, the department of La Paz, the city of El Alto, the zone.

FIVE *HOW THE GODS TOUCH HUMANS (AND VICE VERSA)*

This chapter continues the story of the construction of community and a sense of collectivity in Rosas Pampa and considers how the forms of sociality modeled and mediated by religion affect citizenship.[1] The first section elaborates upon models of sociality and the self provided and reflected by what Olivia Harris (2006) has called "colonial Catholicism," focusing in particular on the importance of the body and ingestion in the fiesta and popular religious rites. The second section counterposes this with the Evangelical anticommunity constructed in opposition to colonial Catholicism. The latter project is a modernizing one, which relies upon a clear distinction between the public and the private and a correspondingly bounded notion of the individual self. It involves quite a lot of work on the self and the body for Evangelicals and can lead to fractures between residents of Rosas Pampa. However, Evangelicalism is only partially successful as a modernizing project of personhood, not least because it relies upon the inability of people to conform entirely to that absolutist version of personhood. Perhaps fortunately, the investment in Evangelicalism is never quite as complete as the missionaries themselves say they would like, and the model of citizenship promoted by them is constantly undermined by ordinary people's flexible and hybrid approach to the sacred.

COLONIAL CATHOLICISM: THE FIESTA, ALCOHOL, AND THE SACRED

In chapter 4, I looked at what is probably the most intense and explicit expression of community in Rosas Pampa, the annual fiesta. I argued that there is a compulsory quality to the fiesta celebrations, coupled with a sense of euphoria and pride in the well-being of the zone. Yet even this moment of collective effervescence needs to be analyzed, since it provides scope for the expression simultaneously of difference, of discord, and of competition (quite apart from those who refuse to participate at all). In this section I discuss other aspects of religious worship—the elements that have typically been associated with the construction and reproduction of community by Andean ethnographers—in order to explore ethnographically how community operates on a day-to-day basis. As we shall see, there are many shared values which link the migrants of Rosas Pampa to their pueblos and express a similar sense of the sources of power that ensure their collective well-being. In turn, these inform the vecinos' understandings of their relationship to each other and to the zone.

Devotion and Dancing   As well as being a social rite of community, the fiesta is, of course, a religious ritual, and the community thereby experienced as sacred. Fiestas are about honoring the pueblo's or zone's saint through dancing and gaining his or her blessing for individuals and the collectivity for the coming year. This religiosity is tightly linked to the consumption of alcohol. Prior to September, both Morenadas in Rosas Pampa held Catholic Masses to inaugurate their rehearsal periods. In one, four months before the fiesta, the priest reminded the dancers that they were dancing out of devotion and not just to get drunk. He proceeded to deliver a sermon about how people should better their lives, part of which included a discourse on relations between husband and wife, stressing communication and the sharing of domestic tasks, a noteworthy point given the frequent connection between drunkenness and domestic violence (Harris 2000a [1978]; Harvey 1994a, 1994b). Many more people went to the dancing and drinking in the churchyard after the Mass, but a good forty or so adults attended the service, the most I ever saw in that church during many visits over the year.

The debates that surfaced about dancing the Kullawada well illustrate the role of devotion and spirituality in dancing. When I started telling friends that my partner and I were going to dance the Kullawada, a number tried to discourage me because the Kullawada is notoriously *khincha* (bad luck). I heard that the pasantes were having trouble getting people to dance and had had to threaten fines. When I asked why the Kullawada was *khincha*, people told me that couples who dance the Kullawada will subsequently separate, and I was told of a number of incidents where this had happened. On the other hand, the women who wanted me to dance had a number of responses to this basic objection. One said that the problem was for single people, "but you already have your husband, don't you? Single women [cholitas] might get carried off, but you'll be carried off by your husband, so you'll be fine!" More frequently, though, people said things along the lines of Doña Betty's response: "That's something from the past, you shouldn't believe that."

One of the pasantes said, "The others didn't want [to dance the Kulla-wada], it's khincha, they say, but I organized it in the campo [countryside] and did it do me any harm? In fact it brought me money." Her husband said that we were dancing for El Señor (by which he meant El Señor de Exaltación, the saint being commemorated), and that this would override any bad effects from such "superstitions" or beliefs "like in Satan, in the devils." In general, they all thought that if I did not believe in the super-stition, then there would be no problem. One woman shopkeeper said to me, "Well, it might happen for these warmis, but not for you—you're not dancing for devotion, are you?" Warmi is Aymara for woman, and she was, somewhat dismissively, attributing the effects of the belief only to Aymara peasant women. In any case, since I was dancing for fun rather than faith, she thought I would be safe from any possible ill effects.[2]

The nature of devotion in dancing was of course very important, as the centrality of the saint's images and devotional Masses to the festivities show. However, there were disputes about the exact obligations of danc-ers. Although not strictly appropriate, it was acceptable to dance purely for fun, particularly for me as a gringa, and fun and enjoyment were seen as central to devotion itself. My status as nonbeliever did not prohibit me from dancing and may indeed have helped me avoid the effects of bad luck. Nonetheless, the sacrifice of dancing usually illustrates and enacts one's devotion, which is viewed as active and requires constant reiteration. One is supposed to dance for the saint three times in a row (Bigenho 2001); one friend told me that I should dance three times for Santiago in Quilloma or I would have bad luck. Not everyone agreed with her, how-ever, and her sister berated her for saying this to me.[3]

However, the actual object of devotion was rather less clear to me. For some people, the devotion was focused on the actual icon of the Señor de Exaltación carried at the head of the procession during the Entrada and worshipped during the Masses on Friday and Saturday. Because of this, the pasante viewed as superstitious those people who had warned me against the Kullawada. However, for them, the dance itself was an object, or at least had the power to bring risk. His wife saw the Kullawada in a similar way, but as having the power to bring luck, when she argued that it had actually brought her money. Others agreed that although the dance might bring bad luck, that belief would have power over me only if I believed in it myself. Thus, religious belief, although strong, cannot be assumed to be constant and unquestionable. Even the best-established and most explicitly devotional elements of the fiesta are subject to debate, scrutiny, and doubt.

Alcohol—Sociality—Spirituality Alcohol was central to my personal experience of dancing in the fiestas, and it is a very important force for creating a sense of community among vecinos. At rehearsals, the organizers circulated with jugs of trago, on the understanding that it would make all of us dance. During the Entradas and the Dianas, we took frequent breaks to drink, and after they were finished, we drank and danced with our comparsa in the football pitch. Fiestas are movement, costumes, applause, dust, exhaustion, devotion, but it will be clear from the descriptions in the previous chapter that drinking alcohol plays just as crucial a role in fiestas as all of these. Of course, not everyone drinks, but all the dancers, band members, and the majority of the audience do. When we arrived in Quilloma, we were met by a small truck filled with beer crates, at least half of which were emptied at the end of three days. Quilloma itself has at most one hundred families, many of whom do not consume alcohol. Most of the drinking was done by the fifty or so couples who went there to dance. Some people drank for three days, to alarming states of inebriation. Most went off to sleep when they felt they had become too *duro* (drunk, literally, "hard"), returning when they felt better. The Rosas Pampa fiesta was similar: a few people I knew were still staggering around drunk on Monday morning.

Alcohol is the third point in a triangle that connects sociality with spirituality. Alcohol is clearly an important aspect of sociality, and various anthropologists have pointed out that the consumption of alcohol and the behavior that results are culturally variable (see edited volumes by Douglas 1987; McDonald 1994; Gefou-Madianou 1992). Anthropologists of Europe have highlighted the role of alcohol consumption in encouraging conviviality, particularly among men (Cowan 1990; Gefou-Madianou 1992); Dwight Heath (1987: 25) points out that "on Latin America, virtually every ethnography has some allusion to drinking and drunkenness." Penelope

Harvey (1994b) makes a similar point for the Andes, where ethnographers generally acknowledge alcohol to be of comparable cultural importance and religious significance to coca (Carter and Mamani P. 1989 [1982]; Abercrombie 1998; Allen 1988).

In altiplano Bolivia (excepting in very wealthy households) the connections between alcohol, sociality, and spirituality are underlined by the conventions around drinking beer, which is the most common drink in urban areas like Rosas Pampa. Generally speaking, whoever has bought the bottle or had bottles given to them, for example when someone is nominated godparent, will pour out a small cup of beer for everyone. They then ask people to drink up, at which point everyone ch'allas Pachamama by dropping some beer on the ground, then either drains their beer or drinks half the cup. As Carter and Mamani (1989 [1982]: 320) point out, alcohol consumption "almost always occurs in a social context." This can be quite literal: you do not sip continually from your glass, but drink up when others are drinking.

I often heard people saying "They made me drink," which at first I thought was just an excuse. However, I soon realized that there was a strong element of empirical truth in this, since there is a lot of pressure around drinking. It is almost impossible to refuse a drink because people just will not hear of it. When people buy you a bottle of beer, you have to reciprocate, that is, buy them one and drink it that evening with them. If poured a drink, you must drink along with everyone else. It is very hard to refuse an offer of any drink, but one solution to the problem of getting overly inebriated is to ch'alla as much as possible to Pachamama before drinking. At the end, you can also tip out the remaining few drops of drink, which is another opportunity to regulate yourself. I was once told that Bolivians ch'alla to Pachamama so that they don't become drunk, but I was often caught out when I attempted these tricks, and people would refill my glass and ensure that I drank the whole amount.[4] Of course, it is possible to get around these types of pressure, and those more discreet than I do, and they also manipulate the conventions of alcohol drinking, as Catherine Allen's (1988) work on Andean Peru shows. But just like the experience of community described in the previous chapter, the conviviality of alcohol consumption has a "compulsory quality," as Jane Cowan (1990) puts it for northern Greece. And this is not just for men. In Bolivia, drinking and getting drunk is the preserve of both men and women, although women are expected to be more self-controlled than men. Often it is women and children who suffer from the effects of excessive alcohol consumption by men, in terms of domestic violence and the loss of hard-earned cash (Harvey 1994a, 1994b; Harris 2000a [1978]), but this certainly does not stop women from consuming impressive amounts themselves.

The centrality of alcohol in fiesta celebrations is symbolized by the fact that the pasantes dance at the front of a comparsa with their jugs of trago in hand, even if they have hired a waiter to do the actual serving for them. Provision of alcohol is one of the biggest expenditures a pasante has to cover, even though dancers will also buy one or two crates of beer, for themselves, the pasantes, or the band; but during the rehearsals, pasantes need to circulate with tragos for the dancers. Alcohol is also linked with ritual obligations in rural areas (Carter and Mamani P. 1989 [1982]; Buechler 1980; Abercrombie 1998); when we danced in Quilloma, the village authorities made a point of circulating among the dancers to offer us tragos, notoriously stronger than tragos made in the city. During the fiesta, alcohol consumption helps create a sense of commonality of actions and experiences. The reciprocal arrangements around buying beer or liquor confirm friendships and demonstrate generosity to fellow members of the community. Alcohol also regularly leads to the expression of disputes, often fights between vecinos and kinspeople. For all these reasons, alcohol is central to the fiesta: lubricated by alcohol, the collectivity of people dancing and watching becomes a community.

Alcohol and Religiosity as a Model of Power Relations: The Ch'alla and the Misa/ Mesa   Alcohol is not only central to the communality of the fiesta, but also forms relationships between kin and between humans and the supernatural. The provision and acceptance of alcohol makes people (and spirits) participants in very powerful gifting relationships based upon commensality. While alcohol has the power to provoke a sense of obligation in the receiving party, this is neither a straightforwardly reciprocal arrangement as envisaged in much Andean ethnography, nor is it based upon rights and responsibilities as in liberal and communitarian citizenship theory. In the Andes, alcohol consumption both oils conviviality and has a heightened significance because of spiritual and religious associations. Carter and Mamani (1989 [1982]: 320) consider alcohol to be even more sacred than coca for the Aymara peasants of Irpa Chico because, while coca can be consumed in individual and secular instances, alcohol "is reserved only for social occasions, and generally for occasions which have to do directly with the sacred." This is not entirely the case in Rosas Pampa, unless watching the Saturday football matches can be considered a sacred experience. But alcohol consumption in the zone is certainly a very social act, governed by formal conventions, as discussed earlier. Drink is shared not only with fellow vecinos, but also with Pachamama, emphasizing and reinforcing the link between person and land (or zone, or pueblo).

Alcoholic drink is a sort of payment. This is the case not only for fiestas: when making a special request of someone, you nearly always have to take drink, usually beer.[5] When my neighbors were asked to be *padrinos de matrimonio* (marriage godparents) for a relative, the mother and future godson came around with a basket of fruit and a couple of crates of beer. The evening turned into a long drinking session, the fruit remaining untouched until the following day. Doña Emiliana was not happy about the potential expenditure of being a godmother, but she had been put in a position where she could not refuse.[6] In the Andes, alcohol is like coca in the power it has to mediate reciprocity in all kinds of relations, not only between kin but also between people and the spirits. Special ritual occasions, like the *Irpaqa, rutuchas,* and offerings to Pachamama and the *achachilas* (spirits) are always accompanied by drink, not just because they are special, but also because they have to do with expected reciprocity: you are making a request of the achachilas, Pachamama, the padrinos, the woman's family.[7] The model for such relationships is feeding, which is made evident in the way people talk about the ch'alla. When people ch'alla by dropping alcohol onto the ground, they are feeding Pachamama as well as including her in the convivial circle. Sometimes this is done to request specific things from her. For example, my family's clay oven had been taking a very long time to cook things, so they ch'alla'd to Pachamama (as manifested in their courtyard and the oven, made of the same substance) with alcohol, asking that it work better. Their request was answered, although the repair may have occurred because they prevented the children from urinating on the ground near the oven while it was cooking. Allen (1988) argues that ch'allas are about the ways objects are imbued with life force, and food and drink need to be shared with them. There are also more ceremonial ways of ch'allaing. Each year at Carnival time, people put up streamers, balloons, and flags to decorate, and spray their houses, cars, and offices with beer in order to ch'alla them, for luck and success over the next year (see figure 13).[8] At the festival of Alasitas in January, when people buy miniature versions of things they want for the next year, the yatiri (ritual specialist) conducts a ceremony that involves burning incense, chanting incantations, and, finally, dropping alcohol over the object.[9]

In August, specific offerings to Pachamama for luck and well-being over the next year involve spraying neat alcohol on fires and at different parts of the house and yard, especially at the entrance and exit points, as a ch'alla. At that time of the year, the harvest is over and the earth is still open and particularly hungry (Fernandez Juarez 1995; Carter and Mamani P. 1989 [1982]; Abercrombie 1998). When I asked what was going on, the yatiri in charge explained to me, "It's so that she [Pachamama] can eat too. We don't sleep in the street do we? We sleep in a house." Another participant elaborated, telling me that it was the same as if she did not give me food one time, I might complain and not give anything back to her. The house is the same: "With trust I give to the house. I have to attend to her well, and if I do, she might collaborate with me." If my friend forgets to "attend to her," she may fall when she enters the compound and her desires will not come true. However, because she pays with "trust, warmth, and emotion" (confianza, cariño, y emoción), so far, in her current house, almost everything she has wished for has happened, and there is still time for the rest to come true. If we feed Pachamama well she will give luck. The August ritual is an offering to the house, and to Pachamama within it: Pachamama can be at the same time Mother Earth more generally and the earth within the particular household, explained to me as both a Virgen and a Virgencita (Virgin and Little Virgin).[10]

The specific Spanish word for such rituals is either mesa (table) or misa (Mass). They get mixed up in part because Aymara does not distinguish between the e and i sounds, usually vocalizing i as in "fist" unless it comes after the consonant q or x, at which point it sounds more like the Spanish e as in "end." But of course there is more going on, as the misa/mesa is an offering to the deities in much the same way as the Catholic Mass is. The "table" translation also underlines the fact that what is being offered to the deities is food (Fernandez Juarez 1995). Misas/mesas are conducted not only in August, but on any number of occasions: to ask for luck, a safe journey, or a job or to protect oneself against sorcery, for example. Tuesdays and Fridays are reserved for black masses, which aim to hurt someone.[11] When ch'allaing and placing sugar objects, wool, and incense onto the paper altar, yatiris and ordinary people appeal for health, luck, or wealth to achachilas, saints, Jesus, and God. Abercrombie (1998) argues that the ch'alla is a poetic form, a pathway that names the social universe of

13. Ch'alla of the author's
room for Carnival

14. An August misa/mesa
for Pachamama

those participating. Through the ch'alla the K'ulta people, an Aymara-speaking group who live near Oruro, organize space concentrically, libating intimate spirits first and progressing outward to more distant deities. The ancestors and deities form part of the social universe, and sharing alcohol with them through the ch'alla is "a significant medium of organized social interaction" (346). Moreover, it is an extension to supernatural beings of the obligations of reciprocity that mediate human relationships. The ancestors, deities, and human beings are all "co-participants in a gifting relationship" (349).

That gifting relationship is not necessarily one of reliable, direct, and commensurate return implied by the notion of reciprocity as it is often understood in Andean anthropology (Mayer 2002b).[12] An obligation to return the gift (Mauss 1999 [1950]) is not automatically a feature of the gift of food during the misa/mesa and the ch'alla. I was often told that ch'allas are asking Pachamama (or the achachilas) for luck (suerte). The libation sequences documented by Abercrombie (1998) always end with an appeal to luck, which was also absolutely central to my experiences of ch'allas and Aymara rituals. Luck is important because the spirits may not respond as they should; they can be capricious, and they might not reciprocate. Gerardo Fernandez Juarez (1995) argues that luck is a particularly important aspect of household ritual activities in the city, a place which requires more of an orientation toward luck in order to accumulate money and success, whereas in the countryside ch'allas and other rituals are aimed at seeking to control the generative processes of the surrounding environment (see also Abercrombie 1998; Sallnow 1987; Harvey 1996). The contrast between country and city may not in fact be quite so stark, as the generative processes in the rural environment are also highly capricious and the spirits there need frequent feeding in order to persuade them to reciprocate.

Feeding involves something more than an expectation of direct return. Olivia Harris (1982) has argued that there are kinds of exchange relationships in the rural Andes that are based more on commensality than reciprocity. While some forms of labor exchange such as *ayni* are directly reciprocal, other forms rely upon the power that eating together has to underline and institute mutual obligation, between both kin and nonkin. Force-feeding is a particularly important aspect of Andean ritual and "opens up" the participants in the commensal relationship to each other; Penelope Harvey (1996) argues that in the Cusco region of southern Peru, feeding relationships can be both one-way (between kin) and two-way (between nonkin). The latter require some sort of return, but in both, "feeding was generally understood to open up the possibility of co-substantiality and was thus a way of making powerful connections with others" (92). Feeding relationships involve power and obligation in combinations rather more complex than a limited notion of reciprocity enables us to explain. Importantly, the participants are defined through those relationships, a point to which I shall return later.

Another important element is faith. Whether Pachamama, God, or the saints would respond—and whether good or bad things happening was directly their fault—is uncertain. However, it is important to believe, and I was told by a yatiri that if you believe they will always give what they can. She told me that you always have to do the Masses "in God's name" (con su nombre del Señor) and ask the achachilas and pachamamas (i.e., the particular instances of the Pachamama) for luck. When I was part of a misa/mesa to ask for a safe return to England, I knelt by the fire where the offering was being burned to pray and watch the request going up to God. The interplay between God, Jesus, the saints, Pachamama, and the achachilas was confusing to me at the time, particularly when I was told that Pachamama was another Virgin.[13] However, I think this can be explained in two ways. First, the yatiris were engaging in cultural translation for me, that is, explaining things in what they considered to be my terms. Second, although the deities are located in different places—the earth, the sky, or mountains—and some are more effective than others, they are in essence similar beings.

Different people have different achachilas that they appeal to in misas/mesas, with some, like the mountain peaks Mururata, Illimani, and Huayna Potosi, being commonly worshipped. But people also appeal to achachilas near their pueblos and to saints such as Tata Santiago and virgins such as Mama Copacabana (the Virgin of Copacabana) and Mama Remedios.[14] In explanations to me, the distinctions between saints and achachilas were rather blurred, but they were often all subsumed under the heading of Catholicism. Once, my family was discussing the August offering, and the very Catholic daughter said that she didn't believe in such things. Her mother turned to her and said, "Well, why do you go to church then, if you don't believe?" For her, they are all one, and God is simply "bigger than the achachilas."

A final element in the relationship between spirits and humans is sacrifice. Thomas Abercrombie (1998) has pointed out the centrality of the llama sacrifice to the ch'alla sequence and to rural fiestas, where llamas and human beings become equivalent and the sacrifice of the llama substitutes for a sacrifice of humans.[15] He considers the extreme level of intoxication during fiestas to be another offering of the body. Llama fat is a central part of Aymara Masses, and a llama fetus integral to the August feeding of Pachamama, so in some sense they are also human sacrifices. Fears about spirits eating people, for example the infamous Kharisiri who sucks blood or fat from humans or Pachamama eating people who have accidents, combine with this logic of sacrifice to create an understanding of deities that are, or can be, "cannibalistic" (Fernandez Juarez 1995).[16]

Fernandez Juarez's use of this term is particularly instructive, because it brings into the open the nature of people's relationships with the spirits and thereby their locality. The spirits are inherent in physical aspects of the locality: people explained the achachilas to me as the mountain peaks themselves. The important point is that they are not distant or removed, nor are they inanimate; they are immanent, in the sense of "indwelling, or inherent" in specific physical incarnations.[17] The relationships between yatiris and achachilas are personal, but also professional. One person I knew was wondering whether to become a more professional yatiri and provide her services outside of her immediate circle of family and friends. One time we were discussing with her mentor the need for yatiris to "marry" an achachila so that they can practice their profession, and I asked whether male yatiris could marry male achachilas. I was told that they could, because the important thing with achachilas is that they are like lawyers, who will take on a case from a man or a woman. Tristan Platt (1997: 223) has also noted the importance of legal language and ideas for providing a "literate framework within which the oral procedures of the [ritual] are inscribed." However, although most yatiris are male, some people felt that since Pachamama is female, she would receive female yatiris better, and they were more likely to be successful.

Returning to Abercrombie's point, the spirits are social beings, with social characteristics such as capriciousness and favoritism, organized in a web of relationships with humans. That web of relationships is mediated by alcohol consumption, which connects conviviality with the sacred in a form of sociality much influenced by that of the campo. I started my discussion of this with the fiesta because it is the most intense experience of this model of sociality, but I have also aimed to show that the fiesta is only one example among many.

This section examines a contrasting model of the relationship between humans and the supernatural which is promoted, with considerable effort, in an almost directly oppositional religious sphere—that of the growing Protestant churches. I explore it in order to demonstrate the competing models of personhood which the vecinos of Rosas Pampa reconcile in their everyday lives and to demonstrate that the sense of community fostered by them differs profoundly from that expressed in the ritual practices of colonial Catholicism. Numerous scholars have noted the rapid growth of Protestant churches (usually Pentecostal) in Latin America since the 1960s (Stoll 1990; Martin 1990; Bastian 1992; Garrard-Burnett and Stoll 1993; Lehmann 1999). The more general surveys focus on Chile, Brazil, and Central America as the centers of this development, and Bolivia has usually been seen as something of a latecomer to the new religions (Martin 1990). However, the Evangelical movement in Bolivia has grown considerably in recent years. In 1960, about 1 percent of the Bolivian population was Evangelical (Bastian 1992). By the time of the 1992 census, this figure had grown to approximately 10 percent (Canessa 2000), and by 2001, the Bolivian media was reporting a figure of about 25 percent, although the census did not ask about religious affiliation. Pentecostalism and Evangelicalism are taken here to mean more or less the same thing. The elements of Pentecostalism that distinguish it from earlier forms of Protestantism, such as the Methodists and Baptists, are a focus on the Holy Spirit and spirit possession (often accompanied by speaking in tongues or faith healing) by the Holy Spirit, as well as a generally effervescent form of religiosity. Evangelical is the term most often used, or *hermano/a*, by Bolivians themselves, so I use this terminology. Sometimes the Evangelicals call themselves Christian.[18]

My survey of Rosas Pampa showed that about 23 percent of the vecinos were hermanos. Given that Evangelicals attend church more conscientiously than Catholics, a significant proportion of religiously active people in Bolivia are Evangelical. My census showed that 28 percent of Catholic households went to the local church, which would make churchgoing Catholics about 21 percent of the total population and the proportions of Catholics to Evangelicals roughly equal among those people who attend church.[19] Some Catholics said that they went to churches in other zones. Given that this survey was conducted by members of the local Catholic youth group, the figures for Catholic attendance at church were almost certainly inflated, and this would accord with my personal observations of church congregations, the majority of which were children and one or two elderly people, except for the Masses celebrated in honor of the fiesta. Furthermore, Evangelicals attend *cultos*, or services, once or twice a week, whereas Catholics will generally attend for more infrequent occasions, such as the fiesta, a baptism, or a marriage.

Evangelicalism and Community: Relating to Other People   Community maintenance is an explicit theme of Evangelical cultos and of the scholarly literature on Evangelicalism. Certainly, community maintenance was a central part of most of the cultos I attended in Rosas Pampa, run by the Misión Evangelica de Bolivia, a branch of the Evangelical Methodists of Indianapolis, Indiana. In the United States, they have 130 churches and about ten thousand members. In Bolivia, they had about fifteen hundred members in 2000, making them one of the smaller Evangelical groups (*sectas*) in the country.[20] The group would welcome new people, discuss upcoming events, celebrate birthdays, and organize visits to sick hermanos. I was welcomed effusively, and on two occasions went up to the microphone at the front to explain why I was there. People came up to me one by one and welcomed me in, calling me hermana, despite the fact that I had made it clear that I did not intend to be converted. They never entirely gave up hope, wanting me to "take the *Evangelio* to England," but they were happy to include me and ask me questions about England and about religion in England. The practice of calling members hermano/a makes for a strong sense of togetherness, cementing membership right from the first meeting. In Rosas Pampa, the way you *saludar* (greet) people is extremely important: many a dispute between neighbors comes out in the open when people do not greet each other on the street, and it is considered very important that children learn to greet adults they know politely; it is a sign of good manners. Altiplano Bolivians are in general initially reserved with strangers, and people do not usually use informal forms of address when they first meet. So the familiarity of *hermana* as a greeting is immediately noticeable, and the warmth quite unusual. Calling fellow Evangelicals brother and sister is by no means peculiar to Bolivia, but in the context of El Alto it has a particular resonance.

Scholars of Latin American Evangelicalism tend to agree on the strength of community developed by Evangelicals, arguing that people in a state of insecurity and lacking family connections in the city seek to replace their rural ties of community and family with another kind of belonging (e.g.,

Ströbele-Gregor 1992; Goodman 1988; Martin 1990). The rural category of compadrazgo is replaced with hermano/a, and a supportive, tight-knit community ensues. Migrants can draw on networks of hermanos in the city for economic support, just as they draw on solidarity networks based upon kinship or provenance from a particular pueblo (Long 1984). Women, and in particular single women (Gill 1990) alone in the city, look to the community of hermanos for emotional support and friendship. However, the hermanos that I knew did not conform to the rather needy image painted in much of the literature, of poor migrants at sea in the currents of uncontrollable social change and cut loose from personal ties as a result of the move to the city.[21] They were adults who had made decisions that they found fulfilling and were very proud of the fact that they had developed a strong sense of community within the church.

Their sense of community was localized to the members of the church, but hermanos also felt a sense of belonging to a wider Evangelical community; the celebration of the first anniversary of the founding of the Rosas Pampa group included members of the same sect from different zones in El Alto, and the services in the Tent of the Holy Spirit (discussed below) attracted hermanos from all over El Alto. Conscious work to develop identification at a level beyond peoples' immediate place of residence, the zone, has been a recognized part of missionary strategy in Latin America for some time now (e.g., see Greenway 1973). In some ways, consciousness of being alteño is more marked in Evangelicals than in others, who more often see themselves as either Bolivians or paceños from the Department of La Paz, or vecinos of Rosas Pampa. So, although the Evangelicals are promoting a mediated form of citizenship, they are creating a different set of mediations from the nested affiliations described in the previous chapter. These mediations map differently onto the same geographic space and consist of, broadly, membership in a church, then membership of that church in El Alto, then Bolivia, then the relationship between that church and its "father," usually in the United States. At all levels, a contrast is drawn between those who are Evangelical, regardless of specific church affiliation, and those who are not.

However, the Evangelical community in Rosas Pampa is not simply an alternative community; it is an antagonistic version that runs on its own rules and attempts to grow at the expense of the Catholic and syncretic community. Although the experience is a very positive one for individual hermanos, the Evangelical community constructs itself and is constructed by others negatively, by concentrating on what it does not do. Even for many members, one of the principal benefits of being an Evangelical is that they or their husbands no longer drink alcohol. Given the role of the fiesta in asserting community togetherness and the importance of alcohol in mediating sociality, Evangelical prohibitions on drinking alcohol, dancing during fiestas, watching the dancing, and conducting misas/mesas show the extent to which the Evangelical churches are attempting to induce profound cultural change. In Rosas Pampa, friends who came up from La Paz to watch us dance in the Entrada told us later that when the dancers had gone for the social gathering in the Catholic church, an Evangelical group began telling people through loudspeakers that they should go to their houses and not stay out on the streets drinking. The growth of Evangelicalism has provoked some tensions and unease in Rosas Pampa. Many Catholics thought that Evangelicals considered themselves to be superior, not least because they repeatedly and publicly proclaim their belief that they have a superior (or the only) route to salvation. One friend asked me whether I thought the Evangelicals had it right about the Second Coming and the need to be an Evangelical to be saved. Other people feel disapproved of in the presence of Evangelical discipline and sobriety, and they are not being paranoid in this. However, people also roundly disputed the superiority of Evangelicals through comments, for example, about how the hermanas are especially haughty, gossipy, and malicious.

The Evangelical "projects of community" are not entirely successful either, and people's membership in any Evangelical community is neither absolute nor consistent. Nor do Evangelicals necessarily withdraw from other aspects of the collective life of their zone or families. Thirteen percent of Rosas Pampa households consisted of both Evangelicals and Catholics, and extended families often split between the two religions. Doña Emiliana's family is a case in point. One sister and brother-in-law were Evangelical, along with their daughter, but their two sons had remained Catholic. Another sister and her daughter (Doña Josefa and Victoria) had been hermanas for a while but had left a couple of years previously. A third sister and her husband remained Catholic. The Evangelical brother-in-law was still padrino to his niece Victoria, and therefore compadre to Doña Josefa. When his (Catholic) son, Rubén, acted as pasante for the Quilloma fiesta, there was some concern within the family that he would disapprove. In the end, though, he was highly supportive and proud of Rubén, coming along to rehearsals and helping with the organization. He did not drink alcohol until the last day of the fiesta, when he could presumably resist no longer and succumbed tearfully to inebriation. He continued to be an Evangelical, though.

People slip in and out of Evangelicalism, thus undermining its project of community building. The Catholic catechist Don Roberto told me that Evangelicals will get their children baptized in their churches but go to another zone to get a Catholic baptism "because they still want a party," then they return to their culto to weep and beg forgiveness for sinning. Although the fluid nature of Evangelical groupings is recognized in the literature (Green 1993; Martin 1990; Stoll 1990), I would argue that it is one of the more important characteristics of the move to Evangelicalism, in Bolivia at least, and underresearched. Lesley Gill (1993) describes people trying out different Evangelical sects before settling on the one they enjoy, but in general, mention of lapsing is remarkably thin on the ground. The churches themselves have very effective ways of dealing with lapses. At one of the last cultos I attended, a hermano got up to beg forgiveness from God and the congregation for sinning and for not attending the church for a while. He had been visited by some hermanos previously, and they had persuaded him to return, following the pastors' exhortations that if a hermano falls, the others should visit his house and bring him back. His long tearful speech told of how God had appeared to him to make him come back, and his participation during the service was fervent. He had been brought back into the community at least temporarily.

Evangelicalism and Individuals: Working on the Embodied Self   A discussion of lapsing moves us from Evangelicalism as a project of community to Evangelicalism as a project of the self, highlighting the hard work involved in such projects. Lapsing is particularly important because it shows the side of Evangelicalism that is characterized by discipline and regulation, contrasting with that side of the congregation which welcomes new people warmly, greets members effusively, and celebrates each hermano's birthday. Various prohibitions are part of this authoritarian character. Being a hermano involves following a very strict set of instructions. As one Catholic schoolgirl said to me, "If you're an Evangelical, everything you do is a sin." Her comments were echoed by a number of people who felt that it was simply too difficult to be a proper Evangelical. It is impossible to live up to the behavior expected of you, which I suspect is part of the point: there is always a deficit for which to beg forgiveness. This appeals to two sides that people have: a side that likes the drama, even the melodrama, of begging forgiveness and a side that wants to be told clearly what to do.

The Catholic Church, at least in Rosas Pampa, does not satisfy these aspects of people's characters to the same extent. The priest's sermons at the Masses I attended told people how they ought to behave but presented these instructions almost as options, as though people needed to be persuaded through rational argument to adhere to them. Ultimately, the responsibility for compliance rests with each individual; I never heard of Catholics going to a fellow congregation member's house to persuade him or her to come back to Mass. Although being an Evangelical requires a great deal of willpower, membership in an Evangelical community is strangely passive in that it requires little independent judgment.

The paradox is that this is contradicted by a philosophy of a more active relationship with God and the Holy Spirit and involvement in religious worship, unmediated by a priest.[22] But this is deceptive. Another characteristic of the Evangelical services I attended was a strong educational element, for example, when the American missionary conducted a course entitled "The Basics of Christian Life." He attempted to ask open questions where the correct answer was not immediately obvious and even to lead them to the wrong answer so he could tell the congregation where they had gone wrong. The responses he got left me feeling that people wanted to be told what to do and what to think; their study of the Bible was for them like studying an instruction book for life. They appeared to feel that those with more education than they needed to tell them how to interpret this instruction book. This accords with the structure of Evangelical churches noted in 1969 by Christian Lalive d'Epinay, who found that the Chilean churches reproduced the authoritarian patron–serf structure of the hacienda.

What is important about the form that Evangelicalism takes in El Alto is that the authoritarianism is focused upon individual bodies. Hermanos are not supposed to drink alcohol or to smoke, nor should they dance in fiestas, or take part in misas/mesas to Pachamama or the achachilas, or have pictures of saints or virgins in their houses. The characteristic that defines hermanos for the vast majority of people is not drinking alcohol, and for many, this is a major reason for joining. One friend of mine was thinking of going back to an Evangelical church; she had been an hermana when single. She told me that she'd stopped because her husband drank, but she did not want her children to grow up wanting to drink like their father. She thought that once they had fulfilled the ayni of beer bought for their wedding she would try to persuade him to join, "because sometimes life goes badly, doesn't it?" Some men are unwilling to join precisely because it means they will not be able to drink alcohol, according to their wives. However, the content of the services that I attended did not include express prohibitions on drinking alcohol or dancing, which I found quite surprising.

The "techniques of the self" (Foucault 1990 [1984]) promoted by the churches do not therefore function in an explicit way. It is more likely that hermanos tell stories to each other about, for example, their heroic struggle with smoking and how God helped them to give it up, as I experienced from one preacher. Perhaps the prohibitions are so well known and the desire for help with self-regulation so often the reason for joining a sect that it is not necessary to prohibit alcohol consumption explicitly during cultos. The argument that alcohol consumption is bad has usually been won before people choose to become hermanos. The cultos themselves focused much more on preparing the self/body for when Jesus returns, like a thief in the night. The emphasis was on creating a personal relationship with Jesus, opening your heart to Him, and cleansing your body of sin in preparation for His coming, largely through begging Him for forgiveness. That personal relationship is hierarchical, framed in a rhetoric of love and also punishment, a fatherhood that is quite different from the relationships that people develop with achachilas or Catholic saints. Worship of Jesus through praying and singing with conviction, along with study of the Bible, were the main religious activities, according to the rhetoric of the services. The Devil is sin and the Holy Spirit the guide, but the appropriate way of behaving was not explicitly elaborated during these particular services.

However, the American missionary did stress the importance of characteristics such as not arguing, not gossiping, not being selfish or envious. At the climax of the services, the group exhorts the Devil, along with various undesirable qualities such as laziness and failure, to "leave now" (sal ahora). So people know the kinds of selves they need to construct, and they attempt to do this through their prayers to Jesus. The church responds to the desires of the congregation for instruction, but its form of enforcement is a mixture of group and individual self-regulation in a Foucauldian sense. The regulation functions through the impossibility of ever living up to the image of the good, proper, or pure person: the essential sinfulness of human beings, for which they repeatedly need to beg forgiveness. This is obviously a central part of the Judeo-Christian tradition, but its repetition within Evangelical churches is just astounding, as is the force with which people are repeatedly told that they do not match up.

Yet it seems to work for many people. One area in which the discipline is much appreciated is gender roles and family life. All over Latin America, women have been the first to decide to join Protestant sects, bringing their husbands in later (Martin 1990; Stoll 1990). This has been attributed by some to the kinds of gender roles encouraged by the Evangelicals (Gill 1990; Brusco 1993). Men are encouraged to take a more active role in family and household life. The prohibition on drinking means they have to behave themselves better than usual, and their wives can feel less vulnerable to domestic violence precipitated by alcohol. The people I spoke with backed this up; one woman delightedly said, "It's a joy to go along this road, because before my husband drank a lot, and we fought [*pelea-bamos*].[23] Now we're fine, there's no argument." A male congregation member said that he used to drink and fight with his wife, but now he thinks of his family and is much happier; his children no longer suffer from his drinking either. His wife said that he had become more home-loving (*más hogareño*). In the words of those who had made the decision to become hermanas there is a very clear *antes* (before) which has to do with drinking alcohol: "Before, my husband drank really badly" (*Antes, mi esposo grave tomaba*). Now they feel much better. Whether this means that they have more money to spend on the household or not, the refocusing of their husband's attention on the family was very important to them (cf. Brusco 1993).

This hints at an important contrast with the more communal version of sociality expressed in the popular religiosity of the fiesta and the ch'alla. Evangelicals' relationship with the spirits is dyadic: between the individual and Jesus. Although not a bounded view of the self, because the self is permeable to the Holy Spirit, the emphasis upon the private, personal individual contrasts with the view of the self as an unequal participant in a web of social relationships that includes the supernatural beings described earlier. This is evident in conversion stories. Most hermanos I spoke with initially stressed their individual revelation, how Jesus had come into their lives and shown them the true path, despite the fact that it was often also the case that their insertion into social networks had an important role in bringing them to the church; with a little probing it was usually possible to identify a sister-in-law, cousin, or parent who had been important in their conversion. Wives almost always are instrumental in converting their husbands; most women in the group had either succeeded or were still trying. Conversely, I never met a married hermano whose wife was still Catholic.

Effervescence and Worship   The focus on the personal as a source of religious experience is brought to the fore in an examination of forms of worship in Evangelical churches, which is often ignored in the literature in favor of sociological data. The intensely embodied nature of the Evangelical experience is no better observed than during the services themselves. Evangelical services can be quite disturbing for observers, or at least they were for me. One fortnight, just before I left Rosas Pampa, the Tent of the Holy Spirit (Carpa del Espiritu Santo) arrived in the zone. They held nightly services attended by people from all over El Alto, so I went along one night. The Evangelical church that runs this tent is from Villa Dolores and occasionally runs these kinds of campaigns, according to them in order to rescue people from alcoholism, drug addiction, and gangs. Although the tent was only half full, I would estimate that there were more than three hundred people present, packed in close to the stage. The preacher on the stage told stories in Spanish and Aymara using Bolivian examples, and every so often a group of singers would start to sing hymns of praise, and the audience would join in. When the preacher had given his main sermon, he began to pray, accompanied first by the singers, then keyboard music, then drums. The praying gradually built in intensity and volume, to the point where the singers took turns to scream into their microphones, which were set at pop-concert decibel levels, exhorting the Devil to "sal ahora, sal ahora" in dramatic, emotive voices. The audience joined in, exhorting laziness, problems, hatred, addiction, prostitution, abortion, debt, failure, witchcraft, all to "sal ahora." It was loud, fast, and repetitive, the volume working on the physical body as well as the emotions.

Then they shifted, after a short pause, to exhorting the Holy Spirit to enter, calling on those present to receive the Holy Spirit in order to be healed. Several women at this point shook all over as though possessed and collapsed on the floor. Members of the church went through the audience to pick out these women and accompany them to the front stage, where they met the preacher. They were lined up on the stage and the preacher got each individual to tell the audience what had happened to her: they felt the Holy Spirit, they had been cured of chronic stomach pain, and so on. After they had given their testimony, he rubbed his hands together and placed one near to their foreheads, not touching, at which point each one stiffly keeled over backward and fell with a thud to the floor. They then got up and walked off. It was astounding to watch.[24] The Tent of the Holy Spirit was clearly an intense bodily experience for all present, who were living devotion and faith through the body in a manner comparable to the experience of fiesta dancing. For me, both experiences were extreme, yet both are quite normal for many alteños.

The effervescence I witnessed in the Tent of the Holy Spirit had an unpleasant and frightening overtone for me. It is hard to avoid the feeling that many Evangelical churches are seeking to take advantage of people when they are vulnerable and suggestible.[25] Although I would not attempt to provide a purely physiological rationale for conversion and religious experience, the role of illness and emotional crisis in a number of people's conversion stories may indicate a certain amount of emotional vulnerability for some at the point of conversion, although it is also the case that conversion stories can be narrated only in terms of extreme crisis. One hermano told me that he had promised to go to the Evangelical church when his father died, but he hadn't—until his mother became paralyzed and the power of prayer had healed her again. An hermana had wanted to become Evangelical but could not persuade her husband until he fell ill. William Sargant (1973) argues that in dissociative states, people are extremely suggestible. He claims that Evangelical pastors manipulate this state of suggestibility, which results from extreme emotional trauma provoked during the service, through frightening sermons, dance, music, and repetitive rhythms. In his opinion, susceptibility to the emotional trauma of the service may be connected to illness or emotional crisis.

Of course, the Evangelicals' explanation is far more benign: they say that they are seeking to help people suffering from trauma and bring them to the gospel. On a more general level, it is possible to argue that there are groups of people in Latin America who may be vulnerable because of the structurally violent effects of poverty, and Evangelical missionaries certainly target them: "Certain sectors of the city population can be discipled and churches planted in greater number during the present period of rapid urbanization" (Greenway 1973: 12). It is in this sense that the sociological explanations for the growth of Evangelicalism work, with their emphasis on the ways the religion helps its adherents, particularly migrants from the countryside, to cope with rapid social change and economic hardship (Martin 1990; Ströbele-Gregor 1992; Annis 1994). On the other hand, these explanations can only go so far: the majority of people cope—and even do well—without the aid of Evangelicalism, and there are Evangelicals at all strata of Bolivian society.

The Evangelical mission on my street ran their twice-weekly services

15. The Tent of the Holy Spirit, visiting Rosas Pampa

along similar lines as the Tent of the Holy Spirit, although on a much smaller scale. Worshippers would arrive, greet those already there, and sit down, ready to begin singing the hymns of praise, shouting, dancing, and clapping where appropriate. Services were led by members of the family who own the building in which the mission is based, as well as ordinary members of the congregation. After singing a few hymns we would sit down to hear the sermon. Both the sermons and hymns were accompanied by shouts by the leader or preacher, to which there are set replies from the congregation. There are many of these, such as when the leader or preacher says "To His name!" and the congregation replies "Glory!"; then the leader might say "To His glory!" to which the response is "More glory!" Sometimes the leader asks for "a war cry," at which point the congregation will whoop. Once, the owner of the building gave a sermon, but it was more often an experienced preacher from another group of the same association in El Alto, or the American missionary who ran the Bolivian arm of this mission. The sermons usually led into a collective prayer, during which women would approach the front stage and the preacher, and kneel down and beg Jesus for forgiveness for their sins, crying and wailing. It is at this point that the Holy Spirit comes to visit or possess the devotees. The prayers also included exhortations to the Devil, laziness, and failure to "sal ahora," along the same lines as in the Tent of the Holy Spirit, only with fewer people and therefore less sound.

Instead of the intense experience of crying because of drunkenness during the fiesta, the tears, indeed wails, of a truly good Evangelical come twice a week from devotion, the power of prayer, the emotion of begging Jesus to forgive him or her. Dancing, singing, rhythm, and emotion are not confined to social events or the annual fiesta, but are part and parcel of biweekly worship sessions. The millennial stress during the service on the imminent return of Christ heightens the experience. Whatever the reasons for their initial experiences of the Holy Spirit, the women in particular enjoy the catharsis of the tearful prayer each week and *feel* the presence of the Holy Spirit while they pray. Felicitas Goodman (1988) argues that Pentecostalism results from a conflict inherent in Christianity from its very inception. The story of doubting Thomas (John 20:29) highlights the tension between the need to experience God, to see, and the imperative for faith without seeing: Jesus says, "Thomas, because thou hast seen me, thou hast believed: blessed are they that have not seen, and yet have believed." Pentecostalism responds to the very human need for ecstatic *experience* of God and religion (63).

As with the fiesta, it is the immediate experience and emotion inherent in performing devotion that make it real. And that experience is felt *internally* in the individual body. Hermanos, their pastors, and their God combine to work on the bodies of the worshippers. The body is the site for struggles within the self between sin and purity, sickness and health, salvation and condemnation. It is also where the Holy Spirit enters. Although Evangelical religion is a collective endeavor, the ecstatic experience is very individual. The Spirit infuses the body. The self is bounded, but permeable to the workings of the Holy Spirit. The individual, private experience creates the individual as ontologically prior to the collectivity.

HYBRIDITY, HYPOCRISY, AND THE SELF

Andrew Canessa (2000) makes a similar point when he argues that the Evangelicals are especially enthusiastic in their embrace of "Western-oriented" modernity. He maintains that Evangelicals come out of groups of people "at the forefront of modernization" who are rejecting identifications based upon "relative and shifting categories" (120) and opting for more essentialized forms, rejecting paganism.[26] The Evangelical explosion has led to non-Evangelicals questioning their own religious beliefs. Some are worried that the Evangelicals might indeed have the right God—they might be right about Jesus coming again, and where would that leave those who are not Evangelical? Don Víctor once said that he was worried about what the Evangelicals told him, but that he'd been Catholic all his life, so it would not be right to change. Others have decided that Evangelicals and Catholics pray to the same God, and there's only one for everyone, just different ways of being close to Him. The problem is that the traditional Andean response, which would be syncretism, or hedging one's bets,[27] is not easily assimilable to the rhetoric of the Evangelicals, precisely because of its absolutism.

Nevertheless, Evangelicalism would probably not work if people were not hypocritical in practice, since the deficit for which to beg forgiveness would not exist. Sinning and begging forgiveness from Jesus are absolutely central to Evangelical worship. On the surface, Evangelical churches preach against superstition. Yet I was told by a friend that her yatiri's biggest client was a large Evangelical church that hires him to conduct misas/mesas so that it will gain more income and more converts. Hypocrisy is also one of the characteristics that Catholics ascribe to hermanos, for example when they make comments about the malicious nature of hermanas, their propensity to gossip and comment on others' behavior, or the impossibility of not sinning since everything is a sin, and about how hermanos go to Catholic churches for weddings, baptisms, and other ceremonies. Andrew Canessa (2000) argues that Evangelicals, like Aymara indigenous activists, choose essentialist categories of identity in order to confront or deal with modernity and their own liminal (and low-status) position as rural–urban migrants. While this argument may work in rhetorical terms, in practice, being an Evangelical is perhaps simply a different form of hybrid, "hypocritical" identity. The fluidity of people's relationships with the Evangelical church and the issue of lapsing is the way that hybridity functions.

At the heart of the contemporary religious picture in El Alto is a contest over how deities touch people, a concern which was central to the first wave of evangelizing in the sixteenth and seventeenth centuries (MacCormack 1991). Different religious experiences meet and clash, creating multiple possibilities for people to experience God. This chapter has only examined two in detail, but Catholic revivalism would be equally worthy of attention. Out of the mix comes one of the most peculiarly alteño struggles of today, which is fought on both geographical and bodily terrain. Colonial Catholicism relates directly to place, and the fiesta dancing moves through space to reinforce that, while Evangelical groups make incursions using rooms in people's houses, then sound and PA systems mark their territory as the singing and praying are audible all around the church, or posters go up, pamphlets are distributed, signs advertising video shows appear, and the orange and blue Tent of the Holy Spirit takes up residence for two weeks.

Evangelical identity is so closely associated with what people do with, and put into, their bodies that it demands a quite profound change in its adherents. One might ask whether, if dancing and drinking are so central to communal life and Bolivian identity, the Evangelical movement is de-Bolivianizing cultural identity. Not even Muratorio's (1980) "alienated folkloric consciousness" experienced during the fiesta appears to be available to Evangelicals, who are told that "the madman dances and the idiot watches" (el loco baila y el sonso mira). On the other hand, the use of Aymara in Evangelical sermons and hymns creates and underlines a different kind of ethnic identity, one which paradoxically bypasses the mestizo, Bolivian, nation-building project in favor of an orientation toward the North American father church. There is debate about the role of Evangelicalism in encouraging some forms of indigenous ethnic consciousness. Some authors seem to feel that it is at least in part an example of North American cultural imperialism (Stoll 1990), a position with which I am sympathetic. Others have shown that some people use Evangelicalism to promote and assert their indigenous identity (Muratorio 1980; Rappaport 1984). This is clearly an issue that depends on the context. In the case of Rosas Pampa, any promotion of an Aymara consciousness by Evangelical groups seems to be largely on the American missionaries' terms and focuses people's sense of belonging more on the city of El Alto than on the zone of Rosas Pampa, although it is possible that the encouragement of lay preachers may lead to a future Bolivianization of Evangelicalism, as is happening elsewhere in Latin America (Martin 1990).

However, the overall Evangelical cultural project is likely to be limited in its success precisely because of the hypocrisy or frailty of the hermanos. As one hermana said when she heard that I was going to dance in the fiesta, "Of course we'll come out and watch you, we're going to sin on that day!" People often only partially adhere to Evangelicalism. This is somewhat peculiar, because it would seem to be logically inconsistent to have an absolutist and essentialist approach to identity (such as a concern for what might be the true religion), and at the same time to hold two or more of those identities concurrently or sequentially. Hybridity would seem to be possible only if the identities that exist together are porous, undecided, and shifting. But in El Alto, hybridity can consist of different fundamentalisms or absolutisms. People do not and usually cannot make the choice between the two religious domains in a once-and-for-all way.

The relationships that people have with supernatural beings both model and mediate other power relationships; as such, the forms of sociality and the self promoted by competing religions in Rosas Pampa are central to a discussion of citizenship. Colonial Catholicism presents a model of relating to those in power that incorporates their capriciousness, greed, and particularism, and thus sits uneasily with a universal model of citizenship based upon an abstract set of rights. Furthermore, colonial Catholicism highlights a very real relationship between people and localized notions of places, physical entities in the natural environment, which are active beings. A vision of *unmediated* national citizenship depends upon a sense of imagined community with fellow Bolivians (humans) who are located only in a generalized place, that is, Bolivia, as created on maps and TV, in the census and newspapers (Anderson 1991), and this is undermined by the strong connection with place experienced in popular religiosity.

The model of sociality and the self that is revealed through an investigation of colonial Catholicism as it operates today does not therefore fit with liberal notions of citizenship. Neither is it fully captured by communitarianism, because both assume a model of the individual person as bounded and autonomous, something which is contradicted by the imbrication of humans and spirits implied in the kinds of gifting and feeding relationships described earlier. In contrast, contemporary Evangelicalism's project of the self focuses on the individual. This does not mean, as some have argued, that Evangelicalism promotes individualism; in fact, it places great emphasis on the construction of community. However, the personal and private focus of Evangelical religious experience constitutes the individual worshipper as permeable only to Jesus or the Holy Spirit in a dyadic and unmediated way. Thus, individuals are ontologically prior to the collectivity and bounded and autonomous in relation to other members of their community. This accords with the notions of the person characteristic of both liberal and communitarian citizenship theory, for even though communitarian theorists stress the importance of community, their concept of the self is prior to the collectivity and shaped by it, rather than created in dialectical relation to other selves within that collectivity.

Evangelicalism is on the surface an aggressively modernizing project which condemns colonial Catholicism as superstition and traditional and considers itself supremely true and rational. The Evangelical view of modernity consists of a form of community that is detached from localized place—the Tent of the Holy Spirit can set up anywhere. Its project of the self requires a great deal of work on the bodies of hermanos as they are enjoined to stop drinking and dancing and learn to worship in a very physical way. However, the absolutist rhetoric is blurred in practice. Evangelicalism uses existing networks embedded in place to draw in new recruits and relies upon lapsing (the sin–forgiveness nexus) for its power. People make choices, for example using Evangelicalism to help their husband stop drinking. They draw on the resources provided by apparently conflicting models of the self in variable ways and to different extents throughout their lives. Hybridity and hypocrisy soften the edges even of one of the most absolutist projects of the self operating today.

PART II

This part of the book explores another of the hinges in the mediated relationship between individual citizen and the state in El Alto, namely, trade unions, with a special focus on the Federation of Street Traders (Federación de Trabajadores Gremiales, Artesanos Comerciantes, Minoristas y Vivanderos de la Ciudad de El Alto—La Paz; Federation of Organized Workers, Artisans, Small Traders and Food Sellers of the City of El Alto—La Paz). The dynamic of the chapters inverts that of part 1, beginning with an examination of the subjective processes of the construction of collective selves and moving to political and philosophical discussions of the nature of democracy in Bolivia today. The chapters place my discussion of citizenship practices in the context of the aftermath of the neoliberal assault on collective citizenship based on class that took place during the 1980s and 1990s. Neoliberal hegemony did not, however, result in the replacement of collective politics with individual politics: the late twentieth century saw a flowering of collective identity–based politics, as the growth of the indigenous movement at that time attests. My argument here is that, contrary to expectations, even the "old" class-based forms of collectivity have not disappeared; indeed, the working class in Bolivia is reconstituting itself as a political subject, albeit not in its traditional form.

Trade unions are flourishing in the informal economy of El Alto today and form a crucial part of the structure of civic organization that is parallel to the state and that shapes multitiered citizenship in the city. They do so in a context where economic competition between individuals is painfully exaggerated and where one would therefore expect political collaboration to be difficult, if not downright impossible. In chapter 6, I explore the practices by which unions overcome those tensions and promote a collective sense of self, which in turn enables them to be effective political subjects in their confrontations and negotiations with the state. The collectivity is created through the assertion of particular dominant values, principally of participation and obligation, as well as through embodied practices such as the mediation of conflicts and participation in dances, demonstrations, and civic parades. The ideology of collective identity through participation in political practice, which is promoted through the notion of *vida orgánica* (organizational life), exposes individual-collective tensions within understandings of leadership. As with the place-based organizations discussed in part I, the grass roots membership, or *base*, attempts to assert collective values in the face of leaders' perceived individualism. In practice the assertion of such values is often more about the operation of factional politics than about an opposition between base and leadership. Nonetheless, it reveals the practices and values conceived of as ideal.

Leadership is one of the important themes of these chapters, in part because of its centrality in ethnographies of the Andes more generally and in claims currently being made about the potential reinvigoration of Bolivian democracy based upon popular and indigenous traditions, which I discuss in chapter 8. Leadership is a critical arena for the struggle (or perceived struggle) between collectivism and individualism, identified by Xavier Albó (1977) as the paradox of Aymara solidarity and factionalism. We can see such tensions and dynamics in trade unions in El Alto, as well as in community politics and authority structures in the rural altiplano. In making this argument, I differ from the contemporary scholars who tend to analyze the "trade union form" and "the communitarian form," to use the words of Garcia Linera (2001), as distinct traditions (Garcia Linera et al. 2000, 2001; Gutierrez et al. 2002; Rivera Cusicanqui and Equipo THOA 1992; Rivera Cusicanqui 1990; Albó 1977). In some parts of Bolivia, especially northern Potosí, trade unionism was a (Western, alien) means of exercising power over indigenous communities (Rivera Cusicanqui and Equipo THOA 1992). However, in the northern altiplano, communities tended to appropriate the trade union form in a kind of political syncretism, and I would argue that this was one of the most important sources of Katarismo's vibrancy as a political organization, at least in the 1970s. The MAS has continued that syncretic appropriation of political traditions, drawing on trade unionism, populism, and indigenous democratic values and practices. It is the creative mixing of these different threads that has enabled El Alto to overcome its political marginalization at the national level and take center stage.

Chapter 7 explores these processes as they affect everyday politics and moves from the discussion of subjectivity to analyze citizenship as political agency through a detailed examination of one case. The competition between rival associations of fish-sellers and fishermen illustrates two key aspects of contemporary alteño citizenship: first, the complex relationship between the state and civic organizations like trade unions, and second, the relationship between El Alto and its rural hinterland. Both of these relationships shape the politics of the extraordinary moments of national and even global significance that have been so notable in recent years. Both are difficult and conflictual as well as harmonious and respectful at different times and where different interests are at stake. That ambiguity derives from the liminality of the subjects of these chapters: the trade unionists are both mediator between citizen and state and substitute for the state, and as market traders they connect the rural economy with the national economy. Even their cholo ethnicity is a fluid and "in-between" one (Seligmann 1989). Finally, in a practical sense, El Alto lies in between La Paz and the rest of the country, giving the social movements there considerable political power, as we saw during the blockades of October 2003.

This liminal position therefore is of considerable importance for citizenship in the city and at a national level. However, the unions constantly attempt to counter that liminality and assert their position as separate from the state. In the sphere of everyday politics, this translates into a defense of their right to regulate economic activity without state interference. They make a stark separation at the level of rhetoric between the state (which is equated with party politics) and the civic organizations. This kind of dynamic is a long-standing feature of Bolivian politics, where the trade unions, and lately the social movements more generally, have long maintained an interdependent but oppositional relationship with the state. Laurence Whitehead (2001) contends that the corporatist tradition has been as essential to Bolivian politics as the more liberal, individualist one familiar to Western readers. The latest cycle of upheavals in Bolivia is the contemporary expression of the struggle for legitimacy between the two traditions, where claims about the kinds of democracy that operate within each have become central. Politicians and intellectuals participate in this claim making as well as trade unionists; indeed, the potential revitalization of democracy in Bolivia based upon popular and indigenous traditions is a common theme in contemporary Bolivian political philosophy. For many, Evo Morales's government is an opportunity to translate those ideas into actual political practice. I argue that the popular movements, including the trade unions, are the most important sources of creativity in the imagination of alternatives to liberal Western democracy in Bolivia today. The development of alternative democracies is probably most evident in the practice of the organizations themselves, which are the subject of the final chapter. Here, I discuss in particular the general assembly and the relationship between leaders and the grass roots, both more commonly analyzed in the scholarly literature as expressions of "ayllu democracy," but both just as central to trade unionism. Practices such as these combine with the encouragement of a strong sense of corporate political subjectivity and the organizational structure of the nested affiliation of an alliance of associations, each one with local forms of accountability. They all form the foundation of the social movements' strength in Bolivia and are crucial to the reinvigoration of citizenship and democracy in the country today.

These chapters are principally based on fieldwork conducted between April and September 2003 and a follow-up visit from December 2003 through January 2004. I was privileged to be able to spend a considerable amount of time with the Federation of Street Traders, attending public meetings, demonstrations, and parades as well as more private discussions of the Executive Committee and between them and the mayor of El Alto. I sat in the Federation's central office while members of the Executive Committee attended the constant stream of leaders of individual associations coming to air their complaints. I followed up a number of specific problems and conflicts and also attended association meetings, discussions among the leadership committees, and meetings with state officials. I also had conversations with both the association and the Federation leaders. I formally interviewed most of the most active members of the Federation Executive Committee, sometimes twice, because I wanted to ask them about the events of October 2003 when I returned at the end of that year. At that time I also interviewed some members of the executive committee of the FEJUVE, and I consulted all the available editions of the newspaper *el alteño* for the period of September through mid-October 2003. In mid-2003, I taught a short course in urban sociology at the UPEA, thus getting to know students and staff in the sociology department there, and participating in departmental activities such as a trip to the countryside and a demonstration in favor of autonomy for the university. I also attended several political meetings held in youth and cultural centers in El Alto, some associated with the UPEA while others were organized to discuss political issues arising from the events of February 2003. The very politicized students and other people I met through these two kinds of activities have profoundly informed my analysis of the politics of El Alto beyond the more sectoral concerns of the Federation of Street Traders. While conducting this part of my fieldwork, I also returned to Rosas Pampa to live and to carry out the more ephemeral kind of participant observation that happens during basic conviviality, informal conversations with friends, journeys home after meetings, and participation in events such as funerals and parties.

SIX

**COMPETITION, INDIVIDUALISM, AND
COLLECTIVE ORGANIZATION**

Trade unionism appears to be remarkably strong within the alteño informal economy today and shapes the citizenship of many alteños just as much as those place-based citizenship practices discussed in the first part of this book.[1] In most of Latin America throughout the twentieth century, trade unions were a crucial aspect of ordinary people's citizenship because of the importance of corporatist politics. They were criticized from one side for co-opting the poor into dominant governmentality projects and from another for inhibiting economic development. Following the latter ideological project, the neoliberal restructuring of the economy represented a serious onslaught on trade union power globally. Actual government repression (Gill 1998, 2000; Nash 1992), deformalization of the economy, increased competition, and the promotion of active and individual citizenship (Rose 1999, 2000; Lazar 2004) have all weakened trade unions. However, in Bolivia at least, these processes have paradoxically also shaped (neoliberal) collectivities, which are one of the most important counterweights to neoliberal political, economic, and governmental projects. Organized labor has not been entirely broken but is beginning to reconstitute itself as a political subject. As Hardt and Negri (2005) argue, this political subject is not the working class as we traditionally understand it, but the urban poor; and in Bolivia that urban poor is indigenous.

As with the juntas vecinales, trade unions both mediate between their members and the state and substitute for the state. The two kinds of organizations are part of the structure illustrated in figure 4, a state-like structure parallel to the formal state which shapes the multitiered version of citizenship (Yuval-Davis 1997) that is the subject of this book. The focus of this chapter is on the ways the unions create a sense of collectivity among their members in an environment—the informal economy—often characterized as one primarily of competition between individuals, which may make collaboration difficult or even impossible. I explore how the street traders unions construct themselves as collective political subjects with the capacity to confront and negotiate with the state, as they did in October 2003 and the first half of 2005. As with previous chapters, I highlight the embodied and physical nature of these processes without assuming their automatic success. I take the discussion of the individual–collective tension further through the example of leadership, where we see how people attempt to assert values of collectivity in the face of the (perceived) pursuit of individual interests to the detriment of the group.

The chapter thus develops the discussion of the self in the previous chapter with an investigation of the processes of construction of the collective self within the specific context of the informal economy in early twenty-first-century El Alto. In an influential article published in 1977, Xavier Albó identified "the Aymara paradox" as the existence of a strong communitarian ethic within Aymara peasant communities alongside a tendency toward individualism and factionalism. He partially resolved the tension by proposing the concept of "individualism within the group," whereby the group manages to "synchronize the interests of the different individuals through reciprocal help or common enterprise, in which in the last instance particular interests are unified through a common institutional matrix" (21, my translation). My ethnography shows this process not as a structural principle regulated through ritual practices such as ayni and the ayllu, but as a political process riven with tensions, failures, and difficulties as well as some notable success. In the case of political organization in the urban Aymara context of El Alto, the struggle between collectivism and individualism is absolutely central. Individualism plays an important part in trade union leadership and is a considerable source of tension, as the conduct of leaders becomes a crucial arena for the assertion of collectivity as an ideal in the face of (perceived) individualism. That assertion may not always be very successful, of course. This links to the study of office-holding, which has been key to much Andean ethnography, although mostly simply as an expression of collectivity and obligation to the group.[2] As chapter 8 discusses in more detail, the nature of leadership in the Andes is one of the key themes in claims currently being made for the potential revitalization of Bolivian democracy based upon indigenous and popular traditions.

Why should the issue of collectivism or individualism be important today in El Alto? The process of individuation accompanying the growth of cities has been a persistent trope of urban sociology and anthropology, expressed in early twentieth-century urban sociology as the loss of *Gemeinschaft* in favor of *Gesellschaft*, for example. In the case of Bolivia, scholars have stressed the individualism, stratification, and fragmentation of city life in contrast to the strength of the rural community, or of the class-based community of miners (Gill 1997b; Canessa 1998; Rivera Cusicanqui 2002). Scholars usually link individuation in the city to the structure of the urban economy. Olivia Harris (1995: 368) argues that in the rural Andes, collective organization is oriented usually to subsistence, the "nonmarket sphere," while "intervention in markets is an affair for individuals" and households. Markets are not confined to Bolivia's cities, but they are associated with urban spaces, and more generally a common assumption is that competitive market economies are individualistic (Colloredo-Mansfeld 2002), not least because this is how economists have historically approached the study of markets (Hart 2001). Of course, much economic anthropology has been devoted to outlining the embedded nature of markets, following the substantivists' lead (Polanyi 1957 [1944]; Dalton 1971; Granovetter 1992 [1985]). In work on informal economies, however, the social relations underpinning market transactions have not always received as much attention as they deserve, as Keith Hart admits of his seminal article defining the informal sector in Accra (1973). The picture he painted then, and one that retains much power in contemporary literature, was of many individuals or small groups developing multiple and individual (or household) strategies for economic survival. In later works, he has done much to outline the social processes lying beneath supposedly individualized and abstracted market exchanges, such as the extension of credit (Hart 2001; see also Basile and Harris-White 2000).

Individuation is associated with competition, and competition in the informal economy of El Alto has become acute in recent years. The neoliberal restructuring so enthusiastically implemented in Bolivia from the mid-1980s onward had two principal effects. First, on the demand side, the popular classes saw a decrease in their wages in real terms and were fired from their jobs or moved into temporary contracts. Initially, the circulation of cocaine money in the Bolivian economy alleviated this problem (Sanabria 1999; Blanes Jimenez 1989), but by the end of the 1990s, Bolivian governments had achieved considerable success in reducing the illegal growth of coca, and so the money was drying up. Second, on the supply side, the number of vendors increased as workers and miners were fired and migrated to El Alto in the mid-1980s. More recently, cheaper products manufactured in Chile, Brazil, and China are increasingly arriving in Bolivian markets, both legally and as contraband. Many vendors I spoke with talked about how their earnings were good in the 1970s and 1980s, but how competition has now increased to the point where their markups are tiny:

> Yes, effectively things have changed radically; for example, before there were more sales, we had more income. In contrast, now because there is quite a lot of competition and more traders, the sales themselves have really lowered, too much. Where you used to sell 100 percent of your stock, now you sell 20 percent. And profits too, we've also had to lower our prices in order to compete, for example before, from a [sachet of] shampoo, let's say, we earned at least 2 Bolivianos, now a sachet only earns me 50 cents, sometimes 20 cents. And so we have to sell so that the money circulates and doesn't stagnate.

> What you used to sell for 100 Bolivianos now you sell at 20 or 30 Bolivianos. Now it's not like before, because before there was money in circulation, a worker earned, had [money] in order to buy from the streets, and bought from us. But now no, now it's reversed, we only buy and sell between ourselves. For example, you, Doctora, you'll sell books, I sell batteries, you buy batteries from me, and I buy exercise books from you—that's all we do now.

Another common complaint among street traders is that there are more vendors than consumers, and that money simply circulates between them, as one woman said, like a *pasanaku*, a communal credit scheme. Accumulation is no longer possible; traders can only "live from day to day."

Whether neoliberal deformalization and the consequent increased competition within the informal economy have meant a decrease in worker solidarity beyond the household is a matter of some debate, however. Agadjanian (2002: 261), for example, argues that "increased competition in the swollen marketplace, combined with a sanctification of private initiative and self-reliance by the dominant class ideology, undermines workers' collective strategies both by alienating them individually and by reinforcing compartmentalistic small-scale solidarities and alliances within various subgroups of workers." In a concrete sense, some groups of workers have been severely weakened, the organized miners being the paradigmatic example. From their position as the most powerful proletarian organization in the twentieth century, the Miners Federation suffered a brutal onslaught from the state during the 1980s, as thousands were fired and hundreds massacred in the restructuring process (Sanabria 1999). Yet newly powerful groups of the "popular classes" have also emerged: the coca growers (cocaleros) of the Chapare region, led by Evo Morales; the peasants of the altiplano; and the residents of El Alto, as both workers and vecinos (residents, neighbors). All of these new groups share a set of relations of production that should mean they are less vulnerable to state predation than were the miners, an argument made by Harry Sanabria for the cocaleros. He points out that their "social organization of production hinges on relatively autonomous and shifting production units" (556), in contrast to the way the miners were concentrated in intensive and accessible production sites. This is also true for peasants and the petty capitalists (microcapitalists) working in small family-based businesses in El Alto and selling in different and relatively fluid street markets. This kind of household production model is of course common, even typical, under neoliberalism in countries of the global South. As Hart (2001) argues, the model of economy that rigidly separates production (in the factory, office, etc.) from reproduction (in the home) is the exception rather than the rule, historically speaking.

Related to this, globally street markets are often viewed as acceptable places for women to work precisely because they blur the distinction between house and workplace and are compatible with women's roles in the reproductive economy (Lessinger 2001). In El Alto, women form the clear majority of those engaged in small-scale commerce,[3] even though the dominant discourse is of women working mainly in the home; in my survey of Rosas Pampa, 20 percent of women said that they were comerciantes, or traders, and 33 percent said they were housewives. Many of the women I knew who called themselves housewives would also go out and sell goods occasionally, or would knit or weave commercially from their homes. The high level of involvement of women in commerce cannot be entirely attributed to increased numbers of female-headed households or to the economic crisis of the late twentieth century, the factors usually outlined in the feminist literature (Berger 1989). These have played a major part, but in addition, urban Aymaras are drawing on indigenous cultural codes about female-male complementarity in labor (Harris 2000a [1978]) and a long history of female responsibility for commerce in the Andes (Weismantel 2001; de la Cadena 1996, 2002; Larson and Harris 1995).

The way the household model of production and exchange articulates with competition in the marketplace will be one of the forces that shape collective organization, rather than necessarily making it disappear altogether. Neoliberalism thus helps to create particular forms of collectivity alongside its well-recognized promotion of the active individual citizen operating rationally in the marketplace (Lazar 2004; Rose 1999: 167–193).[4] Such contemporary forces also operate alongside and in interaction with more long-standing experiences of organization: in indigenous communities, the miners' trade unions, and the trade unions of domestic workers, teachers, market sellers, and others.

CREATING THE COLLECTIVITY THROUGH VALUES AND PRACTICES

Given these kinds of contradictory pressures, the street traders associations and the Federation need to put a considerable amount of work into maintaining and constructing a sense of collectivity among their members. As Iris Young (1990) pointed out, an assumption of homogeneity and unity of purpose within any given collective would be mistaken, but the recognition that collectivities incorporate members with competing interests does not necessarily mean that methodological individualism is the only or indeed the best way to understand collective politics. While it is certainly possible to analyze group cohesion in terms of a set of contracts between individuals based upon the conferment of rights in return for fulfillment of duties, such an analysis provides only part of the picture. As the ethnography presented below shows, a recurrent value in how trade union leaders and members talk about membership is that of the "organic," by which they mean the contribution of each part to the organic whole of the trade union or federation. That contribution is usually taken for granted: it is presented as simply what one does as a member, not necessarily an exchange of an obligation for a set of rights that can be evaluated according to how closely it fits with each individual's interests. The organic view of the relationship between the part and the whole is important because it is far more useful than a more contractual approach as a way of explaining the power demonstrated by the various civic organizational structures in El Alto in recent years, as the following chapters elaborate. First, though, I discuss some of the values and practices that are the foundation of this construction work, from the very practical mediation of competition and conflict between traders to the philosophical and then physical and embodied bases of self-construction as collective political subjects.

Mediating Conflicts between Affiliates　One of the most important functions of street traders associations and the bulk of the day-to-day work of the Federation is the mediation of conflicts between traders, between traders with stalls and those without, and between traders and other associations or the civic authorities. General secretaries of street traders associations often deal with arguments (or fights) between affiliates as they happen; one time I was conducting an interview with a particularly experienced general secretary when she was called over urgently to another stall to calm down the protagonists of a drunken argument that had spilled over into a fight. If conflicts are particularly stubborn and cannot be resolved by day-to-day mediation, they will be brought to a general assembly (the meeting of all the members of the association) or the Federation.

Conflicts between individuals and with other groups and traders associations obviously have many causes but tend primarily to involve problems of competition, price-fixing, and, most important, encroachments on a vendor's or association's territory, including when a competing stall has grown beyond its allotted space into walkways or other people's stalls. Sometimes, ambulantes (traders without a fixed stall) take over empty spots, and the stall's owner objects. Within the context of increased competition and economic hardship, such problems are frequent. The initial offense is often exacerbated by defamation or physical violence during the *cruces de palabras* (arguments) that ensue, which can become by far the most important aspect of the conflict. There is an understanding that vocal argument and defamation is something to which women are particularly prone—modern-day scolds, as the interview extract below indicates:

> Are female leaders different from male leaders?
> Yes, they're different. Sometimes our [female] comrades think that we can find a solution through shouting, or with the loudest voice. . . . The majority of female leaders try to solve things by shouting, or in anger.

Gender tensions run through conflicts in other ways too, for example when women become the figurehead for male ambition. It is usually the woman who is the affiliate or who actually runs the stall, and if her husband's family is interested in the stall problems can occur. For example, one conflict happened because a woman had lent her kiosk to her daughter, who would not give it up when her mother asked for it back. Both women were affiliated with the association, as the daughter had another, nearby stall in her own name. The mother argued that she needed to be able to pass on her own kiosk to another of her nine children. The daughter's husband appeared to be encouraging her into the conflict with her mother, which the Federation delegate mediating this conflict quickly realized. When he demanded that mother and daughter reconcile and agree to an ocular inspection by members of the Federation Executive Committee, the daughter glanced at her husband as if to ask him if she should give her mother a hug. At this point, the Federation delegate reproached her, saying, "Your husband is for a little while [un rato], your mother forever." This particular problem was very difficult for the Federation delegate because it was difficult to work out whether the conflict was a family problem, a trade union problem, or a problem for the police to resolve. He felt that the association and Federation should become involved only if it was the second of the three. The conflict was also particularly knotty because, although the daughter did not legally own the stall loaned by her mother, she had maintained it well and conscientiously fulfilled her obligations to the association, as had her mother. It was thus difficult to distinguish between the two conflicting parties according to the dominant values of what makes a good affiliate, a point I return to later.

Federation leaders often discuss problems with the association *directorio* (leadership committee) in the Federation's central office and give them advice on how to manage the situation. The next step would be to convene a meeting at the office between the two parties to the conflict, as happened in the above case. Much of the Federation's mediation involves persuading the different parties to take their grievances to a general assembly, where the directorio can make a recommendation. A member of the Executive Committee of the Federation often attends this meeting as a mediator and guide to give the directorio increased legitimacy in front of their affiliates and to advise the *bases* (grass roots) on what course of action to take. As with every conflict that they mediated, in general assemblies the Federation representatives usually prefaced their comments on the situation with a declaration that they could not be partisan, and that the maximum authority was the bases. In fact, they often were very partisan, supporting different parties according to moral values I discuss below. The practices of conflict resolution described here also indicate dominant processual values within trade unions: first, the importance of group solutions to conflicts, initially in the group meetings at the Federation offices and ultimately in the general assembly; second, the role of deliberation and discussion of grievances, sometimes over a considerable amount of time as each party makes its case to the Federation delegate or the bases in the general assembly. Finally, conflict resolution processes highlight the importance of scales of hierarchy, as in the first place the directorio should attempt to resolve conflicts, in which they are often successful. If they are unsuccessful, the Federation delegate has the authority to recommend a solution; the final authority is that of the bases in the general assembly. These processual values are part of what many see as unionism's contribution to the potential revitalization of Bolivian democracy currently under way.

Responsibility and Vida Orgánica   When resolving conflicts between individuals or groups, both individual associations and the Federation operate from the same basic set of values, which are constructed and enforced in different ways. Principal among these is the concept of *vida orgánica* (organizational life), which refers to participation in union activities. Thus, if one party to the conflict fulfills the obligations of vida orgánica, which include attending meetings, demonstration marches, and civic parades called by the association, they have a greater call on the protection provided by that association. Where both *hacen vida orgánica* ("do" vida orgánica), as in the example of the mother and daughter, resolving the conflict is more complicated because both are equally conscientious members of the association. To be considered conscientious, individuals should also pay their affiliation quotas and maintain their stall, that is, go out to sell regularly. It is not necessary for the affiliate herself to go out to sell; she can send a family member instead. Vida orgánica therefore has a very important physical dimension of disciplining bodies to attend their stalls regularly, which can be physically demanding when the weather is bad. People must also attend general assemblies that usually last over four hours, and demonstrations and parades that can take up a whole day.

One level up, associations can be classified into those that fulfill vida orgánica and those that don't. When I asked for the number of associations affiliated with the Federation, people always made this distinction, so that the Federation has about 350 affiliates, but around 200 fulfill vida orgánica. The definitive list they gave me for 2003 was based upon those associations that had attended the Independence Day parades on 6 August. The Federation is more willing to defend associations that hacen vida orgánica in any conflict with the authorities, and Don Braulio Rocha, the executive secretary, frequently upbraided petitioners who seemed to appear in the office only when their association had problems that needed Federation help. The Federation leaders also see longevity as providing an association with greater legitimacy.

Fulfilling vida orgánica can strengthen the hand of parties in a dispute, such that we can speak of a dynamic of obligations and rights operating between the association and its members. However, more generally and in nonconflictual circumstances, vida orgánica is not spoken of as an individualized exchange of duties and rights, as might be the case in other trade union contexts. Among the street traders, the overt discourse was that there are certain things that one just does if one is a member of an association; it is taken for granted.[5] Research into citizenship in Cochabamba conducted by Karen Monasterios and Luis Tapia Mealla (2001) found that people spoke more of their obligations in relation to their civic association or trade union than to the state. But a contract of rights and duties as in the Western legal tradition does not adequately describe the exchanges that occur within an association of traders.

For one thing, the notion of vida orgánica includes a sense of a gradation of rights that corresponds to how conscientious the conflictual party has been, and in practice to how well they know the people mediating the conflict. For another, there is general acceptance of what might appear to be coercive measures to enforce vida orgánica. Affiliates are usually fined if they do not attend a general assembly of their association. At the end of the assembly, the directorio distributes paper tokens, and in the case of those who sell in the 16 de Julio market, the following Sunday they demand to see each trader's token and fine those who do not have one. Under normal circumstances, people also considered it an obligation to participate in civic parades, demonstrations, and strikes, and this is often enforced by the practice of taking attendance and fining those who are absent.[6]

These measures are sometimes used by members of the upper classes to argue that demonstrators are not participating of their free will but are obliged to do so by the fines or by threats from other protestors. For example, the right-wing paper La Razon ran an article on mobilizations on 23 April 2004 with the title "Fear Closed Stalls in Some Markets." In fact, there is a delicate balance that goes on inside an organization which mobilizes its members on demonstrations. Leaders are expected to fine those who do not participate in protest marches, but that fine should not be too heavy. For example, Don Antonio, a member of the Federation Executive Committee, disapproved of the 2003 president of the Federación de Padres de Familia de El Alto (Federation of Parents Associations) because he fined his members about 30 Bolivianos if they did not participate in marches.[7] This meant that people had no choice but to participate:

> Yes, he has the power to decide, and it's not like he doesn't deserve it, he has it because he convenes marches that his bases attend. Because there we have to pay a fine of 30, 40 Bolivianos, and in this last [economic] crisis, you just can't find this [money], so we're forced to attend the march. It's more drastic than the juntas vecinales, more drastic than the Federation of Street Traders, because when you want to register your child [in school], they say "you haven't attended this many [marches or other events] and the fine is around 90 to 120 [Bolivianos]." So it's like paying, we parents just have to attend.

In other instances, the fine is not too heavy, so that people can decide whether they will go along, because whatever happens their participation will cost money—in lost income, food, or transport to the meeting point. My interpretation is that some form of support, either through the fine or through physical participation, is obligatory. The Federation of Butchers is another organization that charges high fines for nonattendance. One of its members who lived in Rosas Pampa (Doña Patricia) circumvented this rule by paying her friend Sofia half the cost of the fine to attend demonstrations and occasional meetings in her stead. From Sofia's perspective it was a good deal, as she quite enjoyed demonstrations and earned 30 Bolivianos for a day's work, while Doña Patricia saved money on the 60 Bolivianos fine and did not waste her time going to marches or lose shop income through her absence.

The Federation of Street Traders has no coercive power to enforce vida orgánica among its affiliated associations, although their central office is furnished with desks, bookshelves, chairs, and benches that have been bought with fines levied on associations that did not fulfill vida orgánica and subsequently wanted to return to the Federation. In their day-to-day activities the Executive Committee members tend to use more positive methods, such as mentioning the most conscientious associations at the official party to celebrate Independence Day. This gives considerable prestige to the directorio of those associations and is often marked by the giving of certificates or diplomas of honor. They also give certificates to those who participate in civic parades. Nonetheless, if the Federation is politically effective—that is, unified, with committed leadership, able to resolve conflicts, and not too compromised with the municipal government—then associations tend to see vida orgánica as worthwhile. This of course creates a cycle where the more associations that fulfill vida orgánica, the more effective the Federation as a whole can be, and the more associations it attracts.

Convocatoria: The Dance, the Parade, and the Demonstration   A crucial part of vida orgánica at individual and association levels is participation in ritual events, which in many ways are embodied practices of collectivity with important ramifications for politics and citizenship in El Alto. The street traders unions organize events throughout the year, such as the Carnival festivities, when people ch'alla their workplace—their office, vehicle, stall—for luck and prosperity over the coming year. Most unions will also coordinate their members' participation in parades on important civic dates and in the dancing for the anniversary fiesta of the zone in which they work, as well as in demonstrations called by the Federation. These three related practices—the demonstration, the civic parade, and the fiesta Entrada—construct and express collective political agency. They are linked through the concept of *convocatoria*, which can be glossed as the power of numbers or the ability to get large numbers of people on the streets; paper notices of demonstrations and parades are also called convocatorias. Indeed, there are a number of important similarities among Entradas, parades, and demonstrations, and they are practices which enact and constitute similar physical understandings and performances of political agency through the interaction among the three as they cite or mimic each other.

In general, associations feel a strong responsibility to dance in the anniversary fiestas organized by the junta vecinal in the zone where they work. In the runup to the largest fiesta in El Alto, that of the 16 de Julio zone, the Entrada was on the agenda of all the association meetings that I attended. Not all participated directly—one paid for a group of musicians, for example—but participation of some sort was important to them. This was in part because it would gain them the goodwill of the vecinos, but also because collaboration in this way is one of the things an association just does, in the same way that individuals recognize the importance of attending a demonstration or contributing financially. Participation in the Entrada is one way of expressing and strengthening the ties between local association and the junta vecinal in a particular zone. The traders' participation enables the junta vecinal to put on a good show, and the gratitude that is then due the associations can be traded for support in other areas. It also makes the traders part of the zone: they *belong* to it, as do the vecinos who participate.

A similar process of affirming and experiencing collective belonging happens in the civic parades which occur quite frequently in El Alto and all over Bolivia to commemorate city and departmental anniversaries, Independence Day, Labor Day, and other important dates. Adults and schoolchildren march along the main roads of a city or neighborhood in groups according to their school year, in the case of the children, or their membership in a junta vecinal or trade union, in the case of the adults. These parades revere special anniversaries of the nation, city, or urban zone through the bodies of their participants and drill that reverence into their bodies from an early age, with the participation of children as young as five in the schoolchildren's parades (see figure 16). The parades are not quite as effervescent or exciting as the Entrada, but they do draw large crowds, and many of the participants in the parades feel a sense of pride in the *civismo* (civic virtue) they display. For the civic parade is explicitly part of citizenship practice, an obligation of citizens to the state. In the runup to the Torchlight parade on the evening of 15 July 2003, which honors the department of La Paz, representatives from affiliated associations of street vendors came to the Federation office to be allocated a numbered place in the parade. Some murmured that they were not keen to participate on what was likely to be a very cold evening and asked if they could get permission to miss the event, but the secretary responded to them by saying, "No, there's no permission [to be absent]. As citizens of La Paz [*ciudadanos paceños*] we have to honor our fallen heroes. It's not like you're Chilean, are you [*acaso eres chileno*]?" Bolivian nationalist ideology paints the Chileans as particular enemies because of their victory in the War of the Pacific of 1879, when they took Bolivia's coastline. It is a perception widely shared, as indicated in the opposition to the export of natural gas through Chile in recent years. Thus only a Chilean would not wish to honor the Bolivian nation or the department of La Paz. In the event, over one hundred associations took part, some mobilizing up to two hundred members. I would estimate that about four thousand people participated in total, a significant number.

For the parades on Bolivia's Independence Day that year (6 August), 180 associations and probably about nine thousand individuals participated.

16. Schoolchildren parade in El Alto for Independence Day. The youngest children in the school lead the parade in costume.

The procession of street traders took several hours to pass by the official stage at the end of the route. At the time of organizing both these events, relationships between the municipal authorities and the Federation were very strained. However, there was a clear understanding that the street traders should participate, both in honor of some higher ideal (as citizens of La Paz or for Bolivia) and also because if they were to make demands of the municipal government later and had not put on a good show, the mayor would have something to hold over them. This was explicitly discussed in the meetings of the Executive Committee of the Federation.

The parades are also a way of demonstrating to the state authorities the power of convocatoria wielded by the different organized social forces in El Alto. This power is especially visible in street demonstrations. Often, and particularly on 1 May, civic parades shade into protest marches. This was evident in the Torchlight parade, when leaders of the Federation and individual associations shouted slogans to which the participants responded, in the form that slogan chanting takes in street demonstrations.[8] Once, they even chanted, "This is not a parade, it's a protest march!" Other clues to their similarity can be found in the ways they are organized; once a meeting has decided to call a protest march, the Federation organizes the march in exactly the same way as it does the civic parades: they send out a convocatoria calling for participation, and the general secretaries of affiliated associations come to the central office to collect the number that denotes their place in the demonstration. The Federation leaders note down which association has which number and take attendance at the end of the march.

In addition, there are important similarities in the physical form of all three of these practices. (See video at http://www.sianlazar.net.) Chapter 4 described the Entrada, where the comparsas parade in turn along a specific route, led by the guides at the head of the subgroups. The bare physical form of the civic parade is very similar to that of the Entrada, as corporate groupings move through space in a unified way with banners at the front identifying themselves. Schoolchildren march as their school, and within that their year, with boys and girls separate, as in some of the Entrada dances; adults march in blocks of union affiliation or as members of a junta vecinal or junta escolar. Both the Entrada and the parades are viewed by an audience lining the streets through which they progress, and they both culminate in the real show in front of distinguished guests at the palco, or stage. During the parades, the display at the palco must be the most disciplined possible, with more emphasis placed upon keeping neat rows and marching in step and raising the arm at the appropriate time, similar to how the dancers demonstrate all their steps in front of the judges at the palco at the end of the Entrada. Often, as with the Entrada, the end of the parade is the cue for the participants to break up into their separate groups in order to mark attendance lists and to drink together. The latter was particularly the case for the Torchlight parade of 15 July, when participants notoriously *amanecen*, that is, stay up drinking until dawn.

The physical form of the demonstration is also remarkably similar to that of the parades and the Entradas. The focus on discipline, neat lines, the organization into corporate blocs delineated by banners advertising belonging, are all the same, and strictly observed, as I experienced in a number of demonstrations. For example, often the UPEA students are more anarchic than older demonstrators, but during the demonstration that I participated in, the director of the Sociology Department frequently exhorted us to keep to our lines as if we were in a parade, especially when we proceeded down the main street of La Paz. Like the Entrada dances, the frequent demonstrations congregate groups of people moving through

17. Civic parade in El Alto, passing the dignitaries on the stage

18. An impromptu demonstration by the Federation of Street Traders

space in a highly disciplined and coordinated manner, organized into lines and with the same purpose, shouting out their demands in unity.

The overall impression for spectators of the Entrada, the parades, and the demonstrations is one of groups of people moving forward in disciplined uniformity, which has implications for how people experience their political agency. In all three forms, a diffuse agency rests in the collectivity as an organic whole. This is underlined by their aesthetics, which require some measure of conformity, most notable in the Entrada, where stepping out of line or getting out of sequence breaks the flow and the overall impression of the performance. And those aesthetic values work on those involved to create a collective purpose and experience. The aesthetics of unity in forward motion map out people's collective relationship to their zone or city, whether that is as a vecino or as a member of an associated trade union. The experience is physical and embodied, as dancers and demonstrators take great care to follow the lead of those at the head of the group in order to pattern the movement of others, shout slogans in unison, keep to neat lines, get tired together, and have fun together.

The Entrada, parade, and demonstration are a means for individuals to define and physically experience the collectivity, creating a shared sense of identity through movement. They experience this sense of collectivity as a series of "nested affiliations," evident for example in the organization of the neighborhood Entrada, when citizenship in the zone is dependent upon insertion into smaller communities which are differentiated by sound, movement, and costume. Citizenship in the imagined community of Bolivia is experienced similarly, as evident in the organization of parades for Independence Day, when the citizens participated as part of their trade union (or junta vecinal), their Federation, their city, and their country. Thus, as with economic activity (Mayer 2002a), political activity is structured along the lines of households, specific occupational group affiliation or zone, city, department, and country. In a parallel case, Gary Urton (1992) identified these patterns as "differentiation within communalism" for the case of the ayllus that made up the Cusqueño community he studied.

Given their physical similarities, we might even propose that these three citizenship practices lie on a continuum, from the highly stylized Entrada to the street demonstration. The physical experience of participating in one of these citizenship practices is not only about relating to one's fellow union members or vecinos, but also about the relationship to place that develops. Place—the earth, the city, the zone, the streets—is active, in many ways part of the collectivity. Alcohol consumption is less central to parades and demonstrations (although it is not absent), but the ways that these cite the Entrada hints at a similar understanding of place as active, as a participant in the parade or the demonstration. Moving through space during an Entrada and a parade constitutes the relationship of person to locality, which is reinforced by the sharing of alcohol with other vecinos or fellow traders and with the local manifestation of the Pachamama through the ch'alla. During demonstrations, the disciplined and synchronized flow through space asserts the presence of collectivities in the face of those who ignore and exclude them. It visibly marks their collective claim on the physical territory through which they move and makes and remakes the relationship between the collectivity and the space they inhabit.

LEADERSHIP: INDIVIDUALISM IN THE GROUP?

From an emphasis on the construction of selves through collective values and practices, I move in this section to the role of individualism within trade union politics, in light of Xavier Albó's (1977) concept of "individualism within the group." I discuss individualism in street traders associations and the Federation through an examination of different narratives or discourses of trade union leadership: from the leaders' own rhetoric of sacrifice for the group to the ways the bases control their leaders. These discussions prefigure those of chapter 8, where such philosophies are shown to impact directly on understandings of political life and democracy. Here, I emphasize that leadership is the terrain for struggles between collectivity as an ideal and the practice of self-interested action by individuals.

Trade union leadership is a source of both hardship and pride for the men and women involved. The Executive Committee of the Federation nominally has over one hundred members, but only about forty to fifty are active at any one time. Of those, about twenty-five come to the central offices very regularly and attend general assemblies of associations as a representative of the Federation. A few key people work extremely hard to resolve legal problems and internal conflicts for associations, coming to the office every day to deal with petitions, attending the long general assemblies, convening meetings between complainants in the central office, and typing up the (often considerable) documentation that is a part of every conflict. Others are more politically inclined, assisting the executive secretary in his dealings with the alcaldía, typing up the resolutions of an *ampliado* (a meeting of general secretaries of associations or trade unions), or composing the convocatoria notices calling the street traders to demonstrations and civic parades. Still others distribute the convocatorias, photocopy resolution sheets or *convenios* (covenants) agreed with the mayor, receive letters, assign delegates to meetings, and clean the office. None of them receives payment for this work. They are usually able to work for free because family members (usually a wife) are attending their stalls or because they come to the office when they are not selling. Some sell in the evenings, early mornings, or Thursdays and Sundays, in the case of those who work in the 16 de Julio street market.

Although the vast majority of street traders are women, at least half of the general secretaries at association level are men, a majority of the active Executive Committee members in the Federation are men, and men hold all of the most senior posts. However, there are female general secretaries, many of whom are long-lasting and highly accomplished leaders. As one would expect, there is a dominant gendered notion of appropriate activities, whereby men should take responsibility for legal and political matters while women are seen as their helpers. Don Alberto hinted at this when he said, "Only about 10 percent of the [female] comrades [in leadership positions] are patient in this way, have this sociability, this way of assisting their [male] comrades." The other men I interviewed did not talk so explicitly, but some women complained about it: "The male leader always treats us as if we were just his helper; they don't want a woman to head things up, they are always at the forefront, with the female leader as assistant." While I was there, the female Executive Committee members took responsibility for organizing meetings, for example registering attendance, bringing food to those running the meeting publicly, and blocking the exit when people wanted to leave a particularly long meeting. In general assemblies of associations women from directorios, ex-directorios, and the bases frequently do speak up, sometimes using Aymara so that everyone can understand. In the Federation ampliados, it is more usual for men to speak, but women do also contribute from time to time.[9]

In interviews, street traders spoke of leadership at both association and Federation levels as very difficult. Both men and women talked of financial hardship and of the amount of their time that was taken up with leadership responsibilities. Don Braulio even maintained that he had lost two daughters as a result of being a union leader. They had run away or been kidnapped, something he attributed in part to his neglect. Other difficulties that people mentioned were the criticism from their bases due to lack of understanding or associated with the fact that the leaders are not paid:

> Well, it's pretty difficult, because a lot of people simply think that the leader would be taking advantage [of the situation]. First, in order to be a leader you have to have money in your pocket. If there's no money in your pocket, then one is going to have to go around hungry perhaps, or perhaps you might have a worse problem in your home because there's no money, right? So first, in order to be a leader you have to have money; then you have to be secure in your business, so that the business provides for you and you're not short of money at home. [Because] the leader takes up his time being in different places. Sometimes being a leader is wasting time, without having a salary, without having anything.

> Managing an organization is not easy, it's really difficult because the comrades, well, there are comrades who understand you, there are comrades who don't. There are comrades who value the work, there are those who don't. They say you're a thief, that you want to be a leader only for that [reason], that there is a lot of money. It's not like that, it's not like that. For my part, no, I've never charged money, for example. When I need some to pay the lawyer, then I charge, but if I don't need it, I don't charge.

In recorded interviews, leaders stressed the difficulties of working for free, as one might expect in the context of an interview with a foreigner who might be a future source of development assistance. Nonetheless, the cost of community office-holding has been noted in many Andean ethnographies, a few of which have discussed its attendant problems and tensions (e.g., McEwen 1975).

Even so, for many being a leader was also a source of pride, which comes largely from their position as servant to the bases:

> The only thing is that it brings pride [orgullo], the pride of saying "I, as a leader, I achieved this, I defended that person, or I spent time with that person." And some day, some meeting or some assembly, some place, perhaps they'll reward you with a round of applause. Or perhaps a comrade will recognize, will say "thank you comrade, because thanks to you we are unified." There are times when one says "I'd like to stop being a leader." But you can't. Many times when you hear some problem that is happening in some place, or someone is work-

ing against the traders, or an authority is wanting to attack them, you say "why can they attack? If I were a leader, I could defend [the traders]." So, there's no chance of easily letting down our comrades in the streets.

Despite the often florid protestations of selfless service in my interviews, in less formal contexts and in some interviews, leaders used the word orgullo (pride) as a gloss for a prestige that comes from fulfilling an obligation to their community. Some of the older women in particular stressed that it was orgullo to work for the Federation, even if it was at times difficult for them. They had been nominated for that position, and therefore they were responsible members of the Executive Committee. For them, the one followed from the other, and orgullo was the ethical value that made it possible, rather than a calculation of individual self-interest. While such calculations are also important, I think we should take seriously the comments of leaders about how they could not refuse the position, and how they felt they should do the job properly, as well as the fact that becoming a leader was quite taken for granted. Doña Antonia Narvaez said that she took up the position of secretary general of her association, which was formed by vecinos who sell outside their houses, for the following reason: "Since I had never done anything for the zone or for the association, well, all of a sudden they nominated me secretary." I suggest that, as in the campo, taking on a leadership position in the city is partly viewed as an element in the development of full adult personhood. As with the campo, not everyone will be a "good comunero" (Rasnake 1988), that is, fulfill their responsibilities properly, and many simply abandon their position. However, enough do the job of leadership conscientiously to make it work, especially when the Federation is in a strong position politically.

Suspicion of the Leaders, Corruption, and Party Politics   Having said that, as Albó (1977) identified for Aymara peasant groups, in the street traders organizations there is a very strong desconfianza, or group suspicion of the leaders. This often takes the form of accusations or rumors of corruption, rather like the rumors and gossip surrounding junta vecinal leaders. In a similar way, these tend to accuse leaders of serving their personal interests (intereses personales). This might be through corruption, understood principally as robbery of group income, or through alliances with political parties. As I discussed in chapter 2, the discursive use of personal interests as a motivation for different forms of corruption has the effect of delimiting what group interests are. Corruption talk constructs and polices the frontiers between public and private if corruption is viewed primarily as people stealing public resources for their private interests. In this case, making this distinction discursively connects the public to the group and the private to the individual and has the effect of emphasizing a collective sense of self as more moral.

As with the juntas vecinales, corruption talk is also a form of preemptive accountability in associations and the Federation, so that incoming leaders know how they should act. Moreover, it is one of the most important ways of "doing politics." Accusations of corruption are one of the most frequently used ways of attempting to remove a leader who is refusing to leave his or her position, and they are often very effective. When one faction within an organization is gathering adherents in opposition to the present leaders, they often do so by accusing them of corruption. When the balance has shifted in favor of the opposing faction, the leaders will fall, whether the accusations are actually true or not.

Indeed, it is often very difficult to assess the truth of the accusations. Leaders are expected to put in a great deal of work and make many sacrifices without pay, so it is unsurprising that sometimes they use association resources to make payments to themselves, especially if they need money urgently. Furthermore, associations tend to demand highly detailed financial reports, rendiciones de cuentas, from outgoing leaders, which are challenging for even the most conscientious to provide. Association leaders may not be fully literate, and almost certainly cannot afford to hire an accountant to produce their reports. Sometimes the only measure of whether a leader has been more or less honest is if there is a largish amount of money left in the association account. In one association, despite the existence of a comision revisadora (supervisory commission), the clearest indication of the nefarious dealings of the previous leader was that he had left a sum of us$200 in the bank account at the end of the year, whereas his successor had left us$1,609. The corruption or potential corruption of previous directorios or general secretaries was one of the sets of problems that leadership committees of associations most frequently brought to the Federation.

At Federation level, the issue of party political alliances is also a means of understanding and doing politics and working through the tensions between individualism and collectivism, and is discursively linked to corruption. A dominant theme of my interview discussions with members of the Federation Executive Committee was how many leaders allow themselves to be bought by political parties, often expressed as "selling oneself for a plate of lentils." When leaders talked about this, it was universally expressed as a bad thing; many ascribed the problems of factionalism that the Federation had suffered throughout its history to *intromisión política* (political interference), or simply *la política*. Many spoke of an initial period when the Federation "worked organically," followed by a highly politicized period during the 1990s when the Condepa administrations coopted many Federation leaders and factionalism was rife. By 2003, the Federation had unified and the leaders on the Executive Committee were overwhelmingly committed to working as trade unionists rather than "selling themselves" to political parties. The exact chronologies presented to me depended on when the interviewee had joined the Federation, with the common thread that all felt the present to be less politicized than the past. All emphasized their own commitment to *sindicalismo* (trade unionism) over *la política*.

In talking about the Federation's history, several members of the Executive Committee argued that earlier eras were "less political" and "more *sindicalista*" and that they wanted to work "organically" (*organicamente*), not politically.

The previous executives served their bases. They never liked politics. Of course, there must have been about 20 or 10 percent oriented toward politics, but not like now, when 50 percent are politicized, perhaps even more, right? Since politics is now fashionable, it's embedded in the trade union sector. There are political parties that have a good conscience, that manage institutions, help them, and cooperate with them. There are politicians who work in good faith, there are politicians who abuse their power, whose aim is to destroy the union representatives of the city of El Alto.

I'm going to talk at a political level now. In this aspect, when all municipal governments are elected they want to manipulate us at a political level. We're completely *sindical*, all the political parties always try to get ahead for themselves, and nothing more, nothing for us. It's for this reason that we don't support any political party.

We're not like before, when we were manipulated in politics. We can't sell ourselves for a plate of lentils, we can't be politicized. We don't want this, [so] we women will struggle. We women are going to struggle to the bitter end because we're not going to let them do politics to us like this.

As with corruption, it is usually someone other than the speaker who has "sold themselves" to a political party. When interviewees admitted their experience with political parties, they tended to say that they were not a "militant" but a "sympathizer," or to downplay their involvement by simply not discussing it. A surprising number of members of the Executive Committee had previously worked as civil servants, either in the municipalities of La Paz and El Alto or in national ministries. This means that they had been members of political parties, as civil servant jobs depend upon party affiliation and *aval político* (for a discussion of which, see chapter 3). Don Juan was one of those, but he said that he had left the MIR because he felt that they had betrayed their name (Movimiento Izquierdista Revolucionaria, or Leftist Revolutionary Movement) and were nothing more than "servants of Yankee imperialism." Although I later saw him at the front of a demonstration by the MAS party, he did not mention this affiliation when I asked him about party politics in our interview. Another sympathizer of the MIR, Don Alberto, stressed that he was no longer a member but retained his personal connections with the MIRista congressman for El Alto, Irineo Espinoza. The only interviewee who did not play down his party membership was Don Juan Melendres, the leader of the COR at the time and an ex-executive secretary of the Federation, largely because his party political colors were well known to everyone, as he had been a candidate for the MAS in the 2002 elections. In the end, he lost the MAS candidature for the 2004 municipal elections, so he stood as a candidate for the Movimiento Sin Miedo (Fearless Movement).

At the time I conducted my interviews, the Federation was thinking about forming their own political party, with Don Braulio as the leader, which appeared to me to be mostly the idea of one of his deputies, Don Roberto. Many of the Executive Committee members professed their enthusiasm for that in interviews, for example Don Luciano:

> Making a "political instrument" from within the family of street traders is a
> very good idea . . . because really, at least in my view, the political parties have
> never taken us into account. Nor have they taken into account our children,
> who are also graduates; we have lawyers, doctors, we have engineers, we have a
> lot of graduates among our children. But our children as likely as not work only
> as assistants, or perhaps in an office thanks to a political connection; but our
> graduates, the children of our [social] class, of our background, have never
> taken charge of running a municipality or the country. In reality I'm thinking of

simply forming [a political party] together with all the civic organizations [of El Alto] for the next municipal elections. But with the children, the children are the most important. Thinking through it, we should try to form a political party, a [political] instrument of the street trading family, and see from here on in what we could actually achieve, and how we could defend our interests from within [the political system]. But imagine if one of our number became the mayor. It would be really good to bring participation in politics inside [the control of] the street trading family.

On the whole, though, interviewees thought that it was not helpful for the Federation to be allied with political parties, saying, "We mustn't ally ourselves with any political party, we have to work organically." In the end, the Executive Committee felt that it would cost too much to pursue this particular course of action, and the plan fell by the wayside.

Leaders of civic organizations "protect" themselves from party political influence by maintaining a rhetorical emphasis on the importance of preserving the separateness of the trade union sphere from that of the state and politics. This separation has the backing of the Constitution, as the protection of the *fuero sindical* (art. 159) illustrates.[10] The fuero sindical is a kind of diplomatic immunity for trade union leaders, and something frequently stressed by trade unionists. For example, one of the most important initial demands of the peasants who went on a hunger strike in September 2003 was freedom for a community leader who had been jailed for murder, arguing on the basis of fuero sindical. Fuero sindical has its roots in the colonial system of different courts or fueros for different professions, such as the church and the military.[11] A contemporary version of that fuero system (although not explicitly named as such) operates through an agreement between the local police service and the Federation, that the police will send any trade union conflicts or problems to be addressed at least in the first instance within their trade union structure. Hence the concern of the Federation leader for the appropriate jurisdiction under which to assess the conflict between the mother and daughter described earlier.

Politics (party politics) was understood as something that pollutes and corrupts, a perception that is common globally (Castells 2004).[12] Don Eugenio said:

Really the people who go with the political parties do so really for jobs, personal capriciousness, right? Now we see that people are tired of politics here in

Bolivia. I think that it's not the same politics as before. It's politicking, so that ordinary people are simply the servants for those who are there on the career ladder [i.e., politicians].

Don Luciano added his personal experience:

Sometimes people from the alcaldía offered me money but I didn't accept. I can't sell myself for a few Bolivianos. I can't do that to my family of street traders. I'm going to continue struggling. . . . I will defend the interests of my base, that was always my goal. In reality the political parties don't run things in that way. . . . Whatever party they belong to they work for personal interests. That's really what we don't like. I especially don't like people swindling me. I've never liked them swindling me, I've always been transparent.

Accusing a leader of party political allegiance functions as a way of delegitimizing him or her. It may be that the rejection of party politics is in some sense a contemporary version of the anarchosyndicalist thought that was dominant in trade unionism in La Paz, particularly that of the market women, in the 1920s (Lehm and Rivera Cusicanqui 1988). Trade union and civic leaders are accused of joining political parties because of their individual and personal interests, in contrast to the group interests of the bases whom they serve. It is perhaps ironic that in serving their individual interests, they replace one affiliation not with a highly individualistic form of political action, but by joining a competing group, that is, the political party.

MAKING COLLECTIVE CITIZENSHIP

The political party may be a good example of Albó's "individualism within the group," where the group coheres because of common interests. In contrast, I argue that there is a slightly different dynamic at play in the street traders unions, without going so far as to argue for an overdetermination of individual behavior by the group. We might find an indication of what this is in the gender understandings that are sometimes brought into play with regard to corruption. Frequently, although not always, women are said to be less corruptible than men, and sometimes more radical politically. Doña Leonor once said matter-of-factly, "Men are always weak." Don Alberto thought that women might be argumentative, but "the majority of our male comrades are looking to serve personal appetites, aren't they? They have become leaders only in order to be [electoral] candidates, only to work in some place [in government]—that's what they're after. But the female comrades are genuinely striving to make social demands [reivindicación social]." The contrast made between "personal appetites" and the interests of the group brings to mind some of the feminist work on women's relational or social sense of self. Whether it is attributed to biological essence, early psychological development, socialization, or necessity because of our structural position in the reproductive economy, some feminist scholars posit a gender differential in the development of a more social or collective sense of self (Gilligan 1982; Chodorow 1978). This accompanies the philosophy of the "ethic of care" and a greater ability for empathy and solidarity with the marginalized and oppressed (Hekman 1997; Harding 1986). Such characteristics may not actually be gender specific, but are often seen as more feminine than masculine, at least in Western political thought. Thus within the street traders associations, one often gets the impression that the collective is attempting to draw out the characteristics which some Western feminists see as the "feminine" (social/collective) aspects of its members' selves against their more "masculine" (individual) impulses. And to a certain extent, these gendered expectations are shared by the street traders themselves.

We may remain agnostic about their actual gender ascription, but the emphasis on the social and collective as opposed to the individual is undoubtedly a central feature of trade union life. The fact that it needs reemphasizing in the various ways discussed in this chapter points to its fragility and contingency. However, it also points to the fact that the value of communalism is, as Gary Urton (1992) argues, widely shared at least as an ideal or goal. That notion of communalism is based upon a particular interpretation or experience of the self which is beyond that of individuals pursuing self-interested strategies, as one might expect given the scholarly emphasis on individualism within the market economy and especially the informal economy in places like El Alto.

Individualism and rational calculation of self-interest does play its part in people's decisions to join a union or association. However, in many senses, the bonds that make the collectivity also just are: you just are a member of the union, a vecino, or a parent, and that requires you to do certain things, to act "organically." That this goes without saying is constituted and reinforced by the physical experience of togetherness and commonality of purpose expressed and constituted in the kinds of organizational values and practices I have described in this chapter. One of their effects is that people experience their citizenship as mediated by a set of nested affiliations, from kinship or occupational group up. The organizational structure of the trade unions mirrors this nested kind of citizenship and is reinforced during the dances, civic parades, and demonstrations in which citizens participate. Citizenship here is bound up in the relationship of the part, that is, individual selves, to the particular collectivity that at any one point mediates their relationship to the state and the nation. Viewing that relationship as a commoditized exchange of duties for rights illuminates only part of the picture and fails to explain the political power that such organic relationships between individual and collective can wield from time to time, as the following chapters demonstrate. It is paradoxical that such powerful collectivities have arisen at a time when the dominant economic model stresses competition and individual interest. They should be seen both as a reaction to the neoliberal assault on more traditional class-based political entities and a product of the concomitant reorganization of the economy. Instead of disappearing, class-based political formations of the poor have reshaped themselves, drawing strength from past traditions and present circumstances.

From the previous chapter's emphasis on political subjectivity and collective selfhood, I move in this chapter to another central aspect of citizenship: political agency and the specific relationships between citizens and the state in El Alto. I examine this through a case study of one street traders association, the Asociación de Comerciantes Minoristas de Pesca y Acuicultura Central Pescaderas Norte, Sud, Interprovincial e Interdepartamental de la Ciudad de El Alto, or the *pescaderas*, the fish-sellers, whose market is located at Final Los Andes in the northern part of the city. They have a history of problems with the municipal authorities and in 2003 were embroiled in a particularly difficult conflict with a federation of fishermen from the provinces. Their story illustrates some of the tensions that can result from the intermediary position of the unions between traders and the state. I explore the ways that the multitiered trade union structure works in practice and how at all levels problems arise from the dual function of associations and federations as both substitute for the state and mediator between citizens and the state. I also investigate the political relationship between El Alto and its rural hinterland, a relationship that has become particularly salient in the extraordinary events of recent years. An examination of its dynamics on a more day-to-day level helps us to appreciate some of its complexities and ambiguities.

The competition between the pescaderas and a rival union for state (and development agency) patronage fractures along the lines of urban and rural jurisdictions, as both organizations span the two. State actors seek to uphold freedom of trade as expressed in the infamous Decree 21060. However, they also need to seek partners in order to control commerce in El Alto, partly because of the power of the unions, partly because of their own preconceptions. The result is that they look to one of the rival organizations to supervise the trade in fish, while assuring the other that its members will be free to sell in the same site. The organizations for their part attempt to play off different parts of the state against each other to preserve what they feel to be their rights of jurisdiction over commerce in the area. The case study therefore provides insight into the tensions of labor organization and citizenship under neoliberalism. The promotion of privatization and free trade happens in a context in which the state and unions are interdependent: the state needs the unions to regulate economic activity, and the unions need the state to confer legitimacy. This relationship between state and civil society shapes citizenship in El Alto today. Negotiations between the two sides are often conflictual and difficult, and trade union politics is as much characterized by factionalism, rumor, and intrigue as is state politics. So the case study has two main threads: an examination of some of the intricacies of trade union politics and an ethnography of a small part of state bureaucracy from the perspective of its partner organizations.

The pescaderas' case also illustrates the relationships between commerce, ethnicity, and political agency in El Alto more generally. Linda Seligmann (1989) has highlighted the importance of the intermediary position of market traders as they connect the rural economy with national and metropolitan markets. She argues that being "in between" in this sense gives them considerable political power, which is linked to their chola ethnicity. Geographically also, El Alto lies in between La Paz and the rest of the country, as all but one of the four roads out of the capital city that can take reasonable levels of traffic go through El Alto, and the main roads converge at the Ceja. Thus, if alteños choose to blockade the few roads down to the city of La Paz, as they did in September and October 2003, they can wield significant political power. These different kinds of "in-betweenness" as experienced by the fish-sellers are central to alteño and national political life and citizenship.

BACKGROUND AND HISTORY OF THE CONFLICT

Don Alberto Mamani, a member of the Executive Committee of the Federation of Gremialistas, filled me in on the history of the pescaderas' association.[1] The commercialization of fish is relatively recent in Bolivia; about twenty years ago, fish was mostly eaten only by those who lived in the provinces around the banks of Lake Titicaca, to the north of La Paz. At that time, a few (around five) women traveled from the lake to the Ceja, to sell fish "directly from the producer [the fishermen] to the consumer." They founded an association in the Ceja but were moved a few years later, in the mid-1980s, to a site on the road to Oruro, opposite the traffic police station. As the population of El Alto grew, so did the market for fish, and by the late 1980s, a system of intermediaries had developed. The women who went to the lake, bought fish from the fishermen there, and then transported the fish to El Alto became wholesalers. In the city, they sold the fish to a further level of intermediaries, women who sold small quantities in other markets in the city, called *detallistas*. In the early 1990s, the pescaderas had to move for a second time. They went to the Avenida Chacaltaya, a particularly good site for them as it was at the main entrance to the 16 de Julio market. However, it was also opposite the prestigious air force base, and the authorities were unwilling to grant them legal permission to sell in that area. So the pescaderas moved once more, to Final Los Andes, where they have stayed since, putting considerable energy into organizing themselves as an association. The association of pescaderas gradually grew; they had begun with members from one or two sectors, and by 2003 had twenty-three sectors in five provinces of the department of La Paz, comprising over two hundred members.

In 1997, they declared themselves independent from the Federation of Street Traders, something that Don Alberto clearly felt was a mistake; as a result, he said, the pescaderas had nobody who would defend them from the municipal authorities. This became a serious issue when Jose Luis Paredes was sworn in as mayor in early 2000. His municipal authorities repeatedly sent the police out to remove the pescaderas from Final Los Andes. Officially, this was at the behest of the local vecinos, but Don Alberto thought that it had more to do with the influence that a rival union leader had in the alcaldía. She had previously been a candidate for the MIR, and in 2003 was notorious for setting up parallel associations in the Ceja. Many affiliates of her association in the Ceja sell fish, so she had a clear interest in removing their competition from Final Los Andes.

Eventually, some "brave comrades" from the pescaderas' association came back to the Federation, saying that they could not defend themselves against the municipal authorities without their support. By mobilizing his friendship with Irineo Espinoza, a municipal councilor at the time for the MIR,[2] Don Alberto managed to get the authorities to back off, at least for a while. With some of the pescaderas, he helped depose the leader who had declared independence from the Federation, Don Felix Quispe. Doña Veronica took over in 2000 but resigned after two years, and Doña Maria Quispe then took over as general secretary. In 2003, the pescaderas had some suspicions of financial mismanagement during Doña Veronica's term of office.

Unfortunately the pescaderas' problems did not stop with the removal of Don Felix, as Don Roberto Quispe, the executive of the Departmental Federation of Fishing Workers of La Paz (Federación Departamental de Trabajadores Pesqueros de La Paz), then came on the scene. In early 2002 he led a protest march, demanding, among other things, a "fish terminal" in El Alto, where fishermen from the provinces could sell directly to consumers. By mid-2003, the La Paz departmental prefect's office appeared to be taking this demand seriously. When I went to the relevant prefect office to investigate, Don Roberto Quispe was there. He had been told that a gringa was supporting the pescaderas and was eager to tell me his side of the story. He contended that the Final Los Andes pescaderas had not demanded anything like this from the prefecture themselves, that only when it subsequently appeared that the prefecture was responding to his demand did they want to be involved. He said that there was a large amount of money belonging to the association which had simply disappeared and which could have bought a piece of land to be a commercial center had they really wanted it, clearly a thinly veiled accusation of corruption on the part of the Final Los Andes leaders.

He also said that the pescaderas had intimidated women who occasionally came from Lake Titicaca and Oruro to the city to sell fish, preventing them from selling directly to consumers. According to him, they demanded that women who sold fish only occasionally should affiliate with their association, for substantial amounts of money. He argued that the Final Los Andes pescaderas were middlewomen who earned a good profit, possibly 15 to 20 Bolivianos per arroba (25 pounds), which was money that the fishermen themselves should be earning.[3] Both his affiliates (i.e., the fishermen) and the detallistas (i.e., the smaller-scale intermediaries in El Alto) wanted to bypass the Final Los Andes wholesalers. Furthermore, the Final Los Andes association had demanded that the detallistas affiliate to them, but it was not possible for them to do so, as they were also affiliated to the markets where they sold their products and could not afford to belong to two. Don Roberto Quispe also said that the pescaderas had obliged affiliates to dance in fiestas and had suspended some of those who had not danced. "Nowhere in the Constitution does it say that dancing is obligatory," he said, hinting at the importance of dance as citizenship practice. The pescaderas themselves did not deny this, but they said that these kinds of things had happened under previous leaders of their association and would not happen again.

Don Alberto Mamani (from the Federation) argued that many of the participants in the protest march of 2002 led by Don Roberto were in fact pescaderas from Final Los Andes. The pescaderas there were also angry with Don Roberto for using photographs of them in his application to the Spanish Embassy for funds for the proposed fish terminal, pretending that they were members of his association. According to the pescaderas, Don Roberto had also begun to harass them. He told fishermen not to sell to those who belong to the Final Los Andes association, and "his" people attacked "their" people, overturning and spoiling their merchandise in Batallas, a town near the lake. In a meeting of the pescaderas in early July, some also accused him of sexual harassment. Part of the reason for accusing Doña Veronica (the leader of the pescaderas' association between 2000 and 2002) of financial mismanagement was probably that she was involved in the establishment of a parallel pescaderas association located in Nueva Jerusalen and allied with Don Roberto. Both sides accused the other of high-handedness and *buscando sus apetitos personales* (seeking [the fulfillment of] their personal appetites, i.e., being corrupt); both vigorously denied that they were either.

In mid-2003, it looked as though the prefecture was ready to find land for the fish terminal. The political context for this was the success of the Aymara peasant mobilizations of 2000 and 2001, one of the results of which was the prefecture agreeing to grant Felipe Quispe's Confederación Sindical Única de Trabajadores Compesinos de Bolivia (CSUTCB) control over land in El Alto for two "peasant markets," where producers could sell directly to consumers. The office of the Servicio Departamental Agropecuario de la Prefectura (SEDAG; Prefecture Departmental Service for Agriculture and Fisheries) had made arrangements to find land for the construction of a fish terminal with financial assistance from the Spanish Embassy. Because Don Roberto Quispe was friends with the people in SEDAG, he was best placed to control the proposed fish terminal. Rumors had it that he was planning to charge an affiliation fee of US$500 to each person who wanted to sell fish there, but he energetically denied this, saying it was "calumny and lies."

The Final Los Andes association argued that they should be in charge of any terminal, which in their opinion should be called a "commercial center of fish," because their association had supervised the sale of fish in the city for over twenty years. The difference in terminology is significant, because Quispe was arguing in favor of a direct producer–consumer relationship, while the pescaderas wished to preserve their position as intermediaries. They might have had a stronger case in the eyes of the state authorities if they had had full documentation as an association, specifically an *ordenanza municipal*, which is a municipal order conferring on an association the legal right to trade in a certain location. The problem was that successive municipal administrations were not happy with the locations chosen by the pescaderas for their markets: fish markets are smelly and unsightly and particularly likely to provoke opposition from local vecinos. They had not therefore granted the ordenanza municipal and had indeed repeatedly tried to move the pescaderas on. However, the pescaderas did have legal personhood, which helped them make their case, and the Federation of Street Traders was prepared to vouch for their longevity.

By August 2003, the pescaderas and Roberto Quispe had signed a convenio under the supervision of the prefecture, promising mutual respect. That meant that women from Don Roberto Quispe's federation would not be prevented from selling their fish at Final Los Andes, although according to Don Alberto they would be expected to support the activities of the association with occasional but small financial contributions. In return, Quispe promised not to harass the pescaderas from Final Los Andes. However, the dispute over who would control the commercialization of fish in El Alto remained. When I interviewed Don Alberto, he said that the mayor was more or less amenable to the creation of a commercial center for fish supervised by the Final Los Andes pescaderas but accessible to members of Don Roberto Quispe's federation. On the other hand, SEDAG (at the prefecture) remained convinced that Quispe should run the terminal. However, both the mayor and the prefecture stressed that neither organization could charge extortionate amounts to those who wanted to sell in areas they controlled, because that would go against the free trade provisions of the 21060 law.

The location of the fish terminal or commercial center also remained under discussion. The alcaldía proposed land on the road to Laja, but Don Alberto Mamani pointed out that most of the fish-sellers arrive in El Alto via the road to Copacabana (i.e., Lake Titicaca). It was not economically viable for them to pay two fares, one to get to El Alto and then another to get to the terminal/center. It was not practical either to do this journey with several tins of fish. As he remarked, the commercialization of fish needs a lot of care, as the product does not last much over twenty-four hours and hygiene is extremely important. Therefore a central location on the road to Copacabana would be much more appropriate. They had some ideas of land that could be used and were going to propose them to the authorities in a series of future meetings.

"ESO ES LUCHAR SINDICALMENTE": *SUBSTITUTING FOR THE STATE*

The pescaderas were asserting their rights to oversee the wholesale marketing of fish in El Alto and to substitute for the state in the regulation of this sphere. As in other parts of the world, the street traders associations seek to protect their ability to self-regulate as far as possible (Basile and Harris-White 2000). This is also compatible with the neoliberal "solution" to the informal sector that has inspired Bolivian governments since the 1990s, namely deregulation, as advocated in Hernando de Soto's influential book *The Other Path* (1989). De Soto argued that the costs of being legal in developing countries were too high for poor traders, largely because of the bureaucracy involved in setting up a stall, getting a permit, and so on. His solution was to reduce state regulation in all sectors of the economy, which would have the effect of merging the informal with the formal. Governments thus have two main options for dealing with the black market: either try to instigate a clampdown in order to force people to formalize or legalize their businesses, or allow (parts of) the informal sector to self-regulate, thus delegating the costs of regulation to entities such as the trade unions, who become de facto state agents. Bolivian national governments did not follow de Soto's advice in its entirety, but they did remove sales tax for those with small amounts of capital and left the regulation of street trading in the hands of local governments and trade unions.[4] The trade unions defend this situation fiercely because it places them in the position of negotiator with and therefore partner of the state, a position that gives them considerable power within the commercial sector itself. However, it can lead to some insecurity for the unions, as what are essentially ad hoc arrangements are vulnerable to the kinds of conflicts outlined earlier. In a conflictual situation, there is always the danger that affiliates will choose to abandon the organization they perceive to be on the losing side (as electors do with political parties).

Under everyday circumstances the street traders associations have considerable regulatory responsibilities. They control how many traders can sell in their part of the street or fixed market and formalize the ownership of particular stalls: overseeing changes in ownership and defining and regulating the size of the stall and what products are sold. The directorio monitors whether vendors are not attending their stall regularly, keeping it orderly, or helping to clean their part of the street. In the past few years, they have also taken on the responsibility of organizing the policing of their market through raising quotas to hire private security. The problem for the pescaderas by 2003 was that they were not fully able to control or regulate their sphere. Substitution for the state is a process that can be riven with tensions and difficulties, and in this the pescaderas' experience is not unusual. The conflict with Roberto Quispe meant that the pescaderas were highly vulnerable to internal division and the setting up of parallel associations, as Doña Veronica had done in Nueva Jerusalen. Parallel associations can ingratiate themselves to those in authority by paying taxes or bribes or by promising support in future elections. Although this is common, the Nueva Jerusalen group had not, to my knowledge, done so, but their power came from their more amicable relationships with Don Roberto Quispe. He was encouraging members of his federation to sell fish to the Nueva Jerusalen pescaderas instead of to the Final Los Andes women. He enforced that ban by preventing those who contravened this order from going out on the lake to fish. The Final Los Andes pescaderas were very upset that they were losing trading partners at the lake.

The conflict between the pescaderas and Don Roberto Quispe revolved around accusations of abuse of power by the leaders. The pescaderas accused Quispe of physical and even sexual harassment. Quispe himself contended that the pescaderas' accusations were defamatory. The conflict became highly personal, as the accusations of corruption on both sides testify. Quispe hinted that the pescaderas' leaders had embezzled association money, while the pescaderas contended that Quispe had a reputation for corruption in previous trade unions he had headed, particularly the truck drivers union. All these allegations indicate the importance of rumor and suspicion of the leaders by the bases in trade union politics: each side tried to impugn the other's personal character by suggesting that they were "buscando sus apetitos personales." Quispe's accusation that the pescaderas' former leaders had obliged association affiliates to dance in fiestas was also important. His contention that "nowhere in the Constitution does it say that dancing is obligatory" was one that I heard frequently in general assemblies that I attended. The general opinion was that it was wrong to oblige affiliates to dance, largely because of the cost of costumes, quotas for the band, and beer. Although it was acceptable to fine members who did not attend demonstrations and civic parades, dancing was less obligatory. My suspicion is that the constant rhetorical emphasis on the voluntary nature of dancing hints that some feel dancing to be obligatory in the same way as demonstrations and parades are. However, the widely acknowledged effects of the economic crisis, and more particularly the rise of Evangelical Protestantism, have meant that it is now less acceptable than before to oblige people to dance and drink alcohol. As the previous chapter argued, the dance is one of the ways that associations reinforce their communality and bind members together. Dancing is not an obligation that you fulfill in exchange for certain rights or protections from the organization, but is simply something you do by virtue of being a member. So the assertion of the right not to participate is a political act, and it highlights the ways that changes in cultural norms are undermining some collective behaviors. When Quispe and others refer to the Bolivian Constitution to make this claim, they are drawing on legalistic rights-based discourses that conflict with more communal understandings of association membership.

The tensions resulting from competing understandings of the relationship between traders and unions are also revealed in the issue of affiliation itself. Quispe accused the pescaderas of preventing women from the provinces from selling at Final Los Andes unless they paid to affiliate with their association, and of demanding that detallistas who bought from them affiliate with their association. For their part, the pescaderas said that Quispe was proposing to demand US$500 from new affiliates of his association once the fish terminal was built and he was in charge, an allegation that he denied vigorously. Despite the civil servants' emphasis on the importance of the freedom of trade, nobody questioned the need to pay to affiliate with an association or the importance of having an association in charge of a market space. Their concerns were more about the details: the detallistas could not pay to affiliate to the Final Los Andes association because they would already be paying quotas to the association of traders where they sold the fish; the amount of US$500 would be the abuse of Quispe's power, not the fact of charging for affiliation per se; and the women from the provinces could not afford to pay as much as the Final Los Andes association was alleged to have demanded from them. The agreement in August 2003 protected the provincial women from high charges but did leave it open for them to be charged a small amount for each day that they sold at Final Los Andes. Furthermore, both sides in the conflict scoffed at the suggestion from civil servants that both associations could control the fish terminal, albeit perhaps partly as a negotiating tactic, an acceptable solution of last resort. Without a doubt, both sides recognized that controlling the terminal would bring power and money for their organizations, as fish-sellers would be likely to leave the losing union and affiliate with the other.

The Role of the Federation and Relations between the Federation and the Associations The Federation provided crucial support for the Final Los Andes pescaderas in their fight for the right to regulate their particular area, support that depended on the individual personalities involved on both sides. The way this worked reveals much about the nature of leadership in these trade unions, an important cross-cutting theme of this part of the book. As Don Alberto recounted to me, the pescaderas had dealt with many problems throughout their history. His emphasis on the ins and outs of their relationship to the Federation of Street Traders indicates the importance he placed on the protection that their affiliation with the Federation would give. The Federation Executive Committee understood their protective role as conferring increased legitimacy on the association as well as the provision of practical assistance. Don Alberto's ability to protect the pescaderas from police harassment came partly from his legal knowledge and the confidence to stand up to police officers, and partly from his friendship with Irineo Espinoza, a municipal councilor at the time and Don Alberto's neighbor.

Various Executive Committee members assisted the pescaderas in their dealings with the state, for example accompanying them to the prefecture, demanding access for them, and presenting their case in terms that the prefecture's people would understand. Don Braulio Rocha (the Federation executive secretary) also convened a meeting with Roberto Quispe to try to resolve the issue without the interference of the authorities. One meeting was aborted because Quispe and his directorio came to the street outside the Federation offices but then went to Nueva Jerusalen and communicated by cell phone with the Federation leaders and Doña Maria to try to persuade them to meet them there, at the site belonging to the rival pescadera association. They used the excuse that there were too many of their people to fit in the Federation offices. The Federation Executive Committee was well aware of the implications of this symbolic politics of space and were angry at Quispe's demand, so the meeting did not take place. In July, though, they managed to convene another, which Quispe did attend and which was in the appropriate location, the Federation offices, reinforcing their own claims to jurisdiction over commerce in El Alto. The final convenio between the two associations was signed at the offices of SEDAG.

Federation leaders were also very involved in the internal politics of the pescaderas' association. Throughout the conflict with Don Roberto Quispe, Don Alberto Mamani also advised Doña Maria and her directorio on what they should do when confronted with rumors of spies in general assemblies, people spreading rumors about them, difficulties with their husbands, and other problems. For example, in early July, a group of five members of the directorio, including Doña Maria, came to the Federation's office very concerned because they had found out that some land had been given over to Quispe, they thought for the purpose of building a terminal. One woman was close to resigning; she pointed out that she had lost her *caseros* (regular clients) because of having been so busy with this conflict and not going out to sell enough. They were all very frustrated and anxious about the situation. Don Alberto took them into the inner office and began to advise them on the best way to pursue their struggle. He recommended that Doña Maria organize commissions to go to different places and find out what was going on, then to return and inform the rest. He said that these commissions should go everywhere: if Roberto Quispe enters into a bureaucrat's office, then they too should go in right behind him. For official hearings, all should go. In general, the directorio should be unified and not show any doubts or conflicts. He told them that being a leader is like being husband and wife: they can fight, but must not do so in front of the children, and their bases were their children. The important thing was for them to "be strong. I know you're a revolutionary compañera. They [Roberto Quispe and allies] have capital in money, we have human capital." He told them not to be put off by the "psychological war" of rumors and gossip which was seeking to turn the members of the directorio against each other, given that this was an inevitable part of being a leader. He told them that their aim was to get to the point where people decided not to struggle any more, and so would negotiate, and advised them to discuss what they might be able to agree to if and when this happened, assuring them that the struggle could not continue forever.

Don Alberto's mixing of military and revolutionary and family metaphors is quite notable here, and typical of Federation discourse. Aside from that issue, the importance of this incident is twofold. First, it is clear that prosecuting such complex and difficult conflicts was an extremely stressful experience for the directorios, and they relied upon the Federation for assistance and reassurance. Doña Maria was finding it very difficult, which was compounded by the fact that her husband was starting to become annoyed at the amount of time she was spending on association business. Second, the main thrust of Don Alberto's advice consisted of encouraging Doña Maria to lead more effectively, from practical advice that she should tell her directorio where they should go and what they needed to find out, to the encouragement that she should be strong and not listen to malicious gossip. Although the dominant rhetoric around leadership is that leaders serve their bases, this position was not inconsistent with a need for strong leadership in times of trouble. The bases make the final decisions, but on a day-to-day basis the general secretary has to be able to make quick decisions about what his or her directorio should do, and enforce those decisions. Don Alberto was training Doña Maria as a trade union leader; he told her, "This is the trade union struggle" (*eso es luchar sindicalmente*).

Part of the present directorio's problem was probably that they had been going to different advisors in the Federation. As a result, a number of members of the Executive Committee were involved in this complex and long-running dispute. It appears that one was also advising Doña Veronica, although another member of the committee told me that he was doing this for Doña Veronica's personal benefit and not for that of the bases.[5] Meanwhile, it appears that Doña Maria did not entirely trust Don Alberto to help them, so had appealed to another member of the Executive Committee, Don Eugenio Awircata. When I asked Don Alberto about this, he told me that it was fine because he and Don Eugenio both had different skills, and he did not always have the free time necessary to devote to this particular problem. As he said, it was their case, and it was up to them whom they chose to advise them. He did not speak of the third member of the committee who was assisting Doña Veronica.

Don Alberto was an experienced trade unionist, with a background in peasant unions and as executive secretary of a federation of workers who sold their products at the annual Alasitas market in El Alto.[6] He had attended various training sessions run by the Cuban Embassy and was politically well connected. Don Eugenio had previously worked in the La Paz alcaldía, so was especially experienced in judicial and municipal matters. Don Eugenio worked particularly hard, coming into the Federation office almost every day to mediate problems, give advice, and type up official documents connected to associations' business. Other Federation delegates assisted the pescaderas when they attended hearings with the state authorities and in explaining the situation to their affiliates in general assemblies. They prepared mountains of documentation to back up the meetings, including letters to the prefect and the mayor, various *votos resolutivos* (resolution votes), and a declaration of a state of emergency, not to mention letters to and agreements with Quispe, denunciations to the Federation, and witness statements.

Members of the Federation Executive Committee are often highly experienced people working on very complex issues with very little qualified legal assistance and no salaries. It is indeed quite remarkable that people had the energy to work like this, and the pride that comes from serving one's community in such a way was very important for them. The recognition of this was all that Don Alberto said he wanted during the discussions described here. He asked the women, "What interest do I have in damaging you [with bad advice]?" and replied to his own question, saying, "My only interest is in helping, and one day enjoying a respectful greeting" from them. The pescaderas also used particular cultural practices to make the Federation leaders help them. Just before their hearing at the prefecture, they came to the Federation's central office with a huge *apthapi* meal of different kinds of fried fish, eggs, potatoes, *chuño*, and *tunta* (two types of freeze-dried potato). An apthapi is a communal meal where every participant contributes some food. The contributions are put in a big pile on an awayu on a table (or the ground), and everyone eats whatever food they like. With the pescaderas, all of those present shared the meal, eating our fill from the mountain of food. After we had all gorged ourselves, Don Braulio made a speech to thank the pescaderas. Like the rituals described in chapter 5, the apthapi at the Federation offices was a means of gaining assistance from the Executive Committee through the obligations created by the sharing of food, in a further example of the importance of commensality in the creation of agency (cf. Harris 1982). The apthapi was more than preemptive payment to the Federation for their future support of the association when they were due to go to the prefect's office. It created the obligation on the part of the Federation to fulfill this role effectively, and can be seen as one of the ways in which the relational notions of selfhood described in the previous chapter are actualized in collective practices to create particular understandings of agency and obligation.

The bond between the leaders of the Federation and their bases, who are the directorios of individual associations, is thus forged in both everyday practices of problem solving and ritual practices of sharing food or, more commonly, soft drinks. The food and drink may be seen as payment for services rendered, especially given the fact that trade union leaders do not get a salary. However, the practice of sharing food and drink has strong ritual parallels with the ways that people relate to the spirits (see chapter 5). In some sense the relationship thus constituted through exchange is also similar: it is an unequal one between those with more power or knowledge and those who need their assistance. Commensality encourages a sense of obligation and exchange between those sharing food, but does not absolutely guarantee that those being appealed to will respond. Trade union leaders who do work hard do so for different reasons, such as the prestige that comes from doing a good job, personal conviction, or because they have no other job at the time. But being a trade union leader can be very tiring and involve a considerable amount of effort. The complexities of conflicts that arise can also lead to high levels of stress, which arise from the tensions and factionalism involved in processes of self-regulation in the place of the state. The conflict discussed here has shown some of the practical implications of the decision to take on a leadership role (and to do it well) that some leaders spoke about in the abstract in the previous chapter.

THE STATE: MEDIATION AND NEGOTIATION

Legally speaking, the conflict between the two associations was about the freedom of trade. Some of the civil servants involved argued that if either side were to control a fish terminal and charge extortionate fees to prospective affiliates, they would be infringing the free trade provisions of Decree 21060.[7] However, the people from the municipality and the prefecture did not take the notion of free trade so far as to assume that the existence of a union controlling access to the terminal made trade unfree, or that it was more properly the role of the state to control access. They were more than ready to negotiate with representatives of the producers and wholesalers and distributors of fish, and some were prepared to support the claims of one association over another. Through the implementation of neoliberal economic policies and laws, the Bolivian state reinforced the necessity of collective organization because its agents cannot negotiate directly with the household-based units of production produced through economic restructuring. Trade unions and the state are interdependent: the state gives legality to the union and needs organizations to do regulatory work in its stead (Cross 1998); trade unions seek to defend their members against the measures of a sometimes predatory government when they consider that it is attempting to overregulate (Clark 1988). As Foweraker (1990) has pointed out, the unions' ability to solve practical problems for their members usually requires some sort of negotiation with the state. In Bolivia, state actors will not (or cannot) negotiate with individuals, thus collective organizations become necessary as counterparts.

The pescaderas' struggle highlights two important ways that associations of traders mediate between their members and the state in its different guises. First, it illustrates how Bolivian citizens relate to the state through protests. In the pescaderas' case, as a functionary explained to me, the reason that SEDAG were so willing to help Roberto Quispe was because they were responding to one of the demands in a petition (pliego petitorio) presented during a protest march that he headed. In the context of pressure from the national government to respond to the demands made by the peasants of the CSUTCB during their blockades of 2000 and 2001, it was very important that SEDAG respond as far as they could to a similar set of demands. If this meant that they went against the interests of another group of people (who, as Don Alberto pointed out, had participated in the march), then that was perhaps an unfortunate side effect. The pescaderas' discussions at different points in the conflict about holding a march or a hunger strike were a sensible response to this aspect of their relationship with the state. As their rival, Don Roberto Quispe, said to me, "Every citizen has the right to demand his needs" (cada ciudadano tiene todo derecho de exigir sus necesidades).

Second is the relationship that traders associations and the Federation have with the state bureaucracy and the role of personalism in that relationship. This section examines how state bureaucracies operate in Bolivia. I was present one afternoon when the pescaderas went to see the prefect. They were particularly concerned to be early for their 3 P.M. appointment because they had been five minutes late for the previous appointment and were sent away. One of the prefect's people, a young man, came out while they were preparing themselves outside to tell them that the prefect would not see them and that they should go to the offices of SEDAG, in El Alto. However, they persisted and went in to the prefect's office in a group of around fifteen, the members of the directorio. The secretary in the reception area explained to them that their case was being decided in the SEDAG offices in El Alto and that there would be a hearing there the following Monday. They remained, though, and Don Alberto Mamani went into the inner office with another secretary to see if they could get a hearing with the prefect. Don Alberto was later joined by three other members of the Federation Executive Committee, who were all allowed straight through.

The rest of us waited in the reception office until the Federation delegates came out to say that the prefect's people wouldn't receive us, and we all barged in to wait in the corridor between the reception office and the civil servants' rooms. We waited there for about two hours. Various officials came out to talk to the Federation delegates or to try to move us along. We were put in one office to wait, but then told to vacate that because they were having a meeting. One woman brought chairs for us to sit on in the corridor. The pescaderas sat, chatting, eating surreptitiously, talking on their mobile phones, discussing how they might have to hold a hunger strike or go to the press in order to be listened to, and later on giggling and making jokes. Eventually, we were ushered into the meeting room and met with one of the prefect's top advisors. Don Alberto explained the pescaderas' case clearly and relatively concisely at the beginning, while the members of the pescaderas' directorio overcame their initial nerves at speaking. He discussed what he felt to be key points and gradually stepped back as the pescaderas' directorio, particularly the men, took a greater role in the discussions. The women focused initially on the harassment they had suffered at the instigation of Roberto Quispe. Although the advisor told them that this was out of his jurisdiction and should be taken to the relevant legal bodies, the meeting probably helped to make the prefecture take the pescaderas' case more seriously.

The advisor's principal focus was the various legal competencies of the different entities involved. For example, he said that it was not the prefecture's responsibility to recognize one federation or association instead of another, that this was up to the Federation of Street Traders to agree with the body above Don Roberto Quispe's federation, which he thought was the CSUTCB. The advisor argued that the prefecture could only be an intermediary between the different parties, and that the case was the responsibility of SEDAG. Don Alberto and the pescaderas pointed out that the people from SEDAG had taken Don Roberto Quispe's side in their supervision of this dispute. They also explained their allegations about Quispe's behavior toward them, and said that he was misusing the prefect's name, saying that the prefecture had authorized some of his attacks on the pescaderas. In fact, the advisor was not fully cognizant of the details of the case. He was, for example, wrong about Quispe's federation being part of the CSUTCB. To his credit, his aim was to persuade the petitioners to deal with SEDAG, which did know all the particulars. He promised that he would try to attend the upcoming meeting himself, or send another delegate, in order to avoid any partisanship from the prefecture. He also explained the political context of the agreement between the national government and the CSUTCB in August 2001 for the establishment of the two peasant markets in El Alto.[8]

In many ways, the pescaderas and Don Alberto put the prefecture's advisor in a difficult position: they wanted to meet with the prefect himself, or for him to be the mediator between them and Roberto Quispe. They wanted to go straight to the top, in part because of the prefect's power to overrule subordinates, in part because of the structure of the bureaucracy more generally. This strategy was not peculiar to the pescaderas: in an unrelated discussion about whether the mayor would agree to meet with the Federation, Don Jorge eloquently said, "Why would we want to talk with the clown? We have to talk with the owner of the circus" (¿Cómo que con el payaso nos vamos a hablar? Con el dueño del circo tenemos que hablar). Everything revolved around the prefect; seemingly all decisions were made by him, and all functionaries spoke in his name. For example, the advisor at this meeting repeatedly said that the prefect himself would understand the pescaderas' problems, and that he respected them because he had experience of union leadership himself; the advisor was speaking to us in the name of the prefect, not in his own right. At a general assembly of the pescaderas, another representative of the prefecture told them, "The prefect is so generous, so good, he's helping everyone, all the people. . . . The prefect does not want anyone to suffer." In the case of the prefect of the time, Mateo Laura, there was a third reason for seeking to talk directly to him. Laura is of indigenous background, and the pescaderas felt he would understand their situation. One woman said that they wanted to speak directly to Laura because "he's like us, he's people, basically" (es como nosotros, gente nomás es). Here, gente is a Spanish translation of the Aymara word jaq'i, meaning an Aymara person (see Canessa 1998). Roberto Quispe had also noted this, once calling the prefect a provinciano, meaning someone from the provinces, the campo. Laura's ethnicity did give him a substantial amount of credibility with many alteños. Unfortunately, at that particular time, he was too busy to meet with the pescaderas, according to the various functionaries who did speak with them. Yet, according to the pescaderas, they had been promised a hearing with Laura and this particular event was their third time trying. They had been repeatedly turned away by the prefect's people and told to return on another date.

The experience in the prefecture is typical of many Bolivians' experience of state bureaucracy. The various layers of politicians' people spend much of their time gate-keeping, controlling access to the real source of power, and do not have the authority to make decisions themselves. It is the functionaries between the petitioners and the politician who turn away the petitioners, never the politicians themselves. In this way a dynamic is created where the politician can be beyond reproach, because it is always possible that he (it is usually a man) is being shielded from the truth by his people, even though they might be speaking in his name. Thus, if they say something good, they are speaking in his name; if not, they are shielding him from the truth. Petitioners, the representative of the state authority, and the politician himself collude in this belief, at the level of explicit discourse anyway. Another example of this was at a hearing between the Federation and the mayor in mid-August, when all participants maintained the fiction that the mayor's subordinates were at fault and not the mayor himself. It is difficult to tell how self-conscious this is, because people did not tend to make explicit any doubts they had. Certainly several people I spoke to genuinely thought that the mayor was being advised badly by the people around him.

The civil servants also treat the petitioners so badly (in my view) that the potential meeting with the politician takes on an aura of the miraculous: after two hours of waiting at the prefecture, we were all rather light-headed and giggly, and Mateo Laura took on the aspect of a magical and long-awaited end to this particular trial of strength and patience. Actually getting a meeting would have been an achievement in itself. I was surprised at the pescaderas' patience as they doggedly waited for what they saw as their right, an official audience with the prefect. They would be mollified only by being able to raise their concerns with a very senior advisor, certainly not a lowly functionary or secretary, despite the fact that the senior advisor told them precisely the same as what the lower status people had said, namely, that their case would be dealt with at SEDAG.

The issue of the partisanship of SEDAG was also an important aspect of the personalization of the bureaucracy, because the pescaderas knew that Roberto Quispe had become friends with one of the functionaries there. They were convinced that it was because of this that the prefecture was so willing to help him; they held no illusions of bureaucratic impartiality (Herzfeld 1992). However, they did feel that if the prefect himself would only listen to their petition, then somehow he would be able to be impartial. Practically speaking, they also needed to appeal above the head of the SEDAG functionary. In other ways too the pescaderas' story shows the importance of person-to-person contact, for example their concern that the harassment from the authorities was in part the result of the influence that the leader of a competing association had in the municipality. Don Alberto eventually managed to mobilize Jose Luis Paredes in favor of the Final Los Andes pescaderas. His ability to do so was in part due to his connections with Irineo Espinoza, the former councilor and then in 2003 a congressman for the MIR. Mateo Laura was also a MIRista, and it is possible that Irineo Espinoza was in communication with him at some point.

The story of the pescaderas is an example of personalism in action as part of the day-to-day operation of the bureaucracy. The way that story was told to me over time shows that politics and the ordinary activities of the state are about the actions of individuals, rather than the functioning of an impersonal bureaucratic system. Of course, the idea that "the system" should function as such, independent of individual personalities, is a Northern European and North Atlantic idea that is quite culturally specific and probably exceptional, as argued by Michael Herzfeld (1992). In the Bolivian case, the personalization of bureaucracy does have some negative effects. The hierarchical structure of state agencies means that decisions can become concentrated in one person, hence slowing down decision making and conflict resolution. Furthermore, the frequent changeovers in personnel due to the political nature of appointments at all levels can mean a loss of continuity on the part of the state. Continuity comes more from the long-term involvement of the Federation with the pescaderas' association and the historical memory of Don Alberto and the pescaderas' directorio than from the different branches and departments of the state. Nonetheless, the prefecture was in the end able to negotiate some sort of resolution of the conflict. Following the meeting with the advisor, the prefecture involved a different department, that of Citizen Security, because of the allegations of harassment. That department was clearly concerned to sort things out amicably, and their involvement probably did mean that Roberto Quispe was pushed into a position where he had to come to an agreement with the pescaderas. The alcaldía also appeared to be thinking about who should supervise the selling of fish in the city, even though they at first proposed sites for the fish terminal that were totally unsuitable. They were more amenable to the Final Los Andes pescaderas' claims and were a counterweight to SEDAG's support of Quispe.

Jurisdiction: Rural and Urban   One of the key issues for all the bodies involved in the dispute was how to negotiate the rural–urban relationship. Federation leaders persisted in articulating the dispute as a split between rural and urban. They argued that the Final Los Andes association had been selling fish in the city of El Alto for twenty years, and jurisdiction over any urban activities belonged to them. Don Jorge, for example, said in their general assembly, "They're two things—one is urban, the other rural. . . . Are we urban or are we rural?" He used the fact that their association "belonged" to the urban Federation of Street Traders to underline this point. At the same meeting, Don Eugenio said that the members of the parallel association of Nueva Jerusalen should affiliate with the Final Los Andes association because they were in the urban area, "which is our jurisdiction." When Don Braulio met with the pescaderas, he consistently emphasized that he did respect the federation of fishermen, but only in their place.

It is certainly the case that both sides organized themselves in different spheres: one focused on the urban space where the fish was sold, while the other focused on the catching of the fish, mainly in Lake Titicaca. However, of necessity the two regions shaded into each other. The Final Los Andes women had to go to the lake to buy fish, and Roberto Quispe's federation wanted the right to bring fish from the lake into El Alto to sell there. The matter was further complicated by the fact that the women and men of the Final Los Andes association did not all live in El Alto. Some of them had dual residence, some lived in the provinces. Those who lived mainly in the city usually had their pueblo in the lake area and bought fish from their family members and countrymen (*paisanos*) who lived there. Quispe's affiliates were probably in a similar situation. Quispe himself certainly spent much of his time in the city, going through all the legal processes associated with the dispute. It is understandable that, according to one of those involved, the mayor thought that Don Roberto Quispe's federation and the Final Los Andes association were one and the same. Certainly it was easy for Quispe to convince the Spanish Embassy that they were.

The distinction was quite subtle, being focused on individual personalities within the different organizations as well as on the central locus of the legal "personhood" of each organization. Legally and politically, however, the distinction was crucial, not least because the different areas fell largely under different state jurisdictions: the El Alto municipal government was responsible for the city, while the prefecture (especially the SEDAG office) was responsible for the provinces. The different trade unions attempted to play one part of the state off against the other, the pescaderas using Don Alberto's personal connections to influence the mayor, while Quispe used his friendship with the SEDAG functionaries to influence the prefecture (cf. Cross 1998). The conflict was essentially a dispute between rival associations of fish-sellers and organizations of fishermen, both of which spanned the rural and the urban. However, when it suited their purpose, members of the two different bodies did make a distinction between urban and rural, and they wanted it respected. One man said in a meeting at the Federation's office, "As a migrant [*residente*], I'm a vecino of the city of El Alto. I defend my province, yes, but over there. Here [in the city] I defend myself." Others argued that the fishermen of the provinces had their own markets in the campo where they could sell their produce and that the urban area was properly under the jurisdiction of the Federation and the Final Los Andes association.

At the heart of the conflict was a struggle over the position of commercial intermediaries. The Final Los Andes women were most aggrieved at the fact that Quispe was preventing people who lived by the lake and with whom they had a special trading relationship from selling fish to them, especially since their trading partners were in many cases also their kin. When fishermen did sell fish to the pescaderas, Quispe apparently prevented them from going out to fish. By agreement with the prefecture, his federation was responsible for organizing the environmental regulation of fishing in Lake Titicaca, which meant that he could easily enforce his sanctions against those who sold to the Final Los Andes pescaderas instead of to their rivals. However, he was presenting his demands as the demand for the right to sell from (rural) producer direct to (urban) consumer, and the functionaries at SEDAG considered this to be an important principle. Florence Babb (1988) describes a similar case in Peru in the 1970s, when state agencies attempted to bypass the market women and create fairs where producers could sell directly to consumers. There, the campaigns were unsuccessful, as producers generally preferred to sell in bulk to sure buyers rather than spending their time selling small quantities. They recognized the value the market women added to the products they sold in the considerable work of packaging, transporting, building up a client base, and so on. The Final Los Andes pescaderas pointed out that fishermen generally do not catch enough fish to warrant spending the time and money to travel to El Alto; instead, they combine small amounts from different sources in order to make it worthwhile. As one would expect, Don Braulio and the Federation leaders were utterly opposed to the bypassing of commercial intermediaries. Don Braulio said in a meeting, "We can't defend the direct sale from the producer to the consumer; what a disgrace when there are no jobs around." His point reflects another argument made since Hart's (1973) seminal article, which is that employment in the informal sector absorbs the surplus labor of the formal sector, a crucial function in the present economic crisis.

Don Braulio was also asserting a sense of the Federation's social responsibility to protect jobs in the city, in contrast perhaps to Roberto Quispe's more commercially efficient proposition. Some of the accusations against Quispe implied that he was more like a businessman than someone acting in the interests of his affiliates: he sought to streamline the business process by selling directly from producer to consumer and charge high rates for access to the terminal, in dollars, both of which would mean that people would lose their livelihoods. They also accused him of looking to serve his individual interests rather than those of the collectivity. Not only was the conflict between the organizations one about territory and political power, but it was also about competing business interests, which were discussed using the script of jurisdictional difference. Although each side in the conflict was both entrepreneurial and had a sense of social responsibility to its members, they had an interest in painting their opponents as more commercially motivated than interested in serving their affiliates or the wider good.

The pescaderas' position as commercial intermediaries is a difficult one, fraught with factionalism and conflict. They cross geographical and cultural boundaries between the country and the city, their associations mediate political boundaries between the state and the citizen, and they are adept at manipulating the different spheres. They present themselves as representing their members and as having a sense of social responsibility rather than valuing entrepreneurial efficiency. They also place considerable emphasis on organizing themselves as a collectivity, struggling against the pressures of factionalism and individualism and emphasizing organic belonging over a membership based upon rights and responsibilities. However, their strength and coherence as an organization relies upon their ability to mediate with the state and to resolve conflicts within their association and between their association and its rivals. This is no easy task in the fractious sphere of competing business and political interests that is commerce in El Alto.

In the story of the pescaderas we see the complexities of the liminal position of commercial intermediary; I want to conclude this chapter by drawing back from their specific case to assess the political importance of this for El Alto as a whole and returning briefly to the events of September and October 2003. In doing so, the links between ethnicity, commerce, and political agency come to the fore. The pescaderas' story highlights one way in which ethnicity and commerce relate to each other in El Alto and the surrounding provinces. At first glance, it appears to be a conflict between the fishermen and the chola market women, who are the classic intermediaries between the peasants of the provinces (the fishermen) and the mestiza (or chola) consumers in the urban sphere. However, look more closely and we see that in the first place, the Final Los Andes pescaderas are part of a much longer chain of commerce in the urban sphere. They do sell to some consumers, but they also sell to the detallistas, the women who go to markets in El Alto and La Paz and sell small quantities to consumers there. They buy their fish from fishermen in the provinces, but these are frequently their family members. Alternatively, they may actually base themselves in the provinces and come to sell at the market of Final Los Andes a few days a week, perhaps staying with relatives in El Alto or owning one house in the city and one in the provinces. Their ethnic identity shifts as they move from the countryside to the city and back again, and the boundaries between the two are blurred. Yet at the same time they make a distinction between the two spheres for political purposes in order to defend their right to work and to sell. This dynamic of rhetorical separation between rural and urban, and the practical porousness of the boundaries between the two, is not confined to groups such as the pescaderas, but is a key characteristic of El Alto in general, one that has important political implications.

Commerce in the Andes is ethnically marked (Larson and Harris 1995; Seligmann 1989, 1993; Weismantel 2001; Rivera Cusicanqui 2002; Peredo Beltrán 1992). Market women in El Alto and La Paz are known as cholas, and El Alto is a cholo city: most of its inhabitants or their parents have migrated from indigenous rural areas, and 27 percent of adults over fifteen work in commerce, a remarkable statistic and likely an underestimation, as people often engage in occasional commercial activity even while considering themselves primarily housewives or students. As such, El Alto is in the middle of several sets of flows of people and objects, as goods produced in the provinces are brought to the city to sell, alongside contraband transported from the borders with Chile and Brazil. As Linda Seligmann has argued, that intermediary position can be a source of political power. She points out, "The capacity of the cholas to (a) speak and understand the language and behaviour of the peasants; (b) withdraw the services they provide to the mestizos; and (c) ally themselves with the indigenous peasantry increases their prospects for successful political resistance to the existing economic and social order" (1989: 717). The urban mestizos and whites are dependent on the cholas for produce such as fish and other foodstuffs. The cholas' linking of the peasant economy and the national market make them "crucial nodes of the national economy" (707). The cholas fiercely defend their broker position, as the pescaderas opposed the direct sale from producer to consumer. The combination of this broker position and El Alto's position as the link between the city of La Paz and the rest of the country means that concerted action to blockade the city of La Paz by well-organized groups can result in a situation where food supplies simply cannot enter the city and people cannot get out. The siege tactic has a long historical pedigree, at least as far back as the indigenous revolt of 1780 led by Tupac Katari.

A siege or blockade affects different classes and ethnicities differently because of the way that marketing and food provisioning is organized in La Paz and El Alto. People of all classes do the majority of their shopping in markets, even the very wealthy, who tend to complement their market shopping with produce from the growing number of supermarkets. Those from the wealthier classes tend to buy fresher goods more frequently. Their diet is richer in vegetables and fruit, for example, which they buy on a weekly basis, whereas ordinary residents of El Alto often buy staples like potatoes, chuño, rice, and pasta in bulk, or bring potatoes and other vegetables from their fields in the countryside. Between 2000 and 2003, families I knew in El Alto increased the proportion of these kinds of staple foods in their diet and reduced their meat consumption because their economic situation became more difficult. So when there is a blockade, although poorer alteños suffer more from price increases for food and do not have refrigerators to preserve goods, they do have greater stocks of food available to rely upon, and their diet changes relatively less than that of residents of the wealthy parts of La Paz. During the blockades of April 2000, my landlady said to me, "As far as I'm concerned, it's fine. That way, perhaps the government will think a little bit. We're fine here—we have potato, chuño, meat. It's the people who live in Obrajes and Calacoto [i.e., the rich areas of La Paz] who will suffer, because they buy their food each week, don't they?" Furthermore, ordinary alteños mobilize their relationships with the countryside to bring back vegetables for family consumption; groups such as the pescaderas can use the commercial relationships with kin and paisanos that they have developed over the years. Those who are from the areas where the peasants are protesting are frequently let through the blockades because they know the protestors and can therefore bring back provisions for their families, whereas trucks transporting supermarket goods are prevented from proceeding along the main roads, and the supermarkets have to shut down.

Seligmann assumes that cholas will identify with the peasants in any political struggle between whites and Indians. In fact, in Bolivia, "cholo politics" has tended to favor urban populist leaders more than indigenous or peasant movements, although this may be changing. Alteños' relationship with the peasants and the countryside is not quite as straightforward as an automatic identification, as the conflict discussed here illustrates. Many do strongly support the peasants when it comes to political mobilization, yet on the whole they feel that they are different from the people who live in the countryside, largely because they have become accustomed to city life. Nevertheless, although the peasants from their birth villages might be different—they might drink more, eat better food, be stronger or work harder—they are still kin, both figuratively and literally. This can be compared with the strong kin relations that even the most urban fish-sellers had with the fishermen of Lake Titicaca.

For many of those who migrated from the countryside, and often for their children, their affiliation with their pueblo (village of birth) is stronger than that with their place of residence in El Alto, even if in practice they spend more of their time as vecinos than as peasants. Many alteños have strong emotional attachments to their pueblos, and to the countryside in general. When I asked women and children in interviews about the relative advantages and disadvantages of the countryside and the city, they generally considered the countryside a good place to live, at least when the harvests were relatively good. They appreciated that you could produce all that you needed to eat without having to spend money on food, and complained about the necessity for money in the city, saying things like "With money you have to leave the house, and with money enter it." On the other hand, they also recognized that life is very difficult and insecure in the countryside when crops fail, and they told me of the importance of the services available in the city, such as schools, health centers, and transport systems. They said, for example, "Everything is good in the countryside. Except the children's education, that's why we came here"; and "The good things [of the city] are that we have the convenience of public transport. We have electricity, water, sewage systems, toilets, all that. That's the positive aspect, these comforts." But I often felt that if the countryside had these services, many people would prefer to live there than the city, and a number of people even said that to me.

The peasants themselves have an ambiguous relationship with those who have migrated from their village, as the conflict between the provincial fishermen's association and the urban pescaderas also illustrates. David Llanos Layme (1998) has studied the effects of return migration on the rural community of Chari. While many return migrants reintegrate into the community well, some create resentment, as they express attitudes of superiority and individuality and try to enjoy all the rights accorded to community members without being prepared to fulfill their responsibilities. These tensions occur also when migrants visit their pueblos, but equally, migrants can be seen as members of the community even if they spend relatively little time in the pueblo, as long as they attend the important fiestas and are present for planting and harvesting (Canessa 1998).

Few political movements have effectively capitalized on the links between alteños and their pueblos. The most important Aymara movement in Bolivia, Katarismo, has in the past not directed its appeal to ordinary urban Aymaras in El Alto or La Paz. Katarismo has targeted its political efforts at rural areas since its inception in the late 1960s. Despite the fact that many of its leaders were educated urban Aymaras, its rhetoric appealed to indigenous people as noble peasants with an alternative social, political, and economic logic based upon either the ayllu or the peasant union (e.g., see Untoja 2000; Quispe 2001). There is a sense in which the rural–urban migrants are seen as already assimilated into Hispanic society, by virtue simply of having moved to the city, at best a sort of bastardized category of Aymara, lying outside of the essentialized scheme of identification that is perhaps necessary for indigenous politics. Katarismo has found it difficult to deal with the ordinary people like the pescaderas who are both rural and urban and who move between the two spheres with relative facility.

But, as I argued in chapter 1, September–October 2003 was something of a turning point, when the links between city and countryside in El Alto became much more politicized. The most radical parts of El Alto were those in the northern part of the city, which are some of its newest (and poorest) neighborhoods. The residents of these zones tend to be people who have migrated more recently and who therefore have especially strong ties to the provinces. However, alteños throughout the city reacted in particular to the massacre at Warisata. Don Braulio Rocha described that reaction as follows: "That was where the problem was born. The government sent military and police forces to Warisata, where . . . they unleashed a great fury in order to save the tourists. There were deaths, injuries, and this problem affected [*salpicó*] El Alto; and in El Alto we organized support for our peasant brothers." When leaders in El Alto talk of "our peasant brothers," they make use of the rhetorical distinction between urban and rural which enables them to make claims upon an indigenous authenticity in opposition to the (Hispanic) governing elites. The use of the kinship term "brothers" indicates one way that alteños relate to the countryside, kin relations powerfully felt all over El Alto, a fact that political parties and civic organizations are increasingly acknowledging. Thus, for inhabitants of El Alto, the peasants both are and aren't "us"—they are our kin, but not us. El Alto is in the middle, between the rural provinces and the city, and this strategic location, in both a geographical and ethnocultural sense, makes the city a force to be reckoned with when it irrupts into national political life.

However, this was not an automatic unification of cholos and peasants, as Seligmann proposes, and there is a gap between the rhetoric and the actual ability of these groups to unify. As the pescaderas' story shows, the high degree of civic and trade union organization in El Alto can lead to fractious and conflictive relationships as well as to strong and unified action. People perform the rhetoric of kinship with their peasant brothers in a conscious way, using such rhetorical devices to position themselves as collectivities in the context of the economic ties that drive the myriad relationships between city and country. The potential for confrontation over who controls the market for different products in the city is as great as (if not greater than) the potential for unification and thus political power. Specific political circumstances are necessary for the latter to occur at particular moments in time. The point here is that liminality in its different forms—between city and countryside, state and individual, producer and consumer, and Indian and mestizo—is a state that is both powerful and difficult to manage.

This chapter continues the story of the complex relationship with the state that is the context for Bolivian trade unions' political agency and assesses the implications of this for how we understand democracy in Bolivia today. As the previous chapter showed, the street traders unions' principal struggle with different state agencies is over who will control or have jurisdiction over commercial activity; the emphasis placed upon the differentiation between rural and urban spheres was important because of how the various parties to the conflict attempted to exploit what were in practice overlapping state jurisdictions and to assert their rights to be the state's counterpart in particular areas. Other disputes, especially over municipal taxation, demonstrate the Federation's desire to assert their right to regulate "their" sphere, according principally to the values described in chapter 6. Previous administrations in El Alto accepted that separation: Condepa appears to have given more leeway to street traders, granting many associations legal permits to sell and then largely leaving them alone. In that sense, the structure of regulation at the beginning of the twenty-first century has grown up largely in the (partial) absence of the state from that particular sphere, and it is an absence that the street traders seek to defend. They maintain the distinctiveness between the two spheres through the rhetoric of state predation and corruption, as we saw in chapter 6 when trade union leaders distinguished between corrupt politics and organic trade unionism, and through their analysis of the problems that occur when the boundaries between politics and sindicalismo become too porous. Yet in the previous chapter we saw how the trade unions inevitably encounter and negotiate with the state. Part of their ability to do so effectively relies upon the rhetorical separation between the two spheres, which is of particular salience in the contemporary political context and has become a common theme in the discourse not only of ordinary trade unionists but also of politicians and intellectuals. That assertion of difference rests especially on claims about how democratic the two spheres are. In recent years, as the social movements have increased in strength to the point where they became part of the government in December 2005, the political salience of these claims and dynamics is undeniable.

MODELS OF DEMOCRACY

Nicolas Mendoza, an alteño student at the UPEA, argued in a research report he prepared for a course in urban sociology that the mass democracy of community meetings was much more democratic than liberal representative democracy. He illustrated his argument with a description of two elections that occurred in his zone, one for the junta vecinal and one for the junta escolar. In the former, the election was by secret ballot, so different political parties put up slates and there were rumors of ballot-stuffing. For the junta escolar, he said, the people putting themselves forward for election to different posts came up to the front of the hall, and voting was done by standing behind them. He argued that this system was more democratic than the secret ballot because it was more transparent: no one from outside of the zone could vote because people would have expelled them from the meeting, and everyone could see who won. I was struck by his analysis because of the emphasis placed on secret ballots in my own political education and democratic practice.

Throughout this book, I have argued that collective organizations in El Alto both model and enact a type of democracy that looks very different from that assumed by liberal political science, where political agency is individualized. As David Nugent (forthcoming) has argued, democracy is "vernacularized" in different sociocultural and historical contexts. A political science informed by modernization theories flattens those differences into a simple line from less to more democratic, such that democracy can be brought to countries simply by importing liberal institutions. Bolivian intellectuals quite often counterpose the *democracia asambleistica*, or "assembly-based democracy" (Gutierrez et al. 2002; Garcia Linera et al. 2000, 2001) of the social movements to the unrepresentative democracy of the neoliberal political institutions of the state and political parties. However, in-depth analysis of assembly-based democracy is rare, and here I explore the ways street traders associations model democracy through two principal aspects: the relationship between the leaders and their base (the grass-roots members) and the importance of the general assembly. These particular elements are also key to "ayllu democracy," the direct democracy of the ayllus that is usually counterposed to Western systems of representative democracy. The latter is often equated with trade unions, the principal organizational rival to the ayllu in the altiplano countryside (Rivera Cusicanqui 1990; Albó 1977). In El Alto, the distinction is not so stark, and the direct democracy of the trade unions builds upon understandings of democracy derived from the experience of the ayllu, as well as other influences such as anarchosyndicalism and even civic republicanism. The creative combination of many different traditions is the source of what many see as a revitalization of Bolivian democracy associated with the contemporary power of popular politics.

Leaders and Bases   Along with the top-down aspects of leadership described in chapter 6, a dominant theme of the discourse of trade union and community leaders is the philosophy that leaders do not lead, they implement the decisions of their grass roots. As expressed by Mauricio Cori, the president of the FEJUVE in 2003, "Mauricio Cori fulfills the demands of his base." This version of democratic action builds directly upon the notion of leadership as service to the community that is inherent to ayllu democracy (Rivera Cusicanqui 1990; Ticona Alejo 2003). It is also evident in one of the most common analyses of the events of October 2003, that it was the people, *el pueblo*, which revolted. My informants often used the phrase *el pueblo rebasó a los dirigentes*, meaning that quite quickly there came a point where the leaders had to follow the will of their bases, since *rebasar* is the verb used to indicate when water overflows its container. I translate it here as "overrule." The following quotes illustrate this tendency:

> We were no longer an executive, the people didn't take any notice [of us]. The people rose up, until the point when seventy deaths accumulated, when therefore the alteño people and the peasants, we asked for—or the institutions, the people in general, the Bolivian people, asked for the resignation of Sanchez de Lozada. (Braulio Rocha, executive secretary, Federation of Street Traders)

> We didn't get rid of him ourselves, the leaders, it was the Bolivian people that threw him out, because they're now tired—so, so, so many things that are

happening, well, so the Bolivian people were no longer in a position to continue with him. . . . We were—as leaders, we had to obey, because we obey orders also, [orders] from the people. . . .

The Gas War is not a triumph, it's not a triumph belonging to Mauricio Cori [president of the FEJUVE], it's not a triumph of the COR, of Roberto de la Cruz [a COR leader and member of Movimiento Indígena Pachakuti (MIP; Indigenous Pachakuti Movement)], it's the triumph of the Bolivian people, that's to say of the people from here. They triumphed, not us [the leaders]. We simply obeyed orders. (Doña Roxana, member of Executive Committee, FEJUVE)

Trade union leaders tread a fine line between leading their members and administering a structure that expresses group decisions, as Don Alberto's advice to Doña Maria of the pescaderas in the previous chapter shows. Although the leaders' explicit discourse is one of serving the bases, only doing what they say and faithfully reflecting their position, I have seen instances when the leaders have manipulated the decision of a mass meeting. One tactic that the Federation Executive Committee used was to place members of the committee in among the general audience instead of at the table at the front of the meeting where the executive secretary sits. Those in the audience would then shout out proposals or make speeches in favor of a certain position. At one meeting of the Federation, a general secretary of an affiliated association complained about this, but one of the Executive Committee members in the audience responded that he had every right to be there and to give his opinion, as he was also general secretary of his association. After the meetings, the printed resolutions that are produced for each one are written by one of the Executive Committee members, giving some leeway in the development of an official interpretation of the discussions. On occasion, resolutions are added or altered in some way or one particular side of the discussion is played down. In subsequent meetings, there is an opportunity to contest the minutes and resolutions, but this rarely happens.

Nonetheless, it is certainly the case that if leaders do not do a good job of persuading their bases that their demands are just and that they are reflecting their opinion reasonably faithfully, then the bases have ways of showing their displeasure. They will vote out leaders of whom they disapprove, for example, or whistle at them when they stand up to speak at a public meeting. Another tactic is to form breakaway associations or even federations. In 2003, parallel associations appeared throughout the city, where leaders allied to the MIR (according to the Federation Executive

Committee members) had formed new associations, and in some instances instructed their members to begin paying taxes against the federation's instructions. The power of any association comes from its power of convocatoria: at the time of greatest disunity within the Federation, the leaders that could convene the most people for civic parades and protest marches were seen as the strongest. Thus, if the bases disapprove of the leaders, they may also stop coming to meetings or demonstrations, thus undermining the leaders' power of convocatoria.[1]

Furthermore, the bases tend to be inherently suspicious of their leaders, especially the higher up they are in the union structure, and this suspicion is expressed in the constant rumors of corruption and party political allegiance. Some scholars consider suspicion to be evidence of ordinary people's disillusionment with their leaders, and therefore a force that undermines collective organization (e.g., Agadjanian 2002), but it may better be viewed as one of the ways that the politics of trade unionism is conducted. Suspicion and rumor are also often a form of preemptive control over the leaders, as in the case of the juntas vecinales, and may also keep those who are tempted to *buscar sus apetitos personales* (search for their personal appetites) somewhat more in check than might otherwise be the case.

Regardless of actual practice, at the core of the model of democracy proclaimed as ideal by the associations is the idea that the leaders enact the will of the bases, and that frequently, although by no means always, the bases have the means of disciplining leaders who do not do this adequately. Indeed, this was precisely how one treasurer of a junta escolar described Goni's resignation in October 2003; she said that she knows, as a leader, that if she acts inappropriately, her bases would "give her a thrashing," and that was what had happened to him. Nonetheless, the constant presence of suspicion of the leaders belies the fiction of a community without internal conflict that is a much criticized aspect of communitarian political thought. The assumption behind much communitarianism is that if there is any contestation of the leaders' ability to embody the will of that community, then the community disintegrates and becomes a conglomeration of individuals. In contrast, members of trade unions are perhaps modeling the kind of "agonistic" democracy proposed by Chantal Mouffe (1993), which does not assume that consensus within a community is always possible or even desirable.

One of the ways that scholars believe Andean communities guard against leaders gaining too much power is the rotative nature of the leadership system in the communities. A central feature of most Andean ethnographies, the *cargo* system or *thaki* in rural communities, is run such that leaders remain in position usually only for a year (Isbell 1978; Carter and Mamani P. 1989 [1982]; Abercrombie 1998; Rasnake 1988; Skar 1982). Leadership is an expensive obligation to the community, and this system ensures that the expense of being a leader is not too overwhelming for households. It is often also painted as a highly democratic feature of Andean authority structures (e.g., see Gutierrez et al. 2000; Ticona Alejo 2003; Rivera Cusicanqui 1990), even though, as Nancy Postero (2006) points out, short terms of office can sometimes tend toward short-termism and even corruption among leaders. Some trade unions function along similar lines, with leaders holding office for only one or two years, but there are also many leaders in the Federation who have been in position for years, some even for one or two decades. The practice of holding onto a leadership position for a long time is known as *vitalicismo* (life-long-ism). Leaders who do this are very vulnerable to criticism and suspicion of their intentions, but it is also the case that the ordinary bases are often happy to keep a good leader in position. They recognize that it is a very difficult, expensive, and time-consuming job, and therefore reelect a leader every two years with little complaint. Vitalicismo may be a feature of the "forma sindicato" (Garcia Linera 2001) that demonstrates its antidemocratic nature, even (implicitly) its anti-Aymara nature. Yet the cacique system is just as much a feature of Aymara history as the more democratic community thaki systems (Harris and Platt 2006; Thomson 2002). Silvia Rivera Cusicanqui (1990; Rivera Cusicanqui and Equipo THOA 1992) also points out that hierarchy of some kind is inherent in the thaki systems of northern Potosí, as some authority positions are restricted to particular categories of community members, although there is some flexibility in how people can change category.

It is important therefore to recognize the centrality of hierarchy within the community of street traders and collective organizations in general. The frequent use of family metaphors to describe the bond between leaders and bases provides an entry point into understanding the nature of such hierarchies. Executive Committee members constantly referred to the *familia gremial* (family of organized street traders), and this phrase was a particular favorite of Don Braulio's. He frequently explained problems with associations as family problems, saying that there are always problem children, or badly behaved children within any family. The Federation was in the parents' position, where he was the father who loved his children but also disciplined them. He once explained parallelism (i.e.,

19. Don Braulio Rocha, executive secretary, and Don Rodolfo Mancilla, general secretary, in the Federation central office

the establishment of a rival association) as "rebellious children looking for another father." Another Executive Committee member explained that the Federation leaders could not appeal directly to individual affiliates, but had to go through the association; they could not go directly to the "grandchild," "because it's your child that you have to defend, the directorio has to look after the base." An affiliate said to the Executive Committee member present at an assembly, "You have to back us up, we're your children."

It is of course not unusual to describe political systems through the metaphor of the family (e.g., see Arendt 1998 [1958]), but understandings of family hierarchy are culturally specific. According to German Guaygua et al., authors of *Ser joven en El Alto* (2000), Aymara families are very authoritarian in terms of the expected relationship between parents, especially fathers, and children. Certainly, threatened corporal punishment in the form of the *chicote*, a small whip, is an important part of family life and the disciplining of young children. And according to official and NGO statistics, El Alto has a high incidence of domestic couple violence (Perez de Castaños 1999). Parents and older family members are also expected to be very involved in the life decisions made by their children; for example, they have a central role in approving who their children marry and in attempts to resolve marital difficulties for young couples (Lazar 2002a). How authoritarian this actually is in practice is undoubtedly highly variable, and there has been little detailed ethnography on such matters. Some ethnographers would argue that parent–child relationships are not really authoritarian at all, and that the chicote is far more often threatened than used.[2] The interest that parents have in helping their children to live well is in my experience most often represented, as one might expect, in terms of love, duty, and concern. There is also considerable emphasis placed rhetorically on the sacrifice that parents, especially mothers, make for their children. When Don Juan was mediating the conflict between the mother and her daughter described in chapter 6, he constantly repeated that parents would do anything for their children. In one particular rhetorical flourish, he said that he could kill for his children, that we all struggle in life only for the sake of our children; they did not ask to be born and we must love them. The corollary is that children must respect their mother and father. Families are not generally perceived as democratic institutions, in El Alto as elsewhere (cf. Dietz 1985), but discipline and authority are balanced by sacrifice and service.

Within the street traders unions, the emphasis on family pulls against the more egalitarian relationship of compañero/a drawn from leftist discourse, which is equally if not more common. Both are cultural resources that people draw on to understand and manage social relations, making claims for support from those higher up in the hierarchy, or alternatively giving advice to those less experienced. We might propose that different kinds of relationships dominate different levels of collectivity, certainly ideologically. The levels might be family, community or association, and federation, or even politics, where the family (parent–child) relationship is as described above, the community or association relationship is one between social equals, and the relationship between ordinary people and the federation leaders or politicians is characterized by that between the cacique/caudillo and his followers.[3] Such a delineation would certainly work on an ideological level, but the ethnographic material shows the picture to be rather messier: at different times and for different purposes, all three of these kinds of relationships come to the fore as people draw on their extensive cultural repertoires to advance their interests and desires most effectively. It would therefore be unwise to take at face value the claims that leaders purely serve their bases and that associations are entirely egalitarian; conversely, it would also be wrong to view the relationship between leaders and base as completely one-directional.

Assembly-Based Democracy   Along with rotative leadership, the most persistent theme in the claims made by activists and intellectuals for a more democratic popular sphere is the community meeting or trade union assembly. For example, Gutierrez et al. (2000: 170) describe the culmination of the Water War in Cochabamba in the meeting held in the main square as follows:

> In a few hours, in what will become the most extraordinary pedagogy of *democracia asambleistica*, with the square replete with workers from the city and the country, and through telephone and megaphone communication, [the people] follow the course of the negotiations between their leaders and the governmental commission. The points of the agreement are approved or rejected by the same council that at the end of the day takes control over its decisions. . . . Today, the gathered multitude deliberates directly; it proposes, rejects, modifies and approves. The leaders only transmit. Once more, the power of decision-making is reappropriated by the social structures, which, in their act of radical political insurgence, they removed the delegative habit of state power, to exercise [power] themselves.

An assembly features in almost every one of the indigenista filmmaker Jorge Sanjines's films as a practice that is crucial in defining the "other Bolivia" and that is inherently representative of the will of the community. In *Los Hijos del Ultimo Jardín* (2003) the emphasis on government corruption is explicitly contrasted with the morality of the community assembly when a small community decides not to accept money stolen from a corrupt politician. The community assembly is a central part of many discussions of ayllu and community democracy (e.g., Klemola 1997; Ticona Alejo 2003; Albó 1977). Esteban Ticona argues that "the communal assembly . . . is the maximum authority and the centre of the communal life of the *ayllu*. . . . Through the level of participation and the sense of mutual respect, [the assemblies] constitute the principal stage for the practice of *thaki* or the democracy of the ayllu" (125).

In the case of the street traders associations and other trade unions, the general assembly of the bases is the highest authority of any association. For the Federation, the equivalent is the *ampliado*, the periodic meetings of the general secretaries of member associations. General assemblies of associations are held from once a month to once a year, but if the association does not have any problems, they are usually held every three to four months. Federation delegates attend general assemblies when an association has problems with internal conflicts or corruption issues. More mundanely, they also make reports to the bases about Federation decisions, activities, and negotiations and confrontations with the municipal authorities.

General assemblies and ampliados are about public speaking and the reaction of the crowd to what they hear. In the meeting, the aim is usually to reach some sort of consensus as people take turns to speak in favor of or against a particular argument. The meetings are held in *locales* (rooms hired out for parties), which are arranged with a desk and chairs at the front for the directorio of the association and the Federation delegates plus other visitors. The audience sits on chairs against the walls of the hall or stand at the back (in the case of the men) or sit on the floor (in the case of the women). Women bring awayus to sit on, along with food, drinks, and knitting or spinning to keep them occupied. Some of the men clutch exercise books or leather folders. Young children thread through the audience or sleep on their mother's lap. The meetings open with a report from the secretary general and any delegate from the Federation who is present. They report on their activities and relevant political events in long and uninterrupted speeches. They may be questioned at the end, but most discussion occurs over specific agenda items, when people stand up in turn to give their opinion on the issue in question. They do this by making a speech that will quite often repeat the arguments made by others with whom they agree prior to making their own point, if they have one. Each speech can take between five and ten minutes, and people express themselves in a very formal manner, opening by greeting the authorities and all present respectfully, using formulae such as "Pido la palabra" (I request the word), and taking their time over their sentences.

Consensus is built through repetition, as the argument moves, speech by speech, to one predominant viewpoint and the leaders eventually make a decision that the majority of speakers have taken one position. They also assess the audience's reaction to each speech—whether they have expressed shock, shouted their disagreement, clapped, or murmured their approval to their neighbor. On that basis they ask the general members to approve it: "¿Aprobado?" (Approved?). If the audience is silent or some shout out yes, then the motion or decision is approved. It is rare to hold a vote, but if one does happen, it is usually the case that no one will vote for

20. An ampliado of the Federation of Street Traders

the losing position and between a majority and everyone will vote for the winning one. The careful process of building consensus usually takes a very long time and is spread over several assemblies, giving people a chance to discuss the issues in between meetings, as Klemola (1997) found for the countryside. The creation of public opinion informally in this way is also one of the more important means by which women influence the process of decision making. However, that is not to say that the meetings themselves are a speedy ratification of decisions already taken. The general assembly is a more gradual process that airs viewpoints formally and provides moral guidance (in terms of the general view of the base) and material for the subsequent informal discussions and decisions to be taken by the protagonists of any dispute. As such, they can take a long time; the ampliado of 2 June 2003 took five hours, for example. This was by no means unusual; my most vivid memories of the assemblies I attended are of my physical discomfort as they continued seemingly interminably.

Speech is an important part of the process of direct democracy in the unions as in other collective organizations; the punishment for two women who had attempted to set up a parallel association with the municipality was that they could attend meetings but would have *ni voz ni voto*, neither voice nor vote. Speaking publicly is also an important aspect of proving and learning leadership ability; Don Rodolfo Mancilla described to me how he became one of the most important men on the Executive Committee by watching how leaders spoke in meetings and gradually learning how to "speak well" (*hablar bien*) himself. Speaking well is also a category that I have heard used to assess politicians at a national level. Many male *gremialistas* (unionist street traders) have gained the ability to speak through their experience of union membership in their previous jobs, especially those who have been "relocalized" from the mines.[4] Women often talk of themselves as lacking the knowledge necessary to speak publicly. This is sometimes connected implicitly to their ability to speak Spanish, the prime language of formal gatherings such as general assemblies. Isabella Lepri (2003) has argued that the Esse Ejja of lowland Pando avoid political meetings in part because they are uncomfortable speaking Spanish. However, in the case of the street traders, it is quite common in general assemblies and ampliados for women to give speeches in Aymara, which everyone understands. Sometimes, although less frequently, men also speak in Aymara, and discussions continue in Aymara until someone, usually one of the leaders or the Federation delegate, switches back to Spanish.

The importance of speech is one of the indications of the thick conception of participatory democracy that operates within the trade unions. In addition to sharing characteristics with ayllu democracy, it has much in common with civic republican traditions of democracy which ultimately derive from the model of Athenian democracy. In *The Human Condition* (1998 [1958]: 26), Hannah Arendt argued that in the public realm of the polis, the most intensely political activities of humans were praxis, or action, and lexis, or speech: "To be political, to live in a polis, meant that everything was decided through words and persuasion and not through force and violence," and to command rather than persuade was "prepolitical," more characteristic of the household than of political life. For Arendt, human beings actualize themselves through participation in politics, which consists of discussion and deliberation. As Castoriadis (1992) points out, the education of the citizen as person so important to Athenian notions of citizenship was accomplished precisely through these processes. The processual sense in which unionists become better through their experience of speaking in public meetings indicates a similar philosophy. Moreover, in Athens, citizens had both a right and a "commitment" (or duty) to speak their minds on public affairs, which also has parallels with Bolivian practice (Castoriadis 1992). In Latin America, claims for more participatory forms of democracy are not especially new (cf. Nugent forthcoming on mid-twentieth-century Peru), but they are undergoing a resurgence, being expressed in the demands of social movements from the late 1980s onward (Dagnino 1998) and through initiatives such as participatory budgeting in Brazil and Argentina. They build upon the deep political traditions of public meeting democracy that came from the Greeks to Latin America through the circulation of civic republican political thought among intellectuals influenced by the French and American revolutions, and earlier, through the translation of the citizenship practices of medieval Spanish and Italian cities during colonization (Herzog 2003). Of course, these European practices combined with indigenous forms of self-government and direct democracy. The combination of such external influences with more indigenous traditions is what gives them their power and particular character as citizenship practices today, a point I return to later.

Mass action during meetings is a counterpoint to the speeches. At every meeting I attended, people began to shout "¡Hora!" (Time!) when it had gone on too long, or when the important matters had been discussed and they wanted to go home. The leaders usually heed this call once it is no longer a few isolated individuals, unless they have something very important that has not yet been discussed. Any business left over is either postponed until the next meeting or dealt with very quickly, because people usually have to stay to the end of meetings in order to collect the token that certifies their attendance. One good example of democracy by numbers in this sense happened in a meeting where it seemed to me that the prevailing opinion in terms of the spoken debate was that there should be an election for a new directorio. People criticized the general secretary's vitalicismo and there appeared to be a sizable group who wanted to replace her. She defended her position, saying that she needed to stay in order to steer the association through a court case it was involved in with a rival association. The debate proceeded until the point where a decision on whether or not to have an election that meeting was imminent, at which time large groups of affiliates simply stood up and left, thus giving a very clear and effective indication that that they did not want an election, whatever the conclusions of the spoken discussions. At supper after the meeting, the general secretary said that it was only a few trouble-

makers who wanted her out, while the majority supported her, something borne out more by the physical dynamic of the meeting than by the
spoken debate.

The balance between public speech-making and this physical dynamic
is gendered. Women do speak formally less than men but play a greater
role in the encouragement of mass action. They form the bulk of the
members of an association and have a keen understanding of how that
group acts politically in a physical sense. When someone says something
with which they disagree, individual women may speak out publicly, but
others will make comments to their neighbors, and it is possible to get a
sense of their view from the tone of those conversations. They are also not
afraid of shouting out "¡Hora!" if they want to leave. As always, it would be
foolish to overplay the extent of gender equality in the street traders associations, as it is men who dominate the leadership and the formal spheres
of decision making. Outside of such spaces, though, women play very
important roles in the politics of the associations on a day-to-day level as
well as during extraordinary events. Largely by being the ones selling the
produce they know what is going on in the marketplace and are the ones
involved in the daily conflicts among affiliates and between affiliates and
the local government. They are also often thought to be more radical
politically and less corrupt than most of the men, and they make those
views known.

Assembly-based democracy as it is practiced in the street traders associations is complex. It defies both the romanticization of intellectuals and
the disdain of those who are unaware of its subtleties and who therefore
dismiss trade union members as masses manipulated by their leaders.[5] It
is not always easy to interpret the mood of the meeting, because it rests on
a delicate balance between what people stand up to say in a formal, public
sense and the comments they make to their neighbors and in shouted but
unattributable interjections as well as in their body language and physical
movement. Long-standing trade union leaders are highly skilled at interpreting all these different signals. The assemblies are run on the basis that
all who want to can and should speak, but it is well understood that this
will not necessarily happen. Nonetheless, those who do not wish to commit themselves in a formal speech have ways of expressing their approval
or disapproval during and outside of the meetings. They do so within a
hierarchical framework, where some management of the mood of the
meeting is undoubtedly possible and where there is room for interpretation by the leaders. However, the bases are by no means docile masses that

follow their leaders largely unwittingly or simply because they are forced to do so, as some would like to believe.

CORPORATISM AND BOLIVIAN POLITICS

The complexities of internal trade union democracy are important because at the beginning of the twenty-first century social movements in Bolivia and elsewhere in Latin America appear to be stronger than they have been at any time since the end of the dictatorships. While earlier scholarly literature on new social movements debated how democratic social movements are (A. Escobar and Alvarez 1992), what is important in the current wave of literature and activism is the explicit claim that popular democracy is more democratic than institutional politics. For many, the vitality of social movements today raises the possibility of a reinvigoration of normative political life, which is seen as corrupt and decrepit. After the attacks on the popular classes represented by structural adjustment, collective organizations are gradually developing new and more effective forms of struggle against neoliberal hegemony, on a local and a global scale. Their ability to do so relies upon their creative combination of different collective traditions and histories, from indigenous forms of organization to the strong local trade unionist traditions. This of course does not happen in a uniform way across some kind of homogeneous sphere of civil society, but is a fraught process riven with factionalism, competition, and co-optation. It is not my intention to romanticize the alternative visions of democracy and the state proposed by different social movements, including the street traders, or to overstate their chances of success. Their struggle is tough, and possibly unrealistic, but there have been some small victories against seemingly unassailable foes such as large multinational utility companies and U.S.-backed governments. I would argue that such victories derive in large part from the combination of older traditions with new collective forms through innovation and communication and because of changes in the organization of labor. Thus we should perhaps no longer speak of the "return of the Indian," as was hailed in the early 1990s (Wearne 1996), but of the "return of plebeian Bolivia," the title of a recently published book (Garcia Linera et al. 2000). This section of the chapter assesses the nature of that particular return and the nature of the relationship between citizens and the state that has developed as a result.

Trade Unionism in Bolivia In a paper given at the 2003 Bolivian Studies Congress, Juan Claudio Lechín (2003: 14) argued that the Miners Federation (FSTMB) and the Central Obrera Boliviana (COB; Bolivian Workers Center) are "states in miniature," or "an alternative state with people, mechanisms of representation and government, organized and unified leadership structure, and a territory superimposed over that of official structures." He points out that these structures have survived for over fifty years, a longevity that is quite remarkable once we recognize the volatility of the official "establishment" (he uses the English word) of the Bolivian state. His argument that the organizational forms of trade unions influence and are influenced by other contemporary organizational forms, such as juntas vecinales, is compelling. For example, the practice of public speech-making in turn is certainly common to most, if not all, collective gatherings at which I have been present, from junta vecinal assemblies to dance rehearsals and family events such as funerals. These ways of reaching agreement are common across rural and urban Bolivia.[6]

Lechín (2003: 15) also suggests that trade union organizational forms are a mixture of European and Latin American syndicalist traditions with the colonial cabildo as well as the ayllu, despite the common assumption that Bolivian trade unions are strong because of the "natural and ancestral associative spirit of the indigenous, quechua and aymara." Without a doubt, indigenous community forms have been more thoroughly studied than the trade unions, which, depending on the part of Bolivia under study, were often seen as unwelcome Western imports, especially the peasant unions (Rivera Cusicanqui 1990, 2003 [1984]). A picture of El Alto would not be complete without a discussion of both influences, however, and the trade union form may even be the more powerful. As Lechín (2003: 16) points out, even if the contemporary COB and FSTMB are a shadow of their former selves, "the emerging trade unions, those that now have the power of *convocatoria* and political power, as is the case for *cocalero* peasants and peasants in general, . . . have revived the mechanisms and the organic structure of the historic Trade Union, as well as its methods of struggle."

Although in Latin America trade unions typically have been mechanisms for government control of the working classes through corporatism, the history of trade unions in Bolivia has been less consistent in this than in other countries of the region, beginning in the 1920s, when anarchosyndicalism gained ground within several trade union organizations, especially those of the market women in Oruro and La Paz (Lehm and

Rivera Cusicanqui 1988; Lora 1977). The Miners Federation, which was formed in 1944, helped organize the revolution of 1952 alongside the MNR party, and then set up the COB. At the beginning, the COB was led by members of the governing party (MNRistas), but it and the Miners Federation always had a strong Trotskyite faction, articulated most notably by the Partido Obrero Revolucionario (Workers Revolutionary Party). Because of this, there was consistent opposition to the MNR leaders and the worker-ministers of the first government. State control over the trade unions of the COB was effective only for a few years; after the military coup of 1964, a majority of the COB unions moved into opposition to the government. During Banzer's dictatorship of 1971–1978, the government attempted to replace the COB with "workers' coordinators" but failed, and the COB, particularly the miners, once again led the opposition. Since the transition to democracy, all the main political parties have attempted to control the COB Executive Committee.

The peasant unions supported the government for considerably longer than the miners, particularly because of the agrarian reform of 1953; then in 1964, General Barrientos signed the Peasant-Military Pact, winning the peasants to a pro-government position until the 1970s. However, oppositional tendencies began to take over the peasant unions from the late 1960s, as young Aymara nationalists, who became known as the Kataristas, gradually rose to prominence (see Rivera Cusicanqui 2003 [1984]; Hurtado 1986). By the late 1970s, after the repression that followed the massacre of the peasants of Tolata in 1974, the peasant unions were at the forefront of the opposition to the dictatorship alongside the COB. From 1979 onward, the Kataristas ran the unified peasant confederation, the CSUTCB (Rivera Cusicanqui 2003 [1984]). Now different factions of the Kataristas vie with the MAS for control over the CSUTCB leadership committees. The majority of the street traders in El Alto are either ex-miners or ex-peasants, so, given this history, it is unsurprising that the Federation should currently style itself in opposition to the governing political parties, although we should also recognize other important political influences, especially the populism of Condepa and the Unión Cívica Solidaridad (UCS; Civic Solidarity Union). Condepa dominated all aspects of the alteño political scene in the 1990s, including the Federation of Street Traders and the other civic institutions, such as the FEJUVE (Quisbert Quispe 2003).

Any oppositional position is always threatened by the possibility that some party or other has "bought" enough leaders to neutralize the upper echelons of the trade union movement, a frequent occurrence. However, the ability of the state to control the workers, street traders, and peasants through corporatist organization depends on the historical conjuncture. There are times when the unions are fragmented and weak and vulnerable to control, or at least to divide-and-rule strategies, from government. Occasionally, though, they manage to slip out of state control and unify in opposition. It is no coincidence that the October protests in El Alto happened at a time when the FEJUVE, COR, and Federation of Street Traders were all relatively strong: compare the existence of four rival federations of street traders in La Paz. Both the FEJUVE and the Federation of Street Traders have divided into competing factions throughout their histories; the Federation of Street Traders managed to unify itself most recently only in 2000. It is also the case that in 2003, the main political parties (especially the MIR) failed to co-opt leaders of most of the civic organizations in El Alto in the way that Condepa had managed during the 1990s. Those who had been bought were in any case overruled (rebasados) by the base. An example is the MIRista leader of the fourth main civic organization in El Alto, the Federacion de Padres de Familia de El Alto (Federation of School Parents of El Alto), who had to hide from the protestors for his own safety. One friend told me in January 2004 that he had heard that the political parties were trying to buy civic leaders in order to prevent a repeat of the events of the previous October. By April, some political activists suspected that the MAS was involved in this process, as Evo Morales and his advisors stressed the importance of the electoral route to power and focused their attention on the municipal elections of December 2004.

Thus, under normal circumstances collective organizations can certainly be the means by which Bolivian governments control their citizens. Yet political participation (or even perhaps the flow of power) can also be two-directional. There are structures in place which allow citizens to contest policies and laws they consider to be against their interests, as the previous chapter has shown. The normal balance of power between the two groups is greatly in favor of the political elites who usually govern; however, in the past few years, this has become slightly more fragile than usual, in Bolivia and throughout the region. Democratic governance in Bolivia has always included direct state negotiation with organized corporate groupings, known as the "social sectors." However, since at least 1997, successive Bolivian governments have failed to implement any coherent strategic plan of government. Instead of making policy, they became reactive, only able to respond to pressures from the International

Monetary Fund on one side and increasing volumes of social mobilization on the other. Based on megacoalitions of sometimes up to five different political parties, they were weak in institutional terms, compounded by the fact that the majority of the political parties represented the interests of the Bolivian elites rather than ordinary people. The extent to which these sets of interests are opposed to each other cannot be understated: the cleavage within Bolivian society between the elite classes and the popular classes is undoubtedly deep. Although members of the (urban) popular classes often know how the wealthy live because they have been their maids or gardeners, they consume their media, and they sell to them, the wealthy have almost no knowledge about the conditions of life of most Bolivians. Encouraged by the IMF and Harvard-educated Bolivian economists, the political elites wanted to implement what they thought were the best (and correct) economic policies for their country, without realizing that such policies were utterly unacceptable to the majority population. They created a situation in which both of the forces pressurizing them, the IMF and the social movements, were demanding unrealistic economic policies: increased market liberalization from the former and much greater state control of the economy from the latter.

The Strength of the Multitude   Using Hardt and Negri's (2000, 2005) terminology, we could say that governments of Bolivia find themselves between Empire and multitude, a position that may be increasingly common for democratically elected governments globally. The extent of Empire (as represented in Bolivia by the alliance of local political and economic elites with the IMF, the World Bank, and the U.S. Embassy) is well known. What has become notable at particular moments in the past few years is the relative strength of its counterpart: the multitude, or social sectors. Undoubtedly, some agnosticism about the usefulness of the term "multitude" is necessary; certainly in Hardt and Negri's formulation the concept itself is loose enough that almost any popular oppositional movement that is not the organized industrial working classes or vanguardist political parties could count as part of the multitude. Nonetheless, some aspects of their analysis are useful in understanding the renewed political vigor of the Bolivian popular classes in recent years, particularly as the concept has been taken up and concretized by a group of Bolivian intellectuals who publish under the insignia of the *grupo comuna* (e.g., see Garcia Linera et al. 2000, 2001; Gutierrez et al. 2002).

Along with the continuity with older trade union and community traditions, it is also important to recognize the extent of the rupture with older forms of collective organization of labor. The trade union sphere has changed considerably in Bolivia as a result of the neoliberal economic policies of the mid-1980s, which irrevocably weakened the traditional power base of the COB, the miners. Some commentators (e.g., Sanabria 1999) have seen this as an outright defeat for trade unionism, with the cocalero unions of the Chapare region as its only remnants. However, in recent years it has become clear that while one sector of the working classes was indeed defeated, the destruction was not as complete as feared by the most pessimistic. What has happened is that new kinds of trade union structures have emerged alongside the cocaleros, especially those of the peasants and informal sector workers in the cities. One thing these different sectors all have in common is a particular relationship to their means of livelihood. As I discussed in chapter 6, the new unions are one set of (work-based) collectivities that have emerged with neoliberalism and the post-Fordist organization of labor (Hardt and Negri 2000; Garcia Linera 2001). They are based upon coalitions of smallholders, even micro-capitalists, who do not work for one boss in one place, where they can be easily targeted by the army (Sanabria 1999). Their household model of production allows for fluidity of associational life, but has also enabled them to form alliances and organizations based upon territorial location: the street where they sell, the village or region where they live and farm, and, with the addition of the vecino-based organizational structures in the cities, their zone. The previous chapter showed this to be a complex and fluid territorial affiliation, but the relationship between people and place that has been a continuous theme of this book makes it extremely strong nonetheless.

Individuals and household units are affiliated with one or more associations or organizations; the associations themselves come together in networks, federations, and alliances at city, regional, and national levels. They are a true multitude of "plural singularities" (Hardt and Negri 2005: 99) that coalesces at particular moments, such as April 2000 in Cochabamba, the peasant blockades in the altiplano of April and September 2000, February and October 2003 in El Alto and La Paz, and January–March 2005 in El Alto. Outside of those moments, the social movements often fall prey to severe factionalism and infighting between rival figures —remember Xavier Albó's (1977) analysis of Aymara solidarity and factionalism. It is a weakness that is commonly mentioned (e.g., see Crabtree 2005) and is certainly a problem when the elites are generally so coherent, in terms at least of their ability to sustain agreement on what constitutes the best economic and political system for Bolivia, even if they are split among themselves on more specific questions of policy. We should probably expect factionalism and division among the popular classes and counterhegemonic forces, since the development of fully coherent alternative economic and political visions could not happen in a short space of time, and may indeed never happen (since that may be the point, diversity of visions being perhaps more progressive and fairer). The demands for the social movements to present entirely coherent and well-thought-out economic and political programs are probably misplaced, since action will always move faster than theory. What we can say at this stage is that the social movements do come together increasingly frequently and are beginning to build a more coherent ideology out of the particularity of the different sectoral demands along two connected lines of principle: first, the issue of the protection of the means of social reproduction (Garcia Linera 2001), and second, a particular vision of the state and their relationship to it.

As Alvaro Garcia Linera (2001) has argued, some of the key demands of the various protests of the first years of the twenty-first century have been articulated around questions of control over resources, in particular water and natural gas. In Cochabamba, localized control over water provision was much more advanced than in El Alto, but in both cities protesters objected to its privatization, especially given the foreign ownership of the utility companies involved; the main shareholders in Aguas del Tunari of Cochambamba were Bechtel, a U.S. and German multinational, and Abengoa SA, a Spanish company, while that of Aguas del Illimani in El Alto was Suez, which is French. The question of foreign control over the revenue from the export of natural gas was key to the standoff between governments and the social movements between October 2003 and May 2006. For Garcia Linera (who became vice president in December 2005), such questions, namely "that of the management of water, access to land and the price of basic services," are principally about the material means of sustaining social reproduction (43). However, we should be wary of reducing this to a simple equation of protest as a response to poverty. In the inevitable simplifications that accompany the international flow of information, the contemporary political developments in El Alto and Bolivia have been understood through narratives of desperation and economic crisis, or the image of a noble and naturalized indigenous concern for Bolivian sovereignty over natural resources. But it would be a mistake to view the mobilizations as simply a politics of desperation. Although it would also be foolish to try to maintain that people are not responding to a situation of increasingly acute hardship in the midst of a severe economic crisis, the protests are also a politics of surplus and creativity, a point recognized by Hardt and Negri (2005: 212) for the multitude: "Deprivation . . . may breed anger, indignation, and antagonism, but revolt arises only on the basis of wealth, that is, a surplus of intelligence, experience, knowledges and desire." The protesters have positive proposals, for example in their assertion of a sense of Bolivian sovereignty over natural resources (Albro 2005). Gutierrez et al. (2000: 176) maintain that the Coordinadora's proposals for the local control over water in Cochabamba have "demolished the fallacy of the duality between privatization and state ownership which had guided contemporary political proposals." They argue that such new proposals can have arisen only through the operation of genuinely democratic decision-making processes, and in their view represent a clear alternative proposal for the "recomposition of political life" (181).

This may be somewhat optimistic, and the extent to which proposals are thought through in the case of water in Cochabamba is certainly not generalizable across the whole spectrum of oppositional social movements. However, coherent visions of the state and of democracy are emerging in the theory and practice of the social sectors and popular classes. As David Nugent (forthcoming: 16) argues, the absence (or dysfunction) of the state can create as much of a "state-effect" as its presence, as in the case of mid-twentieth-century Chachapoyas in Peru, where local elites' success in consolidating regional power and holding the nation state at bay "created the illusion (and illusion it was) that a liberated nation-state existed in a different spatial domain. . . . It was possible for the popular classes to conceive of the liberated nation-state not only as a 'thing' that could arrive from afar, but also as a thing whose arrival was being thwarted by the elite." In a similar vein, much talk about corruption in Bolivia today tells the story of elite politicians and businessmen who are betraying a higher ideal of what the state should be, even though people are unlikely to talk about the abstract concept of "the state." They are more likely to use abstract terms such as "our dear Bolivia" (nuestra querida Bolivia) or "the Bolivian people" (el pueblo boliviano), alongside concrete terms referring to politicians in general, the president, the mayor, or the government. With neoliberalism, the Bolivian state has absented itself from some areas, such as the provision of public utilities, while strengthening itself in others, especially the military (Gill 2000; Sanabria 1999).

In the face of this, alteños often articulate specific visions of a strong developmentalist state. The two most oft-articulated complaints about contemporary Bolivian governments are that they are corrupt and that they do not provide jobs for ordinary Bolivian people. For Don Eugenio of the Federation of Street Traders, the entrance of businesspeople into government has corrupted his ideal of a state that is able to give people jobs:

> It's politicking, so that the ordinary people are just the servants, part of the ladder for those people up there [i.e., politicians]. Because the supply of jobs has dried up. It's because really they're more businessmen than politicians—for example, CORDEPAZ [the Department of La Paz Development Corporation] had more people, and then also [people] used to work for the National Roads Service, YPFB [the state petrol company], the ENFE—the railways—all of them no longer exist. Now really the people, the base, now they work for people from above, no longer *for themselves*. Now there is no place where someone can be a public functionary. (My emphasis)

Working for the state is, in his view, working "for themselves" (*por ellos mismos*), instead of working to the profit of the "people from above" (*gentes de arriba*), the owners of private companies. This kind of vision of the state may be quite specific to El Alto, or to urban Bolivians more generally, as in other parts of Bolivia people may feel the state to be remote and want to keep it at bay (Lepri 2003; Goudsmit 2006). Many alteños, particularly those who are politically active in collective organizations, have previously had jobs provided by the state; the alcaldía is the biggest single employer in the city, for example, and many street traders were public functionaries during the 1990s. Others worked for public companies that were privatized in recent decades, such as the mines and the national roads service. It is unsurprising therefore that they wish to return to a situation in which they had a more secure job provided by the state that in some cases even came with benefits such as pensions. Inherent to Don Eugenio's vision is a claim for economic fairness, which should be protected by the state (cf. Nugent forthcoming). Such a view is also expressed in the demand from the altiplano peasants for the government to provide them with tractors and other kinds of development projects. These claims are somewhat paradoxical, because on the one hand people want more state in the form of tractors or jobs, but on the other, one of the main problems that spark off protests is too much state, for example when the state intervenes in previously community-based modes of water provisioning by attempting to sell them to other parties. The other example of too much state is, of course, state repression of demonstrators, actively and also preemptively through laws such as the Law of Citizen Security, which criminalized blockades and the repeal of which was one of the key demands of demonstrators in October 2003.

Thus the call is for a particular kind of state, one that more clearly represents the interests of the people as defined by the people and is therefore more genuinely democratic. The problem with this is a political one: given current international economic orthodoxy and Bolivia's relative poverty in terms of natural resources (it has oil but is no Venezuela), this may just be unrealistic. But there is a vision nonetheless. When imagining such a state, trade unionists and workers use historical referents, in particular the nationalization of Gulf Oil in 1969. The contemporary period shares some interesting parallels with 1969–1971, both being times of notable leftist agitation. With the Asamblea Popular in 1971 and the Asamblea Constituyente today, both periods evidence demands for a democracy that is deeper than that of the official political system—as Hardt and Negri (2005) put it, for the rule of everyone by everyone. These visions of democracy both derive from and deepen existing practices of mediated and collective citizenship in Bolivia.

Luis Tapia (2002) argues that during the 1980s and 1990s, the defeat of the popular, trade unionist, and leftist forces meant that the elite-based political party system took over institutionalized politics at that time, expelling the workers to the *no lugares* or "nonplaces" of politics. With the elections of 2002, the successes of the MAS and the MIP saw the return of the workers and the reentry of the class struggle into parliament, and the elections of 2005 consolidated that process. For Tapia, the proliferation of the nonplaces of politics during the 1980s and 1990s meant "the renovation of the capacity for political life in the heart of the popular classes; [a capacity] for organization and collective action. The non-places have revealed the banality of the places of politics, as well as their anti-national character" (72). He remains agnostic about whether the flow between the nonplaces and the places of politics may ultimately lead to the renovation or democratization of official politics. Nonetheless, the creativity of the popular movements in the nonplaces of politics is not confined to the vision of the state they articulate from that position. The development of alternative democracies is probably most evident and effective in the actual practice of the organizations themselves, which returns me to the ethnographic material at the heart of this chapter. As Tapia argues, it is organization that distinguishes the multitude from the crowd, and as Hardt and Negri (2005) point out, multiplicity that distinguishes the multitude from "the people," which they conceive of as unitary. The nested affiliation of an alliance of associations, each one with local forms of accountability, is one of the sources of the social movements' strength in Bolivia and is crucial to the contemporary reinvigoration of citizenship and democracy. Another is the assembly-based democracy proclaimed by grupo comuna intellectuals. Yet another is the strength of corporate feeling encouraged through practices that work to create collective selves, the subject of chapter 6.

As older debates about new social movements highlighted, such practices are not always very democratic in the sense of being nonhierarchical (A. Escobar and Alvarez 1992). Certainly, the trade unions and other collectivities organize themselves in ways that seem authoritarian and undemocratic if we define democracy as essentially about preserving individual freedoms. But if we view democracy as the will of the people, the corporatist side of Bolivian politics makes sense as one of its most important democratic (albeit not necessarily egalitarian) traditions. My point is not to measure trade union democracy against state democracy, but to argue that their dynamics are different, and that one is not necessarily more functional than the other. The sociologist Silvia Rivera described to me the euphoria after Goni's resignation as a "euphoria of democracy." October 2003 saw the operation of a kind of direct democracy that asserted the common will against a government that was not only intractable and distant, but also murderous. In April 2000 and January–March 2005 multinational corporations that seemed impregnable, such as Bechtel and Suez, were forced to take a loss on their investment in Bolivia and withdraw without compensation. Those victories would not have been possible without the mundane experiences of collective democracy that are part of alteños' day-to-day lives.

Contemporary indigenous-popular movements in Bolivia and across Latin America have created a politics that has coalesced into a forceful and effective critique of the neoliberal state, from Chiapas to Cochabamba. Ethnographic examination reveals that El Alto has been such an important focus for this new politics in large part because of the ways that citizenship of the city is constituted as a mediated relationship between citizen and state that is shaped by the structure of collective civic organization parallel to the state at zone, citywide, and national levels. In 1999, the political party Condepa lost its hold over those organizations and over the city in general, enabling a more oppositional stance to emerge; this coincided with the fact that alteños have been radicalized by increasing economic hardship. The protests of September and October 2003 and subsequent years derive their strength from the combination of these particular political circumstances with much more long-standing processes of identification with the countryside and the construction of a collective sense of self. In this book I have explored these political processes ethnographically and sought to articulate them in terms of a theory of citizenship. What they reveal are the complexities of being indigenous in Latin America at the beginning of the twenty-first century. Citizenship in the indigenous city of El Alto involves a mix of urban and rural, collectivism and individualism, egalitarianism and hierarchy. The alternative visions of democracy that are being produced have reinvigorated national and regional indigenous movements by the ways that they combine class-based and nationalist concerns with identity politics, through the contestation over the ownership of the means of social reproduction (Garcia Linera 2001) and the nature of the state. This helps to forge an inclusive indigenous and popular identity, which can be the source of considerable political strength.

Recent work on citizenship recognizes its multiscalar nature (Isin forthcoming; Sassen 2003; Yuval-Davis 1997; Hannerz 1990). If the state operates at different levels—national, local, and supranational—then political agency and belonging, that is, citizenship, must similarly operate at these various different levels. I have focused in this book on the connections between local or urban citizenships and national citizenships, emphasizing the importance of local-level citizenship. If we can analyze citizenship as a bundle of practices surrounding the relationship between individuals and the state, thus equating citizenship broadly with political participation, then in El Alto at least that relationship requires some consideration of people's memberships in different communities. Adapting and expanding on T. H. Marshall's (1983 [1950]) definition of citizenship, the issues at stake here are what it is that makes someone into a "full member of a community" and what (political) community we might be talking about in any one instance. Whereas Marshall assumed, first, that the community could be straightforwardly equated to the national community and, second, that someone could be granted the status of full member of that community in some legal sense, I have argued that political communities at the local level are equally important for alteños' citizenship and I have investigated the practices that go into making someone a full member of those collectivities or communities. These operate in different ways and with varying levels of success according to how far people choose to participate in any particular political community and to share in its values. The communities I have explored here are based on residence at zonal and city levels, and on occupation at the city level. Other important communities for alteños include political parties (for some) and those based on religion, birth village, the school attended by their children, and possibly generation in the case of youth groups. Most individuals belong to several overlapping communities and some choose not to belong to any.

The collectivities I have examined relate to the state in contradictory ways, especially significant being the relation of mediation between people and the state as well as substitution for the state. The different communities are thus constituted through both the state's presence and its absence. State presence was key for the pescaderas in chapter 7 and the juntas vecinales in chapter 2, when the state required and propelled the formation of particular collectivities in order to channel resources or negotiate the protection of principles of free trade. State absence is also important when the government delegates the responsibility for the regulation of the market, environmental regulation, even local development to private entities such as the trade unions or juntas vecinales. From the perspective of the collectivities themselves, the relationship with the state therefore is one of engagement in practice accompanied by an increasing distance from the state. This dialectic works also on an individual level for many alteños and is particularly evident at election time, when citizens engage with the state by attempting to make clientelist networks work for them and for their zone. They thus endeavor to substantiate their citizenship by trying to make politicians personally accountable to them but at the same time strongly express their feelings of distance from the politicians when they talk about how corrupt they all are and how they forget the poor and the marginalized. Similarly, the trade unions put a great deal of effort into maintaining a rhetorical distance between the two spheres of sindicalismo and la política (i.e., party politics), while in practice engaging in all sorts of personal and professional network relationships with representatives of the state. They could not do their job effectively if one or the other side of the equation were missing.

Engagement with the state can be through day-to-day processes of negotiation and petitioning, as we saw for both the juntas vecinales and the pescaderas. Often frustratingly so, collective groups are in the position of being supplicants for resources from a frequently capricious state, a relationship with those in power that is similar to the relationship with the spirits, who are also able to bestow good fortune if appealed to ("attended to") correctly, but who are also capricious. Collectivities therefore often engage with the state in a conflictual way, principally through demonstrations, when they are demanding that their pliego petitorio (petition) be met. This dynamic has created a cyclical pattern of politics, a tendency which has a considerable historical heritage (Irurozqui 2000; Platt 1982) but which has become significantly more acute since 1997. That cycle begins as popular protest, and moves to negotiation and then agreement with the state. Governments do often give in to the demands of protesters and renegotiate legislation—or make a show of so doing. Examples include the withdrawal of Aguas de Tunari from Cochabamba in April 2000 and the renegotiation of budget surplus requirements with the IMF after the February 2003 riots. On a more mundane level, the conflict between fish-sellers in the provinces and in El Alto shows how the prefecture was proceeding in favor of the provincial fishermen's federation because it was responding to the set of demands presented in a protest march. However, the cycle continues when that concession is followed by the government reneging on all or some of its promises and provoking renewed protest. In October 2003, the cycle broke down once the army started to kill demonstrators, but it was not the social movements that conceded in the end, as Bolivian citizens turned on their government and forced the president and his chief ministers to resign. In March 2005, Carlos Mesa's resignation threat was an attempt once again to break the cycle without either resorting to the authoritarian measures of his predecessor or conceding to the demands of the social movements. He was unsuccessful, leading to the subsequent standoff between the government and the social movements over the question of natural gas exports, and his eventual resignation for real. The important question now is whether Evo Morales's government will be able to manage those tensions better. Certainly at the time of this writing there was considerable optimism among many Bolivians, and alteños at least felt represented by Evo and his government (Charlotta Widmark, anthropologist, personal communication, July 2006).

The point, though, is that the local political communities based upon residence, occupation, and so on are able to negotiate with the state from a position of some strength. Part of what enables them to do so comes from their ability to maintain the perception of two carefully delineated spheres: the people on one side and the politicians and businessmen on the other. They use this distinction to describe their relationship to the state because they maintain the perception that the state or nation ("our dear Bolivia") is equivalent to the former and is being betrayed by the latter. The venal politicians who are the principal criminals betray the higher ideal of a state that serves the people's interest and is the "rule of everyone by everyone" (Hardt and Negri 2005) because they are serving their own individual interests at the expense of those of the collectivity. At the beginning of his government, Evo blurs the distinction between the people and the politicians, which puts him in a powerful position because he enjoys very much more legitimacy than previous regimes have had. But this is risky, because expectations are very high.

INDIVIDUAL AND COLLECTIVE INTERESTS

There is, therefore, an important ideological emphasis on the collective as a shared value, at least as a goal or ideal, when it comes to the state and the responsibilities of those holding public office. This shared value works both at the level of the national government and at the local level of the collectivities discussed here, as the issue of leadership makes clear. At local and national levels, the venality of the powerful is something that is somehow assumed by the majority of the ordinary members of those communities: as politicians will steal public money, junta vecinal leaders will also embezzle funds, and trade union leaders will "sell themselves [to a political party] for a plate of lentils." They do so because they are *buscando sus apetitos personales*, seeking to fulfill their personal, that is, individual, interests, which are constructed in opposition to those of the collectivity. However, the high degree of suspicion and rumor around the supposed misdeeds of those in leadership positions is evidence of the fact that this tendency must be fought. Future leaders are held to account preemptively, with the knowledge that their reputation will be severely diminished if they fulfill their personal interests to too great an extent. Current leaders may keep themselves in check because "people talk"; they may also simply be more effective as leaders because they do not want to be accused of being corrupt. The notion of corruption as the assertion of individual interests at the expense of the collectivity reinforces the common idea of what the collectivity actually is and what its interests are.

Other practices and moral values also create the collectivity and build in people an understanding of themselves as inherently collective, as belonging to specific communities. These practices vary according to the community, as we have seen, and range from ritual practices such as dancing during the fiesta and sharing alcohol with other people and with the spirits, to organizational practices such as the building of consensus through formal speech-making or physical politics during general assemblies or the mediation of conflicts between trade union affiliates. Here, the embodied and physical nature of these citizenship practices is crucial. During the dancing, the physical experience of effervescence and of the discipline of controlled forward motion in concert with similarly regulated others helps create a very strong sense of collectivity, of being imbricated in relationships with others and with the place that the Entrada progresses through. Entradas, civic parades, and demonstrations all take a similar physical form, and through their citation of each other maintain similar notions of collective agency, belonging, and political action. There are two ways that this citation is important for citizenship: first is the sense of collective selves in concert that is maintained through physical movement, and second is the relationship to place that develops. Place is made spiritual in the devotional aspects of the fiesta, which are underlined by the consumption of alcohol (which also plays an important part in civic parades and demonstrations). In rituals at fiesta time and at other moments, the ingestion of alcohol mediates the relationships of commensality between people and local deities that have a very strong association with place: an achachila is located in a particular mountain, in August we must give gifts to the Pachamama located in our yard, the anniversary fiesta is an act of devotion to the zone, which is mapped out by the Entrada. In civic parades and demonstrations, participants are similarly creating a relationship with place made spiritual, asserting their presence as the Bolivian people, and making themselves visible.

During general assemblies, embodiment is similarly important: speeches often seem to be more about the performance than the precise content, and decisions are made on the basis of an assessment of the mood of the meeting that relies upon a keen awareness of the politics of the bodies present. The organizational values that are the foundation of the trade unions' strength are also based upon what people do: whether they attend meetings, demonstrations, parades, or fiestas and uphold the union's power of convocatoria, its power to do mass politics. Perhaps because of the importance of the collective self, such values are upheld rhetorically more by an assertion of the obligations or taken-for-grantedness of such actions than through a calculation of an exchange of the fulfillment of responsibilities of attendance in return for certain rights of protection by the union or more favorable treatment by the leadership in any conflict. Vida orgánica is simply something that one does by virtue of being a good member of the union; similarly, people collaborate at the time of the zone's anniversary fiesta by donating goods because they can and because it is their zone.

However, the conflicts that arise show that reality does not always match up to this ideal version of behavior. It is precisely because some people are more conscientious than others that vida orgánica can be a means of discrimination when it comes to mediating conflicts between trade union affiliates. And alteños also obviously frequently operate as individual selves as well as collective selves, not only if and when they become civic leaders. The Evangelicals are a very good example of a community that is built on the basis of a coalition of bounded autonomous individuals. The extreme competitiveness of the informal economy of the city is another sphere where individualistic behavior is often necessary. Various citizenship projects exist to promote the sense that people have of themselves as individual and self-sufficient citizens operating in the contemporary marketplace, such as microcredit schemes (Lazar 2004) and even schooling (Lazar 2002a). Nonetheless, the collective self remains absolutely central to citizenship and political agency in El Alto today.

Such an assertion should not be taken to imply either that alteños are inherently collectivist or that being collective is the same as being democratic or egalitarian. These assertions are both made quite frequently by enthusiasts of the argument that the organizations of the popular sphere will reinvigorate the (implicitly decrepit, explicitly corrupt) liberal representative democracy of the normative sphere of institutional politics (Garcia Linera et al. 2000; Gutierrez et al. 2002). I agree that some potential does exist, and that the popular organizations are developing alternative notions of democracy and of the state that may be closer to the ideal of the "rule of everyone by everyone" (Hardt and Negri 2005). However, this book has also shown that there exists as much potential for tensions between different collectivities (such as the two fish-sellers organizations) as there does for unification and the consequent power that coalesces at specific political moments, such as April 2000 and October 2003. It has also shown that collectivity does not mean a flattening out of all members of the collective: as in the dances and the fiesta, hierarchies and divisions are a key part of the expression and construction of collective selves; as in the trade unions, authority is as much a part of leadership as the obligation to serve the bases, something underlined by the use of kinship metaphors in explaining that relationship.

Citizenship is a complex experience in contemporary El Alto. Most people experience their citizenship as part of one or more collectivities, which may take the form of nested affiliations, for example the citizen as a member of the local street traders association, which belongs to the zone of 16 de Julio, which is part of the city of El Alto, which is part of the department of La Paz, which is part of Bolivia. Or through another trajectory, where the street traders association is a member of the Federation of Street Traders, which belongs to the Central Obrera Regional, which belongs to the Central Obrera Boliviana. The same person could also exercise his or her citizenship as a vecino of the zone where he or she lives—say, Rosas Pampa—and thus as a member of the junta vecinal, as such belonging to the zone of Rosas Pampa, the city of El Alto, and so on. Experiencing citizenship is not only about a legal status and the ownership of a set of rights and responsibilities associated with that status; in fact, it is highly physical, having to do with participation in a whole series of practices that can encompass the sharing of alcohol, attendance at a meeting, the mediation of a conflict in the central federation office, a dance, a parade, a demonstration, passing on a rumor about the corruption of a leader, and more. It is also highly moral, such that people often feel themselves to be citizens in opposition to the state when it is in the hands of a particularly corrupt group of custodians, the politicians.

Thus citizenship can be experienced *despite* normative institutional politics as well as, necessarily, in negotiation with that sphere. This creates a paradoxical relationship with the state, in which alteños and the popular movements articulate a scathing critique of the neoliberal state along with their vision of an alternative state. They want a strong developmentalist state that is able to provide them with jobs and organize the provision of public services such as health and education, but also water, gas, and electricity. Both the everyday talk of corruption and the extraordinary moments of protest are responses to the cruelty of the neoliberal state of the past twenty years, a cruelty that crystallized in Warisata, Senkata, Villa Ingenio, and across El Alto in 2003. However, alteños do not seem to have entirely lost faith in the state. They are prepared to engage with it, however corrupt they think it might be. They continue to expound a political vision of what could be and to practice their alternative forms of democracy in the kinds of organizational processes described in this book. National governments will need to take these visions and practices seriously if they are to enjoy legitimacy in the eyes of ordinary people.

INTRODUCTION

1. National Statistics Institute, http://www.ine.gov.bo.
2. I follow Begoña Aretxaga (2003) in my use of the term "encounters" between citizens and the state, although she does not discuss citizenship explicitly as such.
3. This gender specificity was underlined later, with the word *virtus* in Latin, which became *virtú* in Italian (Machiavelli), and which derives etymologically from the Latin *vir*, meaning "man" (Oldfield 1990).
4. I follow Elizabeth Frazer (1998) in distinguishing between philosophical communitarianism and political communitarianism. The former is based upon a criticism of the abstract individualism of liberal political thought and represented by philosophers such as Michael Sandel and Alisdair MacIntyre. See the collection by Avineri and de-Shalit (1992) for an overview of this debate. Political communitarianism is most clearly associated with the work of Amitai Etzioni (1993), but see also many of the practices of New Labour in the United Kingdom and some local schemes of community empowerment in the United States, discussed by Rose (1999) and Cruikshank (1999), respectively.
5. For discussion of the Bolivian indigenous movement with a focus on Katarismo, see Rivera Cusicanqui (2003 [1984]), Hurtado (1986), Patzi Paco (1999), Albó (2002), and Hylton et al. (2003).
6. Gonzalo Sanchez de Lozada won with around 22 percent of the vote.
7. National Electoral Court of Bolivia, http://www.cne.org.bo; National Congress, http://www.diputados.bo.
8. The *ayllu* is a form of indigenous community organization in the Andes

spread over different ecological niches. See Ouweneel (2003) for a discussion of the history of the ayllu concept.

9. Although it seems that the hydrocarbons law of 2004, which raised the tax on natural gas to 50 percent from 18 percent against the wishes of the International Monetary Fund and President Carlos Mesa, produced a situation where Bolivia's current account held a small surplus by the beginning of 2006, and Bolivia did not need an extension of the temporary IMF credit facility that was due for renewal later in the year. This may mean that the IMF is less able to pressure the Bolivian government in favor of the extraction of natural gas by foreign companies (Weisbrot and Sandoval 2006), something perhaps borne out by the process of nationalization under way at the time of this writing.

10. Rawls proposed the development of political theory of the common good built upon a procedural model, in which individuals are imagined to be in a contemporary version of the contractarian state of nature, the "original position," and the structures they visualize from this vantage point are the best way of ordering society. The original position consists of individuals behind a "veil of ignorance," where they are unaware of their social positioning, sex, wealth, state of health, and so on when they decide upon such structures. He argued that this would lead to the fairest distribution of the common good.

11. From the late 1980s onward, anthropology of the self, influenced by postmodernism, moved to question a coherent single self as the source of agency and subjectivity (Butler 1990, 1993; Strathern 1988; Rosenau 1992). Recent work has compensated for the disembodying tendencies of the more extreme postmodern positions and asserted the importance of embodiment for our experience of our selves (Moore 1994; Csordas 1999).

12. Larson (2005) discusses the work of Bautista Saavedra, Manuel Rigoberto Paredes, Alcides Arguedas, and Franz Tamayo, all very prominent literary and political figures.

13. In Peru, the cholos famously voted in President Alberto Fujimori in 1990, and there is some evidence to suggest that the children of cholos were the principal source of activists for the terrorist group Sendero Luminoso (Seligmann 1989, 1993; Degregori 1991). In Bolivia around the same time (the late 1980s and early 1990s), the rising importance of the cholos as constituency was underlined by the remarkable success of the political party Condepa (see Lazar 2002b).

14. Indian phenotypal features are also important, especially dark hair, which is usually worn long, straight, and in two plaits.

15. For discussions of chola dress, see Buechler and Buechler (1996), Salazar de la Torre (1999), and Weismantel (2001). Koch's (2006) study of consumption patterns in the cities of La Paz, Cochabamba, and Sucre suggests that dress

may be the way that urban Aymara conspicuously consume in order to increase their status. The study found that Quechua households spent more than poor Hispanic households on conspicuous consumption of consumer durables, specifically TV sets. The difference between Aymara households and Hispanic households was not statistically significant. The author hypothesized that this indicated that Aymara households did not feel the need to "pass" as mestizos through status consumption because of a more powerful sense of ethnic identity than that of Quechua households.

16. *Maya* and *paya* are the Aymara words for "one" and "two," respectively.

ONE **EL ALTO THE CITY**

1. Estadísticas e Indicadores Socioeconómicos del Municipio de El Alto, Nota de Prensa no. 20, Instituto Nacional de Estadísticas. Available at http://www.ine.gov.bo.

2. See especially Albó, Greaves, and Sandoval (1987), Criales Burgos (1994), Rivera Cusicanqui et al. (1996), Llanos Layme (1998), and Paulson (2003a).

3. That is, offered a libation for their stalls. See chapter 5.

4. On New Years Eve, you eat twelve grapes and make twelve wishes for the coming year, one for every month. Red underwear brings love, and yellow underwear brings money over the next year.

5. The sweet lejía found in La Paz softens the bitter taste of coca leaves and activates the alkaloids present in the plant. Cigarettes and alcohol often accompany coca chewing, especially on Tuesdays and Fridays, the most propitious days for malicious spells, when the smoke from a cigarette can "blow away" curses.

6. I am godmother to her child, so we are *comadres*. *Compadrazgo* is a very important kinship relation in the Andes. See chapter 3 for more detailed discussion.

7. *Pueblo* can also be used to describe the birth village of the parents of second-generation migrants.

8. Land in El Alto, especially near the Ceja, is more expensive now than land in La Paz because it is better situated for commerce and distribution of goods.

9. The other main destination for "relocalized" miners was the region of Chapare, where many went to grow coca, encouraged by the buoyancy of the cocaine market during the boom of the 1980s.

10. Estadísticas e Indicadores Socioeconómicos del Municipio de El Alto, Nota de Prensa no. 20, Instituto Nacional de Estadísticas. Available at http://www.ine.gov.bo.

11. In September 2003, the blockade was only really effective in the department of

La Paz, in contrast to the wider extent of the previous blockades over the altiplano. In July and August 2003, a blockade had failed because of divisions within the CSUTCB.

12. *Ultima Hora* 23 July 2000.

13. This council included the university rector, the bishop of El Alto, the executive secretaries of the COR, the Federation of Street Traders, the Consejo Central de Artesanos, teachers' and students' organizations, and the presidents of FEJUVE and the FEDEPAF (Federacion de Padres de Familia de El Alto, Federation of School Parents of El Alto).

14. Chair legs were filled with gunpowder from fireworks, and stones were used as bullets.

15. There is a distinction between those traders who sell at street markets and those who sell every day on a fixed and permanent site in residential zones. The latter are organized into their own federation, and that is affiliated to the COR.

16. This refers to something said by Carlos Mesa, that El Alto was the "centinela" of Bolivian democracy.

TWO CONSTRUCTING THE ZONE

1. This seems to be the case for several parts of Spain, particularly Castile (Nader 1990; Vassberg 1984).

2. Arendt (1998 [1958]) and Castoriadis (1992) both point to the importance of speech for the operations of Greek democracies. I discuss this point in chapter 8.

3. The Law of Popular Participation (Ley de Participación Popular, LPP) of 1994 increased the amount of national revenue directed to local government from 10 to 20 percent and instituted a framework whereby it would be distributed through municipalities and according to population. The "popular participation" element comes in the planning and supervisory mechanisms. In urban areas, delegates from juntas vecinales form supervisory committees to supervise the municipal budgeting; the planning processes for the annual municipal plans are meant to be participatory. The LPP also recognized indigenous authorities, who could register their community as a territorial grass-roots organization (*organización territorial de base*). The education reform of the same year promoted "intercultural education" as well as a number of reforms in the monitoring, education, and payment of teachers. As a result of the popular participation legislation and education reform, responsibility for health and educational infrastructure has devolved to often poorly administered munici-

pal governments, who disburse what money they can find in collaboration with community organizations. See Booth et al. (1997), Albó and Equipo CIPCA (1999), McNeish (2001), and Gray Molina (2001, 2003) for further discussion of the LPP in rural areas, and Gill (2000) for discussion of the LPP and educational reform in El Alto.

4. The juntas are also increasingly finding themselves representing the community to private enterprises, such as the electricity and waste disposal companies. However, my material for this is limited, so I focus here primarily on local government and NGOs.

5. The historical information here is from Musch, Valdez, and Gondrie (1994), a book produced as a result of participatory research conducted in Rosas Pampa by the Dutch NGO APS.

6. The latter two came in 1994, part of the development project that included the participatory research exercise that was published in Musch et al. (1994).

7. Both of these companies provided an appalling service: in one year in Rosas Pampa, not more than one light on my street ever worked, and that in patches. We also had weeks of strikes by Clisa workers (because the mayor refused to pay municipal debts to Clisa, who then did not pay their workers), and a consequent building up of ugly piles of unhygienic rubbish in the streets, as nothing was done to settle the dispute or provide alternative methods of rubbish collection.

8. See Nelson and Wright (1995) for a discussion of participation in development projects.

9. The Law of Popular Participation did lengthen the mayoral term from two years to five, and the recent Law of Municipalities prevents councilors from sacking a mayor before he or she has served two years. In addition, Jose Luis Paredes's party gained a substantial majority on the council in the local elections of 1999. All of these developments provided much-needed stability for El Alto. Furthermore, Paredes's own political ambitions required him to do a good job in and for El Alto, and from the beginning he reasserted municipal control over alteño development. I discuss his election in 1999 in the following chapter.

10. I have no way of verifying if the incident happened, or if the amount I was told was correct or an exaggeration. The point is the nature of the corruption narrative itself (Gupta 1995).

11. A ch'alla is a libation, and the way you open a building, for example: you drop some alcohol onto the floor to feed the Pachamama and for good luck. Chapter 5 discusses ch'allas in more detail. The president who had "misspent" the

money intended for its furnishing was present at this particular ceremony. Nobody commented on his presence or on the issue of misspent funds.

THREE CITIZENS DESPITE THE STATE

1. A key problem for Bolivian party politics. See Gamarra (2003), Gamarra and Malloy (1995), Romero Ballivian (1996), Dunkerley (1998), and Domingo (2001).

2. A *charango* is a small mandolin, used in classic Bolivian folkloric music.

3. I have discussed Condepa and the intertwining of gender politics and the media elsewhere (Lazar 2002b).

4. However, 1990s Latin America has shown that populism is also compatible with neoliberalism, the best example being Fujimori in Peru, but also Menem in Argentina and Collor in Brazil. This has been called "neopopulism" (Crabtree 1998; Weyland 1999).

5. Populism is often characterized as a direct appeal by a leader to the popular sectors, bypassing intermediary organizations such as political parties and interest groups (Crabtree 1998; Blanco Cazas and Sandoval 1993; Dix 1985; Weyland 1999; Conniff 1999). Kurt Weyland calls it a "quasi-direct but hierarchical relationship between a personalist leader and masses of devoted followers" (172), and this characterizes the relationship that developed between Paredes and his voters well.

6. See Schmidt et al. (1977). Gay (1998) argues that much of the misrepresentation of clients as passive subjects of control, common in the political science of Latin America, derives from the fact that the literature analyzes clientelism from a top-down perspective. Recent work is beginning to redress that balance. See, for example, Auyero (2000, 2001).

7. See Terrazas and Dibbits (1994) for an in-depth discussion of alteño women's views on health care.

8. Most Condepistas were fired from the municipal government when Paredes took over. However, his unwillingness to replace them all was a response to pressure from international donor agencies (governmental and NGO) to reduce the bureaucracy of the El Alto municipality in order that it might regain the credit-worthiness lost during Condepa's administration.

9. *Almanaques* are posters with calendars on them. The posters proclaimed "Goni 2002" rather than the name of the MNR candidate for mayor, showing that the MNR priority for that election was in fact the candidature of Gonzalo Sanchez de Lozada for the presidential elections of 2002. As expected, in the elections the MNR gained only one councilor, and that because they have a substantial

following of militantes in El Alto. They were never seriously in the running for mayor, and were well aware of this.

10. The colors of ADN, MNR, and Condepa, respectively. The ADN colors are rather sinister; one friend said he thought the red was for the blood shed during Banzer's dictatorship.

11. He estimated that he spent US$30,000 of his own money, generated from his business interests, especially the TV Channel 24. *Pulso* 19–25 November 1999, pp. 12–13.

12. This personalistic politics is common elsewhere in Latin America (Banck 1998; Conniff 1999; Weyland 1999).

13. *Pulso* 19–25 November 1999.

14. It seems that at first this was a business strategy, whereby he would donate obras in order to protect and expand his market, or regain territory lost to competitors undercutting his prices (Mayorga 1991). Although the UCS's main power base was not in La Paz so much as Cochabamba (among truck drivers) and Santa Cruz, Fernández funded obras all over the country, often allied to the interests of his constituencies. For example, his money paid for the surfacing of one of the roads from El Alto down to La Paz.

15. It is important to note that the concept of the Jach'a Uru, or Great Day, was a particularly powerful one that appealed to a strong Aymara emphasis on hope for change, expressed for example in the concept of *pachakuti*, or "the world turned upside down." In this sense, its resonance for urban Aymaras was particularly strong (Saravia and Sandoval 1991). Paredes understood this, saying in the interview quoted above, "Now I am the one who represents hope, change, modernity" ("Ahora soy yo quien represento la esperanza, el cambio, la modernidad"), reflected well in the translation of the slogan from Aymara to Spanish. In this, Paredes picked up on the aspirational side of many urban Aymaras in El Alto, appealing to those wanting to stress their modernity, the difference between themselves and their *campesino* parents or grandparents.

16. *Pulso* 19–25 November 1999.

17. It is very incongruous on the surface to be seriously weighing up membership of ADN versus MAS. The ADN's economic policies were very orthodox and right wing. MAS is the party of the cocalero leader Evo Morales.

18. Their firm buys land around El Alto, then sells off small lots for people to build their houses. When this is done unscrupulously, without proper legal title to the land or on land that has already been sold, is unsafe because of potential erosion or collapse, or belongs to the municipality, the perpetrators are called loteadores. But Martinez stressed to me that they did their "urban development" legally and according to appropriate studies and plans.

19. Plan Identidad's catchy slogan was "A New Era Has Arrived for the Development of Identity and Citizenship, with Enterprise and Modernity."

20. In both El Alto and La Paz. In La Paz, the entry into the mayoral race of Juan Del Granado, a respected human rights lawyer and parliamentary deputy, led to a media focus on his anticorruption and pro–participatory democracy rhetoric. He eventually won the election by a very small margin.

21. This is the view of Bolivians at all strata of society. For example, a wealthy friend of mine was talking about Ronald Maclean, a candidate in the 1999 elections for La Paz, when another friend said that she'd heard he had been honest in a previous mayoral administration. My friend said, quite matter-of-factly, "No, he must have stolen, but he did things." Ronald Maclean is actually one of the very few mayors of La Paz who is talked about as honest, but for my friend this was inconceivable.

22. Local election campaigns in El Alto and La Paz often focus on the problem of transport between the two cities, since the current motorway takes a long time and cannot carry the amount of people traveling at rush hour. Politicians frequently propose highly expensive and quite ridiculous plans, elaborated at great expense by architects and engineering consultants.

23. *Pulso* 19–25 November 1999.

24. Of course, this is by no means confined to the Andes. See, for example, Roniger and Gunes-Ayata (1994), Schmidt et al. (1977).

FOUR PLACE, MOVEMENT, AND RITUAL

1. With alcohol, which I discuss in the following chapter.

2. See Swartz (1968), Kertzer (1988), Boissevain (1992), Gledhill (1994), Lomnitz (1995), and Banck (1998).

3. Such as Buechler (1980), Albó and Preiswerk (1986), Sallnow (1987), Carter and Mamani P. (1989 [1982]), Abercrombie (1991, 1998), and Bigenho (2001).

4. This is not as frightening as it sounds. The bullfight is held in the football pitch, which is ringed by buses and trucks to stop the bulls from getting out and to provide seating for the audience. The bulls rarely approach the dancers because they are being distracted by the young men taunting them with capes. Although I do not cover the bullfight in detail in this chapter because my data for the dancing is much richer, it is an important part of the fiesta, which requires a fair amount of organization on the part of the junta vecinal and attracts a large audience. Penelope Harvey (1997) argues that the bullfight brings together the powers of state institutions and authorities and of the landscape. Many of her insights would apply to bullfights in El Alto, which are

very similar to that she describes for Ocongate, Peru, with the notable exception that they do not involve a condor playing with the bulls.

5. Carnival is the week of Ash Wednesday, Gran Poder is around 23 June, and the Entrada Universitaria is at the end of July.

6. For example, Sheets-Johnstone (1979), Horton Fraleigh (1987), Ness (1992), Thomas (1993), and Ram (2000).

7. The colors of the Bolivian flag.

8. Kinship and friendship networks are often the same thing because friends usually seal their friendship by instituting fictive kinship categories such as compadrazgo (Wolf 1977; Mintz and Wolf 1977).

9. This is a complex issue. I was not quite a full partner in the sorts of exchange relationships that developed around dancing, so I did not witness extended formal requests to dance. My neighbors asked me if I wanted to join in the comparsa we took to Quilloma in April 2000. They had received an invitation to rehearsals from the pasante (who was their nephew) and hosted one of the rehearsals. I just turned up one evening. For the Rosas Pampa fiesta later that year, people told me that I could dance with any comparsa I wanted, but I knew people in the school and the market better. Once I told friends who sold in the market that I was keen on dancing, the wife of one of the organizers told me where the rehearsals were and what were the quotas, and my partner and I went along. In both instances, the pasantes ensured that I received a formal invitation to participate in the fiesta and also expressed their gratitude to us for agreeing to dance.

10. Who, ironically, were Evangelicals. I discuss their case and the Evangelical view of dancing in the following chapter.

11. Interestingly, the official website of the 2001 Oruro Carnival divides the dances into traditional and popular; the latter category seems to refer to dances that have been created, rather than drawing on autochthonous Andean traditions. The Morenada appears in the popular category (http://www.acfo.org.bo). The distinctions are as follows: Tradicionales: Diablada, Cullaguada, Llamerada, Tinkus, Pujllay, Kallawaya, Incas, Tobas, Negro o Tundiques, Kantus, Tarqueadas, Zampoñeros. Populares: Morenada, Caporales, Ahuatiris, Surisicuris, Wititis, Doctorcitos. The website does not say on what basis the distinctions are made.

12. The costume described is that of chola women, although (of course) of the best quality that they own. Chola dress bespeaks commercial success and status, because even those polleras and shawls that are worn on a day-to-day basis are very much more expensive than Western clothing (Buechler and Buechler 1996; Weismantel 2001; Salazar de la Torre 1999).

13. Jane Cowan (1990) shows how movements in dance reflect and constitute "gendered dispositions" in northern Greece; Zoila Mendoza (1998) demonstrates something similar for race and ethnicity in Andean Peru.

14. I don't know how the baby, or the alegría I was supposed to demonstrate, squares with being a grandmother, but that is what I was told, and Rocha (n.d.) also talks of the Awila, or *vieja* (old woman) as mascot in the Kullawada.

15. The male role in Caporales looks much more fun, and exuberant. The women in Caporales comparsas seem to be there mainly to look pretty and wear very short skirts. They don't jump as much as the men do.

16. Formation of dance associations that participated in 2001: 1900–1949: 9; 1950–1969: 7; 1970–1979: 14; 1980–1989: 10; 1990+: 2 (http://www.acfo.org.bo). Presumably a number of the older associations have ceased to function. General Banzer encouraged the Gran Poder Entrada in its early years by attending in the early 1970s. The role of the nationalist military governments in encouraging folkloric production in Bolivia would bear further research. Thomas Turino (1991) demonstrates the importance of the nationalist de facto government of General Juan Velasco Alvarado for raising the national profile of Andean music in Peru.

FIVE HOW THE GODS TOUCH HUMANS

1. The title of this chapter paraphrases Sabine MacCormack (1991).

2. I was at the time anxious about these possibilities, but I did not know people in any of the Morenada comparsas, and I wanted a more authentic experience than dancing with the school, so I decided to risk it. I felt that I would be protected a bit by my foreign status, and my partner agreed.

3. The discussion took place too late to make a difference to my decision to dance that year.

4. Dealing with my own alcohol consumption became something of a methodological consideration for me: it was extremely hard, and in fact rude, to refuse drinks, and people appreciated the fact that I was willing to drink with them. But I often came across the problem of alcohol and participant observation: the more you participate, the less you can observe. Thomas Abercrombie (1998) makes the same observation. My decision in the end was not to drink excessively so that I was sick, but to enjoy myself. It was, I think, easier for me as a foreign woman to moderate my drinking.

5. Although nowadays it is often possible to substitute soft drinks for beer; it is cheaper, and the influence of the Evangelicals has made it more acceptable for others to ease off the alcohol.

6. One tactic for refusing or avoiding requests of this kind is to not be in when the relatives come to call. I am grateful to Olivia Harris for this observation.

7. The *Irpaqa* is a ceremony where the groom's family "buy" the bride from her family. The *rutucha* is the ceremony that accompanies a baby's first haircut. *Achachila* is the Aymara word for grandparent. These spirits are located in particular features of the local landscape, especially mountains, and the usual anthropological translation for them is ancestors. For a discussion of the various types of deities in rural Bolivia, see Bouysse-Cassagne and Harris (1987) and Abercrombie (1998). People I spoke to did not make the distinction between ancestors and devils that is common in the anthropological literature about rural Bolivia (Harris 2000b; Bouysse-Cassagne and Harris 1987). They explained the achachilas as the mountain peaks themselves.

8. I was told that Carnival time is also the time to ch'alla your animals and fields in the countryside, although llamas have their own special festival.

9. *Yatiri* is an Aymara word meaning "one who knows."

10. See Harris (2000b) for a discussion of Pachamama as earth mother.

11. See Fernandez Juarez (1995) for a detailed description of the different kinds of masses.

12. Mayer does talk about asymmetric reciprocity for situations where the return is less than the original gift, arguing that this is usually the result of inequalities in status between the participants in the relationship.

13. For clarification of the various deities in rural altiplano Bolivia, see Bouysse-Cassagne and Harris (1987) and Abercrombie (1998).

14. Santiago is a manifestation of God and is closely identified with *rayo*, or lightning, a very powerful deity in Andean religiosity (Platt 1997; Bouysse-Cassagne and Harris 1987).

15. See also Fernandez Juarez (1995) for discussion of the llama-human equivalence.

16. Often, white anthropologists (and local non-Indians) in the Andes are accused of being *kharisiris* (Harris 2000c; Abercrombie 1998), but fortunately I missed this particular rite of passage. However, I was warned not to get too drunk when I went to Quilloma to dance because the kharisiris might suck my fat while I was unconscious.

17. Rather than in the sense of "permanently pervading the universe" or being everywhere (*Oxford English Dictionary*).

18. For case studies of Evangelical Protestantism in Bolivia, see Canessa (2000), Ströbele-Gregor (1992), Gill (1990, 1993).

19. This is a slightly difficult statistic because it does not include households where there is a mix of Evangelicals and Catholics (13 percent of total). It is calculated only on the basis of pure Catholic households.

20. The Evangelical Protestants are split into a bewildering number of groups in Bolivia. Assemblies of God and the Seventh Day Adventists are the largest.

21. Which may be reasonably accurate for women who come to La Paz as domestic servants (Gill 1990) but is not representative of the Evangelicals I knew. In a more macro sense they might be seen as psychically vulnerable as a result of their poverty. See below for discussion.

22. One of the key factors in the growth of Pentecostalism in the Latin American countryside is often the small number of Catholic priests, who take a long time to train and are usually foreigners. In contrast, the Evangelical movement has relied much more on indigenous lay preachers (Stoll 1990; Martin 1990; Bastian 1992; Green 1993).

23. When a woman says "Peleabamos" in reference to her husband, it is often a euphemism for "He beat me." I am grateful to Andrew Canessa for this observation.

24. Dissociative states associated with trance or possession seem to be a universal human phenomenon (Goodman 1972). Erika Bourguignon (1994) notes that the experience of sensory overload from the drumming, dancing, hyperventilation, and crowding in these kinds of rituals can often induce dissociation. Rouget (1980) stresses the importance of music and rhythm in what he calls "communal trances," where repetition, accelerando, and crescendo create a state of emotional excitement that leads to trance states. He notes the importance of theatricality to such effervescence.

25. Some of the literature on charismatic religion suggests this directly (Sargant 1973). Of course, such extreme loss of control is also threatening to the cultural expectations of someone like myself who is from a noncharismatic Anglican background.

26. Canessa (2000) compares them in this to Kataristas, who similarly "reject the possibility of a middle ground" of "cultural mestizaje," opting to reject Western cultural models in favor of a revitalized and mythical indigenous past. As he points out, many more have chosen evangelism over Katarismo because of the perception of the higher status of the West.

27. The Catholic Father Arriaga, an "extirpator of idolatry" from the seventeenth century, said in 1621 that the "common error" of the natives "is their tendency to carry water on both shoulders, to have recourse to both religions at once" (quoted in Sallnow 1987: 51).

SIX COMPETITION, INDIVIDUALISM

1. Here I am using a broad definition of the informal economy as characterized by small-scale commerce, production, or transport that is unregulated and untaxed by government, with people mostly self-employed rather than receiving a wage. I acknowledge that it is difficult to define precisely and that there is no clear distinction between formal and informal sectors since they rely so much upon each other (Rivera Cusicanqui 2002; Hart 1973; Peattie 1987).

2. For example, Isbell (1978), Rasnake (1988), Skar (1982), Urton (1992). For ethnographies of the Andes that deal with the issue of social cohesion with a particular focus on the community authorities, see McEwen (1975), Carter and Mamani P. (1989 [1982]), Klemola (1997).

3. Silvia Escobar (1989) shows that, in 1983, women were the majority (71 percent) of those engaged in small-scale commerce in La Paz. See also Rivera Cusicanqui (2002).

4. Neoliberal forms of collectivity would obviously not solely be occupation-based, but could include microcredit groups, NGOs, community survival-based organizations such as communal kitchens, or community groups set up by development agencies for the purpose of project implementation, health promoters, or groups of trainers in human rights.

5. My experience is mostly with leaders and those who fulfill vida orgánica rather than with those who don't. Having said that, I think that it is possible for me to say that I am discussing the dominant discourse of acceptable behavior. If it were not, the Federation and individual associations would not be able to enforce their interpretations of what is acceptable.

6. Taxi drivers have more vigorous means of enforcing strike compliance, as they will puncture the tires of strike-breaking taxis and sometimes whip (huascear) the drivers. Usually the whipping is symbolic, but it is still very effective.

7. He was also a known MIRista, which may have been another reason for Don Antonio's dislike.

8. Examples of these slogans include: "¡Viva la Federación de Gremialistas!" "¡Que viva!"; "¡Viva el 16 de Julio!"; "¡Jallalla Tupac Katari!" "¡Jallalla!"; "¡Jallalla Bartolina Sisa!"; and "¡Gremiales de pie, nunca de rodillas!" (the slogan of El Alto is "El Alto de pie, nunca de rodillas"). Less frequently, I also heard "¡Jallalla Kollasuyumarka!"; "¡Que muera el modelo neoliberal!" "¡Que muera!"; "¡Abajo el MIRismo!" "¡Abajo!"; and "¡Abajo los oportunistas!"

9. See chapter 8 for a discussion of the importance of speech for trade union democracy.

10. "ARTICULO 159°: I. Se garantiza la libre asociación patronal. Se reconoce y

garantiza la sindicalización como medio de defensa, representación, asistencia, educación y cultura de los trabajadores, así como el fuero sindical en cuanto garantía para sus dirigentes por las actividades que desplieguen en el ejercicio específico de su mandato, no pudiendo éstos ser perseguidos ni presos" (http://www.presidencia.gov.bo).

11. I am grateful to Natalia Sobrerilla for this information.

12. In December 2004, Transparency International (2004: 3) reported that public opinion in thirty-six out of sixty-two countries surveyed perceived political parties as the institution most affected by corruption in their country. The next most corrupt institutions were parliament or legislature, followed by the police and the legal system or judiciary. The news received prominent coverage in the Bolivian press.

SEVEN "IN-BETWEENNESS" AND POLITICAL AGENCY

1. With the exception of Don Alberto Mamani, the names in this chapter are pseudonyms. However, I have changed only the first names, as the other main characters all had the surname Quispe, probably indicating that they come from the same area of the countryside.

2. Irineo Espinoza became a congressman for the MIR in one of the El Alto constituencies in the 2002 elections.

3. The pescaderas themselves said that they made around 10 to 15 Bolivianos per arroba (25 pounds). Exact figures for some fish in 2003 are as follows: Karachi: 100 fish bought for 30 Bolivianos; they sell 25 at 10 Bolivianos (so make 10 Bolivianos per 100 they sell). Ispi (whitebait): 30 pounds for 20 Bolivianos; 1 pound sold at 1 Boliviano (so make 10 Bolivianos per 30 pounds). Trucha (trout): arroba (25 pounds) = 135 Bolivianos; 1 pound sold at 6 Bolivianos (so make 15 Bolivianos per arroba).

4. In 2004, the amount was 12,000 Bolivianos. Decreto Supremo no. 27924, 20 December 2004.

5. I cannot confirm the truth of this accusation, as I did not speak either with Doña Veronica or with the Executive Committee member in question.

6. Alasitas is a festival held at the end of January in honor of the deity Ekeko, when people purchase and bless miniature versions of items they would like to get over the next year: miniature trucks, dollars, houses, passports.

7. The use of Decree 21060 was somewhat ironic, as it is a very famous law in Bolivia, its structural adjustment decree. Outside of neoliberal political parties, it is known as the Ley Maldita because it led to thousands of miners and other workers being fired.

8. I was later informed by a prefecture civil servant that the peasant markets had been a project at the prefecture for ten years, which was revived after the peasant blockades. He said that there had been a project for a fish terminal for eight years. Both had languished because of lack of funds.

EIGHT THE STATE AND THE UNIONS

1. See Cross (1998) for a similar argument in the case of Mexico City.
2. Andrew Canessa and Olivia Harris, personal communications, September 2004.
3. I am grateful to Into Goudsmit for making this point.
4. The male leaders that I knew came from a wide range of jobs, not just mining. Many had been traders all their lives, and others had been public employees or truck drivers or worked in a factory.
5. I make no claims for my abilities to understand fully the subtleties of the meetings, which would need years of participant observation to grasp.
6. I am grateful to the anthropologists Isabella Lepri and Into Goudsmit for making this point. See also Klemola (1997).

achachila	ancestral spirit located in particular features of the local landscape, especially mountains
ADN	Acción Democrática Nacionalista, National Democratic Action. Right-wing oligarchic party of General Hugo Banzer, de facto president 1971–1978 and democratically elected president 1997–2001, when he retired in favor of his vice president, Jorge "Tuto" Quiroga. Banzer died from cancer in 2002, and the party disappeared after 2003. Quiroga's successor party is called Podemos, or Poder Democratico Social, Social Democratic Power. It came in second in the elections of 2005.
alcaldía	town hall, municipality
alteño/a	resident of El Alto
altiplano	Andean highland plain
ampliado	meeting of general secretaries of associations or trade unions which are members of a federation such as the Federation of Street Traders. *Ampliados* are called by the executive committee of the federation.
ayni	reciprocal and obligatory service (e.g., beer bought for weddings or other festivities); also labor
base	grass-roots members of an organization
campo	countryside

ch'alla	libation, usually to Pachamama (Aymara term)
cholo/a, cholita	ethnic term for a rural–urban migrant, most often used for women who work in commerce and wear a *pollera*, shawl, and bowler hat. *Cholita* is the diminutive of *chola* and means young single woman who dresses in this way.
COB	Central Obrera Boliviana, Bolivian Workers Center
COR	Central Obrera Regional, Regional Workers Center
cocalero	coca grower
compadrazgo, compadre, comadre	*Compadrazgo* is the relationship between parents of a child and the godparent of that child; *compadre* refers to the men, *comadre* to the women.
comparsa	dance group
Condepa	Conciencia de Patria, Conscience of the Fatherland. Populist party founded by Carlos Palenque, who died in 1997.
Condepista	Condepa activist
conocido/a	well-known
convenio	signed agreement between two institutional parties, such as two associations or federations, or the mayor and the federation. *Convenios* usually settle disputes and have considerable force, even if they are not strictly legally binding.
convocatoria	the ability to get large numbers of people out into the streets for demonstrations, dances, or parades
detallistas	women who sell small quantities of goods in street markets
directorio	leadership committee of an association or trade union
Entrada	procession of *comparsas* along the defined route of the fiesta, in full costume. Usually held on the first day of the fiesta.
FEJUVE	Federation of Juntas Vecinales of the City of El Alto
interesado/a	lit. "interested," used to refer to people who are considered corrupt; also *personalista*
jefe de calle	chief of the street

junta escolar	parents association for a particular school
junta vecinal, junta de vecinos	residents committee; community authorities for a particular urban zone
Katarismo	Aymara political movement, founded in the early 1970s
MAS	Movimiento Al Socialismo, Movement toward Socialism. Party of the *cocaleros*, led by Evo Morales, who became president in December 2005
MBL	Movimiento Bolivia Libre, Movement for a Free Bolivia. Small party.
MIP	Movimiento Indígena Pachakuti, Indigenous Pachakuti Movement. Small party led by Felipe Quispe, the Mallku. Some success in 2002 elections.
misa/mesa	ritual offering to Pachamama, the *achachilas*, and/or the saints
MIR	Movimiento de Izquierda Revolucionaria, Movement of the Revolutionary Left. Party established in opposition to the military dictatorships of the 1970s, but by the 1990s no longer particularly left-wing, and seen as one of the oligarchic parties. Party of Jose Luis Paredes, elected mayor of El Alto in 1999. After 2003, the MIR split, and Paredes formed a party called Plan Progreso. He was elected mayor again in 2004, then prefect of La Paz in 2005.
MIRista	MIR activist
MNR	Movimiento Nacionalista Revolucionaria, Nationalist Revolutionary Movement. Well-established party, leaders of the popular revolution of 1952, but since the 1980s in favor of neoliberal economic policies and decentralization. Gonzalo Sanchez de Lozada ("Goni") was president 1993–1997 and 2002–2003. In October 2003, his vice president, Carlos Mesa, took over, but resigned in June 2005 in favor of a transitory government, which called elections for the following December.
MSM	Movimiento Sin Miedo, Fearless Movement. Small party founded in 1999 by Juan Del Granado, a human rights lawyer; based in La Paz.

mujer de pollera	woman who wears a *pollera*; polite term for *chola*
mujer de vestido	woman who wears Western clothes (i.e., is not *de pollera*)
obra	public works
paceña	someone from the department of La Paz
pasante	organizer of a *comparsa*
personalista	self-interested, used to refer to people who are considered corrupt; also *interesado*
pescadera	fish-seller
pollera	gathered skirt worn over several petticoats
pueblo	birth village, or, for second-generation migrants, birth village of parents; *pueblo* can also mean people, or nation
UPEA	Universidad Publica de El Alto
UCS	Unidad Cívica Solidaridad, Unit of Civic Solidarity. Populist party founded by Max Fernandez in 1989, then led by his son Jhonny after his death in 1996.
vecino/a	resident, inhabitant, neighbor, citizen living in an urban zone; term deriving from medieval Spain, where to be a *vecino* of a town meant being a citizen of that town
vida orgánica	organizational life
vitalicismo	"life-long-ism"; the tendency to be a leader of a civic organization or trade union for a long time
yatiri	ritual specialist; Aymara word meaning "someone who knows"

Abercrombie, Thomas A. 1991. To Be Indian, to Be Bolivian: "Ethnic" and "National" Discourses of Identity. In *Nation-States and Indians in Latin America*, edited by G. Urban and J. Sherzer. Austin: University of Texas Press.

———. 1998. *Pathways of Memory and Power: Ethnography and History among an Andean People*. Madison: University of Wisconsin Press.

Agadjanian, Victor. 2002. Competition and Cooperation among Working Women in the Context of Structural Adjustment: The Case of Street Vendors in La Paz–El Alto, Bolivia. *Journal of Development Studies* 18 (2–3): 259–285.

Albó, Xavier. 1977. *La Paradoja Aymara: Solidaridad y Faccionalismo*. Vol. 8. La Paz: CIPCA.

———. 1991. El retorno del indio. *Revista Andina* 2: 209–345.

———. 2002. *Pueblos indios en la politica*. La Paz: CIPCA.

Albó, Xavier, and Equipo CIPCA. 1999. *Ojotas en el Poder Local*. Vol. 53. *Cuadernos de Investigaciòn CIPCA*. La Paz: CIPCA y PADER.

Albó, Xavier, Tomas Greaves, and Godofredo Sandoval. 1981. *Chukiyawu: La Cara Aymara de La Paz*. Vol. 1. El Paso a la Cuidad. La Paz: CIPCA.

———. 1982. *Chukiyawu: La Cara Aymara de La Paz*. Vol. 2. Una Odisea: Buscar "Pega." La Paz: CIPCA.

———. 1983. *Chukiyawu: La Cara Aymara de La Paz*. Vol. 3. Cabalgando Entre Dos Mundos. La Paz: CIPCA.

———. 1987. *Chukiyawu: La Cara Aymara de La Paz*. Vol. 4. Nuevos Lazos con el Campo. La Paz: CIPCA.

Albó, Xavier, and Matias Preiswerk. 1986. *Los Senores del Gran Poder*. La Paz: Centro de Teologia Popular.

Albro, Robert. 2000. The Populist Chola: Cultural Mediation and the Political

Imagination in Quilllacollo, Bolivia. *Journal of Latin American Anthropology* 5 (2): 30–88.

——. 2003. The Indigenous and the Plural in Bolivian Oppositional Politics. *Bulletin of Latin American Research* 24 (4): 433–453.

——. 2005. "The Water is Ours, Carajo!" Deep Citizenship in Bolivia's Water War. In *Social Movements: An Anthropological Reader*, edited by J. Nash. Oxford: Blackwell.

Allen, Catherine J. 1988. *The Hold Life Has: Coca and Cultural Identity in an Andean Community*. Washington: Smithsonian Institution Press.

Altamirano, Teofilo. 1984a. *Presencia Andina en Lima Metropolitana: Estudio Sobre Migrantes y Clubes de Provincias*. Lima: Pontifica Universidad Catolica del Peru.

——. 1984b. Regional Commitment among Central Highlands Migrants in Lima. In *Miners, Peasants and Entrepreneurs: Regional Development in the Central Highlands of Peru*, edited by N. Long and B. Roberts. Cambridge: Cambridge University Press.

Amit, Vered, ed. 2002. *Realizing Community: Concepts, Social Relationships and Sentiments*. European Association of Social Anthropologists series, edited by J. P. Mitchell and S. Pink. London: Routledge.

Anderson, Benedict. 1991. *Imagined Communities: Reflections on the Origin and Spread of Nationalism*. London: Verso.

Annis, Sheldon. 1994. Introduction. In *Coming of Age: Protestantism in Contemporary Latin America*, edited by D. R. Miller. Lanham, Md.: University Press of America.

Antezana, Mauricio. 1993. *El Alto desde El Alto II: Ciudad en emergencia*. La Paz: Unitas.

Anze O., Rosario. 1995. *Construyendo una Identidad en Zonas de El Alto Sur*. La Paz: CEBIAE.

Arbona, Juan Manuel. n.d. Managing Policy Failures: Neo-Liberal Tensions, Ruptures, and Stabilizations in El Alto, Bolivia. Unpublished manuscript.

Archondo, Rafael. 1991. *Compadres al Microfono: La Resurreccion Metropolitana del Ayllu*. La Paz: HISBOL.

Arendt, Hannah. 1998 [1958]. *The Human Condition*. 2nd ed. Chicago: University of Chicago Press.

Aretxaga, Begoña. 2003. Maddening States. *Annual Review of Anthropology* 32: 393–410.

Aristotle. 1992. *The Politics*. London: Penguin.

Asociacion de Conjuntos Folkloricos del Gran Poder. 1999. *Tradicion pacena: Festividad del Gran Poder*. La Paz: Asociacion de Conjuntos Folkloricos del Gran Poder.

Assies, Willem, Gemma van der Haar, and Andre Hoekema, eds. 2000. *The*

Challenge of Diversity: Indigenous Peoples and Reform of the State in Latin America.
Amsterdam: Thela Thesis.

Auyero, Javier. 2000. The Logic of Clientelism in Argentina: An Ethnographic Account. *Latin American Research Review* 35 (3): 55–81.

———. 2001. *Poor People's Politics: Peronist Survival Networks and the Legacy of Evita.* Durham: Duke University Press.

Avineri, S., and A. de-Shalit, eds. 1992. *Communitarianism and Individualism.* Oxford: Oxford University Press.

Babb, Florence. 1988. "From the Field to the Cooking Pot": Economic Crisis and the Threat to Marketers in Peru. In *Traders versus the State: Anthropological Approaches to Unofficial Economies,* edited by G. Clark. Boulder, Colo.: Westview Press.

Banck, Geert. 1998. Personalism in the Brazilian Body Politic: Political Rallies and Public Ceremonies in the Era of Mass Democracy. *European Review of Latin American and Caribbean Studies* 65: 25–43.

Barron, Anne. 1993. The Illusions of the "I": Citizenship and the Politics of Identity. In *Closure or Critique: New Directions in Legal Theory,* edited by A. Norrie. Edinburgh: Edinburgh University Press.

Barth, Fredrik. 1977. Political Leadership among Swat Pathans. In *Friends, Followers and Factions: A Reader in Political Clientelism,* edited by S. W. Schmidt, J. C. Scott, C. Lande, and L. Guasti. Berkeley: University of California Press.

Basile, Elisabetta, and Barbara Harris-White. 2000. Corporative Capitalism: Civil Society and the Politics of Accumulation in Small Town India. Working Paper No. 38, Queen Elizabeth House, Oxford.

Bastian, Jean-Pierre. 1992. Les protestantismes latino-americains: Un objet a interroger et a construire. *Social Compass* 39 (3): 327–354.

Bayart, Jean-Francois. 1993. *The State in Africa: The Politics of the Belly.* London: Longman.

Berger, Marguerite. 1989. An Introduction. In *Women's Ventures: Assistance to the Informal Sector in Latin America,* edited by M. Berger and M. Buvinic. West Hartford, Conn.: Kumarian Press.

Bigenho, Michelle. 2001. *Sounding Indigenous, Feeling Bolivian: Authenticity in Music Performance.* Houndmills, England: Palgrave.

Blanco Cazas, Carlos, and Godofredo Sandoval. 1993. *La Alcaldia de La Paz: Entre populistas, modernistas y culturalistas 1985–1993.* La Paz: ILDIS-IDIS.

Blanes Jimenez, Jose. 1989. Cocaine, Informality, and the Urban Economy in La Paz, Bolivia. In *The Informal Economy: Studies in Advanced and Less Developed Countries,* edited by A. Portes, M. Castells, and L. A. Benton. Baltimore: Johns Hopkins University Press.

Boissevain, Jeremy. 1992. *Revitalizing European Rituals*. London: Routledge.

Bolton, Ralph, and Enrique Mayer, eds. 1977. *Andean Kinship and Marriage*. Washington: American Anthropological Association.

Booth, David, Suzanne M. Clisby, and Charlotta Widmark. 1997. *Popular Participation: Democratising the State in Rural Bolivia. Report to Sida*. Unpublished manuscript.

Bourguignon, Erika. 1994. Trance and Meditation. In *Handbook of Psychological Anthropology*, edited by P. K. Bock. Westwood, Conn.: Greenwood Press.

Bouysse-Cassagne, Therese, and Olivia Harris. 1987. Pacha: En Torno al Pensamiento Aymara. In *Tres Reflexiones sobre el Pensamiento Andino*, edited by T. Bouysse-Cassagne, O. Harris, T. Platt, and V. Cereceda. La Paz: HISBOL.

Brusco, Elizabeth. 1993. The Reformation of Machismo: Asceticism and Masculinity among Colombian Evangelicals. In *Rethinking Protestantism in Latin America*, edited by V. Garrard-Burnett and D. Stoll. Philadelphia: Temple University Press.

Brysk, Alison. 2000. *From Tribal Village to Global Village: Indian Rights and International Relations in Latin America*. Stanford: Stanford University Press.

Buechler, Hans. 1980. *The Masked Media: Aymara Fiestas and Social Interaction in the Bolivian Highlands*. The Hague: Mouton.

Buechler, Hans, and Judith-Maria Buechler. 1996. *The World of Sofia Velasquez: The Autobiography of a Bolivian Market Vendor*. New York: Columbia University Press.

Butler, Judith. 1990. *Gender Trouble: Feminism and the Subversion of Identity*. London: Routledge.

———. 1993. *Bodies That Matter: On the Discursive Limits of "Sex."* London: Routledge.

Caldeira, Teresa. 2000. *City of Walls: Crime, Segregation and Citizenship in Sao Paulo*. Berkeley: University of California Press.

Calderon, Fernando, and Alicia Szmukler. 2000. *La Politica en las Calles: Politica, urbanizacion y desarrollo*. La Paz: CERES, Plural, UASB.

Canessa, Andrew. 1998. Procreation, Personhood and Ethnic Difference in Highland Bolivia. *Ethnos* 63 (2): 227–247.

———. 2000. Contesting Hybridity: Evangelistas and Kataristas in Highland Bolivia. *Journal of Latin American Studies* 32: 115–144.

———. 2006. Todos somos indígenas: Towards a New Language of National Political Identity. *Bulletin of Latin American Research* 25 (2): 241–263.

Carmagnani, Marcello, and Alicia Hernandez Chavez. 1999. La ciudadania organica Mexicana, 1850–1910. In *Ciudadania political y formacion de las naciones: Perspectivas historicas de America Latina*, edited by H. Sabato. Mexico, D.F.: El Colegio de Mexico, Fondo de Cultural Economica.

Carrithers, M. 1985. An Alternative Social History of the Self. In *The Category of the*

Person: Anthropology, Philosophy, History, edited by M. Carrithers, S. Collins, and S. Lukes. Cambridge: Cambridge University Press.

Carter, William E., and Mauricio Mamani P. 1989 [1982]. *Irpa Chico: Individuo y Comunidad en la Cultural Aymara*. 2nd ed. La Paz: Libreria Editorial "Juventud."

Castells, Manuel. 1989. *The Informational City: Information Technology, Economic Restructuring and the Urban-Regional Process*. Oxford: Blackwell.

———. 2004. Politics and Power in the Network Society. Milliband Lecture on Culture in the Age of Global Communications, London School of Economics, 18 March.

Castoriadis, Cornelius. 1992. *Philosophy, Politics, Autonomy*. Translated by D. Curtis. New York: Oxford University Press.

Chodorow, Nancy. 1978. *The Reproduction of Mothering: Psychoanalysis and the Sociology of Gender*. Berkeley: University of California Press.

Choque, Maria Eugenia, and Carlos Mamani Condori. 2003. Reconstitucion del Ayllu y Derechos de los Pueblos Indigenas: El Movimiento Indio en los Andes de Bolivia. In *Los Andes desde Los Andes*, edited by E. Ticona A. La Paz: Ediciones Yachaywasi.

Clark, Gracia, ed. 1988. *Traders versus the State: Anthropological Approaches to Unofficial Economies*. Westview Special Studies in Applied Anthropology. Boulder, Colo.: Westview Press.

Cohen, Anthony. 1985. *The Symbolic Construction of Community*. London: Tavistock.

———. 1994. *Self Consciousness: An Alternative Anthropology of Identity*. London: Routledge.

Cohen Bull, Cynthia Jean. 1997. Sense, Meaning and Perception in Three Dance Cultures. In *Meaning in Motion: New Cultural Studies of Dance*, edited by J. Desmond. Durham: Duke University Press.

Colloredo-Mansfeld, Rudi. 2002. An Ethnography of Neoliberalism: Understanding Competition in Artisan Economies. *Current Anthropology* 43 (1): 113–137.

Conniff, Michael, ed. 1999. *Populism in Latin America*. Tuscaloosa: University of Alabama Press.

Cottle, Patricia, and Carmen Beatriz Ruiz. 1993. La Violenta Vida Cotidiana. In *Violencias Encubiertas en Bolivia*, edited by Centro de Documentación and Información Bolivia. La Paz: CIPCA-ARUWIYIRI.

Cowan, Jane K. 1990. *Dance and the Body Politic in Northern Greece*. Princeton Modern Greek Series. Princeton: Princeton University Press.

Crabtree, John. 1998. Neo-Populism and the Fujimori Phenomenon. In *Fujimori's Peru: The Political Economy*, edited by J. Crabtree and J. Thomas. London: Institute of Latin American Studies.

——. 2005. *Patterns of Protest: Politics and Social Movements in Bolivia.* London: Latin American Bureau.

Crandon, Libbet. 1985. Medical Dialogue and the Political Economy of Medical Pluralism: A Case from Rural Highland Bolivia. *American Ethnologist* 13 (3): 463–476.

Criales Burgos, Lucila. 1994. *Mujer y Conflictos Socio-Culturales: El Caso de las Migrantes de Caquiaviri en la Ciudad de La Paz.* La Paz: THOA.

Cross, John. 1998. *Informal Politics: Street Vendors and the State in Mexico City.* Stanford: Stanford University Press.

Cruikshank, Barbara. 1999. *The Will to Empower: Democratic Citizens and Other Subjects.* Ithaca, N.Y.: Cornell University Press.

Csordas, Thomas J., ed. 1994. *Embodiment and Experience: The Existential Ground of Culture and Self.* Cambridge Studies in Medical Anthropology. Cambridge: Cambridge University Press.

——. 1999. The Body's Career in Anthropology. In *Anthropological Theory Today,* edited by H. Moore. Cambridge: Polity Press.

Dagger, Richard. 2005. Response to Conference Papers. Paper read at Urban versus National Citizenship, University of Aberdeen.

Dagnino, Evelina. 1998. Culture, Citizenship and Democracy: Changing Discourses and Practices of the Latin American Left. In *Cultures of Politics, Politics of Cultures: Re-visioning Latin American Social Movements,* edited by S. E. Alvarez, E. Dagnino, and A. Escobar. Boulder, Colo.: Westview Press.

——, ed. 2003. Citizenship in Latin America. Special issue of *Latin American Perspectives* 30 (2).

Dalton, G. 1971. Theoretical Issues in Economic Anthropology. In *Economic Anthropology and Development: Essays on Tribal and Peasant Economies,* edited by G. Dalton. New York: Basic Books.

de Certeau, Michel. 1984. *The Practice of Everyday Life.* Berkeley: University of California Press.

Degregori, Carlos Ivan. 1991. How Difficult It Is to Be God: Ideology and Political Violence in Sendero Luminoso. *Critique of Anthropology* 11 (3): 233–250.

de la Cadena, Marisol. 1996. Women Are More Indian: Ethnicity and Gender in a Community near Cuzco. In *Ethnicity, Markets and Migration in the Andes,* edited by B. Larson and O. Harris. Durham: Duke University Press.

——. 2002. The Racial-Moral Politics of Place: Mestizas and Intellectuals in Turn-of-the-Century Peru. In *Gender's Place: Feminist Anthropologies of Latin America,* edited by J. Hurtig, R. Montoya, and L. J. Frazier. New York: Palgrave Macmillan.

de Soto, Hernando. 1989. *The Other Path: The Invisible Revolution in the Third World.* London: I. B. Tauris.

———. 2000. *The Mystery of Capital: Why Capitalism Triumphs in the West and Fails Everywhere Else.* New York: Basic Books.

Diamond, L., J. Linz, and S. M. Lipset, eds. 1989. *Democracy in Developing Countries.* Vol. 4. *Latin America.* Boulder, Colo.: Adamantine.

Dietz, Mary. 1985. Citizenship with a Feminist Face: The Problem of Maternal Thinking. *Political Theory* 13 (1): 19–37.

Dix, Robert H. 1985. Populism: Authoritarian and Democratic. *Latin American Research Review* 20 (2): 29–52.

Domingo, Pilar. 2001. Party Politics, Intermediation and Representation. In *Towards Democratic Viability: The Bolivian Experience,* edited by J. Crabtree and L. Whitehead. Houndmills, England: Palgrave.

Douglas, Mary, ed. 1987. *Constructive Drinking.* Cambridge: Cambridge University Press.

Dumont, Louis. 1986. *Essays on Individualism: Modern Ideology in Anthropological Perspective.* Chicago: University of Chicago Press.

Dunkerley, James. 1984. *Rebellion in the Veins.* London: Verso.

———. 1998. *The 1997 Bolivian Election in Historical Perspective.* University of London Institute of Latin American Studies Occasional Papers No. 16. London: Institute of Latin American Studies.

Durkheim, Emile. 1965 [1915]. *The Elementary Forms of the Religious Life.* Translated by J. W. Swain. London: Free Press. Originally titled *Les formes elementaires de la vie religieuse, le systeme totemique en Australie.*

Edwards, Michael, and David Hulme. 1995. *Non-Governmental Organisations: Performance and Accountability. Beyond the Magic Bullet.* London: Save the Children, Earthscan.

Escobar, Arturo, and Sonia E. Alvarez, eds. 1992. *The Making of Social Movements in Latin America: Identity, Strategy, and Democracy.* Boulder, Colo.: Westview Press.

Escobar, Silvia. 1989. Small-Scale Commerce in the City of La Paz, Bolivia. In *Women's Ventures: Assistance to the Informal Sector in Latin America,* edited by M. Berger and M. Buvinic. West Hartford, Conn.: Kumarian Press.

Etzioni, Amitai. 1993. *The Spirit of Community: Rights, Responsibilities and the Communitarian Agenda.* New York: Crown.

Fernandez Juarez, Gerardo. 1995. *El Banquete Aymara: Mesas y yatiris.* Biblioteca andina series, edited by J. Medina and D. Tuchschneider. La Paz: HISBOL.

Fernández Osco, Marcelo. 2000. *La Ley del ayllu: Practica de jach'a justicia y jisk'a husticia (justicia mayour y justicia menor) en comunidades aymaras.* La Paz: Fundacion PIEB.

Fotopoulos, Takis. 1997. *Towards an Inclusive Democracy: The Crisis of the Growth Economy and the Need for a New Liberatory Project.* London: Cassell.

Foucault, Michel. 1990 [1984]. *The Care of the Self. The History of Sexuality: Volume 3*. London: Penguin.

Foweraker, Joe. 1990. Popular Movements and Political Change in Mexico. In *Popular Movements and Political Change in Mexico*, edited by J. Foweraker and A. Craig. London: Lynne Reinner.

Frazer, Elizabeth. 1998. Communitarianism. In *New Political Thought: An Introduction*, edited by A. Lent. London: Lawrence and Wishart.

Frazer, E., and Nicola Lacey. 1995. Politics and the Public in Rawls' Political Liberalism. *Political Studies* 43: 233–247.

Gamarra, Eduardo. 2003. Political Parties Since 1964: The Construction of Bolivia's Multiparty System. In *Proclaiming Revolution: Bolivia in Comparative Perspective*, edited by M. Grindle and P. Domingo. London: Institute of Latin American Studies and David Rockefeller Center for Latin American Studies, Harvard University.

Gamarra, Eduardo, and James Malloy. 1995. The Patrimonial Dynamics of Party Politics in Bolivia. In *Building Democratic Institutions: Party Systems in Latin America*, edited by S. Mainwaring and T. Scully. Stanford: Stanford University Press.

Garcia Linera, Alvaro. 2001. Sindicato, multitud y comunidad: Movimientos sociales y formas de autonomia politica en Bolivia. In *Tiempos de rebelion*, edited by A. Garcia Linera, R. Gutierrez, R. Prada Alcoreza, F. Quispe, and L. Tapia Mealla. La Paz: Muela del Diablo editores.

Garcia Linera, Alvaro, Raquel Gutierrez, Raul Prada, Felipe Quispe, and Luis Tapia, eds. 2001. *Tiempos de rebelion*. La Paz: Muela del Diablo editores.

Garcia Linera, Alvaro, Raquel Gutierrez, Raul Prada, and Luis Tapia. 2000. *El retorno de la Bolivia plebeya*. La Paz: Muela del Diablo editores.

Garrard-Burnett, Virginia, and David Stoll, eds. 1993. *Rethinking Protestantism in Latin America*. Philadelphia: Temple University Press.

Gay, Robert. 1998. Rethinking Clientelism: Demands, Discourses and Practices in Contemporary Brazil. *European Review of Latin American and Caribbean Studies* 65: 7–24.

Gefou-Madianou, Dimitra, ed. 1992. *Alcohol, Gender and Culture*. London: Routledge.

Gill, Lesley. 1990. "Like a Veil to Cover Them": Women and the Pentecostal Movement in La Paz. *American Ethnologist* 17 (4): 708–721.

———. 1993. Religious Mobility and the Many Words of God in La Paz, Bolivia. In *Rethinking Protestantism in Latin America*, edited by V. Garrard-Burnett and D. Stoll. Philadelphia: Temple University Press.

———. 1994. *Precarious Dependencies: Gender, Class, and Domestic Service in Bolivia*. New York: Columbia University Press.

——. 1997a. Power Lines: Nongovernmental Organizations (NGOs), the State and Popular Organizations in an Urban Bolivian Slum. *Journal of Latin American Anthropology* 2 (2): 144–169.

——. 1997b. Relocating Class: Ex-Miners and Neoliberalism in Bolivia. *Critique of Anthropology* 17 (3): 293–312.

——. 1998. Neoliberalism and Public Education: The Relevance of the Bolivian Teacher's Strike of 1995. In *The Third Wave of Modernization in Latin America: Cultural Perspectives on Neoliberalism,* edited by L. Phillips. Wilmington, Del.: Scholarly Resources.

——. 2000. *Teetering on the Rim: Global Restructuring, Daily Life, and the Armed Retreat of the Bolivian State.* New York: Columbia University Press.

Gilligan, Carol. 1982. *In A Different Voice: Psychological Theory and Women's Development.* London: Harvard University Press.

Gledhill, John. 1994. *Power and Its Disguises: Anthropological Perspectives on Politics.* London: Pluto Press.

Goldstein, Daniel. 2004. *The Spectacular City: Violence and Performance in Urban Bolivia.* Durham: Duke University Press.

——. 2005. Flexible Justice: Neoliberal Violence and "Self-Help" Security in Bolivia. *Critique of Anthropology* 25 (4): 389–411.

Goodman, Felicitas D. 1972. *Speaking in Tongues: A Cross-Cultural Study of Glossolalia.* Chicago: University of Chicago Press.

——. 1988. *How about Demons? Possession and Exorcism in the Modern World.* Bloomington: Indiana University Press.

Goudsmit, Into. 2006. Praying for Government: Peasant Disengagement with the Bolivian State. *Bulletin of Latin American Research* 25 (2): 200–219.

Gow, David, and Joanne Rappaport. 2002. The Indigenous Public Voice: The Multiple Idioms of Modernity in Native Cauca. In *Indigenous Movements, Self-Representation, and the State in Latin America,* edited by K. Warren and J. Jackson. Austin: University of Texas Press.

Granovetter, Mark. 1992 [1985]. Economic Action and Social Structure: The Problem of Embeddedness. In *The Sociology of Economic Life,* edited by M. Granovetter and R. Swedberg. Boulder, Colo.: Westview Press.

Gray Molina, George. 2001. Exclusion, Participation and Democratic State-Building. In *Towards Democratic Viability: The Bolivian Experience,* edited by J. Crabtree and L. Whitehead. Houndmills, England: Palgrave.

——. 2003. The Offspring of 1952: Poverty, Exclusion and the Promise of Popular Participation. In *Proclaiming Revolution: Bolivia in Comparative Perspective,* edited by M. Grindle and P. Domingo. London: Institute of Latin American Studies.

Green, Linda. 1993. Shifting Affiliations: Mayan Widows and *Evangelicos* in

Guatemala. In *Rethinking Protestantism in Latin America*, edited by V. Garrard-Burnett and D. Stoll. Philadelphia: Temple University Press.

Greenway, Roger S. 1973. *An Urban Strategy for Latin America*. Grand Rapids, Mich.: Baker Book House.

Guaygua, German, Angela Riveros, and Maximo Quisbert. 2000. *Ser joven en El Alto*. La Paz: PIEB.

Guerra, Francois-Xavier. 1999. El soberano y su reino: Reflexiones sober la genesis del ciudadano en America Latina. In *Ciudadania political y formacion de las naciones: Perspectivas historicas de America Latina*, edited by H. Sabato. Mexico, D.F.: El Colegio de Mexico, Fondo de Cultural Economica.

Gupta, Akhil. 1995. Blurred Boundaries: The Discourse of Corruption, the Culture of Politics, and the Imagined State. *American Ethnologist* 22 (2): 375–402.

Gutierrez, Raquel, Alvaro Garcia, Raul Prada, and Luis Tapia. 2002. *Democratizaciones Plebeyas*. La Paz: Muela del Diablo editores.

Gutierrez, Raquel, Alvaro Garcia Linera, and Luis Tapia Mealla. 2000. La forma multitud de la politica de las necesidades vitales. In *El retorno de la Bolivia plebeya*, edited by A. Garcia Linera, R. Gutierrez, R. Prada Alcoreza, and L. Tapia Mealla. La Paz: Muela del Diablo editores.

Gutmann, Amy. 1992. Communitarian Critiques of Liberalism. In *Communitarianism and Individualism*, edited by S. Avineri and A. de-Shalit. Oxford: Oxford University Press.

Haller, Dieter, and Cris Shore, eds. 2005. *Corruption: Anthropological Perspectives*. London: Pluto Press.

Hanna, Judith Lynne. 1979. *To Dance Is Human: A Theory of Nonverbal Communication*. Austin: University of Texas Press.

Hannerz, Ulf. 1990. Cosmopolitans and Locals in World Culture. In *Global Culture: Nationalism, Globalization and Modernity*, edited by M. Featherstone. London: Sage.

Harding, Sandra. 1986. *The Science Question in Feminism*. Ithaca, N.Y.: Cornell University Press.

Hardt, Michael, and Antonio Negri. 2000. *Empire*. Cambridge, Mass.: Harvard University Press.

———. 2005. *Multitude*. London: Hamish Hamilton.

Harris, Olivia. 1982. Labour and Produce in an Ethnic Economy, Northern Potosí. In *Ecology and Exchange in the Andes*, edited by D. Lehmann. Cambridge: Cambridge University Press.

———. 1995. Ethnic Identity and Market Relations: Indians and Mestizos in the Andes. In *Ethnicity, Markets, and Migration in the Andes: At the Crossroads of History* and Anthropology, edited by O. Harris, B. Larson, and E. Tandeter. Durham: Duke University Press.

———. 2000a [1978]. Complementarity and Conflict: An Andean View of Women and Men. In To Make the Earth Bear Fruit: Ethnographic Essays on Fertility, Work and Gender in Highland Bolivia, edited by O. Harris. London: Institute of Latin American Studies.

———. 2000b. The Mythological Figure of the Earth Mother. In To Make the Earth Bear Fruit: Ethnographic Essays on Fertility, Work and Gender in Highland Bolivia, edited by O. Harris. London: Institute of Latin American Studies.

———. 2000c. To Make the Earth Bear Fruit: Ethnographic Essays on Fertility, Work and Gender in Highland Bolivia. London: Institute of Latin American Studies.

———. 2006. The Eternal Return of Conversion: Christianity as Contested Domain in Highland Bolivia. In The Anthropology of Christianity, edited by F. Cannell. Durham: Duke University Press.

Harris, Olivia, and Tristan Platt. 2006. Qharaqhara-Charka: Mallku, Inka y Rey en la provincia de Charcas (siglos XV–XVII). Historia antropológica de una confederación aymara. La Paz: Plural.

Hart, Keith. 1973. Informal Income Opportunities and Urban Employment in Ghana. Journal of Modern African Studies 11 (1): 61–89.

———. 2001. Money in an Unequal World. New York: Texere.

Harvey, Penelope. 1994a. Domestic Violence in the Peruvian Andes. In Sex and Violence: Issues in Representation and Experience, edited by P. Harvey and P. Gow. London: Routledge.

———. 1994b. Gender, Community and Confrontation: Power Relations in Drunkenness in Ocongate (Southern Peru). In Gender, Drink and Drugs, edited by M. McDonald. Oxford: Berg.

———. 1996. Bulimia and Force Feeding: Contrasting Techniques of Revealing the Self. Renaissance and Modern Studies 39: 78–94.

———. 1997. Peruvian Independence Day: Ritual, Memory and the Erasure of Narrative. In Creating Context in Andean Cultures, edited by R. Howard-Malverde. Oxford: Oxford University Press.

Heater, Derek. 1999. What Is Citizenship? Cambridge: Polity Press.

Heath, Dwight. 1987. A Decade of Development in the Anthropological Study of Alcohol Use, 1970–80. In Constructive Drinking, edited by M. Douglas. Cambridge: Cambridge University Press.

Hekman, Susan. 1997. Truth and Method: Feminist Standpoint Theory Revisited. Signs 22 (2): 341–374.

Herzfeld, Michael. 1992. The Social Production of Indifference: Exploring the Symbolic Roots of Western Bureaucracy. New York: Berg.

Herzog, Tamar. 2003. *Defining Nations: Immigrants and Citizens in Early Modern Spain and Spanish America*. New Haven: Yale University Press.

Holston, James, ed. 1999a. *Cities and Citizenship*. Durham: Duke University Press.

———. 1999b. Spaces of Insurgent Citizenship. In *Cities and Citizenship*, edited by J. Holston and A. Appadurai. Durham: Duke University Press.

Horton Fraleigh, Sondra. 1987. *Dance and the Lived Body: A Descriptive Aesthetics*. Pittsburgh: University of Pittsburgh Press.

Hurtado, Javier. 1986. *El Katarismo*. La Paz: HISBOL.

Hylton, Forrest, Felix Patzi, Sergio Serulnikov, and Sinclair Thomson. 2003. *Ya es otro tiempo el presente*. La Paz: Muela del Diablo editores.

Irurozqui, Marta. 2000. *"A Bala, Piedra y Palo": La Construccion de la Ciudadania Politica en Bolivia, 1826–1952*. Seville: Diputacion de Sevilla.

Isbell, Billie Jean. 1978. *To Defend Ourselves: Ecology and Ritual in an Andean Village*. Austin: University of Texas Press.

Isin, Engin, ed. 2000. *Democracy, Citizenship and the Global City*. London: Routledge.

———. Forthcoming. City.State: Critique of Scalar Thought. *Citizenship Studies*.

Kaeppler, Adrienne. 1978. Dance in Anthropological Perspective. *Annual Review of Anthropology* 7: 31–49.

———. 1995. Visible and Invisible in Hawaiian Dance. In *Human Action Signs in Cultural Context: The Visible and the Invisible in Movement and Dance*, edited by B. Farnell. Metuchen, N.J.: Scarecrow Press.

Kealinnohomoku, Joann W. 1979. Culture Change: Functional and Dysfunctional Expressions of Dance, a Form of Affective Culture. In *The Performing Arts: Music and Dance*, edited by J. Blacking and J. W. Kealinnohomoku. The Hague: Mouton.

Kertzer, David. 1988. *Ritual, Politics and Power*. New Haven: Yale University Press.

Kittay, Eva Feder. 1997. Human Dependency and Rawlsian Equality. In *Feminists Rethink the Self*, edited by D. Tietjens Meyers. Boulder, Colo.: Westview Press.

Klemola, Antero. 1997. The Reproduction of Community through Communal Practices in Kila Kila, Bolivia. PH.D. diss., Institute of Latin American Studies, University of Liverpool.

Koch, Julie. 2006. Collectivism or Isolation? Gender Relations in Urban La Paz, Bolivia. *Bulletin of Latin American Research* 25 (1): 43–62.

Kruse, Tom. 2004. *Endemic Poverty and State Violence: Social Watch Country Report: Bolivia 2004*. Accessed 12 August 2004. Available from http://www.socialwatch.org.

Kymlicka, Will. 1995. *Multicultural Citizenship: A Liberal Theory of Minority Rights*. Oxford Political Theory series, edited by D. Miller and A. Ryan. Oxford: Clarendon Press.

Lalive d'Epinay, Christian. 1969. *The Haven of the Masses*. London: Lutterworth Press.

Lande, Carl H. 1977. Group Politics and Dyadic Politics: Notes for a Theory. In *Friends, Followers and Factions: A Reader in Political Clientelism*, edited by S. W. Schmidt, J. C. Scott, C. Lande, and L. Guasti. Berkeley: University of California Press.

Lange, Roderyk. 1975. *The Nature of Dance: An Anthropological Perspective*. London: MacDonald and Evans.

Larson, Brooke. 2005. Redeemed Indians, Barbarized Cholos: Crafting Neocolonial Modernity in Liberal Bolivia, 1900–1910. In *Political Cultures in the Andes 1750–1950*, edited by N. Jacobsen and C. Aljovin de Losada. Durham: Duke University Press.

Larson, Brooke, and Olivia Harris, eds. 1995. *Ethnicity, Markets, and Migration in the Andes: At the Crossroads of History and Anthropology*. Durham: Duke University Press.

Lazar, Sian. 2002a. Cholo Citizens: Negotiating Personhood and Building Communities in El Alto, Bolivia. ph.d. diss., Department of Anthropology, Goldsmiths College, University of London.

———. 2002b. The "*Politics of the Everyday*": *Populism, Gender and the Media in La Paz and El Alto, Bolivia*. Goldsmiths Anthropology Research Papers, edited by J. Hutnyk, O. Harris, S. Lazar, and S. Day. London: Goldsmiths College.

———. 2004. Education for Credit: Development as Citizenship Project in Bolivia. *Critique of Anthropology* 24 (3): 301–319.

Lechín W., Juan Claudio. 2003. El sindicato, germen del Estado nacional. Paper read at Bolivian Studies Congress, La Paz, July.

Lehm, Zulema, and Silvia Rivera Cusicanqui. 1988. *Los Artesanos Libertarios y la etica del trabajo*. La Paz: THOA.

Lehmann, David. 1999. Introduction. *Bulletin of Latin American Research* 18 (2): 139–144.

Lepri, Isabella. 2003. "We Are Not the True People": Notions of Identity and Otherness among the Ese Ejja of Northern Bolivia. ph.d. diss., Department of Anthropology, London School of Economics.

Lessinger, Johanna. 2001. Inside, Outside, and Selling on the Road: Women's Market Trading in South India. In *Women Traders in Cross Cultural Perspective*, edited by L. J. Seligman. Stanford: Stanford University Press.

Lister, Ruth. 1997. *Citizenship: Feminist Perspectives*. London: Macmillan.

Little, Adrian. 2002. *The Politics of Community: Theory and Practice*. Edinburgh: Edinburgh University Press.

Llanos Layme, David. 1998. Diaspora Comunal y sistema Productivo Altoandino:

Una aproximacion al impacto de la migracion y Participacion Popular en la
organizacion social y productiva de la comunidad Chari (Prov. B. Saavedra), La
Paz. Master's thesis, Sociology Department, Universidad Mayor de San Andres,
La Paz.

Lomnitz, Claudio. 1995. Ritual, Rumor and Corruption in the Constitution of
Polity in Modern Mexico. *Journal of Latin American Anthropology* 1 (1): 20–47.

Long, Norman. 1984. Commerce and Kinship in the Peruvian Highlands. In
*Miners, Peasants and Entrepreneurs: Regional Development in the Central Highlands of
Peru*, edited by N. Long and B. Roberts. Cambridge: Cambridge University
Press.

Lora, Guillermo. 1977. *History of the Bolivian Labour Movement 1848–1971.*
Cambridge: Cambridge University Press.

MacCormack, Sabine. 1991. *Religion in the Andes: Vision and Imagination in Early
Colonial Peru.* Princeton: Princeton University Press.

Macfarlane, Alan. 1978. *The Origins of English Individualism: The Family, Property and
Social Transition.* Oxford: Blackwell.

MacIntyre, Alasdair. 1981. *After Virtue: A Study in Moral Theory.* London: Duckworth.

Macpherson, C. B. 1962. *The Political Theory of Possessive Individualism: Hobbes to
Locke.* Oxford: Clarendon Press.

Mainwaring, Scott, and Timothy Scully, eds. 1995. *Building Democratic Institutions:
Party Systems in Latin America.* Stanford: Stanford University Press.

Mainwaring, Scott, and M. Soberg Shugart, eds. 1999. *Presidentialism and Democracy
in Latin America.* Cambridge: Cambridge University Press.

Marshall, T. H. 1983 [1950]. Citizenship and Social Class. In *States and Societies*,
edited by D. Held. Oxford: Blackwell.

Martin, David. 1990. *Tongues of Fire: The Explosion of Protestantism in Latin America.*
Oxford: Blackwell.

Mauss, Marcel. 1979 [1938]. A Category of the Human Mind: The Notion of
Person, the Notion of "Self." In *Sociology and Psychology Essays.* Translated by
Ben Brewer. Edited by M. Mauss. London: Routledge.

——. 1999 [1950]. *The Gift: The Form and Reason for Exchange in Archaic Societies.*
Translated by W. D. Halls. London: Routledge. Originally titled *Essai sur le Don.*

Mayer, Enrique. 1991. Peru in Deep Trouble: Mario Vargas Llosa's "Inquest in the
Andes" Reexamined. *Cultural Anthropology* 6 (4): 466–504.

——, ed. 2002a. *The Articulated Peasant: Household Economies in the Andes.* Oxford:
Westview Press.

——. 2002b. The Rules of the Game in Andean Reciprocity. In *The Articulated
Peasant: Household Economies in the Andes*, edited by E. Mayer. Oxford: Westview
Press.

Mayorga, Fernando. 1991. *Max Fernandez: La Politica del Silencio*. La Paz: ILDIS-UMSS.

McDonald, Maryon, ed. 1994. *Gender, Drink and Drugs*. Oxford: Berg.

McEwen, William. 1975. *Changing Rural Society: A Study of Communities in Bolivia*. New York: Oxford University Press.

McNeish, John-Andrew. 2001. Pueblo Chico, Infierno Grande: Globalisation and the Politics of Participation in Highland Bolivia. ph.d. diss., Anthropology Department, Goldsmiths College, University of London.

Mendoza, Zoila S. 1998. Defining Folklore: Mestizo and Indigenous Identities on the Move. *Bulletin of Latin American Research* 17 (2): 165–183.

Michelutti, Lucia. n.d. The Vernacularisation of Democracy: Musclemen, Politicians and Local Politics in North India. Unpublished manuscript.

Miller, Daniel R., and Don Slater. 2000. *The Internet: An Ethnographic Approach*. Oxford: Berg.

Mintz, Sidney W., and Eric R. Wolf. 1977. An Analysis of Ritual Co-Parenthood (Compadrazgo). In *Friends, Followers and Factions: A Reader in Political Clientelism*, edited by S. W. Schmidt, J. C. Scott, C. Lande, and L. Guasti. Berkeley: University of California Press.

Molyneux, Maxine, and Sian Lazar. 2003. *Doing the Rights Thing: Rights-Based Development and Latin American NGOs*. London: Intermediate Technology.

Monasterios, Karin, and Luis Tapia Mealla. 2001. *De la Ciudadania Pasiva a la Ciudadania Activa*. La Paz: Centro de Promocion de la Mujer Gregoria Apaza.

Moore, Henrietta. 1994. *A Passion for Difference*. Cambridge: Polity Press.

Morris, Brian. 1994. *Anthropology of the Self: The Individual in Cultural Perspective*. London: Pluto Press.

Mouffe, Chantal, ed. 1992. *Dimensions of Radical Democracy: Pluralism, Citizenship, Community*. London: Verso.

———. 1993. *The Return of the Political*. London: Verso.

Muratorio, Blanca. 1980. Protestantism and Capitalism Revisited, in the Rural Highlands of Ecuador. *Journal of Peasant Studies* 8 (1): 37–60.

Musch, Mirjam, Ricardo Valdez, and Peter Gondrie. 1994. *Villa Rosas Pampa: Del Valle Kututu a El Alto*. La Paz: Proyecto de Fortalecimiento de la Atención Primaria en Salud Distrito III, El Alto.

Nader, Helen. 1990. *Liberty in Absolutist Spain: The Habsburg Sale of Towns, 1516–1700*. The Johns Hopkins University Studies in Historical and Political Science. 108th Series. Baltimore: Johns Hopkins University Press.

Nash, June. 1992. Interpreting Social Movements: Bolivian Resistance to Economic Conditions Imposed by the International Monetary Fund. *American Ethnologist* 19 (2): 275–293.

——. 1993 [1979]. *We Eat the Mines and the Mines Eat Us*. Centennial ed. New York: Columbia University Press.

Nelson, Nici, and Susan Wright. 1995. *Power and Participatory Development: Theory and Practice*. London: Intermediate Technology Publications.

Ness, Sally Ann. 1992. *Body, Movement and Culture: Kinesthetic and Visual Symbolism in a Philippine Community*. Series in Contemporary Ethnography, edited by D. Rose and P. Stollen. Philadelphia: University of Pennsylvania Press.

Nugent, David. Forthcoming. Democracy Otherwise: Struggles over Popular Rule in the Northern Peruvian Andes. In *The Anthropology of Democracy*, edited by J. Paley. Santa Fe: School of American Research Press.

Obermaier, Rev P. Sebastian M., Roberto Perez Garriga, and Carlos Donoso Paz. 1999. *Documento borrador del Plan Regulador de la Ciudad de El Alto*. El Alto: Presidencia de la Republica, Comision Impulsora Para Combatir la Pobreza en la Ciudad de El Alto.

O'Donnell, Guillermo, ed. 1986. *Transitions from Authoritarian Rule: Comparative Perspectives*. Baltimore: Johns Hopkins University Press.

Okin, Susan Moller. 1991. John Rawls: Justice as Fairness—For Whom? In *Feminist Interpretations and Political Theory*, edited by M. L. Shanley and C. Pateman. Cambridge: Polity Press.

Oldfield, Adrian. 1990. *Citizenship and Community: Civic Republicanism and the Modern World*. London: Routledge.

Ong, Aihwa. 1999a. Clash of Civilizations or Asian Liberalism? An Anthropology of the State and Citizenship. In *Anthropological Theory Today*, edited by H. Moore. Cambridge: Polity Press.

——. 1999b. *Flexible Citizenship: The Cultural Logics of Transnationality*. Durham: Duke University Press

——. 2005. Ecologies of Expertise: Assembling Flows, Managing Citizenship. In *Global Assemblages: Technology, Politics and Ethics as Anthropological Problems*, edited by Aihwa Ong and Stephen J. Collier. Oxford: Blackwell.

Ouweneel, Arij. 2003. The "Collapse" of the Peruvian Ayllu. In *Imaging the Andes: Shifting Margins of a Marginal World*, edited by T. Salman and A. Zoomers. Amsterdam: Aksant.

Paaregard, Karsten. 1997. *Linking Separate Worlds: Urban Migrants and Rural Lives in Peru*. Oxford: Berg.

——. 2003. Andean Predicaments: Cultural Reinvention and Identity Creation. In *Imaging the Andes: Shifting Margins of a Marginal World*, edited by T. Salman and A. Zoomers. Amsterdam: Aksant.

Paredes-Candia, Antonio. 1984. *La Danza Folklorica de Bolivia*. 2nd ed. La Paz: Editorial Gisbert y CIA.

Paredes de Salazar, Elssa. 1976. *Presencia de Nuestro Pueblo*. La Paz: n.p.

Parry, Jonathan. 2000. The "Crises of Corruption" and "The Idea of India": A Worm's-Eye View. In *Morals of Legitimacy: Between Agency and System*, edited by I. Pardo. Oxford: Berghahn Books.

Pateman, Carole. 1988. *The Sexual Contract*. Stanford: Stanford University Press.

Patzi Paco, Felix. 1999. *Insurgencia y sumision: Movimientos indigeno-campesinos (1983–1998)*. La Paz: Muela del Diablo editores.

———. 2003. Rebelion indigena contra la colonialidad y la transnacionalizacion de la economia. In *Ya es otro tiempo el presente: Cuatro momentos de insurgencia indigena*, edited by F. Hylton, F. Patzi, S. Serulnikov, and S. Thomson. La Paz: Muela del Diablo editores.

Paulson, Susan. 2003a. New Recipes for Living Better with Pachamama. In *Imaging the Andes: Shifting Margins of a Marginal World*, edited by T. Salman and A. Zoomers. Amsterdam: Aksant.

———. 2003b. Placing Gender and Ethnicity on the Bodies of Indigenous Women and in the Work of Bolivian Intellectuals. In *Gender's Place: Feminist Anthropologies of Latin America*, edited by R. Montoya, L. J. Frazier, and J. Hurtig. Hounslow, England: Palgrave Macmillan.

Peattie, Lisa. 1987. An Idea in Good Currency and How It Grew: The Informal Sector. *World Development* 15 (7): 851–860.

Peredo Beltrán, Elizabeth. 1992. *Recoveras de los Andes: La identidad de la chola del mercado. Una aproximaciòn psicosocial*. La Paz: TAHIPAMU.

Perez de Castanos, Maria Ines. 1999. *Derechos Humanos y Ciudadanos en El Alto*. La Paz: Defensor del Pueblo.

Pericles. 1999. The Democratic Citizen. In *Political Thought*, edited by M. Rosen and J. Wolff. Oxford: Oxford University Press.

Perlman, Janice. 1976. *The Myth of Marginality: Urban Poverty and Politics in Rio de Janeiro*. Berkeley: University of California Press.

Peterson Royce, Anya. 1977. *The Anthropology of Dance*. Bloomington: Indiana University Press.

Phillips, Anne. 1993. *Democracy and Difference*. Cambridge: Polity Press.

Platt, Tristan. 1982. *Estado boliviano y ayllu andino: Tierra y tributo en el norte de Potosi*. Lima: Instituto de Estudios Peruanos.

———. 1984. Liberalism and Ethnocide in the Southern Andes. *History Workshop Journal* 17: 3–18.

———. 1997. The Sound of Light: Emergent Communication through Quechua Shamanic Dialogue. In *Creating Context in Andean Cultures*, edited by R. Howard-Malverde. New York: Oxford University Press.

Polanyi, Karl. 1957 [1944]. *The Great Transformation*. Boston: Beacon Press.

Postero, Nancy. 2006. *Now We Are Citizens: Indigenous Politics in Post-Multicultural Boliva*. Stanford: Stanford University Press.

Quisbert Quispe, Maximo. 2003. *Fejuve El Alto 1990–1998: Dilemas del clientelismo colectivo en un mercado politico en expansion*. La Paz: Aruwiyiri.

Quispe, Felipe. 2001. Organizacion y proyecto politico de la rebelion indigena aymara-quechua. In *Tiempos de rebelion*, edited by A. Garcia Linera, R. Gutierrez, R. Prada Alcoreza, F. Quispe, and L. Tapia Mealla. La Paz: Muela del Diablo editores.

Radcliffe Brown, A. 1922. *The Andaman Islanders: A Study in Social Anthropology*. Cambridge: Cambridge University Press.

Ram, Kalpana. 2000. Dancing the Past into Life: The Rasa, Nrtta and Raga of Immigrant Existence. *Australian Journal of Anthropology* 11 (3): 261–273.

Ramos, Alcida. 1998. *Indigenism: Ethnic Politics in Brazil*. Madison: University of Wisconsin Press.

Rappaport, Joanne. 1984. Las misiones Protestantes y la resistencia indigena en el sur de Colombia. *America Indigena* 44 (1): 37–60.

Rapport, Nigel. 1997. *Transcendent Individual: Towards a Literary and Liberal Anthropology*. London: Routledge.

Rasnake, Roger Neil. 1988. *Domination and Cultural Resistance: Authority and Power among an Andean People*. Durham: Duke University Press.

Rawls, John. 1972. *A Theory of Justice*. Oxford: Clarendon Press.

Rivera Cusicanqui, Silvia. 1990. Liberal Democracy and Ayllu Democracy in Bolivia: The Case of Northern Potosi. *Journal of Development Studies* 26 (4): 97–121.

———. 2002. *Bircholas: Trabajo de mujeres: Explotaciòn capitalista y opresiòn colonial entre las migrantes aymaras de La Paz y El Alto*. 2nd ed. La Paz: Mama Huaco.

———. 2003 [1984]. *Oprimidos pero no vencidos: Luchas del campesinado aymara y quechua*. 4th ed. La Paz: Aruwiyiri.

Rivera Cusicanqui, Silvia, Denise Arnold, Zulema Lehm, Susan Paulson, and Juan de Dios Yapita. 1996. *Ser mujer indigena, chola o birlocha en la Bolivia postcolonial de los anos 90*. La Paz: Subsecretaria de Asuntos de Genero, Secretaria Nacional de Asuntos etnicos, de Genero y Generacionales, Ministerio de Desarrollo Humano.

Rivera Cusicanqui, Silvia, and Equipo THOA. 1992. *Ayllus y Proyectos de desarrollo en el norte de Potosi*. La Paz: Aruwiyiri.

Roberts, Bryan R. 1995. *The Making of Citizens: Cities of Peasants Revisited*. London: Arnold.

Rocha, Alfonso. n.d. *Tradicion y Cultura, Ano I, No I, El Gran Poder*. La Paz. Unpublished manuscript.

Romero Ballivian, Salvador. 1996. La Cuestion de la Representatividad de los Partidos Politicos. *Claves: Dossier no. 8* (December): 10.

Roniger, Luis, and Ayse Gunes-Ayata, eds. 1994. *Democracy, Clientelism, and Civil Society.* Boulder, Colo.: Lynne Rienner.

Rosaldo, Michelle Z. 1984. Toward an Anthropology of Self and Feeling. In *Culture Theory: Essays on Mind, Self, and Emotion,* edited by R. A. Shweder and R. A. LeVine. New York: Columbia University Press.

Rose, Nikolas. 1999. *Powers of Freedom: Reframing Political Thought.* Cambridge: Cambridge University Press.

———. 2000. Governing Cities, Governing Citizens. In *Democracy, Citizenship and the Global City,* edited by E. Isin. London: Routledge.

Rosenau, P M. 1992. *Postmodernism and the Social Sciences.* Princeton: Princeton University Press.

Rouget, Gilbert. 1980. *La musique et la transe: Esquisse d'une theorie generale des relations de la musique et de la possession.* Paris: Editions Gallimar.

Ruiz, Carmen Beatriz. 1993. *Mujer, Género y Desarrollo Local Urbano.* La Paz: Centro de Promoción de la mujer Gregoria Apaza.

Saignes, Thierry, ed. 1993. *Borrachera y Memoria: La experiencia de lo sagrado en los Andes.* Biblioteca andina series, edited by J. Medina. La Paz: HISBOL/IFEA.

Salazar de la Torre, Cecilia. 1999. *Mujeres Alteñas: Espejismo y simulación en la modernidad.* La Paz: Centro de Promoción de la mujer Gregoria Apaza.

Sallnow, Michael J. 1987. *Pilgrims of the Andes: Regional Cults in Cusco.* Smithsonian Series in Ethnographic Inquiry, edited by I. Karp and W. L. Merrill. Washington: Smithsonian Institution Press.

Salman, Ton, and Annelies Zoomers, eds. 2003. *Imaging the Andes: Shifting Margins of a Marginal World.* Vol. 91. CEDLA. Amsterdam: Transaction Publishers.

Sanabria, Harry. 1999. Consolidating States, Restructuring Economies, and Confronting Workers and Peasants: The Antinomies of Bolivian Neoliberalism. *Comparative Studies in Society and History* 41 (3): 535–561.

Sandel, Michael. 1992. The Procedural Republic and the Unencumbered Self. In *Communitarianism and Individualism,* edited by S. Avineri and A. de-Shalit. Oxford: Oxford University Press.

Sandoval, Godofredo, and M. Fernanda Sostres. 1989. *La Cuidad Prometida: Pobladores y Organizaciones Sociales en El Alto.* La Paz: ILDIS-SYSTEMA.

Saravia, Joaquin, and Godofredo Sandoval. 1991. *Jach'a Uru: La Esperanza de Un Pueblo? Carlos Palenque, RTP y los Sectores Populares Urbanos en La Paz.* La Paz: ILDIS-CEP.

Sargant, William. 1973. *The Mind Possessed: A Physiology of Possession, Mysticism and Faith Healing.* London: Heinemann.

Sassen, Saskia. 2003. The Repositioning of Citizenship: Emergent Subjects and Spaces for Politics. *Berkeley Journal of Sociology* 46: 4–25.

Schmidt, Steffen W., James C. Scott, Carl Lande, and Laura Guasti, eds. 1977. *Friends, Followers and Factions: A Reader in Political Clientelism.* Berkeley: University of California Press.

Secretaría Nacional de Participacion Popular, ed. 1997. *El pulso de la democracia: Participacion ciudadana y descentralizacion en Bolivia.* La Paz: Editorial Nueva Sociedad.

Seligmann, Linda J. 1989. To Be in Between: The Cholas as Market Women. *Comparative Studies in Society and History* 31 (4): 694–721.

———. 1993. Between Worlds of Exchange: Ethnicity among Peruvian Market Women. *Cultural Anthropology* 8 (2): 187–213.

———, ed. 2001. *Women Traders in Cross-Cultural Perspective: Mediating Identities, Marketing Wares.* Stanford: Stanford University Press.

Sheets-Johnstone. 1979. *The Phenomenology of Dance.* 2nd ed. London: Dance Books.

Shweder, R. A., and E. J. Bourne. 1984. Does the Concept of the Person Vary Cross-Culturally? In *Culture Theory: Essays on Mind, Self, and Emotion,* edited by R. A. Shweder and R. A. LeVine. New York: Columbia University Press.

Sieder, Rachel. 2002a. Introduction. In *Multiculturalism in Latin America: Indigenous Rights, Diversity and Democracy,* edited by R. Sieder. Houndmills, England: Palgrave Macmillan.

———, ed. 2002b. *Multiculturalism in Latin America: Indigenous Rights, Diversity and Democracy.* Houndmills, England: Palgrave Macmillan.

Sikkink, Lynn. 2001. Traditional Medicines in the Marketplace: Identity and Ethnicity among Female Vendors. In *Women Traders in Cross-Cultural Perspective: Mediating Identities, Marketing Wares,* edited by L. J. Seligmann. Stanford: Stanford University Press.

Skar, Harald. 1982. *The Warm Valley People: Duality and Land Reform among the Quechua Indians of Highland Peru.* Oslo: Universitetsforlaget.

Sneath, David. 2002. Reciprocity, Corruption and the State in Contemporary Mongolia. Paper read at Understanding Corruption: Anthropological Perspectives, Goldsmiths College, London, 21 June.

Sostres, Fernanda. 1995. *Poder contra poder y sobrevivencia.* La Paz: Centro de Promoción de la mujer Gregoria Apaza.

Spencer, Paul. 1985. *Society and the Dance.* Cambridge: Cambridge University Press.

Starn, Orin. 1991. Missing the Revolution: Anthropologists and the War in Peru. *Cultural Anthropology* 6 (3): 63–91.

——. 1999. *Nightwatch: The Politics of Protest in the Andes.* Durham: Duke University Press.

Stobart, Henry. 2002a. Creative Cacophony: Music and the Politics of Production in the Bolivian Andes. Paper read at a seminar at Institute of Latin American Studies, London, 20 February.

——. 2002b. Interlocking Realms: Knowing Music and Musical Knowing. In *Knowledge and Learning in the Andes: Ethnographic Perspectives,* edited by H. Stobart and R. Howard-Malverde. Liverpool: University of Liverpool Press.

Stoll, David. 1990. *Is Latin America Turning Protestant? The Politics of Evangelical Growth.* Berkeley: University of California Press.

Strathern, Marilyn. 1988. *The Gender of the Gift: Problems with Women and Problems with Society in Melanesia.* Berkeley: University of California Press.

Ströbele-Gregor, Juliana. 1992. Las comunidades religiosas fundamentalistas en Bolivia: Sobre el exito misionero de los Adventistas del Septimo Dia. *Allpanchis* 40: 219–253.

——. 1996. Culture and Political Practice of the Aymara and Quechua in Bolivia: Autonomous Forms of Modernity in the Andes. *Latin American Perspectives* 23 (2): 72–90.

Swartz, Marc, ed. 1968. *Local-Level Politics: Social and Cultural Perspectives.* London: University of London Press.

Tamisari, Franca. 2000. The Meaning of the Steps Is in Between: Dancing and the Curse of Compliments. *Australian Journal of Anthropology* 11 (3): 274–286.

Tapia, Luis. 2002. Movimientos sociales, movimiento societal y los no lugares de la politica. In *Democratizaciones Plebeyas,* edited by R. Gutierrez, L. Tapia, R. Prada, and A. Garcia. La Paz: Muela del Diablo editores.

Terrazas, Magaly, and Inneke Dibbits. 1994. *Hagamos un Nuevo Trato: Mujeres de El Alto Sur hablan sobre su experiencia de dar a luz en centros hospitalarios.* La Paz: Grupo de Solidaridad de El Alto, TAHIPAMU.

Thomas, Helen, ed. 1993. *Dance, Gender and Culture.* London: Macmillan.

Thomson, Sinclair. 2002. *We Alone Will Rule: Native Andean Politics in the Age of Insurgency.* Madison: University of Wisconsin Press.

Thurner, Mark. 1997. *From Two Republics to One Divided: Contradictions of Postcolonial Nationmaking in Andean Peru.* Durham: Duke University Press.

Ticona Alejo, Esteban. 2003. El Thakhi entre los Aimara y los Quechua o la Democracia en los Gobiernos Comunales. In *Los Andes desde los Andes: Aymaranaka, Quichwanakana Yatxatawipa, Lup'iwipa,* edited by E. Ticona Alejo. La Paz: Ediciones Yachaywasi.

Tilly, Charles. 1978. *From Mobilization to Revolution.* London: Addison-Wesley.

———. 1993. Contentious Repertoires in Great Britain, 1758–1834. *Social Science History* 17 (2): 253–280.

Transparency International. 2004. *Report on the Transparency International Global Corruption Barometer 2004.* Berlin: Transparency International.

Triandis, Harry, and David Trafimow. 2001. Cross-National Prevalence of Collectivism. In *Individual Self, Relational Self, Collective Self*, edited by C. Sedikides and M. Brewer. Hove, England: Psychology Press.

Turino, Thomas. 1991. The State and Andean Musical Production in Peru. In *Nation-States and Indians in Latin America*, edited by G. Urban and J. Sherzer. Austin: University of Texas Press.

Turner, Bryan. 1993. *Citizenship and Social Theory.* London: Sage.

Turner, Victor. 1969. *The Ritual Process: Structure and Anti-structure.* London: Routledge.

Untoja, Fernando. 2000. *El retorno del ayllu.* La Paz: Fondo Editorial de los Diputados.

Urton, Gary. 1981. *At the Crossroads of the Earth and the Sky: An Andean Cosmology.* Austin: University of Texas Press.

———. 1992. Communalism and Differentiation in an Andean Community. In *Andean Cosmologies through Time: Persistence and Emergence*, edited by R. Dover, K. Seibold, and J. McDowell. Bloomington: Indiana University Press.

Van Cott, Donna Lee. 1994. *Indigenous Peoples and Democracy in Latin America.* New York. St. Martin's Press.

———. 2005. *From Movements to Parties in Latin America: The Evolution of Ethnic Politics.* Cambridge: Cambridge University Press.

Van Dam, Anke, and Ton Salman. 2003. Andean Transversality: Identity between Fixation and Flow. In *Imaging the Andes: Shifting Margins of a Marginal World*, edited by A. Zoomers and T. Salman. Amsterdam: Aksant.

Vassberg, David E. 1984. *Land and Society in Golden Age Castile.* Cambridge: Cambridge University Press.

Walzer, Michael. 1992. Membership. In *Communitarianism and Individualism*, edited by S. Avineri and A. de-Shalit. Oxford: Oxford University Press.

Wearne, Phillip. 1996. *Return of the Indian: Conquest and Revival in the Americas.* London: Latin American Bureau.

Weisbrot, Mark, and Luis Sandoval. 2006. *Bolivia's Challenges.* Washington: Center for Economic and Policy Research.

Weismantel, Mary. 2001. *Cholas and Pishtacos: Stories of Race and Sex in the Andes.* Women in Culture and Society series, edited by C. R. Stimpson. Chicago: University of Chicago Press.

Weyland, Kurt. 1999. Populism in the Age of Neoliberalism. In *Populism in Latin America*, edited by M. Conniff. Tuscaloosa: University of Alabama Press.

Whitehead, Laurence. 2001. Introduction. In *Towards Democratic Viability: The Bolivian Experience*, edited by J. Crabtree and L. Whitehead. Houndmills, England: Palgrave.

Williams, Drid. 1996. Introduction: Signs of Human Action. Special issue of *Visual Anthropology* 8 (2–4): 101–111.

Wolf, Eric R. 1977. Kinship, Friendship, and Patron-Client Relations in Complex Societies. In *Friends, Followers and Factions: A Reader in Political Clientelism*, edited by S. W. Schmidt, J. C. Scott, C. Lande, and L. Guasti. Berkeley: University of California Press.

Yashar, Deborah. 2005. *Contesting Citizenship in Latin America: The Rise of Indigenous Movements and the Postliberal Challenge*. Cambridge: Cambridge University Press.

Young, Iris Marion. 1990. The Ideal of Community and the Politics of Difference. In *Feminism/Postmodernism*, edited by L. Nicholson. London: Routledge.

Yuval-Davis, Nira. 1997. *Gender and Nation*. London: Sage.

ambulantes: in Ceja market, 38, 40; conflict mediation involving, 184–86

ampliado (trade union leaders meetings), 196; as assembly-based democracy, 241–47; mass action during, 245–46

"Andeanism," criticism of, 9

"Andeanization," migration flows and, 48

anthropological research: on alcohol consumption, 147–48, 276n.4; Andean collectivist politics and, 9; on community, 28–29; on dance rituals, 133–40; on ritual, 118, 129–30; subjectivity and self in, 12–15. *See also* ethnographic research; research methodology

anticolonialism: corruption analysis and, 109–11; indigenous political activism and, 9–10

apthapi ritual, 218–19

Arendt, Hannah, 5, 239, 244

Aristotle: citizenship concept of, 27; civic republicanism theory of, 5

Asamblea Constituyente, 256

Asamblea Popular, 256

assembly-based democracy (democracia asambleistica), 234–35, 241–47

assimilation, in Bolivia, 15–19

associations (asociaciónes) in El Alto, 53–55. *See also* under individual names

authoritarianism: in Evangelicalism, 161–63; political activism and, 261

Auyero, Javier, 58, 94–95, 114

aval político, 96, 201

awayus (carrying cloths), 37

Awircata, Don Eugenio, 217–25, 255

ayllu associations, 10–19, 49–50, 268n.8; as assembly-based democracy, 241; democracy models of, 235; trade unions and, 176–77, 248

Aymara indigenous culture: alliance of El Alto residents with, 25–26; ampliado meetings in language of, 244–47; campaign practices directed toward, 100–103; citizenship issues and, 6–8; consumption patterns of, 268n.15; El Alto residents' identity as, 2, 51–55; ethnicity and commerce and, 231–32; factionalism in, 174, 179, 252–53; female-male labor complementarity and, 182–83; fish-sellers dispute and, 210–12; individualism in, 179; Jach'a Uru (Great Day) concept in, 104, 273n.15; nationalist activities of, 249; political agency of, 23; religious aspects of dancing for, 146–47, 276n.2; rural identity of, 18–19; sacrificial rituals and, 154–55

"Aymara paradox," 179

ayni. *See* reciprocity (ayni)

Banzer, General Hugo, 47, 96, 98, 249, 276n.16

base support: in assembly-based democracy, 241–47; democracy models and, 235–47. *See also* grassroots organizations

Black February uprising, 20

Brazil, clientelism in, 114

breakaway associations, from trade unions, 236–37

Buechler, Hans, 28, 63, 122, 129, 131–35, 140, 149

bullfights, during fiestas, 120–21, 123, 274n.4

bureaucracy: clientelism and, 97–99, 114–17; corruption and, 109, 112–13; fish-sellers' associations and, 215–19, 222–27; juntas vecinales and, 73–75

Cameroon, political culture in, 112

campaign practices: clientelism and, 94–99; face-to-face politics and, 99–103; grass-roots preparation for, 103–4; promises of obras and, 112–13, 274n.22; voter turnout and, 114–17

Canessa, Andrew, 8, 28, 48, 63, 156, 167–68, 180

Caporales (dance), 139–40, 276n.15

Cardenas, Victor Hugo, 7

cargo system, democracy models and, 237–38

carpeta process, 73–75

Carter, William E., 10, 15, 28, 63, 79, 81, 148–51, 238

Castoriadis, Cornelius, 5–6, 27, 244–45

Catholic Church: Aymara culture and, 151–55; citizenship and, 144; dance rituals and, 145–47; fiesta rituals and, 144–55; hybrid identity of, 169, 278n.27; power relationships and, 170–71; revivalism in, 168–69; in Rosas Pampa, 156–58, 161–63, 278n.19; selfhood and, 59; tensions with Evangelicals in, 159–60, 168

Ceja district of El Alto, 34–42

Central Obrera Boliviana (COB), 52, 248–49, 252, 264–65

Central Obrera Regional (COR), 36, 53, 236, 250, 270n.13, 270n.15

Chaco War, 46–47

ch'alla (libation), 86, 88, 148–55, 271n.11, 277n.8

charango (mandolin), 93, 272n.2

china (Morenada dancer), 136–40

ch'iwiña (market stall), 37–38, 269n.3

cholo/a culture: citizenship and, 15–19; commerce and political agency in, 228–32; consumption patterns and, 268n.15; in El Alto, 32; Morenada costumes in, 134–35, 275n.12; political radicalism in, 268n.13; social movements and, 175; stereotypes of sexuality and, 17–19

citizenship: Bolivian political radicalism and, 3–4; in Cholo culture, 15–19; collectivity and, 8–19, 57–60, 88–90, 203–5, 259–65; convocatoria as tool of, 189–95; cultural context for, 23–24; dance as practice of, 140–43; definitions and theories of, 4–8; in El Alto, 26–29, 264–65; Evangelical form of, 158; fiesta rituals and role of, 131–40; history of, 27–28, 63, 270n.1; indigenous political activism and, 258–65; individualism vs. collectivity and, 8–19; national vs. local forms of, 27–29; nested affiliations and, 140–43; personalization of politics and, 106–8; political agency and, 175, 206–32; state and role of, 23, 70–72, 91–117; subjectivity and self identity in, 12–15; trade unions and, 173–79; vecindad and, 63–64; voting practices and, 94–108 civic mobilization, 104; citizenship and, 19–20; in El Alto, 50–55; by street traders, 187–89; tradition of, 5–8; vida organica and role of, 189–95

civil service: political patronage jobs in, 95–99, 272n.8; trade union leaders in, 201–3. *See also* bureaucracy

civil society: historical concepts of, 27–28; ritual and, 118, 120–22; vida orgánica and, 187–89

class stratification: citizenship rights and, 6; collectivity and, 173–77; corruption and role of, 110–11; ethnicity, commerce, and political agency and, 229–32; individualism and, 180; labor mobilization and, 187–88; vecinos and, 64–65

clientelism: in Brazil, 114; bureaucracy and, 114–17; campaign practices and, 95–99; government wages and, 113; impact of international agencies on, 97, 272n.8; populist politics and, 94, 272n.6; pragmatics of, 94–108; state-citizen relations and, 91–92

Clisa (rubbish-collecting company), 71, 270n.7

coca growers (cocaleors) movement, 2, 182

coca leaves: alcohol consumption vs. use of, 147–50; consumption during fiesta of, 126; market sale of, 40

Cochabamba: citizenship in, 187; political activism in, 3, 7–8, 27, 51, 253–57; Water War in, 2–3, 19, 51, 241

"collective self," anthropological research and role of, 13–15

collectivity: citizenship and, 8–19, 57–60, 88–90, 203–5, 259–65; civic organization in El Alto and, 53–55; competition and, 180–83; conflict mediation and, 184–86; convocatoria as tool of, 189–95; dance as medium for, 118–19; democracy models and, 233–47; economic organization and, 22; in El Alto, 33–34; fiesta rituals and, 122–29; individualism vs., 174–79, 261–65; leadership and, 58–60, 76; nonparticipation in fiestas and, 130–40; political agency and, 250–51; trade unionism and, 173–79; values and practices for creation of, 183–95

colonialism: influence on trade unionism of, 248–51; urban outlook of, 63–64

commerce: in Ceja market, 35–42; ethnicity and political agency and, 228–32; fish-sellers as intermediaries for, 226–27; political agency and, 22–23; women's role in, 182–83

communalism, trade unionism and, 204–5

community: assembly-based democracy in meetings of, 241–47; authorities in, 57–60; citizenship and, 4–8, 26–29, 259–65, 267n.4; civic organization in El Alto and role of, 52–55; control mechanisms in, 62; corruption of leaders in, 78–83; dance as agency for, 125–29; Evangelicalism and, 157–60; juntas organizations, 65–68; Latin American tradition of, 62–63; of migrant groups, 48–50; pre-Columbian authenticity issues and, 10–19; religious aspects of dancing and, 145–55; ritual and, 118–19; subjectivity and self and, 12–15; vecindad as, 63–64; Western cultural view of, 28–29

compadrazgo relationship, 105–6, 158, 269n.6, 275n.8

comparsas (dance groups): fiesta organization and, 131–40, 275n.9; for the Morenada, 136–40

competition, individualism and, 180–83

comuneros, 64

Condepa (Conciencia de Patria party), 101, 268n.13, 272n.8, 273n.10; campaign practices of, 104; clientelism of, 91–99, 113; corruption and, 109; decline of, 258; populist politics and, 249; street traders and, 233; tramite process and, 73–75

Confederación de Pueblos Indígenas de Bolivia (CIDOB), 7

Confederación Sindical Única de Trabajadores Compesinos de Bolivia (CSUTCB), 50, 269n.11; fish-sellers dispute and, 210–12, 221–27; Kataristas and, 249

conflict mediation, collectivity and, 184–86

consensus-building, at ampliados, 242–47

convocatoria: impact on leadership of, 237; vida organica and concept of, 189–95

Coordinator for Water and Life, 3, 7–8

Cori, Mauricio, 235

corporatism: Bolivian politics and, 247–57; electoral politics and, 21

corruption: accountability and, 109–11; assembly-based democracy vs., 241; of community authorities, 62; cultural specificity of, 112–13; in El Alto, 92–94; fish-sellers' accusations of, 209–12; obras and, 83–88, 108–13; political disillusionment and, 92; in Rosas Pampa, 76–88; rumors and accusations of, 76–83; suspicion in trade unions of, 198–203

costumes for the Morenada, 134–35, 275n.12

crime, in El Alto, 33, 42–43

cruces de palabras (arguments), confliction mediation and, 184–86

cultos (Evangelical services), 45, 157, 162–63

cultural practices: collectivity created through, 183–95, 262–65; corruption and, 112–13; Evangelical Protestantism and, 165, 169–71, 278n.25; of fishsellers, 218–19; rituals and, 119

dance: dissociative states and, 278n.24; ethnographic study of, 21–22; in Evangelical services, 166–67; experiential authenticity of, 125–29; fiesta rituals and, 118–22, 274n.1; fish-sellers' requirements for participation in, 209–10, 213–19; as language, 133–34; national identity and, 140–43; nested affiliations through, 58–60, 140–43; as religious ritual, 145–47; social relationships and, 131–40; vida organica and role of, 189–95; zone construction and, 48–49

tions and, 91; voter turnout and, 113–17

Electropaz, 71, 270n.7

elites: citizenship rights and, 6–8; corruption and role of, 109–11; strength of multitude vs., 251–57

Entrada rituals, 120–22, 126–29, 134–43, 147; trade unions' organization of, 189–95

Espinoza, Irineo, 208, 215, 280n.2

essentialism: Evangelical Protestantism and, 167–71; indigenous identity and, 9–19

ethnicity: cholo cultural identity and, 18–19; citizenship and, 8–19; commerce and political agency and, 228–32; Evangelical Protestantism and, 169–71

ethnographic research: on alcohol consumption, 147–49; on community leadership, 81–83; on fiesta rituals, 130–40; individualism vs. collectivism in, 179, 279n.2; on political activism, 258–65; on rotating leaderships, 237–38; subjectivity and self in, 15

Evangelical Methodists of Indianapolis, 157

Evangelical Protestantism: "anticommunity" promoted by, 22; Catholicism and, 156–57, 278n.19; citizenship and, 144; community activities of, 60, 119, 157–60; dissociative states in, 164–67, 278n.24; education and, 161–63; faith and, 154–55; fiesta obligations mitigated by, 133, 214, 275n.10; growth in Latin America of, 156, 278n.22; humansupernatural relationships in, 156–

67; hybridity, hypocrisy, and self in, 167–71; individualism and, 160–63, 263–65; sectoral division in Bolivia of, 157, 278n.20; selfhood and, 59

exchange relationships: alcohol consumption and, 150–55, 276n.5; cholo culture and, 17–19; clientelism and campaign practices and, 95–99; fiesta dancing and, 131–40, 275n.9

experiential authenticity, of music and dance, 125–29

face-to-face politics, campaign practices and, 99–103

family structure, Bolivian political system as, 239–41

Federación de Padres de Familia de El Alto (FEDEPAF), 188, 270n.13; political agency of, 250–51

Federation of Juntas Escolares, 66

Federation of Juntas Vecinales (FEJUVE), 36, 54–55, 270n.13; citizenship practices of, 62; community leadership and, 80; democracy models and, 235–36; fiesta rituals and, 120–22; political activism of, 250–51; research on, 176–77

Federation of Street Traders, 20–22; ampliado meetings of, 241–47; collectivity created by, 183–95, 264–65; Condepa politics and, 249; conflict mediation by, 184–86; Consejo de Desarrollo Institucional and, 270n.13; corporatism and, 255–57; corruption suspicions concerning, 199–203; dances, parades, and demonstrations held by, 189–95; Executive Committee of, 185–86, 195–

276n.15; in trade union leadership,
196–203

general assemblies: collectivity created
through, 263–65; of junta organization, 66–67; of street traders associations, 235, 241–47

"getting people" process, electoral
politics and, 95–108

gifting relationships, ch'alla consumption and, 151–55

Gill, Lesley, 26, 32–34, 48, 63, 75, 158,
160, 163, 178, 180

globalization, Bolivian economy and,
180–83

Goldstein, Daniel, 22, 26, 28, 31, 33

gossip, about corruption in Rosas
Pampa, 76–83

grass-roots organizations: democracy
models and role of, 235–47; juntas
as, 68, 270n.3; of street traders,
185–86

Gregoria, Doña, 59–60; on clientelism, 98–99; on corruption in Rosas
Pampa, 77–88, 109, 111

gremialistas, in Federation of Street
Traders, 207–12, 244–47

group rights, citizenship and role of, 6–8

grupo comuna concept, strength of,
251–57

Gulf Oil, nationalization of, 256

Gutierrez, Raquel, 11, 68, 174, 234,
238, 251, 254, 264

Hardt, Michael, 11, 178, 251–52, 254,
257, 261, 264

Harris, Olivia, 9–10, 67, 140, 144–45,
149, 153, 180, 182–83, 228

Harvey, Penelope, 9, 145, 147–49, 153,
274n.4

hermana/hermano, Evangelical use of,
157–58

hierarchical structure: in ayllu associations, 11; community authority and,
58–59; in Evangelicalism, 162–63;
fiesta rituals and role of, 130–40;
populist politics and, 272n.5; of
state agencies, 223–27; in street
trader associations, 238–41

house registrations (formularios maya
y paya), 20

humanitarian aid, corruption in
Bolivia and, 109–11

hunger strikes: electoral politics and,
93–94; of migrant workers, 50

hybridity, of Evangelical Protestantism,
167–71

hydrocarbons law (2004), 268n.9

identity-based politics, trade unionism
and, 173–77

"imagined community," citizenship
in, 58–60

in-betweenness: commerce and ethnicity and, 22–23; political agency
and, 206–32

Indian characteristics, cholo cultural
identity and, 268n.14

Indianist movement, migrant workers
and, 50

indigenous political activism: academic debate concerning, 9–10; in
Bolivia, 2–3, 7–8, 258–65; corporatist politics and, 247–57; electoral
politics and, 8–9; Evangelical Protestantism and, 169–71; migrant
workers and, 50; trade unions and,
174–77

individualism: citizenship and, 8–19;

individualism (*continued*)
collectivity vs., 174–79, 261–65;
competition and, 180–83; corruption and, 78–83; Evangelicalism
and, 160–63; leadership and, 195–
203; rural-urban migration and
growth of, 62–63; trade unions and,
204–5
informal economies. *See* economic
conditions and policies; market
economy
intellectuals: democracy models of,
234–35; indigenous identity and,
10–19
interesados (self-interested people): as
corrupt, 110–11; in Rosas Pampa, 76
intereses personales (personal interests), of trade union leaders, 198–
203
internal colonialism, indigenous political activism and, 10
International Monetary Fund (IMF):
Bolivian budget surplus and, 2; collective groups and, 260–61; indigenous political activism and, 11–12,
268n.9; influence in Bolivia of, 251–
57; social mobilization and, 250–51
international solidarity activism, Bolivian political activism and, 7–8
intromisión política, 200
Irpaqa ritual, alcohol consumption
during, 150, 277n.7
Isin, Engin, 26–28, 259

Jach'a Uru (Great Day) concept, 104,
273n.15
jefes de calle (chiefs of the street), 65–
66, 71–72, 123
Julián, Don, 81

juntas escolares, 53–55; clientelism
and, 98–99; corruption in, 76–83;
electoral politics and, 234; obras
produced by, 85–88; state relationship with, 57–60; structure and
activities of, 66–68
juntas vecinales: citizenship and, 259–
65; clientelism of, 98–99; corruption charges against, 77–83; electoral politics and, 74–75, 234; fiesta
rituals and, 118–43; gender balance
in, 67–68; Law of Popular Participation and, 68, 270n.3; local development in, 69–72; local government
and, 72–75; organization and
activities of, 52–55, 65–68; state
relationship with, 57–60; trade
union ties to, 189–95
Junta Vecinal de Villa Rosas Pampa, 44

Katarismo movement, 278n.26; ethnicity and commerce and, 231–32;
political activism of, 7; rural identity
of, 18–19; trade unions and, 174–
77, 249–51
Kharisiri spirit, 155, 277n.16
kinship networks: alcohol consumption and, 149–55; commercial relationships and, 229–32; in El Alto,
32–34; fiesta organization and,
132–40, 275n.8; for migrants, 158;
politics and, 105–8; vecinos and,
64–65
Klemola, Antero, 63, 79, 81–82, 241,
243
Kullawada (dance), 119, 125–28, 132,
139–40, 145–47

labor organizations: fiesta rituals as
tool of, 122–29; migrant workers

and, 47, 50, 269n.9; political agency
of, 22; rupture of trade unions with,
252–57. See also trade unions
land prices, in El Alto, 46–47, 49,
269n.8
language: at ampliado meetings, 244–
47; dance as, 133
La Paz (Bolivia): El Alto's links to, 30–
31, 36–37, 47–49; electoral politics
in, 274n.20; protests in, 25–26
La Razon (newspaper), 187–88
Larson, Brooke, 15–16, 183, 228
La Tribuna Libre del Pueblo (radio show),
93
Laura, Mateo, 222–24
Law of Citizen Security, 20–21
Law of Popular Participation, 68, 73,
270n.3; corruption charges and, 82–
83, 109–11
leadership: avoidance of, 80–83; base
suspicion of, 237–47; corruption
suspicions concerning, 198–203;
democracy models and role of, 235–
47; economic costs of, 196–203;
fiesta rituals and role of, 122–29,
132–40; fishsellers' dispute and role
of, 213–19; incumbency in Rosas
Pampa of, 77–83; individualism vs.
collectivism and, 195–203, 261–65;
payment issues concerning, 81–83;
in Rosas Pampa, 76–88; street
traders and vida organica and, 187–
89, 279n.5; trade unions and role
of, 174–77, 281n.4
Lechín, Juan Claudio, 11, 248
Ley de Exvinculación (Law of Disentailment), 15
liberal citizenship: definitions of, 4;
subjectivity and self and, 13–15

lightning (rayo), Andean relgiosity
and, 154, 277n.14
local government: clientelism and,
94–108; corruption in, 111–13;
electoral politics and, 114–17;
fish-sellers' dispute and role of,
208–12; political patronage jobs in,
95–99, 272n.8; popular participation and, 72–75; wage budget of,
113
loteadores, 273n.18
Loza, Remedios, 93, 101, 113
luck, rituals concerning, 153–55

Mallku, the, 8, 50
Mamani, Don Alberto, 207–12, 216
Mamani P., Mauricio, 10, 15, 28, 63,
79, 81, 148–51, 238
Mancilla, Don Rodolfo, 239, 244
March for Territory and Dignity, 7
market economy: Ceja market, 35–42;
cholo culture and, 17–19; individualism and competition in, 180–83;
regulation of, 212–19; in Rosas
Pampa, 45–46
Marshall, T. H., 4, 259
Martínez, Jose Luis "Tren," 107–8,
110–11, 273n.18
mascots, in ritual dances, 139–40,
276n.14
mass action: during ampliados, 245–
47; state and strength of, 251–57
Mauss, Marcel, 13–14, 153
media, politics and, 93, 99–104
mediation and negotiation, state role
in, 219–27
Mendoza, Nicolas, 234
Mesa, Carlos, 2, 26, 52, 261, 268n.9,
270n.16

neoliberalism: citizenship and, 13–15, 173–77; democracy models and, 234–35; economic policies of, 21; El Alto social structure and, 34–35; informal economic sector and, 212–13; local construction in Rosas Pampa and, 70–72; market impact of, 181–83, 279n.4; migration flows and, 47–50

nested affiliations: dance and, 58–60, 140–43; of trade unions, 194–95

nongovernmental organizations (NGOs): in El Alto, 32–33, 44; exchange relationships with, 96; impact on clientelism of, 272n.8; juntas and, 68–69, 270n.4; local development in Rosas Pampa and, 68–75; obra rituals and, 86–88

Obermaier, P. Sebastian M., 47, 72

obras (public works): accountability and corruption and, 83–88, 108–13; importance of, 88–90; juntas vecinales responsibility for, 66; political jobs in, 96–99; as political tool, 102–6, 273n.14; privatization in Rosas Pampas of, 69–72

occupation-based identity, Ceja market and, 35–42

Ong, Aihwa, 4, 58, 75, 97

"organic values": collectivity created by, 183–84; of trade unions, 200–205

orgullo (pride), as motive for leadership, 198

Oruro Carnival, 134, 141–43

Pablo, Don, 82–83

Pachamama rituals: alcohol consumption during, 150–55; selfhood and, 59

padrino de promoción, 104–5, 107–8

padrino de televisión, 105

padrinos de matrimonio, 150

Palenque, Carlos, 93, 103–5, 113

Palenque, Veronica, 93

parades, vida orgánica and role of, 189–95

Paredes, Jose Luis (Pepelucho), 97, 272n.5, 273n.15; corruption charges against, 111; fish-sellers dispute and, 208; grass-roots organization of, 99–108; local government of El Alto and, 72–73; paternalism of, 108; populist politics and, 92–94

parental involvement: in juntas escolares, 66–68; in local development, 71–72

participatory budgeting, 5

party politics: corruption in, 202–3, 280n.12; role in Bolivia of, 115–17; trade union leadership and, 198–203

pasante (dance group organizer), 49; alcohol consumption by, 149; fiesta organization by, 130–40, 275n.9

patronage politics: campaign practices and, 99; trade unions and, 206–7

peasant blockades, 50, 182, 229–32, 252, 269n.11, 281n.8

peasant unions, state and, 249

peleabamos (wife beating), 163, 278n.23

Pentacostal churches, growth in Latin America of, 156, 278n.22

Pericles, 27

personalization of politics: compadrazgo networks and, 105–6; corruption and role of, 110–11; electability and, 106–8; fish-sellers' personalization of politics (*continued*) relations with state and, 223–27; media role in, 102–3, 273n.12; in Rosas Pampa, 76, 78–83; voter turnout and, 114–17

pescaderas. *See* fish-sellers (pescaderas)

Plan Identidad, 107, 274n.19

Plan Progreso (MIR), 101, 108–13

political agency: Bolivian model of, 2–3; citizenship and, 206–32; collectivity and, 89–90; commerce and, 22–23; communitarianism and role of, 12–13, 268n.11; corporatist politics and, 247–57; ethnicity and commerce and, 228–32; fiesta rituals as tool of, 118, 122–29; of fish-sellers and fishermen's associations, 175; of indigenous groups, 23; individualism and leadership and, 195–203; trade unions and, 174–77; zone construction and, 58–60. *See also* protest activities

political subjectivity, selfhood and, 195–203

political system in Bolivia: citizenship and, 5–8; clientelism and, 114–17; corporatism and, 247–57; corruption and, 110–13, 274n.21; hierarchical structure of, 239–41; inclusion and exclusion in, 6–8; local government and development and, 72–75; subjectivity and self in, 12–15; trade unions and, 8, 248–51

pollera, as chola cultural signifier, 18–19; in the Morenada, 136–40

populist politics: in Bolivia, 93–94, 272nn.4–5; cholo culture and, 230–32; trade unions and, 175–77

power relations: alcohol and religiosity as model of, 149–55; convocatoria and, 191–95; Evangelical Protestantism and, 169–71; of intermediaries, 229

pre-Columbian era, indigenous cultures as survivors of, 9–10

prestes, fiesta organization by, 131–40

private enterprises, juntas and, 68, 71–72, 270n.4, 270n.7

private security guards, in Ceja market, 38

production, collectivity and, 182–83

Projecto de Fortalecimiento de la Atención Primaria en Salud Distrito III—El Alto (APS), 44, 70–72; community leaders' alliance with, 77–83

protest activities: in Bolivia, 258–65; in fish-sellers dispute, 209–12; trade union control of, 187–89

public opinion: female networks and formation of, 88–90; formation at ampliados of, 243–47

public sphere, cultural concepts of, 27–29

public works. *See* obras (public works)

pueblos (birth villages): fiesta rituals in, 119; migration flows from, 46, 48, 230–32, 269n.7

Quechuas: cholo cultural identity and, 268n.15; political activism of, 8; rural identity of, 18–19

quillomeños network, 48–49

Quispe, Don Roberto: Federation and association relations and, 215–19; fish-sellers' dispute and, 208–12;

regulation of street traders and, 213–19; state relations with fish-sellers and, 220–27

Quispe, Felipe, 8

racial stratification, in El Alto, 32

Rawls, John, 12–13, 268n.10

rebasar (overrule), democracy models and, 235–36

reciprocity (ayni): alcohol consumption and, 153–55, 277n.12; community and, 119; personalist politics and, 105–6

regional indigenous movements, 6–8

religion: alcohol consumption and, 149–55; citizenship and, 144; fiesta rituals and role of, 119–22, 144–55, 275n.5

relocalized (relocalizados) miners, 47, 269n.9

representativity: corruption and accountability and, 109–11; lack of, in Bolivian political system, 92, 272n.1

research methodology, 19–24; on Federation of Street Traders, 176–77; fieldwork activities, 59–60

residentes association, of migrant workers, 48–50

responsibility, vida orgánica and, 186–89

Reyes Villa, Manfred, 111

ritual activities: Evangelical Protestantism and, 164–67; of fishsellers, 218–19; for obra inauguration, 86–88; zone construction and, 58–60. See also fiesta rituals

Rivera Cusicanqui, Silvia, 10, 48, 63, 174, 180, 228, 235, 238, 248–49, 257

Roberto, Don, 59–60, 84; on corruption in Rosas Pampa, 77, 109, 116; on Evangelicalism, 160

Rocha, Don Braulio, 56, 187, 196–97, 218–19, 225–27, 232, 238

Rolando, Don, 78–79, 83–84, 86

Rosas Pampa (El Alto), 20–21, 42–46; absence of state in development of, 69–72; alcohol consumption in, 123–29; Catholic Church in, 156–58, 161–63, 278n.19; citizenship practices in, 61–62, 264–65; community authority in, 57–60; Community Center project in, 83–88; Evangelical Protestantism in, 156–67; fiesta rituals in, 118–43; gender balance in juntas of, 68; leadership, accountability, and corruption in, 76–88; local development and self-construction in, 68–88; migrant workers in, 48–50; patron-client relations in, 91–92; vecinos in, 64–68; voter turnout in, 113–14

Rose, Nikolas, 28, 70, 72, 178

rotative leadership systems: allyu association with, 11; citizenship and, 28–29; in community organizations, 79–83; democracy models and, 237–47

Rousseau, 6, 27, 118

rumor: about corruption, 76–83; about leadership, 237

rural identity: alcohol consumption and, 149; cholo culture and, 18–19; commercial relationships and, 229–32; migrants in El Alto and, 48–50; rural-urban jurisdictions and, 225–27; trade unions and, 206–7 sacrifice, fiesta rituals and role of, 154–55

saludar (greeting), Evangelical practices of, 157, 164–67

Sanchez de Lozada, Gonzalo, 19, 25–26, 272n.9

sanitation companies, in Ceja market, 38

secularism, fiesta rituals and, 120–22

self-construction of Rosas Pampa, 68–88; local government inefficiency and, 72–75

selfhood: community activity and, 59–60; Evangelical Protestantism and, 156–71; political and anthropological theory and, 12–15, 268n.11; in ritual dances, 140; trade unions and, 173–74, 179

Seligmann, Linda, 17–18, 23, 175, 207, 228–31

Sendero Luminoso: cholo support for, 268n.13; rise of, 9

sensuality, in Bolivian politics, 102, 273n.10

Servicio Departamental Agropecuario de la Prefectura (SEDAG), 210–12, 216, 220–21, 223–27

sexual harassment accusations, in fish-sellers' dispute, 208–13

social movements, corporatist politics and, 247–57

social relations: alcohol consumption and, 147–55, 277n.6; economic production and, 182–83; in El Alto, 12–15, 33–34; Evangelicalism and, 163–67; fiesta rituals and, 130–40; of migrant workers, 48–50; in Rosas Pampa, 45–46

sociocentric self concept, 14

solicitud letter, 73

speech: at ampliados, 242–47; importance in juntas of, 67, 270n.2

spirituality, alcohol consumption and, 147–49

state: absence of, in local development, 69–72; citizenship and role of, 23, 91–117, 258–65; civic organizations' negotiations with, 53–55; clientelism and, 116–17; community authorities and, 57–60; corporatist politics and, 247–57; deregulation and neoliberal policies of, 212–19; fish-sellers associations and, 212–19; mediation and negotiation in role of, 219–27; political patronage jobs and, 97–99; power of convocatoria vs., 191–95; role in El Alto of, 51–55; social sectors in, 250–51; strength of multitude and, 251–57; trade unions and, 173–79, 206, 233–57

stereotypes: of cholo culture, 17–19; of citizenship, 28–29

street demonstrations, as face-to-face politics, 99–103

streets and roads: junta organizations and, 65–66; lighting in Rosas Pampa for, 71–72, 271n.7; paving of, 73–75; in Rosas Pampa, 44–45

street traders: collectivity created by, 183–95; conflict mediation by, 184–86; dances, parades, and demonstrations held by, 189–95; democracy models of, 235–47; hierarchical structure in associations of, 238–41; individualism of, 195–203; political agency of, 22, 206–32; regulatory responsibilities of, 212–19; responsibility and vida orgánica of, 186–89 strike activities, vida orgánica and, 187–95, 279n.6

student strikes, at UPEA, 51–52, 270n.14

subjectivity, political and anthropological theory and, 12–15

Suez Corporation, 253

symbolic activities: dance as, 133–40, 145–47; politicians' use of, 103–8; zone construction and, 58–60

Tapia Mealla, Luis, 11, 187, 256–57

taxi drivers, strike activities of, 279n.6

tax increases: ethnographic research concerning, 20–21; riots against, 2

teenagers: in Ceja market, 37–38; in Rosas Pampa, 45–46

Tent of the Holy Spirit, 158, 164–67

thaki (rotating leadership), 237–38

Theory of Justice, A, 12–13, 268n.10

Thucydides, 5

Ticona Alejo, Esteban, 10, 28, 81, 235, 238, 241

Tinkus (dance), 132, 139–41

Tiwanaku Manifesto, 7

Tobas (dance), 139–40

Tocqueville, Alexis de, citizenship theory of, 5

toma de nombre ceremony, 104–5, 107–8

trade unions: as assembly-based democracy, 241–47; Bolivian political activism and, 8, 248–51; breakaway associations and, 236–37; citizenship and, 173–79, 259–65; civic organization in El Alto and, 52–55; collectivity created by, 183–95, 203–5; corporatist politics and, 247–57; dances, parades, and demonstrations organized by, 189–95; economic importance of, 178, 279n.1; individualism in politics of, 195–203; repression of, 178–79; rupture with older labor organizations, 252–57; state relations with, 173–77, 219–27, 233–57

trago (alcoholic drink), 125–26

tramite process, 73–75; corruption charges concerning, 82–83

Tribuna Libre del Pueblo (TV show), 106

Tupac Katari rebellion, 25, 229

Turner, Victor, 58, 129

Unión Cívica Solidaridad (UCS), 103, 106, 249, 273n.14

United States, influence in Bolivia of, 251–57

Universidad Mayor de San Andres (UMSA), 31, 51

Universidad Pública de El Alto (UPEA): establishment of, 51–52; factionalism in, 20; research on democracy models at, 234; trade union ties to students at, 192–95; urban sociology research at, 176–77

urban identity: cholo culture and, 18–19, 230–32; local government inefficiency and, 72–75; rural-urban jurisdictions and, 225–27; trade unions and, 206–7; vecinos and, 64–65

Urbanización Villa Dolores, 47

urbanization: El Alto patterns of, 46–50; individualism fostered by, 180–83

value systems, collectivity created through, 183–95, 262–65

vecinos/vecindad: citizenship practices of, 61–62, 116–17; community lead-

vecinos/vecindad (continued)
ership and, 80–83; defined, 22, 63–
64; Evangelical Protestantism
among, 156; local development and,
68–69; nested affiliations of, 140–
43; in Rosas Pampa, 69–72; self-
identity and, 22
Velasco Alvarado, Juan, 276n.16
vida orgánica (organizational life),
174; collectivity created through,
263–65; convocatoria and, 189–95;
street traders and, 186–89, 279n.5
vitalicismo (life-long-ism), 238
voceadores, in Ceja market, 41
voting patterns: citizen-state relations
and, 91; clientelism and, 94–108; democracy models and, 236–37; turnout rates, 113–17; vecindad and, 64

water contracts: in El Alto, 44–45;
political radicalism over, 2
Water War (Cochabamba), 2–3, 19, 51,
241, 253–57
wealth accumulation, political corruption as means of, 112–13
Western culture: citizenship status in,
23–24; democracy models of, 234–
35; self concept in, 13–15

women: alcohol consumption by, 147–
49, 276n.4; assembly-based democracy and role of, 243–47; in cholo
culture, 17–19, 228–32; clientelism
and campaign practices and, 95–99;
corruption of, 203–4; in Evangelicalism, 163; as fish-sellers, 208–
12, 216–19, 226–27; hermanos network for, 158, 278n.21; in market
economy, 182–83, 279n.3; as Morenada dancers, 136–40; networks
of, 88–90; role in juntas of, 67–68;
as street traders, 196. See also gender
issues
World Bank, influence in Bolivia of,
251–57
worship practices, Evangelical Protestantism and, 164–67

yatiri (ritual specialist), 39–40
Young, Iris, 29, 183
Yuval-Davis, Nira, 5, 12, 72, 178, 259

zone construction: absence of state in,
69–72; citizenship practices and,
61–62; collective political agency
and, 58–60; in El Alto, 63; fiesta rituals and, 122–29

SIAN LAZAR is a university lecturer in the Department of Social Anthropology and an affiliated lecturer of the Centre of Latin American Studies at the University of Cambridge.

LIBRARY OF CONGRESS CATALOGING-IN-PUBLICATION DATA

LAZAR, SIAN.

EL ALTO, REBEL CITY : SELF AND CITIZENSHIP IN ANDEAN BOLIVIA / SIAN LAZAR.

P. CM. — (LATIN AMERICA OTHERWISE)

INCLUDES BIBLIOGRAPHICAL REFERENCES AND INDEX.

ISBN 978-0-8223-4129-1 (CLOTH : ALK. PAPER)

ISBN 978-0-8223-4154-3 (PBK. : ALK. PAPER)

1. AYMARA INDIANS—BOLIVIA—EL ALTO—SOCIAL CONDITIONS.

2. AYMARA INDIANS—BOLIVIA—EL ALTO—POLITICS AND GOVERNMENT.

3. STATE-LOCAL RELATIONS—BOLIVIA—EL ALTO. 4. EL ALTO (BOLIVIA)—SOCIAL CONDITIONS. 5. EL ALTO (BOLIVIA)—POLITICS AND GOVERNMENT. I. TITLE.

F2230.2.A9L39 2008   305.898'32408412—DC22

2007032554